YOU CAN'T
KILL A MAN
BECAUSE OF
THE BOOKS
HE READS

YOU CAN'T KILL A MAN BECAUSE OF THE BOOKS HE READS

Angelo Herndon's Fight for Free Speech

Brad Snyder

W. W. NORTON & COMPANY

Independent Publishers Since 1923

For information about permission to reproduce selections from this book,
write to Permissions, W. W. Norton & Company, Inc., 500 Fifth Avenue,
New York, NY 10110

For information about special discounts for bulk purchases, please contact
W. W. Norton Special Sales at specialsales@wwnorton.com or 800-233-4830

Manufacturing by Lake Book Manufacturing
Book design by Lovedog Studio
Production manager: Lauren Abbate

ISBN 978-1-324-03654-8

W. W. Norton & Company, Inc.
500 Fifth Avenue, New York, NY 10110
www.wwnorton.com

W. W. Norton & Company Ltd.
15 Carlisle Street, London W1D 3BS

1 2 3 4 5 6 7 8 9 0

To my brother, Ivan

CONTENTS

INTRODUCTION

Angelo Herndon in a publicity photograph

THE FIRST NIGHT IN HIS ATLANTA JAIL CELL, ANGELO Herndon could not sleep. The stench of feces was so strong that he vomited. There was not even a toilet. He did not know what crime he had been accused of or what would happen to him. During the past year, the eighteen-year-old Black Communist Party organizer had been arrested, jailed, sentenced to the chain gang, kidnapped, beaten, and falsely accused of murder. Each time, he had escaped serious harm; the truth, thus far, had set him free. This time, however, was different. Georgia officials had raised the stakes. They vowed to eliminate communist-led demonstrations, interracial coalitions of workers, and the organizing of their young leader.

During the depths of the Great Depression, nearly 22,000 people in Atlanta found themselves "without bread, many without shelter, ragged and ill." They depended on state and local governments to keep them from starving. After days of rumors in the newspapers, the Fulton County board of commissioners cut off funding to the Community Chest administering relief to the poor, and on June 18, 1932, the relief office closed. "Hunger and misery today," the *Atlanta Constitution* declared, "is stalking through the capital city of Georgia."

The leader of Atlanta's Unemployed Committee, Herndon seized the moment. He and his small group of communist colleagues printed 10,000 leaflets calling for an interracial demonstration at the county courthouse. "Thousands of us," the leaflet said, "together with our families, are at this minute facing starvation and misery and are about to be thrown out of our houses because the miserable charity handout that some of us were getting, has been stopped!" The leaflet declared that T. K. Glenn, the president of the Community Chest, made $10,000 a year and executive director Frank Neely made $6400 a year, yet families on relief received only $2.50 a week. It decried a recent proposal that the police round up the city's unemployed workers and return them to Georgia farms— where there were no jobs, no money, and rampant poverty. And it ridiculed County Commissioner Walter C. Hendrix's claim that "there were no starving families in Atlanta" because he had not seen any. The leaflet urged Black and white workers to arrive at the county courthouse at 10:00 a.m. on June 30 to "show this faker that there is plenty of suffering in the city of Atlanta and demand that he gives us immediate relief!" The leaflet was signed by the Unemployed Committee of Atlanta, P.O. Box 339.

At 10:00 a.m. on June 30, about 150 white and Black men, women, and children arrived at the courthouse. "They had come to town," according to a protester, "to let the rich know they was hungry." They marched up to the fourth floor of the courthouse and demanded a meeting with one of the commissioners. A commissioner agreed to meet with only the white protesters. During the meeting, he claimed that there was no money left in the budget for unemployment relief and advised them to return to Georgia farms. Outside the courthouse, the other demonstrators peacefully picketed on the sidewalk for more relief. No one spoke. No property was damaged. Nobody was injured. The police stood nearby and talked amiably with the protesters.

The next morning, the County Commission met and agreed to increase unemployment relief by $6000. Herndon and his Unemployed Committee declared victory yet wanted more. "While we have gained something by showing the bosses we will not starve peacefully, this is not enough!" they insisted in a follow-up leaflet. They demanded to know what had happened to the $600,000 that the county had cut from the salaries of government officials as a way to reduce the budget. They rejected the idea of returning to farms and called for more interracial demonstrations: "The biggest surprise handed the bosses who have been starving us out was when they saw Negro and White workers come down together to fight for relief." The committee promised to hold another meeting to create a list of additional demands and instructed people to contact C. Jones at P.O. Box 339, Atlanta, Georgia.

On the evening of July 11, Angelo Herndon stopped at the post office to pick up the committee's mail in Box 339. Two police officers were watching the mailbox and waiting for someone to open it. As soon as Herndon did, they grabbed him from behind, whirled him around, and placed steel handcuffs on his wrists. When Herndon asked why he had been arrested, they said that John A. Boykin, the Fulton County solicitor general, wanted to see him. Before the officers took him to the police station, they searched his rented room without a warrant and seized communist books and literature.

With the radical literature in hand, the officers drove Herndon to the police station and led him up a dark flight of stairs into a small, unlit room. They turned on lighted red skulls that made him laugh. They kicked him in the shin, sat him in a fake electric chair in the center of the room, and attached some wires to the steel chair. They grabbed him by the throat and demanded a confession. Herndon did not know whether he would leave the room alive. He told them they might as well as kill him. Instead, they bashed him in the head with a flashlight and took him downstairs for booking. Held incommunicado for eleven days, Herndon was finally charged with a crime—attempting to incite insurrection—punishable by death.

You Can't Kill a Man Because of the Books He Reads chronicles Herndon's five-year quest for freedom during a time—the 1930s—when Blacks, white liberals, and the radical left joined forces with the Communist Party USA and helped define the nation's commitment to civil rights and civil liberties. It explains how an Alabama coal miner named Eugene Braxton transformed himself into a Cincinnati-born communist organizer, Angelo Herndon. His story inspired brave individuals to champion his cause: Benjamin J. Davis Jr., a young Black Harvard Law School graduate who defended Herndon at trial and discovered his own political voice; C. Vann Woodward, a Georgia Tech English instructor who joined the interracial Herndon defense committee; Carol Weiss King, a radical white New York lawyer who organized his appeal; Whitney North Seymour, an esteemed Wall Street lawyer who twice argued Herndon's case before the U.S. Supreme Court; Herbert Wechsler, a wunderkind Columbia law professor who revived Herndon's First Amendment claims after the Supreme Court had dismissed them; Charles Hamilton Houston, a visionary NAACP lawyer who pulled his organization into the case; Hugh M. Dorsey, a Georgia trial judge with a guilty conscience; and Owen J. Roberts, a Supreme Court justice under fire who wrote the majority opinion in Herndon's case in April 1937. Finally, the book explores Herndon's emergence as a Harlem literary star who befriended Ralph Ellison, Langston Hughes, and Richard Wright as well as Herndon's fall from grace.

You Can't Kill a Man Because of the Books He Reads is the story of a Black man facing a possible death sentence because of his unpopular political beliefs. It is a legal odyssey that illustrates the difference between lawfully objecting to the actions of government officials and unlawfully encouraging people to commit acts of violence. It is about 1930s America, in which a diverse coalition of people opposed racial injustice at home and fascism abroad. It is about how the Supreme Court averted a constitutional showdown with President Franklin D. Roosevelt and a Democratic Congress, not only by upholding their New Deal programs but also by protecting civil liberties. And it is about Angelo Herndon and the courageous individuals who rallied to his cause, took on Georgia's criminal justice system, and established free speech and peaceable assembly as essential rights in a democracy.

YOU CAN'T
KILL A MAN
BECAUSE OF
THE BOOKS
HE READS

CHAPTER ONE

THE COAL MINER

Angelo Herndon as Communist Party activist

GEORGIA PROSECUTORS DID NOT KNOW THE FIRST THING about Angelo Herndon. They bought his story—repeated in his autobiography, in the press, and by historians—that he was born in Cincinnati, had worked in a Lexington, Kentucky, coal mine, and had joined the Communist Party there before arriving in Atlanta. Like many communists, Angelo had taken drastic measures to protect his family by hiding his past: he changed his name, lied about his background, and altered the names of people he knew and places he'd been.

Angelo Herndon portrayed himself as a "Cincinnati Negro" who had descended from a family of coal miners. In reality, he was the son of third-generation farmers from Bullock County in Alabama's Black Belt. Before and after the Civil War, a Black majority worked the region's fertile black topsoil in cotton fields owned by a white minority—first as enslaved people and then as tenant farmers and sharecroppers. Angelo's paternal great-grandfather Paul Braxton was a farmer who had registered to vote in 1867 when Union troops occupied the newly created county. His maternal great-grandfather Frank Herndon worked as a tenant farmer, growing corn and cotton on thirty acres. Both families lived in the southwestern part of the county, known as Union Church, where their children followed them into the fields, as did their children's children. On December 26, 1905, Angelo's parents, Paul Braxton and Hattie Herndon, were married at her family's home. Paul was dark skinned. Hattie was light skinned with "high cheekbones" and "looked like a Black Cherokee." The couple had four boys: Hilliard, Leroy, Milton, and Leo. Their fifth son, Eugene Angelo Braxton, was born on May 6, 1914. He inherited his mother's narrow eyes and light skin. His family called him Angelo or 'Gelo.

A few years after Angelo was born, his father broke the vicious cycle of sharecropping and tenant farming—the seasonal employment, fluctuating cotton prices, and chronic indebtedness to white landowners—to take a job near Cincinnati as a coal miner. His wife and children likely stayed in Bullock County until he could make enough money to bring his growing family north. In early March 1917, however, forty-year-old Paul Braxton contracted pneumonia and died six days later. Angelo accompanied his mother on the train to take his father's body to be buried in Alabama.

Hattie Braxton and her seven children returned to Bullock County and a life of rural poverty. Angelo grew up in a deeply religious family of fire-and-brimstone Baptists. He was baptized at age twelve. A sickly yet intelligent child, he learned to read and write until, like his siblings, he was old enough to work in the fields. His mother had hoped that Angelo might be able to stay in school and to go to college. Tuskegee Institute, the historically Black college founded by Booker T. Washington, was only fifty miles north of their home. Angelo, however, knew that there were too many mouths to feed.

At age thirteen, Angelo ran away with his older brother Leo to find work. In his autobiography, he claimed to have been employed in a Lexington, Kentucky, mine owned by the DeBardeleben Coal and Iron Company. DeBardeleben, however, was a mining operation based in Walker County, Alabama, and operated a segregated company town in Sipsey matching the description of the one where Angelo and his brother lived and worked. The Braxton boys shoveled coal into cars and got paid in script redeemable at the company store based on how many tons they moved. It was dangerous, backbreaking work. One day, Angelo ripped the skin off the back of his hand when one of the cars had jumped the tracks. He and his brother complained about rigged scales and rip-offs at the company store. After nine months, they quit because the company had slashed their pay from forty-two cents to thirty-one cents a ton.

Sometime in 1928 or early 1929, Angelo and Leo moved to Birmingham to live with an aunt and uncle. The "Magic City" was a southern industrial center dominated by coal, steel, and railroad magnates. By the turn of the century, Blacks made up a majority of Birmingham's unskilled workforce. The coal and steel companies relied on state officials to crush strikes and the United Mine Workers' efforts to create an interracial union. They replenished their supply of unskilled labor by hiring Black workers. After a month in Birmingham, Leo found work in a coal mine and bought them food and clothes. His younger brother was not so lucky.

Struggling to find a job, young Angelo trusted an unscrupulous labor agent and found himself trapped in a life of peonage. He was driven to an encampment and joined sickly-looking workers in building a dam on Lock 18 on the Coosa River, a tributary of the Alabama River. Angelo worked in deplorable conditions and discovered his pay to be nonexistent. At midnight, he and several others escaped armed guards by swimming across the river and hiking through woods and swamps. Upon his return to Birmingham, he paid an employment agency three dollars and was promised a $3-a-day job building a new Goodyear Rubber Company plant in Gadsden, Alabama. Instead, he worked day and night shifts operating a cement mixer for $1.75 a day. After receiving no pay for the first week of work because of deductions for his living expenses, he hitchhiked back to Birmingham.

Angelo and Birmingham's other unemployed Black workers soon found jobs even more difficult to come by. In October 1929, the stock market crashed, sending the American economy into free fall and triggering a worldwide financial crisis. The Depression cost American workers their jobs, their homes, their food supply, and their sense of self-worth. President Herbert Hoover provided Americans with little hope and no unemployment relief. State and local governments struggled to fill the void and to keep people from starving to death. The Depression hit Birmingham's mines and mills hard and Alabama's rural areas even harder.

The fifteen-year-old Angelo lied about his age and finally landed a job with Birmingham's largest corporation, the Tennessee Coal, Iron, and Railroad Company (TCI). Owned by U.S. Steel since 1907, TCI employed approximately 25,000 workers, a majority of them Black, and housed many of them in segregated company towns. As a young miner, Angelo worked on the surface of TCI's Docena mine, building transformer lines and cutting a right of way for wires—for $2.70 a day minus expenses. It was hazardous work. A nineteen- or twenty-year-old friend Angelo referred to as Jimmy was electrocuted by an exposed trolley wire and died. Angelo boldly informed company officials about the racist, white foreman who had refused to fix the exposed wires. The foreman was fired; Jimmy's family got paid. Angelo learned about the benefits of speaking up. One day on his way home from work, a handbill caught his eye: "Would you rather fight—or starve?"

The handbill was the work of the local Unemployed Council. During the Depression, the Communist Party USA had begun organizing unemployed Black and white workers by establishing Unemployed Councils or Unemployed Committees in cities and towns. The chapters held mass meetings to appeal to Black workers, often the last hired and first fired, as prime recruits for Party membership. Founded in 1919, the American Communist Party initially operated underground out of necessity. During the Great War, the federal government prosecuted antiwar radicals for violating the Espionage Act. After anarchists bombed the home of Attorney General A. Mitchell Palmer and mailed bombs to the homes of other public officials in June 1919, the Justice Department's Bureau of Investigation, led by a young J. Edgar Hoover, responded by rounding up radical immigrants and deporting them in what became known as the Palmer Raids. The Party's factions and approximately 15,000 members united in 1923 as the Communist Party USA and took their orders from the Communist International, or Comintern, in Moscow. At its Sixth World Congress in 1928, the Comintern predicted the beginning of the end of capitalism, called for the establishment of communist-run trade unions, and declared that the Black majority living in the Black Belt of the Deep South had a right to political and economic self-determination.

The Communist Party USA attempted to challenge the South's political, economic, and social order by recruiting Black and white workers into interracial unions. During the spring of 1930, an interracial band of Party members boldly ventured into the South as labor organizers. Establishing Birmingham as the headquarters of District 17, covering Alabama, Georgia, and Tennessee, they attempted to unionize Black sharecroppers as well as Black and white industrial workers. As a first step, the organizers tried to make Black workers aware of their political and economic power by fighting for more unemployment relief.

On May 22, 1930, Angelo attended his first Unemployed Council meeting, an integrated gathering of about 150 Blacks and 51 whites.

Tom Johnson, a white district organizer, called for Birmingham's Black workers to fight for "industrial and economical equality," to use majority rule to take over state and local governments, and to stop lynching and boss rule. Walter Lewis, a Black former steel worker, described how he had been sentenced to the chain gang for labor organizing in Chattanooga. Lewis and white district co-organizer Frank Burns endorsed racial equality. For Angelo, the meeting was a revelation. White and Black men were speaking the truth about his life as a Black miner in the racially segregated South. He joined the movement, attended a follow-up meeting, and began immersing himself in communist literature.

Concerned for his safety, Angelo's family tried to discourage him from joining the Party and described its meetings as the devil's work. Disregarding their warnings, Angelo took to the streets. On May 29, he participated in his first peaceful protest—about 300 people gathered in Birmingham's Woodrow Wilson Park (renamed Capitol Park later that summer) and marched to the Community Chest headquarters to raise awareness that Blacks received half the amount of unemployment relief as whites. A hundred police officers watched. Community Chest officials met with a delegation of thirty marchers and urged them to return to their agrarian roots, ignoring the fact that sharecroppers and tenant farmers were starving, too. Black newspaper publisher Oscar W. Adams spoke to the protesters in front of the headquarters, disclaimed any interest in racial equality, and urged Blacks and whites not to join the Communist Party. Angelo felt betrayed by Adams and other Black leaders and emboldened by the communists' interracial movement.

The Ku Klux Klan and local law enforcement cracked down on the interracial mass meetings and protests, which threatened white domination of the economic, social, and political order. About 1000 Klansmen marched through the Black north Birmingham neighborhood of Collegeville on June 19 and burned in effigy Oscar De Priest, the Black Illinois congressman who had announced a plan to visit Birmingham, and district organizer Tom Johnson. Two days earlier, the city commission had passed a criminal anarchy law designed to stop communist organizing, with offenses punishable by a maximum $100 fine and 180 days in jail. The law was not strictly enforced, at least not at first. Police officers and detectives monitored a June 24 mass meeting at Wilson Park and declared the speeches "harmless." Four days later, however, they arrested five communists, two whites and three Blacks, at a mass meeting of about 200 people.

Fearing the wrath of the Klan and the police, Angelo's family balked at his communist activity. His aunt Sallie told him never to return to her house if he made good on his plan to join the "Red hoodlums" at the Unemployed Council convention on July 4–5 in Chicago. Angelo went anyway. The morning he left for Chicago, he found a Klan leaflet on his aunt's doorstep: "Communism must be wiped out. Drive the foreigners back to the North and Russia where they came from. Alabama is a good place for good Negroes, but a bad place for bad Negroes who want social equality."

The speeches at the convention in Chicago inspired Angelo and confirmed his decision to devote himself to Party politics. He joined the Young Communist League and began working as a full-time volunteer labor organizer for the Trade Union Unity League—a communist-backed umbrella organization encouraging Birmingham's unemployed workers to fight for more relief and the city's coal miners to join the interracial National Miners' Union. After failed strikes in 1919 and 1920, the United Mine Workers had ended its efforts to organize the city's Black and white miners. A decade later, the Communist Party sought to shatter southern racial norms and to succeed where the United Mine Workers had failed. Angelo joined the dangerous work of union organizing by using his birth name: Eugene Braxton.

As a labor organizer, Angelo took on the most powerful corporation in Birmingham—his former employer, TCI. Though it permitted white miners to join a company-backed union, TCI opposed any efforts to unionize its predominantly Black workforce. Backed by the Klan and local police, TCI cracked down on Angelo and other communists. On July 24, Angelo and fellow organizer Joe Carr were meeting informally with about twenty-five miners near TCI's Hamilton Slope mine when the company's armed security officers ordered them into a car. The security officers forced Angelo and Carr to visit all the company's mines, warned workers not to meet with them, then turned them over to the Birmingham police. Charged with vagrancy and represented by the Party's local counsel, Angelo was found guilty, fined $500, and sentenced to twelve months on the chain gang. He was released on $750 bond paid for by the Party, and on appeal to the circuit court his conviction was dismissed for lack of evidence.

His arrest and conviction and distinctive, light-skinned appearance made Angelo a marked man. Forty to fifty police officers, Klansmen, and members of the American Legion—determined to prevent any interracial meetings in public spaces—watched and waited for him in Capitol Park before a September 1 mass meeting for more unemployment relief. The police beat Blacks entering the park with clubs and arrested Angelo on a nearby street. Klan members identified him from his previous trial. The *Southern Worker*, a Communist Party newspaper, reported that the Klan had kidnapped him, described him as "still missing," and "it is feared that he is in danger of lynching." Instead, police jailed him in the "dog house" with mentally ill prisoners for eleven days, then charged him with vagrancy. Finally, a judge took pity on Angelo. Instead of convicting him, the judge handed him a letter to give to a prominent Klan leader and businessman, W. J. Worthington: "Dear Sir: I am sending you a man that wants to go to work." Instead, Angelo mailed the letter to the *Southern Worker*, which published and mocked it. The judge, whom he later saw on the street, was not amused.

Even without the letter, the Ku Klux Klan knew all about Angelo. Revived in 1915 with a cross burning atop Stone Mountain, Georgia, the Klan peaked in Alabama during the early to mid-1920s yet retained some measure of political legitimacy during the early 1930s with its white supremacy, antisemitism, anti-Catholicism, and hostility to immigrants and communists. In Birmingham, the Klan worked closely with local law enforcement in surveilling and rooting out Angelo and the city's other communist organizers. In November 1930, Klan members openly testified at federal Fish Committee hearings, chaired by rabid anti-communist Representative Hamilton Fish III (R-NY) and held in Birmingham and other southern cities, to investigate and document communist activity. At the Birmingham hearing, Klan leader John G. Murphy testified: "Eugene Braxton, colored, is half Chinese and half Negro; that is what he looks like. It has been testified he was on the [Communist Party] pay roll. His address here is 908 John Street." That was his aunt Sallie's address. During the same hearing, Birmingham police chief Fred McDuff testified that Angelo had spent about six weeks of the fall of 1930 in Chattanooga getting indoctrinated by party officials before returning to Birmingham.

During the first half of 1931, Angelo was arrested wherever he went. On February 5, Birmingham police raided a private home and arrested him and four other communists. The police offered to release them if they left town, but they refused. Instead, city officials planned to charge them under the criminal anarchy law. Later that month, Angelo barely escaped a lynching after speaking to a group of Black sharecroppers near Camden, Alabama, and was arrested and released upon his return to Birmingham. Perhaps because of his penchant for finding trouble or for getting arrested, communist leaders pulled his application to the Party's national training school. "He is a fine boy," district organizer Tom Johnson wrote, "but made some bad mistakes which he will have to suffer for."

In May 1931, Party leaders sent Angelo to New Orleans to assist striking longshoremen and seamen. He was distributing the *Marine Workers Voice* to newly arriving German seamen when some scab workers attacked him. The police arrived and arrested him. After four days, he was released on $150 bond paid by the Communist Party. The *Southern Worker* impossibly claimed that both Angelo Herndon and Eugene Braxton had been arrested.

In New Orleans, Angelo read about the Communist Party's efforts to save nine Black youths—known as the Scottsboro "Boys"—from the electric chair. On March 25, 1931, Black and white youths had fought while riding on a freight train. The white youths summoned the police. An armed posse stopped the train near Paint Rock, Alabama. The police arrested nine Black youths riding on different train cars and took them to the county seat in Scottsboro. Two poor young white women, also hoboing on the train, falsely accused the nine Black youths of gang rape. Ranging in age from twelve to nineteen, several of the Scottsboro defendants testified against one another after police officers had beaten and threatened them. During four trials in four days, all-white, all-male juries relied on the false testimony of the two white women to convict eight defendants and to sentence them to death. The judge declared a mistrial for the ninth and youngest defendant because the jury could not agree on a death sentence.

Several young Communist Party field workers, who had been organizing sharecroppers in central Alabama, read about the arrests and traveled to Scottsboro to attend the trials. Their reports of a "legal lynching" persuaded the Communist Party that the Scottsboro case represented the perfect vehicle to highlight how whites terrorized and subjugated Blacks living in the Deep South and to recruit Black workers into the Party. The International Labor Defense (ILD), the legal arm of the Communist Party founded in 1925 to defend members of the working-class movement, immediately sent lawyers to Scottsboro. First on the scene, the ILD grasped the magnitude of the injustice and recognized that the parents of the incarcerated teenagers would have the most say about who represented the Scottsboro defendants on appeal. The Communist Party's publicity machine turned the Scottsboro case into a national and international cause célèbre.

By winning the trust of the parents and hiring lawyers to represent the Scottsboro defendants on appeal, the ILD had outmaneuvered the nation's leading civil rights organization—the National Association for the Advancement of Colored People (NAACP). In 1909, a coalition of Black activists and intellectuals and white social reformers, including W. E. B. Du Bois, Ida B. Wells, and Mary White Ovington, had founded the organization. Membership in the NAACP appealed to educated, middle-class Blacks. Du Bois edited the monthly *Crisis* magazine. Moorfield Storey and a group of predominantly white lawyers established the National Legal Committee. The NAACP opposed lynching, racial segregation, and unfair criminal trials. In 1923, the organization won an important Supreme Court victory against mob-dominated criminal trials in *Moore v. Dempsey*, a decision that saved Black sharecroppers sentenced to death after the Elaine Massacre in 1919 in Phillips County, Arkansas. Despite its success in *Moore v. Dempsey*, the NAACP was not a grassroots organization that appealed to poor and working-class Blacks.

Horrified by the headlines about Black youths raping two white women, the NAACP hesitated to get involved in the Scottsboro case. After numerous investigations, however, the organization tried to wrest control of the defense from the ILD. NAACP executive secretary Walter White believed that the ILD had duped the parents of the Scottsboro defendants. The ILD treated the parents as equals. White, in contrast, spoke about them in a patronizing way. He assumed that the parents would come to their senses and lined up defense lawyers Clarence Darrow and Arthur Garfield Hays to represent the Scottsboro defendants. The ILD, however, insisted on controlling the case and hired New York lawyer Samuel Leibowitz. The NAACP steadfastly refused to work with the legal arm of the Communist Party.

Angelo dedicated himself to the Party's efforts to free the Scottsboro defendants. In New Orleans, he attended longshoremen's union meetings about the case and joined the city's Provisional

Committee for the Defense of the Scottsboro Boys. On May 31, he joined two white seamen as delegates at the All-Southern Conference for the Scottsboro Defense in Chattanooga. At the conference, he defended the ILD and the Communist Party's commitment to the case and criticized the NAACP's attempts to undermine the ILD. He clashed with NAACP field secretary William Pickens at a June 7 fund-raising meeting in Chattanooga after Pickens denigrated the ILD and claimed that the NAACP had raised more money for the appeal. A member of the Black Ministers' Alliance refused to allow Angelo to speak and tried to call the police. Angelo, however, demanded the floor and denounced the Yale-educated Pickens: "You say you will let me speak here because I am the same color and blood as you. But my blood will never let me go down on my knees to beg the white rulers of Alabama for mercy for these nine innocent boys. These boys cannot be saved by such slave tactics as yours. Instead, I and the organization I represent will carry on a relentless fight to force the legal lynchers to free these boys. To refuse to fight is to condemn these boys to death."

Upon returning to Birmingham, Angelo almost suffered a similar fate. On August 3, 1931, three affluent young white women drove to Shades Mountain outside the Birmingham city limits in Mountain Brook. A Black man, the women claimed, jumped on the running board of their car, ordered them to park in a secluded area, and ranted and raved about white people for four hours. He shot the three women as they attempted to escape. Only one survived. A massive manhunt ensued. During a "reign of terror," Birmingham police rounded up radical Black suspects.

After a long day of organizing coal miners forty miles away, Angelo arrived home to find his room in shambles and his belongings scattered everywhere. The next morning, police detectives arrested him and beat him with a rubber hose to try to coerce him to confess to the Shades Mountain shootings or to implicate someone else. Unsuccessful inside the jail, the officers drove him twenty-one miles into the woods, handcuffed him to a tree, and beat and bloodied him with a hose. Still unable to extract a confession or a lead about a suspect, they returned him to the jail. Within three days of the shootings, newspapers all over the country identified Eugene Braxton as one of three Black men in custody. The surviving white victim, eighteen-year-old Nell Williams, saved him when she refused to identify him as the shooter. Instead, the police charged Angelo with vagrancy. He was fined $25, sentenced to ninety days in jail, and released on $150 bond pending an appeal to the circuit court. After six weeks without an arrest in the shootings, Williams identified a frail, Black war veteran, Willie Peterson, she had seen on the street. He looked nothing like the thirty- to thirty-five-year-old man she had initially described to police. When Peterson refused to confess, Williams's hotheaded brother shot him inside the jail. Peterson, already suffering from tuberculosis, recovered from his wounds and insisted on his innocence. Tried twice, convicted, and sentenced to death, Peterson died in Montgomery's Kilby Prison in 1940 (the governor had commuted his sentence to life in prison).

It took Angelo several weeks to recover from his head injuries. By now, the name Eugene Braxton, a nationally known murder suspect, made him a liability. He could no longer organize miners in Birmingham without putting himself or the miners in grave danger. In September 1931, the Communist Party offered him the opportunity to organize an Unemployed Committee in a new city and with a new name. The Party sent him to Atlanta, a city rife with its own occupational hazards.

For a Black labor organizer in 1931, Atlanta proved to be attractive yet terrifying. On the one hand, the city featured a thriving Black middle class educated at four historically Black colleges: Morehouse, Spelman, Morris Brown, and Atlanta University. These educated, Black professionals made Atlanta a focal point of civil rights activism. On the other hand, Atlanta included a strong Klan presence, a fascist group known as the Black Shirts intent on driving Blacks from the workforce, and a law enforcement community hell-bent on running the Communist Party out of town.

Fulton County prosecutors tried to rid the city of communist organizers by resurrecting an old slave insurrection law. Revised during Reconstruction to omit references to slavery, the Georgia law made insurrection or attempting an insurrection a capital crime because of the fear of armed Black resistance. In 1868, state officials used the law to try and convict John T. Gibson, a Black preacher who had allegedly encouraged about 100 people to break a Black prisoner out of jail. Gibson's conviction, however, was overturned on appeal because the law failed to specify a punishment for the specific crime of attempting to incite insurrection (as opposed to inciting insurrection). As a result, Georgia legislators revised the law again in 1871 to make inciting or attempting to incite an insurrection punishable by death or, if the jury chose to show mercy, by five to twenty years in prison.

Georgia officials never successfully prosecuted anyone under the 1871 insurrection law yet employed it to quell organizing by Blacks and by labor unions. In 1875, a special jury acquitted a Black man, Corday Harris, of attempting to incite insurrection in Sandersville, Georgia, as part of an alleged Black riot in Washington County. In 1916, Fulton County prosecutors unsuccessfully tried William Pollard, a white labor organizer responsible for a streetcar worker strike, for circulating insurrectionary literature. After a jury deadlocked over Pollard's guilt under the insurrection law, county prosecutors tried and convicted him for suborning perjury.

Lacking a sedition or syndicalism law similar to the ones other states had passed to criminalize radical advocacy of violent political or economic change, Fulton County prosecutors invoked the insurrection law in March and May 1930 to charge six communists—two white men, two white women, and two Black men—known as the Atlanta Six. Initially charged with circulating insurrectionary papers and attempting to incite insurrection, the Atlanta Six were released on bail. The prosecutors, however, seemed in no hurry to go to trial. The arrests and pending charges accomplished the goals of the white establishment. The Atlanta Six left the state after their release. The city's few remaining communists lived in fear of "the terror and the Georgia insurrection law."

Angelo Herndon—formerly known as Eugene Braxton—entered Atlanta fully aware of the Communist Party's precarious situation. The Klan, Black Shirts, and Fulton County prosecutors posed only part of the problem. The Party's few remaining organizers in Atlanta showed more interest in attacking one another than in recruiting new members. Young and inexperienced, Herndon found himself an easy target. A district organizer described him as having a "very lazy streak." Herndon wrote to the national office with charges of his own. During the first six months of 1932, he struggled to expand Party membership beyond more than a dozen people. He established two Foster and Ford Clubs in an effort to get the Communist Party's presidential ticket of William Z. Foster and James W. Ford on the November ballot. Yet he had not succeeded in bringing Atlanta's Black and white workers together— not until the county commissioners decided on June 18 to cut off all unemployment relief for nearly 22,000 starving people.

Herndon knew exactly what he had to do and set out to organize the first mass interracial demonstration of unemployed workers in the city's history. In the name of the Unemployed Committee of Atlanta, he and a dozen colleagues produced a leaflet calling people to action by pointing out the large salaries made by Community Chest executives. The leaflet also mocked the county commissioners' suggestions that the city's poor people should be rounded up and shipped to farms and that no starving people lived in Atlanta. Herndon and his colleagues printed 10,000 copies and called for people to gather at 10:00 a.m. on June 30 in front of the county courthouse. They secretly distributed the leaflets house by house to avoid surveillance and intimidation by the Klan and local police.

The night before the demonstration, Herndon could not sleep. He had no idea how many people would show up or whether the demonstration would be successful. The next morning, he arrived at the courthouse an hour early and discovered many people already there. By 10:00 a.m., hundreds of Black and white workers had arrived at the courthouse. The city of Atlanta had never seen such an interracial demonstration. Herndon took pride in the peacefulness of the protest and in the lack of arrests. He also could point to tangible results. The next day, county officials reversed their decision to end relief for nearly 22,000 people and discovered $6000 in additional relief funds in the budget.

Herndon's attempt to organize Atlanta's Black and white workers was gaining momentum. The Unemployed Committee had earned "considerable prestige" from its "partial victory." Yet Herndon and his fellow communists should have been more aware that the Klan and local law enforcement would not permit an interracial alliance of workers to take root. Indeed, he had no clue that on the night of July 10 he would be arrested while opening his mail at P.O. Box 339. This arrest differed from the ones in the past when he had been charged with vagrancy and released on bail after a few days. The police seized the literature under his arm at the post office and from his rented room—all without a search warrant. They beat him and attempted to coerce a confession from him while he sat in a dark room strapped to a fake electric chair. Initially, they refused to tell him why he had been arrested and simply said that the county's chief prosecutor, Solicitor General John A. Boykin, wanted to see him. The booking ledger at the jail included only one word: "C-O-M-M-U-N-I-S-T."

For eleven days, Angelo sat in a filthy cell in the city jail with no charges pending against him. He smuggled a letter via a released prisoner to the ILD. The Party's legal arm relied on a white Atlanta lawyer, Oliver C. Hancock, to file a writ of habeas corpus challenging the legality of Herndon's confinement. On July 21, Judge Virlyn B. Moore denied the writ but ordered Fulton County prosecutors to charge or release Herndon by 2:30 p.m. the next day. As they had done with the six Atlanta communists in 1930, the prosecutors decided to charge him under the insurrection law. An all-white grand jury indicted Herndon for attempting to incite insurrection

on July 16—even though he had been in jail since July 10—for organizing and attending mass meetings, encouraging people to join
the Communist Party and Young Communist League, and possessing and circulating radical books and literature. Attempting to
incite insurrection was a capital crime punishable by death or up to
twenty years on a chain gang. Upon his indictment, Herndon was
transferred from the city jail to the county jail known as Fulton
Tower to await the trial for his life.

What he needed was a lawyer who believed in his innocence and
possessed the skills and courage to defend him before an all-white
jury. Herndon placed his fate in the hands of a Black Harvard law
graduate and young Atlanta lawyer who had never tried a criminal
case.

CHAPTER TWO

ATLANTA'S PRINCE

Young Ben Davis Jr. (*center*) pictured with his father,
Ben Sr. (*left*) and his mother, Jimmie

O N JULY 12, BEN DAVIS JR. READ A BRIEF ACCOUNT OF
Herndon's arrest in the *Atlanta Constitution*. He headed straight
to the city jail. As a member of the Georgia bar, he was permitted
to meet with Herndon. They talked for two hours about Herndon's
life story and the circumstances of his arrest. Impressed by Herndon's sincerity and conviction, Davis offered to represent him pro
bono. Herndon explained that the ILD controlled the litigation but
welcomed Davis's participation. ILD national secretary William
L. Patterson interviewed Davis in Atlanta and offered him a spot
on the legal team. The cash-strapped ILD liked the idea of a Black

lawyer on the case, especially one willing to work for free. Indeed, Davis and his partner, John Geer, sat at counsel's table on July 21, when Oliver Hancock argued that Herndon should be released on a writ of habeas corpus.

At the time, Ben Davis Jr. was making more headlines for his tennis game than his legal skills. At six foot two and 225 pounds, he smashed "fire-ball" serves and regularly reached the semifinals and finals of statewide all-Black tournaments. The city's leading Black newspaper declared him "Atlanta's Prince of the Clay Courts."

On or off the tennis court, Ben Davis Jr. cut quite a figure in Atlanta. A virtuoso violinist and singer at Morehouse, a football star at Amherst, and a graduate of Harvard Law School, he frequently found himself in the Black press's society pages. He favored tailored suits, studs on his shirts, a gold clasp under his collars, and spats over his patent-leather shoes. He took pride in his finely manicured mustache and fingernails, slicked down his perfectly parted hair, and wore sweet-smelling cologne. He could be seen walking the streets with "a gold-headed cane." Men gravitated to him because of his athletic prowess. Women swooned over him because of his musical ability, aesthetic sense, and good looks.

More than a sportsman and a dandy, Ben Jr. modeled himself after his father and namesake, "Fighting Ben" Davis Sr. A native of Dawson, Georgia, Ben Sr. completed his secondary school education at Atlanta University and began a career as a bricklayer before becoming a teacher and principal. He clawed his way to political power through the state ranks of the Grand United Order of Odd Fellows, a Black fraternal organization, as the editor and publisher of the *Atlanta Independent* newspaper, and as the secretary of the Georgia Republican Party. During the 1920s, all Republican federal political patronage in Georgia flowed through Ben Sr. until jealous whites appealed to Herbert Hoover to oust him as national committeeman. In June 1932, his father's political downfall was fresh in Ben Jr.'s mind.

Like his father, Ben Jr. often challenged the establishment. As a secondary school student at Morehouse, he balked at singing Negro spirituals and was briefly expelled for leading a successful student strike over a mandatory two-hour study hall. He applied to Amherst after his freshman year of college to play football and because a family friend, future NAACP lawyer Charles Hamilton Houston, had been a Phi Beta Kappa graduate of that school. Davis, by contrast, was a mediocre student. During his three years at Amherst, he blamed his C and D grades on northern racism. He focused more on football, playing right tackle on the same offensive line as future surgeon and medical researcher Charles Drew and learning blocking techniques from pro football star, actor, and performer Paul Robeson. Davis's only A during his three years there was in music.

The racism at Amherst was subtle yet real. A talented violinist, Davis was barred from the school's music club because it made trips to southern schools. And he was nearly excluded from the football team's game at Princeton, ostensibly because of the opposing team's southern-born faculty and student body. As a Georgia native, Davis knew all about racial segregation and discrimination. Returning home after his first year at Amherst, he was ordered off an Atlanta trolley car and fined for sitting in the whites-only section. He had given his seat to a pregnant woman. His father accompanied him to court, kowtowed to the judge, who blamed the incident on Ben Jr.'s northern education, and paid the fine.

At his father's urging and by virtue of attending an elite college, Ben Jr. gained admission to Harvard Law School. The nation's preeminent law school, Harvard transformed legal education by adopting the case method—teaching students the law not by encouraging them to memorize lectures but by engaging them in Socratic discussions of court decisions. Getting in was the easy part; staying was harder. Approximately one-third of Harvard's first-year law students flunked out. The lowest passing grade was a 55 (D). Davis barely survived—his highest grade was a 72 (B) in civil procedure; his lowest was a 55 in property. All male and almost all white, Harvard Law School enrolled only a few Black students per class. During his second year, Davis protested to Dean Roscoe Pound that the school's Black students found themselves excluded from whites-only law clubs that taught brief writing. He refused to join the Dunbar Club, comprised of Black and Jewish students, and blamed his exclusion from the white law clubs as the reason that he never learned to write a brief. He lived with his Amherst class-mate William Hastie, the second Black member of the *Harvard Law Review* and later the first Black federal judge, and Robert C. Weaver, a Black doctoral student in economics and later the first Black member of a presidential cabinet. Unlike Hastie, Davis was an indifferent law student who needed four years to graduate. He had to retake his trusts exam in 1929 while working in Baltimore as an editor of the *Illustrated Feature Section*, a white-owned syndi-cated weekly insert sold to Black newspapers.

After graduating from Harvard and several years in journalism in Baltimore and Chicago, Ben Jr. returned to Atlanta to study for the Georgia bar. He passed in January 1932 and formed a partner-ship with a twenty-six-year-old Black lawyer, John H. Geer. Born in Greenville, South Carolina, Geer briefly attended Morehouse, worked as a bellhop, and studied for the Georgia bar by taking correspondence courses. The short, bespectacled Geer knew only slightly more about legal practice than Davis. During his first day in court, Davis was fined five dollars for contempt for smoking a cigar in the courtroom. A few months later, charged with driving through a stop sign, he persuaded the judge to reduce his fine from six to four dollars. He had never argued a criminal case.

In defending Herndon, Davis and Geer quickly found themselves on their own. The ILD fired Oliver Hancock. The organization was unhappy with Hancock's strategy of delay in the Atlanta Six cases, his inadvertent forfeiture of $3000 in bail money for one of the Atlanta Six, and his argument in Herndon's habeas corpus hear-ing. In Hancock's place, the ILD hired a respected white Atlanta criminal defense lawyer, H. A. Allen, to represent Herndon. Allen, however, clashed with the ILD over legal strategy. The ILD wanted to challenge Fulton County's systematic exclusion of Blacks from juries. All-white juries made it almost impossible for Black criminal defendants to receive fair trials in southern courtrooms. The law, moreover, was on Herndon and the ILD's side. The U.S. Supreme Court declared in an 1880 decision, *Strauder v. West Virginia*, that a state law barring Blacks from jury service violated the Fourteenth Amendment's Equal Protection Clause. In another ILD-led case in July 1932, Maryland's highest court reversed the capital murder conviction of Euel Lee because of the systematic exclusion of Blacks from juries. Allen, however, refused to be party to a lawsuit attacking the South's criminal justice system and in late November withdrew from the case. He took his $100 retainer with him.

At Davis's suggestion, the ILD approached the most prominent Black attorney in Atlanta, A. T. Walden, about being Herndon's lead counsel. A graduate of Atlanta University and University of Michigan Law School, Austen Thomas Walden began practicing law in Macon, Georgia, before serving in the Great War as an infantry captain and assistant trial judge advocate. After the war, "Colonel" Walden settled in Atlanta, started a family, and established a law practice that made him a pillar of the city's Black community. In January 1932, Walden allowed Davis to work at his firm while studying for the bar and had mentored him during his first few months in legal practice. It was Walden who had paid Davis's five-dollar fine for smoking a cigar in the courtroom. Yet when it came to defending Herndon and attacking Fulton County's all-white jury system, Walden drew the line. The president of Atlanta's NAACP branch, he did not want the ILD to dictate legal strategy and perceived the Communist Party as more interested in scoring political points about all-white southern juries than in winning Herndon's freedom.

Ben Davis Jr.'s willingness to try Herndon's case and to raise the issue of all-white juries was not surprising in light of his fearless attitude toward the Georgia political establishment. In late September 1932, he clashed with Governor Richard B. Russell Jr. about whether he could use the state's law library on a nonsegregated basis. Davis had been thrown out of the library for refusing to change his seat.

A few weeks later, Davis explained the Communist Party's political platform to the 27 Club, a private organization of Atlanta's Black leaders. He claimed that he was not an official member of the Communist Party—which was technically true at the time. Initially, Davis had taken Herndon's case because he believed that the communist organizer had received "a raw deal." Yet, as he interacted with Herndon and read the communist literature seized from his client, Davis realized that this was "no isolated case of 'injustice.'" Davis understood how the white ruling class was using racism to divide the city's "starving" Black and white workers and was punishing Herndon for trying to unite them. The young Black Atlanta lawyer could not wait to tell Charles Hamilton Houston, the vice dean of Howard University School of Law, what he had learned. Davis had begun not only to embrace the Communist Party's ideas but also to immerse himself in its politics. In informing ILD national secretary William Patterson of his 27 Club talk, Davis wrote: "I think I can handle the situation okay considering how uninformed the people in this section are on our principles and philosophy."

As Herndon's new lead trial counsel, Davis prioritized his client's release from Fulton Tower—the county jail known for its 100-foot granite tower and nicknamed Big Rock. Herndon had been transferred to Big Rock immediately after his July 22 indictment. The facility was notorious for its filthy, inhumane conditions. Herndon shared a small cell with a prisoner who was so ill that he died and then was left to rot. The food—peas and beans often littered with small rocks, barely cooked turnip greens, baked grits with a streak of grease, and a few strips of fatback—ruined Herndon's stomach. As the months passed, he became so sick he could not swallow water. The county physician insisted he was fine. Herndon's visitors, however, smuggled in medicine. He yearned to leave Fulton Tower and despaired each time prosecutors delayed his trial. Bail, initially set at $3000, was increased to $5000. Seeking another way to free his client, Davis filed a writ of habeas corpus, an attack on the legality of Herndon's confinement based on the errors in the indictment such as the incorrect date of the alleged insurrection and the constitutionality of the insurrection law, without specifying how it violated the Constitution. On December 3, a Fulton County judge denied the writ. In addition, the prosecution, over the defense's objection, succeeded in delaying the trial until January after Davis informed them that he intended to subpoena numerous county officials and to challenge the all-white jury system.

In early December, Davis filed a second writ of habeas corpus challenging the county's systematic, intentional exclusion of Blacks from Fulton County's grand and trial juries. A Fulton County judge, wise to the sensitivity of the issue, claimed that an illness required him to hold the hearing in chambers rather than in the courtroom. The ruse conveniently hid the December 15 hearing from the eyes of the press and public, the ears of the court reporter, and the pages of the trial record. In the judge's chambers, Davis called half a dozen witnesses, including a judge, court clerks, deputy sheriffs, and jury commissioners, to testify about the jury selection process. He was prepared to call more subpoenaed witnesses until his chief antagonist, Assistant Solicitor John H. Hudson, made a damning admission on the witness stand: "Negroes have been systematically excluded from the grand and petit juries for years." The ILD hailed Hudson's admission as an "important victory."

Hudson was no easy mark. A lay preacher and deacon at his Baptist church, he pursued communists with a religious zeal. He had bragged to the Fish Committee in November 1930 about all the communist literature he had seized during raids. He also described the state insurrection law he had used to indict the Atlanta Six with capital crimes as the "same thing as treason." He had charged Herndon with attempting to incite insurrection after the arrest at the post office and the warrantless raid on Herndon's room. At six foot three and 200 pounds, "partially bald and with deep sunken eyes," Hudson could match Davis in physical stature. The prosecutor often spoke to juries while "flailing his arms like a windmill." Davis, however, was not intimidated and considered Hudson, with his faux religious piety, "one of the most consummate hypocrites." In mid-December, Davis persuaded the judge to reduce Herndon's bail to $2500 over the opposition of Hudson, who had insisted upon $25,000 "so that damn Red will come back for trial."

On Christmas Eve, Herndon was released from prison after five months and three weeks. Two Black Atlanta pharmacists supplied the $2500 bond. Davis offered to find Herndon a place to stay until the January 16 trial. Herndon, however, declined Davis's offer. He stayed with fellow Party members and was determined to return to organizing Atlanta's unemployed workers. Davis was impressed by Herndon's commitment to the cause. Davis's mettle would be tested as well. The Klan tried to intimidate him. They sent him the first of many warnings in an anonymous note with a simple message: "The Klan Rides Again."

After the defense succeeded in delaying the trial, Hudson sought to blunt their attack on the all-white jury system. In an unrelated case beginning January 3, Fulton County officials selected two Black men, a railroad fireman and the owner of a transfer company, for a prospective jury, for the first time since Reconstruction. The case involved a white lawyer accused of defrauding a Black woman of $250. The defendant's counsel used his peremptory challenges to strike the two Black jurors. The ILD declared another partial victory. Davis, however, denigrated the state's move as a "sham" and vowed to attack the all-white jury system at Herndon's trial.

On the morning of January 16, 1933, Davis walked into a Fulton County courtroom packed with more than 100 people to watch two Black lawyers defend a Black communist on trial for his life. Whites dominated the rows of spectators. A few Blacks huddled in the Jim Crow section in the rear. Viola Montgomery of Monroe, Georgia, was among them. Her seventeen-year-old son, Olen, was one of the Scottsboro defendants who had been wrongly convicted of raping two white women. The ILD was fighting for his release from Alabama's Kilby Prison. A fervent supporter of the ILD, Mrs. Montgomery was there to bear witness for her son and to make sure the same thing did not happen to Herndon.

In front of the lawyers-only railing, four prosecutors led by Assistant Solicitors Hudson and J. Walter LeCraw sat at the counsel table to the left facing the judge near the jury box. Davis, Geer, and Herndon, who was wearing glasses and a red striped tie, sat at the counsel table on the right side. Curious white members of the Fulton County bar sat and stood in the front well of the courtroom. They had never seen two Black lawyers attempt to save a Black man from the electric chair by putting the county's all-white jury system on trial.

This time, Davis was determined to get Fulton County officials on the record about their systematic exclusion of Blacks from juries. He did not have a receptive audience. Judge Lee B. Wyatt of LaGrange, in Troup County, Georgia, presided over the trial. An inexperienced judge, Wyatt had been the city attorney of LaGrange from 1923 to 1931 and had encountered few, if any, Black lawyers. He may have been selected as a visiting judge because Davis chose to challenge the all-white Fulton County jury system. Davis knew he was in trouble when Wyatt ruled on his motion to quash the indictment without allowing him to call a single witness. Hudson, recognizing the potential for reversible error, successfully prevailed upon the judge, a fellow Mercer Law School graduate, to allow Davis to call witnesses.

That morning, Davis called twelve witnesses: four jury commissioners, two deputy sheriffs, a superior court judge, a tax collector, the clerk of the superior court, a grand jury foreman, the receiver of tax returns, and Assistant Solicitor Hudson. Many of them conceded that no Black man had ever served on a Fulton County grand jury. The jury commissioners explained that they selected only "the most intelligent, upright citizens" for grand jury service from a pool of about 4000 men, none of them Black. Trial juries were a different story. The witnesses denied excluding Blacks from the trial jury pool. One of the jury commissioners revealed that they typed the names of white men on white cards, and Black men on yellow or pink cards—to make it easier to exclude Black jurors. No Black man had been chosen for a Fulton County trial jury. Hudson, however, took his opportunity on the witness stand to remind Judge Wyatt of the attempt to seat two Black men on a trial jury twelve days earlier. Yet there was not a single Black man on Herndon's trial jury panel, despite many eligible candidates. To prove this point, Davis called two of them as witnesses: David T. Howard, a mortician who had paid taxes for forty years and R. L. Craddock, a college graduate. Neither man had ever been called for jury service. Oddly, Howard's and Craddock's testimony was later excluded from the incomplete trial record.

What happened next, also conveniently excluded from the trial record, nearly got Davis cited for contempt of court. Davis reminded Judge Wyatt that several judicial decisions, including the 1880 U.S. Supreme Court precedent, had declared the systematic exclusion of Blacks from juries to be unconstitutional. "It ain't clear to me," the judge replied. He turned his back on Davis and informed him that he had ten more minutes to make his case. Davis exclaimed that Wyatt's conduct was "unjudicial" and that he expected "the same courtesy you extended to Mr. Hudson." The judge, swiveling in his chair, pointed his gavel at Davis and shouted: "That's enough from you." Davis predicted that if Judge Wyatt did not dismiss the indictment that he would get reversed on the jury issue by the Supreme Court. Hudson objected that the comment was "contemptuous." The judge snapped: "I'll handle this!" Denying Davis's motions, Judge Wyatt adjourned the court and postponed jury selection until the next morning.

As Davis began to exit the courtroom, seven or eight white men confronted him and Geer. "Watch yourself, or we'll string you up," one said. Another, holding a knife in his hand, warned: "Leave the

Klan out of this." And another chimed in: "We'll be here tomorrow and [the] next day. That nigger red better be convicted." A burly Black minister, Reverend J. A. Martin, and two of his parishioners, fearing for Davis's safety, promised to accompany him and Geer to and from the courthouse each day.

The next morning, while walking to his car in front of his family's home, Davis discovered a four-foot-high white cross and a leaflet: "The Klan Rides Again. Get out of the Herndon case. This is a white man's country." Davis pulled the cross out of the ground as a souvenir and showed the leaflet to his father, Ben Sr. The older man informed his son that he had received threats like these for years and was no longer afraid of them. Davis, Geer, and Herndon, escorted by Reverend Martin and several parishioners into the courthouse, made their way into the crowded courtroom.

At 9:00 a.m., Herndon's trial began with jury selection. Davis asked one of the white men on the jury panel whether he was a member of the Klan. The man admitted he was yet insisted that he could be fair and impartial. Judge Wyatt initially denied Davis's request to excuse the juror for cause until Assistant Solicitor Hudson agreed. Even with the Klan member excused for cause, Herndon's jury consisted of all white men.

In a fiery opening statement, Hudson held up communist literature seized from Herndon. He explained that the literature appealed to southern Blacks to "smash the national guard" and to set up their own nation. Finally, he urged the jury, if it found Herndon guilty beyond a reasonable doubt, to show him no mercy: "I expect you to inflict the death penalty."

The prosecution called its first witness, arresting officer F. B. Watson. Watson testified that on July 10, 1932, he and another officer had been instructed to watch P.O. Box 339. They had been there for about an hour when Herndon opened the mailbox. They arrested him and seized a "paste-board box" containing books, papers, and pamphlets from under his arm. They took Herndon to where he said he lived. They quickly discovered that the first address was not correct. At a second address, they confirmed with the landlady which room was Herndon's and seized a box and a suitcase containing communist books, newspapers, and magazines. They brought Herndon and the radical literature to the police station. Watson testified that Herndon admitted during police questioning that he was a Communist Party organizer. On cross-examination, Watson stated that he did not know who was going to show up at P.O. Box 339. He also conceded that he did not have a search warrant either for the mailbox or for Herndon's room. Finally, he denied taking Herndon to a room in the police station with a fake electric chair.

Davis refused to back down when it came to racist prosecution witnesses. Assistant Solicitor E. A. Stephens testified that he had instructed the chief of police to have officers watch P.O. Box 339 after one of the county commissioners had received "a certain scurrilous letter" from that address. Early in his testimony, Stephens began recounting his interrogation of Herndon and referred to him as a "nigger," which Judge Wyatt forced the court reporter to omit or to change to "darkey." Davis immediately objected and threatened to ask for a mistrial because the racial slur was "prejudicial to our case." "I don't know whether it is or not," Wyatt replied, yet instructed the witness to refer to Herndon as the defendant. Stephens, however, kept referring to him as a "nigger" or "darkey" as he testified about the communist newspapers and books illegally seized from Herndon's room.

To counter the idea that the books could be considered "revolutionary material," Davis called two Emory University economics professors, Mercer G. Evans and T. J. Corley. Evans testified that he had examined the communist books in the indictment and that Emory students could check most of them out of the library. Assistant Solicitor Hudson objected that the comment was "irrelevant and immaterial." Judge Wyatt sustained the objection and added: "If Emory University is guilty of anything, we will try them." He then proceeded to disqualify Evans, an economist who earned his PhD at the University of Chicago, as an expert on communist literature.

As frustrating as Judge Wyatt's ruling disqualifying Evans was, the prosecution's questions for Professor Corley truly outraged Davis. On cross-examination, Corley explained the party's interest in "Equal Rights for Negroes" as meaning "equal rights under the law." In response, Hudson asked Corley: "You understand that to mean the right of a colored boy to marry your daughter, if you have one?" Davis objected to the question about racial intermarriage as "irrelevant and immaterial" and because it was not part of the Communist Party's platform. Judge Wyatt overruled the objection. Corley answered that such a marriage would be illegal under Georgia law. Hudson asked him whether he knew racial intermarriage was legal in twenty states. Davis objected again that the question was "irrelevant and immaterial." Wyatt overruled him again and insisted the question was permissible on cross-examination. Davis kept objecting to questions not having to do with the Communist Party platform, the subject of Corley's testimony, to no avail. Wyatt kept overruling him. Like his Emory colleague Evans, Corley was not permitted to testify as an expert on the communist books illegally seized from Herndon's room and included in the indictment.

For Davis, the most inspiring moment of the trial was Herndon's speech on the witness stand. Under Georgia law at the time, a criminal defendant was not allowed to testify under oath but could make an unsworn statement without direct or cross-examination. Feeling "calm and collected," Herndon knew he had nothing to lose because the jurors had already made up their minds to convict him. In an "impassioned" fifteen-minute speech, he explained how he had organized Atlanta's starving and jobless white and Black workers to protest the lack of unemployment relief and how the peaceful demonstration at the courthouse had led to an increase in relief funds. He described his arrest at the post office; eleven days in jail without formal criminal charges; nearly six months of inhumane treatment at Fulton Tower, including the corpse in his cell, inedible food filled with rocks, and denial of proper medical care, which the county jailers and prison doctor subsequently denied under oath.

Throughout his speech, Herndon defended his interracial organizing: "they can hold this Angelo Herndon and hundreds of others, but it will never stop these demonstrations on the part of negro and white workers who demand a decent place to live in and proper food for their kids to eat." He appealed to white jurors struggling to find work during the Depression, declared that capitalism was on the verge of "collapse," and endorsed the communist idea of uniting the working class. He did not profess to know whether this was "insurrection or not." He predicted that "no matter what you do with Angelo Herndon, no matter what you do with the Angelo Herndon[s] in the future, this question of unemployment, the question of unity between negro and white workers cannot be solved with hands that are stained with the blood of an innocent individual."

"Do with me as you will," the *Atlanta Constitution* quoted Herndon as saying that day, "there are thousands more to take my place." The article described his trial as "unique in the annals of Georgia jurisprudence"; the front-page headline declared: "Death of Herndon Is Asked by State." One of the few white reporters at the trial recalled that Herndon had "really talked himself into jail."

Ben Davis Jr. had seen and heard enough. He needed only one day of Herndon's trial to understand that a Black man could not get a fair shake in a Georgia court of law. He described it as "a turning point of my life." In truth, however, his disillusionment had been building for several years. Even though he had grown up as a privileged member of Atlanta's Black middle class, he knew that he would always be a second-class citizen in the Jim Crow South. He had experienced subtler forms of northern white racism at Amherst and Harvard Law School and as a journalist in Baltimore and Chicago. The Republican Party was out of the question for Davis because of the racist whites who had accused his father of illegal patronage and had ousted him as a national committeeman. The Democratic Party was worse because of its embrace of white supremacist southern politicians. The Communist Party was the only political organization willing to fight for Black economic and social equality and had nominated a Black man, James Ford, as its 1932 vice presidential candidate. Davis had been warming to communist ideas for months. In preparation for Herndon's trial, he had read the communist literature summarized in Herndon's indictment, had spoken about the party's platform to a private club of Black leaders, had advised the ILD's William Patterson on party politics, and had been inspired by his client's commitment to the cause. Indeed, Herndon served as Davis's "political mentor." The night after the first day of Herndon's trial, Davis submitted his Communist Party membership application to his client.

The next morning at 9:00 a.m., two communists—a lawyer and his client—arrived at the Fulton County courthouse and sat at counsel's table. Davis needed to make a closing argument he hoped would save Herndon's life. Each side received two hours.

Leading off for the prosecution, Hudson pleaded with the jury to give Herndon the death penalty. The assistant solicitor, Davis recalled, "flailed his arms, preached, snorted, read excerpts from the forbidden pamphlets, pounded the jury box, pointed his forefinger at Herndon, quoted the Bible, painted a picture of threatened virginal white womanhood, swayed his body left and right as if he tried to hypnotize the jury—appealing to them to do their duty by sending this 'black viper to the electric chair.'" The *Atlanta Journal* described Hudson's closing argument as a "fiery speech" that distinguished "between 'philosophic discussion and rank treason.'" As he did earlier in the trial, Hudson read from one of the books seized from Herndon's apartment, *The Life and Struggles of Negro Toilers* by George Padmore, which endorsed the Communist Party's call for the right of self-determination for the Black majority in the South's Black Belt. "Stamp this thing out now," Hudson told the jury, "with a conviction."

Geer spoke next but sat down after only fifteen minutes. Surprised by the brevity of his co-counsel's remarks, Davis rose to the lectern and tried to match Hudson's fury and passion. He portrayed Hudson as acting like a holy man at church on Sundays yet sending innocent Black and white men to the chain gang during the week. He accused Hudson of trying to deceive the jury by reading only the parts of Padmore's book about Black self-determination and not about the lynching of innocent Black men. "This book should have been written in the blood of Negroes who were burned at the stake by mobs," Davis declared. "I say lynching is insurrection. The only offense Herndon committed was that he asked for bread for children—his only crime is his color." As for the books illegally seized from Herndon's room, Davis informed the jury: "Some of the books are considered classics. You can't kill a man because of the books he reads."

During his closing argument for the prosecution, Hudson's co-counsel, Walter LeCraw, denounced Davis's invocation of lynching. A "small, chalk-white, wizened mummy of a man," LeCraw pointed to Herndon's interracial organizing and possession of seditious communist literature as clear proof of attempting to incite insurrection. He reminded the all-white jury of the Communist Party's support for self-determination in the Black Belt. "If you don't send this defendant to the electric chair we will have a Red Army marching through Georgia," he shouted, "which will take all of the land away from the white people and give it to the Negroes!"

To his credit, Judge Wyatt properly instructed the jury about the evidence required to convict Herndon of attempting to incite insurrection. He informed the jury that Herndon could not be convicted for merely possessing insurrectionary literature. The judge also properly instructed the jury about the difference between "mere acts of preparation" and an attempt to commit a crime. Finally, the judge correctly instructed the jury that Herndon could not be convicted of attempting to incite insurrection unless the evidence showed beyond a reasonable doubt that "the advocacy would be acted on immediately" and result in "immediate serious violence against the State of Georgia."

After listening to Judge Wyatt's instructions, the jury deliberated for a little over two hours. All twelve jurors believed that Herndon was guilty. The only question was whether he should pay with his life. On the first four ballots, two jurors held out for the death penalty. On the fifth ballot, one juror changed his mind. Finally, on the sixth ballot, the final juror agreed to a recommendation of mercy.

Upon learning that the jury had reached a verdict, Judge Wyatt positioned sheriff's deputies throughout the courtroom and warned the crowd of whites and Blacks not to create a disturbance. The foreman read the verdict and recommended mercy in the form of eighteen to twenty years on a chain gang. Sentencing, however, was up to Wyatt. When asked if he wanted to say anything before his sentencing, Herndon replied: "Nothing in particular." Wyatt agreed with the jury's recommendation and sentenced Herndon to eighteen to twenty years on a chain gang. "Under the circumstances," he told Herndon, "I think the jury was thoroughly justified in the verdict it returned." Herndon, who had expected to be sentenced to death in the electric chair, told an astonished reporter that the jury's recommendation of mercy was "a Christmas present."

Some Christmas present. Instead of a jolt of electric current, Herndon immediately returned to Fulton Tower and faced eighteen to twenty years of a slow, painful death. The previous year, journalist John L. Spivak had published both a novel and a nonfiction pamphlet after observing several Georgia chain gangs. He had interviewed young Black men who had been sentenced to the chain gang for vagrancy, being unemployed, shooting craps, and talking back to a white man. He had witnessed how they performed backbreaking manual labor from sunrise to sunset; slept in filthy, unsanitary cages chained around their neck and legs like wild beasts; and died of disease, abuse, and torture. That same year, Robert E. Burns published *I Am a Fugitive from a Georgia Chain Gang!*, an autobiographical account of his life on a Georgia chain gang during the

1920s and his escape to New Jersey. New Jersey officials refused to extradite him. Burns's book became an Oscar-nominated movie. Judge Wyatt, during a sentencing hearing in a different case, denied inhumane treatment of Georgia prisoners on chain gangs as northern falsehoods. If Herndon were sent to the chain gang, Spivak predicted that he would not live to see his case appealed to the U.S. Supreme Court because he faced "certain death."

The day after the verdict, Davis returned to Judge Wyatt's courtroom to file a motion for a new trial. Wyatt, who set a hearing on the motion for March 11, denied Herndon's application for bail because the conviction was a capital offense. Though no longer unbeaten, Davis was unbowed. He expected to take Herndon's case to the Supreme Court. "There wasn't one iota of evidence in the case which would justify such a verdict," he told the press. "We expect to fight to the finish."

Herndon's sentence of eighteen to twenty years on a Georgia chain gang made front-page news in the *New York Times*, New York *Herald Tribune*, and other national newspapers. Many Blacks and liberal whites viewed the Herndon verdict as another Scottsboro case and a blight on the South. The *Macon Telegraph*, edited by white liberal W. T. Anderson, deemed it a "shameful verdict." The *St. Louis Post-Dispatch* declared it "a shameful proceeding, masquerading under the forms of law." For the most part, the Black press sided with Herndon. The New York *Amsterdam News* argued that his case "tears away the last shred of Georgia's claim to decency and exposes her foul body to the world." Other newspapers could not get past their skepticism about the Communist Party and its willingness to send Herndon and other Black organizers into the South. The *Pittsburgh Courier* blamed the communists for "callously sending these youngsters down to certain imprisonment and death." The conservative *Herald Tribune* declared that Herndon's sentence was "unnecessarily harsh" and "extremely stupid" because it aided the communist "campaign to convert American Negroes, using the injustices of which Negroes are victims as ammunition" and provided the Communist Party with "another first-class martyr."

Indeed, the Communist Party seized on the national media attention and turned Angelo Herndon's conviction into a cause célèbre on par with that of the Scottsboro defendants. "Angelo Herndon must not die, and Angelo must not be imprisoned for eighteen or twenty years," ILD national secretary William Patterson declared, "even though ten thousand Angelo Herndons rose to take his place."

In Herndon, the ILD had found the perfect symbol of injustice— young, Black, intelligent, and outspoken. During his spellbinding speech on the witness stand, he had espoused Communist Party principles and had insisted that in organizing Black and white unemployed workers he had broken no laws. On January 26, the *Daily Worker* published a jailhouse letter from Herndon urging people to continue organizing and calling for the abolition of the Georgia slave insurrection law.

In Davis, the ILD had discovered a powerful Black spokesman and a fearless, if inexperienced, legal advocate. He had put Fulton County's all-white jury system on trial. He had secretly joined the Communist Party. He had exposed Hudson in open court as a hypocrite, liar, and racist. He had saved Herndon from the electric chair. The ILD rewarded him and Geer by putting them in charge of Herndon's appeal and of defending the Atlanta Six, the two Black and four white communists who awaited their trials for violating the insurrection law. In addition, on January 29 the ILD opened an Atlanta office at 141½ Auburn Avenue where whites and Blacks worked side by side under Davis's supervision. That night, after the office opened its doors, he spoke to more than fifty Black leaders at the 27 Club about the significance of the Herndon and Atlanta Six cases and the importance that all Black people join the fight. After Davis's talk, the club adopted a resolution protesting Herndon's sentence.

On February 4, Herndon arrived at the Fulton County courthouse handcuffed to another prisoner for a habeas corpus hearing challenging the legality of his confinement. The courtroom was a welcome respite from his cell at Fulton Tower. He sat handcuffed to the other prisoner on a back bench while Davis, Geer, and Ansel W. Morrison, a white lawyer who had joined the defense as a volunteer, sat at counsel's table. Geer argued before Judge E. D. Thomas that Herndon's trial was "full of errors" and against the weight of the evidence and would be appealed to the Georgia Supreme Court and the U.S. Supreme Court. Geer requested $1000 bail for Herndon during the lengthy appeals process. Judge Thomas denied the habeas petition and bail request. Furthermore, he "threatened" Herndon that if his conviction were reversed on appeal, he would be retried and sentenced to death.

Back at Fulton Tower on the night of February 16, prison guards accused Herndon and three condemned cellmates of trying to escape. The "proof" was nothing but little pieces of iron that had peeled away from old pipes. Prison officials placed Herndon in solitary confinement. He complained about his cell's leaky, smelly toilet. Later that night, he heard a group of drunken guards approaching his cell, located at the far end of the hall. Herndon thought he was going to be lynched. Instead, the guards searched the cell and returned eight to ten times that night. They looked for hacksaws and read all his letters. After the ordeal, he wrote a letter to the ILD about the alleged escape and solitary confinement, but it took five days for it to arrive at the ILD's Atlanta office. The ILD protested and forced the county council to hold a hearing about conditions at Fulton Tower with Davis, Geer, and Herndon present. The inhumane treatment, Davis worried, might cost his client his life. He was alarmed as Herndon's health deteriorated and his weight dropped thanks to a diet of "stale bread and foul water."

Davis's life was in jeopardy, too. It rankled Atlanta's white establishment that he was working alongside a white woman at the ILD office and was representing two white women among the Atlanta Six. A Black lawyer representing a white woman in Jim Crow Atlanta was taboo. In mid-February, a gang of seven white men approached Davis in the lobby of the ILD office building. "You are too smart a nigger," they told him and promised "trouble" if he continued to represent a white woman. The threats did not scare Davis as much as the metal tube he discovered sticking out of a hole in the wall of his law office. A note tucked into the tube said: "The Ku Klux Klan rides again. Georgia is no place for bad niggers and red Communists. Next time we'll shoot. [Signed] The Ku Klux Klan." The metal tube was the barrel of a gun.

Ben Jr. showed the note to his father. Ben Sr. contacted friends in the police department. It turned out that the police knew about the note and gun. They tried to get Ben Sr. to persuade his son to drop the Herndon case. Ben Davis Jr. refused to turn his back on Herndon or on the Communist Party. He still made headlines for his prowess on the tennis court but had found his calling as a Communist Party activist.

Not all white Atlantans wanted Davis dead or believed that he should drop the case. In fact, an idealistic young white professor joined Davis's interracial movement to set Herndon free.

CHAPTER THREE

THE SON OF THE SOUTH

C. Vann Woodward

AT 5:00 P.M. ON SUNDAY, MAY 7, 1933, ABOUT 700 PEOPLE
packed Atlanta's Taft Hall. Black people. White people. Working-
class people. Wealthy people. Socialists. Communists. Liberals.
Ministers. Professionals. Intellectuals. As part of what the Communist Party referred to as the "united front" of different political
organizations, they responded to handbills advertising a "citizens
meeting" about the Angelo Herndon case and listened to four principal speakers from the newly organized Provisional Committee for
the Defense of Angelo Herndon.

The third speaker that day was a twenty-four-year-old English instructor at Georgia Tech, Comer Vann Woodward. About six feet tall with a deep southern accent he came by honestly growing up in Arkansas, Woodward looked like an insurance salesman and sounded like a son of the South. But he spoke like a striving young intellectual willing to buck Atlanta's segregated social norms. He believed that the insurrection law used to convict Herndon was antiquated and unjust. Woodward explained to the audience how the state of Georgia had enacted the insurrection law as a Reconstruction-era attempt to keep former slaves in a state of peonage.

Southern liberalism was in Vann Woodward's blood. Growing up in Morrilton, Arkansas, he learned about racial injustice from southern liberals who had visited his father, Hugh, the superintendent of the local school district. Vann's favorite guest was his uncle Comer, an outspoken former minister and Southern Methodist University sociologist who opposed lynching and the Ku Klux Klan. Vann idolized his uncle Comer and aspired to be like him. As an underclassman at Henderson-Brown College in Arkadelphia, Vann wrote editorials for the school newspaper protesting the college's overly strict rules and helped organize a student strike that was so effective it cost the president his job.

Before his junior year, Vann transferred to Emory University. His uncle Comer had become the dean of men at Emory University in 1930, and a few years later his father accepted a job as dean of Emory Junior College in Oxford, Georgia. His uncle introduced him to southern liberals, including Howard W. Odum, a white University of North Carolina sociologist who studied African American folklore; John Hope, the Black president of Atlanta University; and Will W. Alexander, the executive director of the Commission on Interracial Cooperation, which often collaborated with civil liberties and civil rights organizations to fight racial injustice. At Emory, Vann fell in with the radical young intellectuals Glenn W. Rainey and Ernest Hartsock, who chafed under the South's social hierarchy and strived to create fulfilling lives as writers and young academics.

Upon graduating from Emory in June 1930 with a degree in philosophy, Vann landed a job as an English instructor at nearby Georgia Tech. He soon befriended J. Saunders Redding, a Brown University graduate teaching English at Morehouse. Redding was the first Black person Woodward had eaten a meal with and "exchanged views as an equal." Through his friendship with Redding, Vann began to make political connections with members of Atlanta's Black community. He also had been following the case of the Atlanta Six, the Black and white communist organizers who had been charged under the insurrection law that spring. In August 1930, Vann joined his uncle and other prominent white liberals in signing a statement that highlighted the importance of free speech and assembly and called for fair trials for the six white and Black communists.

After a year of teaching, Vann took a leave of absence from Georgia Tech upon receiving a $750 Rosenwald Fellowship to obtain a master's degree in the social sciences at Columbia University. At first, he considered studying economics before settling on political science. Woodward was more inspired by his interactions with the leading lights of the Harlem Renaissance than by his studies. In Harlem, he befriended poet Langston Hughes and his friends and acted in *Underground*, an amateur production based on *Uncle Tom's Cabin*, playing the role of the evil white slave owner. At the offices of *Crisis* magazine, Woodward unsuccessfully tried to persuade its editor, sociologist W. E. B. Du Bois, to sponsor his master's thesis on Du Bois's *Souls of Black Folk*. Instead, Woodward wrote about the racist Alabama politician J. Thomas Heflin.

The summer after his master's program, Woodward traveled to Paris, Vienna, Berlin, and Moscow. In Berlin, he lived for a month with a Jewish family and witnessed the rise of the Nazi Party and the persecution of communists and Jews. Germans assured Woodward that the Nazis would never rule their country. Yet in late February 1933, Hitler blamed the Reichstag fire on his political rivals in the Communist Party and permanently suspended all civil rights and civil liberties. In Moscow and elsewhere in Europe during the summer of 1932, people kept asking Woodward to explain the injustice of the Scottsboro case.

That fall, Woodward returned to his instructorship at Georgia Tech a more worldly person, yet still unsure what he wanted to do with his life. He spoke and wrote about life in Russia, continued to make political and social connections across the color line, and viewed Herndon's conviction in January 1933 as another Scottsboro case. He knew he had to get involved because of the potential of Herndon's case to embarrass the United States at home and abroad and because of the injustice of sentencing a Black man to eighteen to twenty years on a chain gang for exercising his First Amendment rights.

Vann Woodward was exactly the type of white liberal Ben Davis Jr. needed on the Provisional Committee for the Defense of Angelo Herndon. For months, Davis and the ILD had been organizing the committee as a way of building a "united front" of people of different races, political affiliations, and occupations. The Communist Party believed that the best way to free Herndon was through a mass movement. "We must draw into this case elements never before reached by us," Syd Benson wrote in the *Daily Worker*. "We must win to us those liberals who have an honest sympathy for Herndon, but who hesitate in the face [of] the terror of the Southern ruling class Bourbons."

Davis started with the people he knew best—Atlanta's Black middle class. On January 24, J. A. Martin and other Black ministers signed a resolution protesting Herndon's eighteen- to twenty-year sentence. A few days later, the 27 Club adopted its resolution after Davis spoke about the significance of the case. The Provisional Committee met in March and included eighteen Blacks and whites from numerous local organizations—as well as a young English instructor from Georgia Tech.

The Herndon case troubled not only C. Vann Woodward and other members of the Provisional Committee but also many Georgians of goodwill. On April 30, more than 800 Black and white Atlantans attended the ILD's Herndon rally and musical event— "with absolutely no segregation"—at Bailey's Royal Theatre on Auburn Avenue. White fiddler John Carson opened the event and performed his song "Can't Live on Corn Bread and Peas," about the food prisoners ate on the chain gang. John Geer, introduced by ILD lawyer Allan Taub, explained the facts of Herndon's case. And Viola Montgomery, the Scottsboro mother who had attended Herndon's trial, vowed to help the ILD set Herndon and her son Olen free.

The ILD was consumed with freeing the Scottsboro defendants— raising money for their legal team and publicizing the injustice of their case. In November 1932, the organization had scored a major victory in *Powell v. Alabama*, when the Supreme Court reversed the Scottsboro convictions because the state had failed to appoint the defendants counsel at their capital trials. Represented by New York lawyer Samuel Leibowitz during new trials in the spring of 1933 in Decatur, the first of the nine defendants, Haywood Patterson, was retried, convicted, and sentenced to death. The all-white jury was unmoved by the shocking testimony of one of the two alleged victims, Ruby Bates, who admitted that she and Victoria Price had not been raped. Bates insisted that the Scottsboro defendants had been framed. Patterson's conviction triggered massive protests in New York and Chicago, with a plan to march on Washington.

On May 8, 1933, a mostly Black crowd of a few thousand people marched down Pennsylvania Avenue to the White House. As they walked, the protesters held signs that read "President Roosevelt: We Demand Equal Rights for Negroes," "Death Penalty to Lynchers," "Free the Scottsboro Boys," and "Free Angelo Herndon." Their goal was to meet with President Franklin D. Roosevelt. Inaugurated two months earlier, Roosevelt was too "busy" and refused to see them. Instead, ILD national secretary William Patterson spoke with Roosevelt aide Louis Howe and presented him with a petition containing 200,000 signatures calling on Congress and the President to free the Scottsboro defendants and to pass civil rights legislation. From his cell in Fulton Tower, Herndon praised the ILD and the march.

For Woodward, despite the clear connection between the Scottsboro and the Herndon cases, his decision to join the Provisional Committee proved to be an eye-opener about the differences among Atlanta's radical left. The May 7 meeting devolved into chaos. The chair of the committee, Mary Raoul Millis, quit before the meeting was over. The eldest daughter of a white Georgia railroad president, Millis was an active member of the Socialist Party. Formed in 1901, the Socialist Party of America fared well in electoral politics with a presidential candidate, Eugene Debs, who won over 900,000 votes in both the 1912 and 1920 elections. The Socialist Party waned when a radical faction left to join the Communist Party USA in 1919 and with its presidential candidate Debs imprisoned for encouraging people to oppose the wartime draft. During the early 1930s, the Socialist Party, with an old guard led by national chairman Morris Hillquit and young militants led by Norman Thomas, attracted new members amid widespread economic hardship. Aiding the Socialist Party's rise in Georgia by opposing communism, Millis objected to the committee's resolution to free Herndon because she claimed it endorsed Communist Party principles. For a time, Woodward was thrust into the role of temporary chair and tried to prevent the meeting from breaking up before the resolution was read and adopted. A month later, Woodward joined Ben Davis Jr. on the three-member executive committee of the Southern League for People's Rights. Woodward was named the organization's executive secretary.

Woodward tried to persuade Will Alexander of the Commission on Interracial Cooperation to take a stand on the Herndon case. A longtime mentor to Woodward, Alexander was reluctant to do so. He disapproved of what he saw as the Communist Party's exploitation of capital cases involving Black men by publicizing them as martyrs rather than hiring the best lawyers to defend them. As a result, he refused to work with the ILD on the Scottsboro case. Frustrated with his mentor's position, the young professor made the mistake of confiding to ILD lawyer Allan Taub that Alexander was "a dear, sweet old man but politically not to be relied on" in the Herndon case. Woodward soon saw his letter reprinted in the *Daily Worker*. Alexander saw it, too. In a note, he enclosed the clipping and chided Woodward that "the cuts of a friend are the unkindest of all."

The odds of Alexander working with Davis and the ILD to free Herndon were low. Before Herndon's trial, Clarina Michaelson and a few other communist organizers had met with Alexander about helping the ILD find a defense lawyer. Because the case involved complicated questions of constitutional law, Alexander suggested William A. Sutherland, an Atlanta lawyer with experience at the Supreme Court and in litigating a capital case. The ILD, however, hired a respected white criminal lawyer, H. A. Allen, with no constitutional law experience because he seemed "interested in the class struggle." The organization also did not hire Leonard Haas, another Atlanta lawyer recommended by Alexander to assist Allen. The whole episode confirmed Alexander's distrust of working with communists.

To make matters worse, Alexander was discouraging other organizations from working with Davis on Herndon's appeal. After Herndon's conviction, Alexander wrote to American Civil Liberties Union (ACLU) president Roger Nash Baldwin, falsely claiming that Davis had not graduated from Harvard Law School (Davis had graduated a year late) and questioning Davis's claim that his mentor A. T. Walden had declined to defend Herndon at trial. Alexander described Herndon's trial as "an argument between Herndon and his lawyers and an ignorant, fanatical prosecutor as to the merits and demerits of communism." And Alexander insisted that Herndon's conviction could be reversed on appeal "by a competent and experienced lawyer."

■   ■   ■   ■

THE MAY 7 MEETING forced Davis to rethink his united front strategy. In the wake of the fractious Provisional Committee meeting, Davis knew that the people of Atlanta could not raise the necessary funds on their own. What Davis and the Provisional Committee really needed was for national civil rights and civil liberties organizations to contribute to Herndon's legal defense.

Wise to Alexander's machinations against him, Davis blasted the NAACP and the Commission on Interracial Cooperation for not joining the Provisional Committee and for undermining him and his ability to raise money for Herndon's appeal. In the *Harlem Liberator*, Davis described himself as "fed up with the cowardice and the suave treachery of such organizations as the N.A.A.C.P. and the Interracial Commission. We know that they betray the Negro workers. We know that they can always be counted on to echo the language and actions of our oppressors. . . . And so we young Negroes take our stand."

As he prepared Herndon's motion for a new trial, Davis and ILD officials pleaded for financial support from Baldwin and the ACLU. Founded by Baldwin and legal and social activists in February 1920 during the postwar Red Scare, the ACLU quickly gained access to substantial funding to defend civil liberties. In 1922, the organization began administering the American Fund for Public Service, or Garland Fund, a million dollars donated by philanthropist Charles Garland and distributed to radical and left-wing organizations. By the early 1930s, the stock market crash had decimated the fund. Yet the ACLU was willing to support the ILD's efforts in Georgia civil rights and civil liberties cases and to overlook differences with the Communist Party USA over legal strategy and publicity tactics. From 1930 to 1932, the ACLU had supplied the bail money and had assisted with the ILD's legal fees for the Atlanta Six, the communists who had been charged but not yet tried under the insurrection law. But the ILD's decision in

December 1932 to fire Herndon's first legal counsel, Oliver Hancock, caught Baldwin and the ACLU off guard. After Herndon's conviction in January 1933, the ILD rejected the ACLU's offer to hire an esteemed northern white civil liberties lawyer, Arthur Garfield Hays, to appeal the case and instead backed Davis and Geer. ILD national secretary Patterson insisted to Baldwin that "our weakness was not Geer & Davis—this was our strength. Our weakness was the absence of a mass movement."

In pouring all its financial resources into the appeals and retrials of the Scottsboro defendants in the fall of 1932 and spring of 1933, the ILD had no money left to pay Herndon's lawyers. At a minimum, Davis and Geer needed $250 to appeal Herndon's case to the Georgia Supreme Court. In May, the ACLU agreed to raise the money by selling an eight-page pamphlet about Herndon's trial, *Twenty Years for Free Speech!* By mid-June, the organization had sent Davis only $100 as his expenses mounted along with his political and legal challenges.

In mid-June, armed members of the National Guard began patrolling the state capitol, supposedly because of the Herndon case. Governor Eugene Talmadge, according to the state treasurer, had been inundated by nasty letters from people upset about Herndon's conviction, including someone who had threatened to blow up the building. The treasurer subsequently admitted that the guards had been there for another reason. Governor Talmadge, locked in a dispute with the state highway board over $2.5 million in funds, had ordered the National Guard to secure the treasury. The bomb scare was a hoax.

With limited funds and no time to worry about hoaxes, Davis worked quickly to lay the groundwork for Herndon's appeal. In his new trial motion, he and Geer raised twenty-five claims of error, including the admission of evidence seized from Herndon's room without a search warrant; Judge Wyatt's failure to certify the two Emory economics professors as experts on communism; the racist questions the prosecutor asked one of the professors; the refusal to dismiss the indictment because of the systematic exclusion of Blacks from the grand jury; Judge Wyatt's denial of a motion to dismiss the trial jury panel because of the systematic exclusion of Blacks; his allegedly erroneous jury instructions; and the prosecutor's racist language on the witness stand. As in their pretrial motion, however, Davis and Geer failed to object to the Georgia insurrection law as a violation of Herndon's rights of free speech and peaceable assembly.

During a three-hour hearing on June 26, Davis and Geer argued that Judge Wyatt should grant their new trial motion because of the exclusion of Blacks from the grand and trial juries. Davis claimed, contrary to any evidence in the incomplete trial record, that he raised "the right of free speech and free assemblage" and that "the State made no argument whatever." The judge did not immediately rule on the motion. But based on the judge's unsympathetic attitude during the hearing, Davis did not expect him to grant Herndon a new trial. Furthermore, during the hearing, Wyatt rejected Davis's request for bail because Herndon had been convicted for a crime that "warranted death."

In Fulton Tower, an "emaciated, tired[, and] obviously worn" Herndon suffered physically from a poor diet and unsanitary conditions and mentally from a lack of reading material. He wrote his friends at the ILD asking them to smuggle Communist Party pamphlets inside newspapers. He asked a journalist visiting him for news about the outside world and pressed him to send books and pamphlets. He was optimistic about his future. "Well," Herndon told the journalist, "I know I'm coming out. I know the things the law is doing to me right now make that certain."

On July 5, Davis was in New York meeting with ILD officials and trying to raise funds when he learned that Judge Wyatt had handed down his decision. As Davis had anticipated, Judge Wyatt denied the new trial motion. Describing Wyatt's ruling as "expected," Davis's partner John Geer vowed: "The case will be carried to Georgia's highest court and, if need be, to the United States supreme court. The fight has just begun."

As they began to work on the appeal of Herndon's conviction, Davis's and Geer's inexperience began to show. All objections to a state criminal conviction based on the U.S. Constitution must be raised in the state trial and appeals courts before they can be made at the U.S. Supreme Court. Yet in filing a bill of exceptions to the trial record on July 13, Davis and Geer neglected to object to the insurrection law on free speech and assembly grounds. They may have incorrectly believed that since the Georgia Supreme Court had rejected free speech objections to the law in three pretrial motions involving the Atlanta Six, it would be pointless to raise the same claims a fourth time.

They also may have figured that they had little chance of winning a free speech and assembly argument before the U.S. Supreme Court—and for much of American history they would have been right. For the first 130 years of its existence, the First Amendment was rarely enforced. In March 1919, the Court rejected the free speech claims of Socialist Party secretary Charles Schenck and two others and affirmed their Espionage Act convictions for statements attempting to obstruct the draft and war effort. Six months later, the Court affirmed the Espionage Act convictions of the anarchist Jacob Abrams and other radicals for circulating leaflets criticizing the decision to send American troops into Russia and attempting to obstruct the war effort. In a pathbreaking dissent, Justice Oliver Wendell Holmes Jr. argued that Abrams's leaflets posed no "clear and imminent danger" to the war effort. The author of the Court's three Espionage Act decisions in March 1919, Holmes chided his colleagues for misapplying the "clear and present danger" test in *Abrams v. United States*. Joined in his *Abrams* dissent by Justice Louis D. Brandeis, Holmes championed the importance of "free trade in ideas—that the best test of truth is the power of the thought to get itself accepted in the competition of the market, and that truth is the only ground upon which their wishes safely can be carried out. That at any rate is the theory of our Constitution."

After Holmes's *Abrams* dissent, modern First Amendment law

slowly began to emerge. During the first half of the 1920s, the Court rejected all free speech and assembly claims and affirmed the criminal convictions of communists and other radicals under federal and state laws. To make matters worse, the First Amendment ("Congress shall make no law . . . abridging the freedom of speech, or of the press; or the right of the people peaceably to assemble") applied only to the federal government, not the states. Yet in a 1925 decision upholding the conviction of radical Socialist Benjamin Gitlow under a New York criminal anarchy law, the Court conceded that the rights to free speech and assembly were fundamental liberties protected by the Fourteenth Amendment's Due Process Clause. State and local governments, therefore, could be held accountable, too.

During the late 1920s and early 1930s, the Court continued to affirm the convictions of radicals under criminal syndicalism, sedition, and anarchy laws, yet it also began to subject states to constitutional limits. In 1927, the Court reversed the conviction of Harold B. Fiske under a Kansas syndicalism law for distributing literature for the Industrial Workers of the World, a radical union. In a companion case affirming the conviction of Communist Labor Party member Charlotte Anita Whitney under a California syndicalism law, Brandeis published a powerful concurrence asserting that a "clear and present danger" of "immediate serious violence" was a constitutional requirement for criminal punishment because of the importance of free speech and assembly in a robust democracy. "Fear of serious injury cannot alone justify suppression of free speech and assembly," Brandeis wrote in *Whitney v. California*. "Men feared witches and burnt women. It is the function of speech to free men from the bondage of irrational fears.

"To justify suppression of free speech," Brandeis warned, "there must be reasonable ground to fear that serious evil will result if free speech is practiced. There must be reasonable ground to believe that the danger apprehended is imminent. There must be reasonable ground to believe that the evil to be prevented is a serious one." Four years after the *Fiske* and *Whitney* decisions, the Court reversed the conviction of communist Yetta Stromberg under a California law prohibiting the display of a red flag "as a sign, symbol or emblem of opposition to organized government." The Court's more recent decisions should have persuaded Davis and Geer to preserve Herndon's claims to free speech and assembly.

Besides their inexperience and seeming lack of awareness of the Court's free speech decisions, Davis and Geer may have been following the ILD's directive to use Herndon's case to challenge the exclusion of Blacks from Fulton County juries. Either way, they objected to the illegal admission and exclusion of evidence, the exclusion of Blacks from grand and trial juries, and Judge Wyatt's jury instructions. They also charged that the trial transcript prepared by Wyatt's court reporter had been "falsified." The prosecutor's racial epithets during the trial had been changed from "nigger" to "darkey." Some of Wyatt's outbursts, Davis's objections, and Herndon's speech to the jury had been omitted. But the incomplete trial record alone could not explain the failure to raise free speech and assembly objections to the insurrection law.

With an appeal to the Georgia Supreme Court looming, Davis attempted to raise $1000 for Herndon's legal defense. The ACLU reached out to its membership and eventually sent another $100. In Atlanta, the Provisional Committee organized a "Herndon Day Celebration" on July 23 at Butler C.M.E. Church featuring speeches by leading Black ministers, the National Urban League's southern field director Jesse O. Thomas, and ILD attorney Irving Schwab. The weeklong fund-raising drive netted only $100. It was hard to raise money from liberal-minded Atlantans at the height of the Depression and in the face of fierce local opposition. In August 1933, the Ku Klux Klan burned a cross in the driveway of the home of two white committee members, Mr. and Mrs. Walter E. Washburn. The Klan did not intimidate them. The secretary of the local electrician's union, Walter Washburn had spoken at many of the same Provisional Committee meetings as Vann Woodward.

For Woodward, the intimidation was more subtle. After the Provisional Committee meeting on May 7, Georgia Tech president Marion L. Brittain gave him a "talking to" about his involvement in the case. A few months later, Woodward was fired along with about thirty other Georgia Tech instructors because of Depression-era budget cuts. Woodward sued the state for $300 in back pay owed under his employment contract and won. For nearly a year, he lived with his parents before enrolling in the PhD program in history at the University of North Carolina, where he planned to write a biography of Tom Watson, a Georgia populist politician.

Woodward had not lost his youthful radicalism. In November 1933, he traveled to Alabama with seven white southerners to investigate the lynching of two Black Tuscaloosa teenagers, Dan Pippen Jr., eighteen, and A. T. Harden, fifteen, who were charged with raping and murdering a white woman. As a new history graduate student in the fall of 1934, he hung out with the "wrong crowd" of Chapel Hill radicals at Milton "Ab" Abernethy's Intimate Book Shop. He also helped Don West, a radical white writer and activist he had met while working on the Provisional Committee for the Defense of Angelo Herndon, rally support for striking Burlington textile workers.

Woodward's mentor, Will Alexander of the Commission on Interracial Cooperation, began to soften his stance on helping Herndon and his lawyers as events in Atlanta took an ugly turn. In August 1933, Herndon described a "plot to murder him" when prison officials put him in solitary confinement because one of his Black cellmates had clashed with a white guard. In solitary, Herndon lacked fresh air, running water, or a toilet. When he was not in solitary, he shared a cell with three men about to be executed. Herndon anguished over the electrocution of his cellmates at the state prison in Milledgeville.

Herndon's lawyer Ben Davis Jr. was under fire, too. On Labor Day in Atlanta, he spoke to approximately 5000 people at the funeral of Glover Davis, a blind Black man shot and killed by a white police officer for allegedly lunging at the officer with an ice pick. At the meeting, Ben Jr. called for whites and Blacks to join forces against police brutality. "The funeral of Glover Davis," he said, "is the funeral of every Negro in this city unless the murderous brutality of Atlanta police is stopped." Ben Jr. promised more interracial demonstrations and to press the issue with the mayor. After the funeral, several police officers threatened to hold Davis responsible for "any disorder" caused by his remarks. They also tried to coerce people into providing their names and addresses, but Davis intervened and stopped them.

Three days after the funeral, Assistant Solicitor John Hudson, the overzealous prosecutor of Herndon and other communists, and six to eight plainclothes officers raided the ILD's Atlanta branch on Auburn Avenue. They immediately began seizing documents and questioning two white Communist Party organizers, Martin Walker and Ruth Mulkey. Arriving at the office in the middle of the raid, Davis inquired whether Hudson had a search warrant (no) and whether the assistant solicitor planned on arresting Walker and Mulkey. "Perhaps so," Hudson replied, "later." After he finished interviewing the two white organizers, Hudson asked them whether they preferred to be arrested now or the next morning. Davis, acting as counsel for the two white clients and insisting they would appear the next morning, knew that they were not under arrest. That night, Walker and Mulkey fled Atlanta. The next day, two bailiffs arrived at Davis's law office asking where his clients were. Davis said he had no idea. Hudson threatened to file a complaint against Davis with the Georgia bar.

The raid on the ILD offices alarmed the ACLU. Before providing Davis and Geer with additional funding, the organization asked them for a full accounting of their expenses. With their firm less than a year old, Davis and Geer were struggling to pay the rent and telephone bill. Nor could they afford a full-time secretary or stenographer.

Davis was so desperate for funds that he appealed to Woodward's mentor, Will Alexander. The two men had spoken after the raid on the ILD offices and must have parted on good terms. On September 9, Davis wrote a three-page letter to Alexander listing prominent Black and white business, religious, and educational leaders on the Provisional Committee. Walter Washburn was the chair, Reverend J. A. Martin was the vice chair, and Jesse Thomas of the Urban League had spoken at mass meetings. "Whatever may be the political affiliations and religious beliefs of the members of this Committee," Davis explained, "they are united on the one issue of freeing Angelo Herndon." Davis denied that the committee was a "rubber stamp" for the Communist Party and explained that he desperately needed funds for Herndon's appeal. Though he declined to join the Provisional Committee, Alexander sent Davis "a check for a small amount."

Rather than spending most of his days in his law office or in court, Davis was "wholly immersed in the mass campaign." That year, he had spoken at rallies in Harlem and Birmingham about the Scottsboro and Herndon cases and had emerged as one of Atlanta's up-and-coming Black political leaders. He knew that the Communist Party needed the support of Vann Woodward and other white liberals in its united front to win Herndon's freedom. Davis and other communists believed that mass protest, not legal strategy, would free Herndon. But the legal strategy mattered, too.

Davis was willing to do whatever it took to win Herndon's appeal before the Georgia Supreme Court. For ten days in September, he holed himself up in his office and tried to research and write the state supreme court brief. As a young lawyer with no brief-writing experience, he knew that the brief he'd written was inadequate and appealed to the ILD for last-minute legal assistance. He didn't have much time. The briefs were due September 26.

A radical lawyer in New York City volunteered to help.

CHAPTER FOUR

THE RADICAL LAWYER

Carol Weiss King

IT WAS EASY TO UNDERESTIMATE CAROL WEISS KING. SHE cared little about her clothes and wore no makeup or lipstick. She had deep-set eyes, thick glasses, and unruly curly hair. She almost never argued in court. But when the ILD needed a legal brief in a hurry, she was the obvious choice. There was no better brief writer, legal strategist, and recruiter of talented lawyers.

The daughter of a prominent New York lawyer, Carol was inspired by the Palmer Raids to use the law to defend the constitutional rights of radicals and immigrants. Her brother Louis graduated from Columbia Law School in 1920, started a law firm that he merged with his father's and that still bears the family name Paul, Weiss. By necessity and inclination, Carol pursued a different path. At the time, the law schools of Harvard and Columbia did not admit women. The Barnard College graduate, therefore, enrolled at New York University Law School. After graduating in 1920, she briefly clerked in the office of Harvard-educated lawyer Max Lowenthal, passed the New York bar, then rented space from and later joined the office of Hale, Nelles & Shorr—radical lawyers challenging the constitutionality of the Palmer Raids and defending immigrants scheduled for deportation.

By 1925, King was a name partner in Shorr, Brodsky & King and frequently collaborated with Joseph R. Brodsky. As the general counsel of the ILD, Brodsky named her one of the stockholders of the communist *Daily Worker* and enlisted her to work on the ILD's high-profile cases. In 1931, she assisted him in appealing the death sentences of the Scottsboro defendants. A year later, the U.S. Supreme Court overturned their convictions because they had been denied the right to counsel.

Working behind the scenes, King made her name in national legal circles as the editor of an influential bulletin about immigration, labor, civil liberties, and civil rights cases. Initially published as the *Law and Freedom Bulletin* for the ACLU, King renamed it the *International Juridical Association Bulletin* when she became the secretary and cofounder of the IJA's U.S. chapter. Lawyers searching for precedents and plotting legal strategy avidly read the *IJA Bulletin* to learn about pending, recently decided, and unreported cases. King somehow managed to edit the bulletin and to defend clients while raising a son as a single mother (her husband, Gordon King, died in 1930 of pneumonia). She employed her brusque charm and relentless advocacy skills to enlist idealistic New York lawyers to contribute articles for the bulletin and to draft briefs. And she earned the reputation as a brilliant legal strategist and brief writer and relentless fighter for her clients.

In agreeing to draft Herndon's brief, King did not realize how quickly it needed to be written and filed with the Georgia Supreme Court. She thought it had to be filed "some time in October" until she received a special delivery telegram from Atlanta on Thursday, September 21, informing her that the brief had to be filed in five days. Unfortunately, she had given the only copy of the trial record to a young IJA lawyer, Victor Whitehorn. After many phone calls, she learned that Whitehorn had taken it with him to Atlantic City on Thursday for the Jewish New Year and weekend. King had to get the trial record back. She phoned the city's larger hotels but could not find him. Finally, King, who did not drive, asked a young IJA staff member to take her to Atlantic City on Friday to track down Whitehorn and the trial record. They arrived at the boardwalk but had no idea the name of his hotel. The city's telephone book listed more than 200. After calling about fifteen hotels, they asked a soda jerk for the names of leading hotels. "Jewish or Christian?" he asked. At the second "Jewish" hotel they called, they found Whitehorn and the record from Herndon's trial.

Arriving back at her office shortly before 6:00 p.m. on Friday night and fueled by coffee, cigarettes, and sandwiches, King worked all night reading the record, writing the brief, and getting it typed. At 4:30 a.m., she left the office and immediately rode to the post office to mail the brief to Davis and Geer. Herndon's Atlanta lawyers made additional copies and a few minor corrections before filing it on the September 26 deadline. Only Davis and Geer signed the brief. King stayed in the background. Tired yet satisfied, she described the brief as "not a perfect job but presentable" and the whole episode as "one of the pleasantest days of my life."

In the brief, King primarily argued that Herndon's conviction should be overturned because the systematic exclusion of Blacks from the grand and trial juries violated the Fourteenth Amendment's Equal Protection Clause. She included citations to several controlling U.S. Supreme Court decisions on the jury issue. The brief also focused on Judge Wyatt's conduct of the trial, contending that he had erred by not allowing Davis and Geer to interrogate individual jurors about their racial biases, by admitting literature illegally seized from Herndon's room without a search warrant, by refusing to allow the two Georgia Tech economics professors to testify as expert witnesses on communism, and by permitting the prosecution to question one of the professors about his views on interracial marriage. Finally, the brief faulted Wyatt for rejecting the defense's jury instructions distinguishing between a lawful "demonstration" and an unlawful "insurrection" under the law and emphasizing that the Communist Party was a legal political party.

In a reply brief submitted a few weeks later, King rejected the state's contention that the evidence supported Herndon's conviction. The evidence, King argued, did not show that Herndon had attempted to incite insurrection, that he had tried to solicit members of the Communist Party, or that he had sought to establish self-determination in the Black Belt. It merely showed that Herndon, in working with the Unemployed Committee, had been seeking unemployment relief for Black and white workers. In her reply, King argued that Judge Wyatt, by instructing the jury that incitement required an imminent threat of violence to the state, had confused jurors into thinking that Herndon was guilty. In the briefs, King did not argue that the Georgia insurrection law violated Herndon's rights to free speech and assembly. For the time being, she adhered to the ILD's strategy of focusing on the systematic exclusion of Blacks from Fulton County juries.

As Herndon's lead trial counsel, Davis welcomed King's participation in the case. He liked her personality and admired her "indefatigable" work ethic and rapid brief-writing skills. He was pleased with how she transformed his arguments "into presentable and legally forceful shape." While King worked on the brief, Davis scrambled to become a member of the Georgia Supreme Court bar the day before the oral argument.

For fifty minutes on October 5, 1933, Davis lectured the six justices on the Georgia Supreme Court as if they were law students.

They did not ask him any questions and watched him with "utter contempt." Then it was Assistant Solicitor Walter LeCraw's turn. The short, pale prosecutor was just as rabid about rooting out communists as his tall, gangly colleague John Hudson. LeCraw argued that the evidence—the books and materials seized from Herndon and his room and his Communist Party organizing—supported his conviction. Davis was so unimpressed that he waived his time for rebuttal. He was confident, perhaps overconfident, that King's briefs and his argument would set Herndon free.

■　■　■　■

INSTEAD OF A QUICK RULING, the Georgia Supreme Court sat on the case for more than seven months. Meanwhile, Herndon languished in Fulton Tower. On December 2, he was again placed in solitary confinement. This time, prison officials accused him of pouring water out of his cell. In solitary, they shut the small blind door to keep him from getting any air.

In January 1934, Herndon returned from solitary confinement to his old cell in alarmingly ill health. His stomach hurt so badly that he could not keep food down and he frequently vomited. He was so weak he could barely lift a book. His eyesight was failing from reading by candlelight. Water and excrement continued to drip from a leaky pipe. Prison officials prohibited other inmates from speaking to him and threatened to make him share a cell with "sexual perverts."

At Herndon's request, the ILD launched a publicity campaign about his mistreatment and deteriorating health. In February, he wrote the ILD requesting an independent medical examination and two dollars a week so that he could join other inmates in ordering meals from outside the prison. The ILD informed ACLU director Baldwin that Herndon was "dying by inches." The publicity— newspaper articles and letters to Governor Eugene Talmadge, chief jailer Bob Holland, and Georgia Chief Justice Richard B. Russell Sr.

(the father of the former governor)—produced action. The leaky pipe was fixed. Two doctors, one white and one Black, examined Herndon yet reached opposite conclusions. The white doctor deemed him fine after a cursory exam. The Black doctor reported problems with his stomach and lungs and "the beginning of a break in health, to say the least." A white woman doctor confirmed the Black doctor's findings of possible lung damage or tuberculosis and requested further tests. A visiting state judge ordered Herndon admitted to Grady Hospital. Four deputy sheriffs escorted him there. X-rays of his lungs revealed some abnormalities but no signs of tuberculosis. The lack of a concrete diagnosis provided an opening for the Communist Party's critics in Atlanta. Socialist Mary Raoul Millis and a former judge, Edgar Watkins Sr., informed Baldwin that Herndon was exaggerating about unsanitary conditions at Fulton Tower and about his health. Davis—in desperate need of ACLU funds for Herndon's bail and appeal—refuted their claims point by point and instructed an ILD official to set Baldwin straight.

At the same time, Atlanta's Black leaders loyal to the NAACP thwarted Davis's fund-raising efforts at home. Ever since the initial outcry over the convictions of the Scottsboro defendants in 1931, the NAACP and the ILD had clashed over legal strategy, public relations tactics, and fund-raising. In the *Atlanta Daily World*, Davis accused Reverend J. Raymond Henderson and other Black ministers of bowing to the "misleaders of the NAACP" for refusing to hold Herndon meetings in their churches and for failing to distinguish between the political aims of the ILD and the united front of local leaders on the Herndon defense committee.

On May 24, nearly eight months after the October 5 oral argument, the Georgia Supreme Court affirmed Herndon's conviction. In a unanimous opinion, the court observed that Davis and Geer had failed to preserve their pretrial objections to the racial composition of the grand and trial jury pools. And, even if they had, the court declared that the jury issue lacked merit because the jury commissioners had denied that "negroes were merely excluded by reason of their race or color" and "were occasionally placed upon the lists for service on trial juries." The court also held that Judge Wyatt had not erred in overruling the defense's various objections. The state supreme court revealed the state of race relations in Georgia in explaining that the prosecutor's use of the term "darkey" to refer to Herndon was "not opprobrious." The rest of the opinion reviewed the evidence against Herndon—his Unemployed Committee literature, his recruitment of Communist Party members, the Party's platform of "the right of self-determination of the Negroes in the Black Belt," and the communist literature found in his room—and determined that it supported the verdict of attempting to incite insurrection.

In upholding Herndon's conviction, the Georgia Supreme Court argued that the threat of violence did not have to be "imminent"—contrary to Judge Wyatt's jury instructions—for Herndon to be found guilty of attempting to incite insurrection. The court interpreted the law to require only that the violence against the state occur "at any time" in the future. The Georgia Supreme Court concluded by quoting at length from the U.S. Supreme Court decision affirming the conviction of radical Socialist Benjamin Gitlow. The state supreme court, quoting from *Gitlow v. New York*, observed that "a single revolutionary spark" was enough.

Unlike Gitlow, Herndon had not raised a First Amendment challenge to the state law—at least not yet. The ILD was counting on King and her team of lawyers "in the North" to figure out how to do it. William Patterson, the ILD national secretary, informed the ACLU's Baldwin of the intent to appeal to the U.S. Supreme Court but with an important caveat: "if we do not go up, it will only be because of the technical impossibility."

On June 2, Davis and Geer notified the Georgia Supreme Court of their intention to appeal its decision to the U.S. Supreme Court. Chief Justice Richard Russell Sr., who had not participated in the case because of illness and indicated that he would have dissented based on the lack of evidence about inciting insurrection, stayed

Herndon's sentence to the chain gang for fifty days. He also summoned Davis to chambers and offered some advice to the young lawyer. The chief justice warned him "never refer contemptuously to the arguments of the state's attorneys" and never take on another case like Herndon's.

Soon after the state supreme court's decision, Assistant Solicitor Hudson set his sights once again on Davis and the city's other communists. Hudson vowed to issue arrest warrants for the Atlanta Six, to try them in June for attempting to incite insurrection, and to send them to the electric chair. "Georgia," Hudson declared, "intends to rid itself of Communism." Hudson knew about local communist activity thanks to a mole on the Herndon defense team. Ansel Morrison, the white Atlanta lawyer who had volunteered to assist Davis and Geer, had been leaking documents and revealing secret locations of communists to state authorities. On May 28, Hudson and five plainclothes officers raided the ILD offices on Auburn Avenue and the home of a white communist organizer. Hudson seized communist literature and sought to arrest white writer and activist Don West. Escaping in the backseat of Davis's Ford covered by blankets and sacks, West left town. A few days later, Hudson and his men raided the homes of several Black communists, asked if they knew Davis, and claimed to have a warrant for Davis's arrest. It was "pure bluff," the *Daily Worker* declared, "as Davis' whereabouts are well-known to the entire Atlanta police force."

Unconcerned by Hudson's harassment, Davis focused on getting Herndon out of Fulton Tower on bail. Herndon encouraged Davis and other ILD officials to continue to publicize his ill health and mistreatment by prison officials. In a two-part series in the *Daily Worker*, Davis recounted his visit to Herndon after the state supreme court's decision. He described how prison officials delayed his client's mail, censored any book or other reading material perceived to be related to the Communist Party, including a Russian-English dictionary, and withheld medicine for Herndon's stomach. Davis concluded by describing Herndon as "one of the most remarkable leaders of the international working-class movement, a type that only the working class could bring forth. His courage grows daily."

Davis was making his own transition from Atlanta lawyer to Communist Party writer and activist. He had been named the new editor of the *Harlem Liberator*, the Party-backed organ for the League of Struggle for Negro Rights. Don West profiled him in the *Daily Worker*. A week later, journalist Ted Poston wrote an admiring appraisal of him in the New York *Amsterdam News* by explaining similarities and differences between "Little Ben" and "Big Ben," his famous Republican Party boss father. On June 24, 1934, Harlem's finest writers and intellectuals welcomed Davis at a banquet at Lido Hall. Addressing the audience, Davis came out swinging. He denounced the Black press, the NAACP, and the Urban League and derided anticommunist Black columnist George Schuyler and *Crisis* editor W. E. B. Du Bois as "literary prostitutes" and Howard University polymath Kelly Miller as an "Uncle Tom." He charged middle-class Black organizations and their leaders with "fooling the Negro masses" and "keeping them from fighting against their real oppressors."

Back in Atlanta, Davis's co-counsel Geer had been negotiating with Assistant Solicitor Hudson on whether Herndon could be released on bail during the U.S. Supreme Court appeal. On June 20, Judge Wyatt agreed to set Herndon's bail at $15,000. Wyatt and Hudson figured that the ILD could not possibly raise that kind of money. The ILD sought to prove them wrong by asking for contributions in the pages of the *Daily Worker*. A "confident" Herndon began packing his things. His jailers thought he was nuts.

To publicize the bail fund-raising drive and to highlight conditions at Fulton Tower, writer John Howard Lawson led a northern delegation to check on Herndon's health. A playwright and Hollywood screenwriter, Lawson grew up in a wealthy, left-wing Jewish family, graduated from Williams College, and embraced radical political and social causes. He joined the Communist Party, contributed articles to the *Daily Worker*, and led five writers and activists from New York to Atlanta and Birmingham to see Herndon and the Scottsboro defendants.

On the morning of July 2, Lawson and his delegation met with Hudson. The red-baiting assistant solicitor berated them as communists and anarchists, asked them how many times they had been arrested, called them "lousy bums," then threw them out of his office. The delegation decided to see the governor. On the surface, Eugene Talmadge was more "cordial and friendly." During a fifteen-minute meeting, the governor accused the northerners of being outside agitators and tried to separate the two Black Atlantans, Davis and Reverend Martin, from the rest of the group. "You boys with them?" Talmadge asked Davis and Martin. The governor needled Davis that he was nothing like his father and praised A. T. Walden, the Black Atlanta lawyer and NAACP branch president who had refused to take Herndon's case, because Walden was as "humble as the lowest farmer." The governor continued, "Ben, you've been sent up nawth to school. . . . You've got too much education to love your own state." He then turned to Reverend Martin: "What about you, Reverend? You seem to be doing all right." Martin recounted the white violence that infuriated Georgia's Black masses and vowed to vote for the Communist Party ticket rather than the white supremacist Democratic Party in the upcoming gubernatorial election. One of Talmadge's men who had been tasked with investigating Herndon's treatment at Fulton Tower informed the delegation that the prisoner was "uppity" and concluded that the "impudent nigger" was feigning illness.

Later that afternoon, the delegation finally saw Herndon and Fulton Tower for themselves. About ten feet away, Herndon sat in a cane-bottom chair smoking a cigarette. Prison guards stood behind him. A half dozen of Hudson's men glared at the delegation from the edges of the room. For half an hour, Herndon described the awful prison conditions and lack of medical care and explained that Hudson had been censoring any reading material considered to be radical. As a test case, the delegation had brought along *The History of the American Working Class*, a book by Anthony Bimba. Jailer Bob Holland told the delegation that Herndon could have the book, but Hudson would have to review it first. After the visit, Hudson and Holland relaxed the restrictions and permitted Herndon access to communist publications such as the *Daily Worker* and *New Masses*, Black newspapers such as the New York *Amsterdam News*, and a Russian-English dictionary given to him by white inmates. The guards began referring to Herndon as a "big-shot nigger." They did not like his lawyer much, either. A few weeks later, prison officials falsely accused Ben Davis Jr. of trying to smuggle Herndon's letters out of Fulton Tower. A white turnkey had read one of the letters, which described the Georgia judicial system as "fascist dogs."

The ILD had until August 3 to raise the $15,000 for Herndon's bail. The organization appealed to the Black and white masses for loans in cash or liberty bonds in the pages of the *Daily Worker*; in articles in *The New Republic*, *The Nation*, and *New Masses*; and in the Black press. The ACLU kept itself abreast of the latest developments. The NAACP, still unwilling to work with the ILD on the appeals in the Scottsboro case, stayed on the sidelines. Nationally, however, the Black masses rallied behind Herndon's cause. On a front step of Harlem's Abyssinian Baptist Church, someone had painted a simple message: "Free Angelo Herndon."

During the final six days before the bail deadline, small loans from hundreds of individuals and organizations poured into the ILD offices. Yet by July 27, the ILD had raised only $5000. During the final three days, the bail fund lurched closer to its goal. It was $7000 short, then $4000, then $2400. The day before the deadline, the organization still needed $1149. On August 3, the ILD—with the fund oversubscribed—declared victory.

Before Herndon was released on bail, a white turnkey had alerted him to a plot to lynch him. A phone call tipped off the ILD and its allies of the Ku Klux Klan's "planned attack" on Herndon on his way out of Georgia. The ACLU wired Governor Talmadge asking him to protect Herndon from mob violence. Novelist Theodore Dreiser, on behalf of the National Committee for the Defense of Political Prisoners, phoned the governor and received assurances that Herndon would not be harmed leaving the state because he had not raped a white woman. That night, Joseph Brodsky, the ILD's general counsel, flew to Atlanta. The next morning, Brodsky and fellow attorney John Geer arrived at Fulton Tower and discovered that there was no formal order for Herndon's release. They drove more than an hour to Judge Wyatt's home in LaGrange, Georgia, to obtain one. With the order in hand, Brodsky and Geer returned to Fulton Tower and presented the order to chief jailer Holland. Brodsky and Geer walked out with their client. As Herndon left the gates of the prison, his fellow inmates yelled out their windows wishing him good luck. A turnkey said: "Hope to see you back for good!"

At 5:00 p.m., for the first time since his lung X-ray at Grady Hospital, Angelo Herndon breathed fresh air. He looked around, praised the ILD for raising his bond, and briefly stopped at Geer's office before heading to the train station. Herndon, Brodsky, and Reverend Martin boarded a Jim Crow car bound for New York City. Two railway detectives accompanied them on the train until they reached Washington. They took a "circuitous route" north to avoid trouble.

In the *Daily Worker*, the ILD announced that Herndon's train would arrive the next day at New York's Penn Station at 6:35 p.m. and encouraged people to greet him there and along the way. Crowds of white and Black people started forming in Washington. Each time Herndon's train stopped at one of the northern stations, hundreds of people waited on the platform to catch a glimpse of him. He wore a brown suit and vest, round horn-rimmed glasses, and a white panama hat cocked slightly to one side. He looked tired, pale, and thin. But when he stepped onto the platform, his spirits soared as he saw the cheering crowds—hundreds of people in Baltimore, Philadelphia, Trenton, and Newark. At the North Philadelphia station, people waited and yelled, "Hurrah for Herndon." Two men carried him out of the second car on their shoulders. A young woman hugged and kissed him before he was whisked back onto the train. When Herndon arrived at the Manhattan Transfer station in New Jersey, Ted Poston of the New York *Amsterdam News* boarded his car. Poston, who had visited Herndon at Fulton Tower, asked how he was treated during his nineteen months in prison. "It was hell," Herndon replied.

Nothing prepared Herndon for his reception at New York's Penn Station. A delegation of Communist Party leaders, including his lawyer turned newspaper editor Ben Davis Jr., met him on the platform. At 6:45 p.m., Herndon disembarked from the train. Party leader Robert Minor and vice presidential candidate James Ford hugged and kissed him. Ruby Bates, the former accuser turned chief defense witness for the Scottsboro defendants, hugged him and put her cheek next to his. Herndon and his older brother, Milton, a fellow Party activist, sized each other up, shook hands, and embraced.

About 500 more people waited near the track entrances. A Black porter alerted them to the track on which Herndon would be arriving. Several communist leaders hoisted Herndon on their shoulders and carried him up the marble stairs and into the south end of the jam-packed main hall. Someone thrust a large bouquet of red roses into his hands. Herndon waved his hat. About 7000 to 10,000 people greeted him with thunderous cheers. People sang the workers' anthem, "The Internationale." After a few brief speeches by communist leaders, the crowd cleared a path so that Herndon could be carried out of the main hall. Police stopped traffic across Thirty-Second Street between Seventh and Eighth Avenues so that Herndon could wait for his ride in a small, empty parking lot. For fifteen minutes, he greeted more communist leaders until his car arrived. He needed a few days of rest and a thorough medical exam before the first of many public appearances. The crowd followed Herndon's car across Thirty-Second Street and turned south on Broadway for a mass meeting at Union Square, singing songs and shouting, "Free Angelo Herndon!"

During his initial public appearance on August 15, Herndon was "quite tense" and "frail" as he walked to the microphone before about 4000 people at Harlem's Rockland Palace. At the podium, he inspired them with his defiant words about the "Southern ruling class": "They can send me to the electric chair, they can wreck my body, but they cannot break my spirit for the working class struggle. It is not a question of unemployment relief, but it is a question of life and death, a question of political power." He advised the mostly Black audience to abandon their misleaders at the NAACP and anticommunist Black columnist George Schuyler and accused them of betraying the freedom struggle. Before about 10,000 people at the Bronx Coliseum on August 22, Herndon appealed for the release of the Scottsboro defendants. He reminded the crowd that the Communist Party was "the only party that dares to go into the South, that dares boldly to take up the struggle for the liberation of the Negro people, for the emancipation of the whole working class."

As a symbol of southern injustice toward Black people, Herndon began to play an active role in the ILD's mass campaign to free the Scottsboro defendants and other wrongfully convicted prisoners. Since the Supreme Court had overturned their convictions in 1932, the Scottsboro defendants had been retried, with Samuel Leibowitz and ILD lawyers representing them. All-white juries had convicted them again, even though Ruby Bates had recanted her testimony. At Fulton Tower, Herndon had asked visitors about the Scottsboro case and read about it whenever he could get his hands on a newspaper. As his train entered New York City, he had peppered Ted Poston, who had covered the retrials in Decatur, Alabama, with questions. Two of the condemned young men, Haywood Patterson and Clarence Norris, wrote from Montgomery's Kilby Prison hailing Herndon's release. Now it was Herndon's turn to advocate for their cause as well as his own. The ILD announced it was sending him on a national speaking tour with Norris's mother, Ida, to raise $15,000 for a Scottsboro-Herndon legal defense fund.

■ ■ ■ ■

AS THE POINT PERSON ON Herndon's defense team, Carol Weiss King was trying to figure out how to appeal the Georgia Supreme Court's decision to the U.S. Supreme Court. Based on the state court's decision, she believed that the best argument lay in challenging Herndon's conviction under the Georgia insurrection law as violating his freedom of speech and assembly. Yet she knew that Herndon's lawyers had not raised free speech and assembly objections before, during, or after the trial. Nor had they asked the Georgia Supreme Court to reverse the conviction on these grounds. Herndon's free speech and assembly claims had to be raised in state court before they could be appealed to the U.S. Supreme Court.

Rather than admit defeat, King consulted Georgia-born Columbia law professor Jerome Michael, who declined to represent Herndon but referred her to two of the school's bright young constitutional scholars, Walter Gellhorn and Herbert Wechsler. A former clerk to U.S. Supreme Court Justice Harlan Fiske Stone, Gellhorn had worked in the solicitor general's office during the Supreme Court's 1932 term before joining the Columbia law faculty. The twenty-six-year-old Gellhorn brought in his close friend and colleague Wechsler, a wunderkind interested in civil liberties and civil rights.

Nearly three years younger than his law school classmate Gellhorn, Wechsler graduated from City College of New York at twenty and was the editor in chief of the *Columbia Law Review* at twenty-three. During the winter of 1930, Wechsler and Gellhorn interviewed with Justice Stone for the same clerkship. Stone selected the tall, fair-haired Gellhorn, a fellow Amherst College graduate. The top student in his class, the short, beetle-browed Wechsler struggled to find a job. A leading Wall Street lawyer, Emory Buckner, advised him to apply to Jewish-run firms. Instead, Wechsler returned to Columbia Law School as an assistant in law with research and teaching responsibilities. He succeeded Gellhorn as Stone's law clerk during the fall of 1932, when the Court reversed the convictions of the Scottsboro defendants because the state had failed to appoint them counsel. The ILD's victory in *Powell v. Alabama* opened Wechsler's eyes to the possibilities of civil rights and civil liberties litigation. Upon his return to the Columbia law faculty in 1933, Wechsler joined the executive committee of the International Juridical Association, led by Carol Weiss King.

As former Stone clerks and up-and-coming Columbia law professors, Gellhorn and Wechsler knew how the Supreme Court operated and how to persuade the justices to hear Herndon's case. At King's request, Wechsler drafted a memorandum about how to raise the free speech and assembly claims before the Court. King also needed someone with unimpeachable credentials to argue the case. Gellhorn and Wechsler suggested an establishment Republican and quintessential Wall Street lawyer—Whitney North Seymour.

CHAPTER FIVE

THE WALL STREET LAWYER

Whitney North Seymour

B Y THE SUMMER OF 1934, THIRTY-THREE-YEAR-OLD Whitney North Seymour already looked and acted the part of a Wall Street lawyer. He was tall with deep brown eyes, a slightly receding hairline, and a crooked smile. A leading litigator, he was the youngest partner at a prominent Wall Street law firm, Simpson, Thacher & Bartlett. He belonged to several of New York City's exclusive private clubs, where he often ate lunch with esteemed members of the bench and bar. And during his two years representing the U.S. government as assistant solicitor general, from 1931 to 1933, he had argued approximately thirty-five Supreme Court cases.

A born advocate, he learned how to be a polished public speaker by watching his father, Charles W. Seymour, an itinerant lecturer. A former New York lawyer, Charles had been so distraught about the death of a fifteen-year-old son from typhoid fever in 1883 that five years later he moved his family to Tacoma, Washington. He made a living as a full-time lecturer, remarried after the death of his first wife, and settled in the Midwest, where his son Whitney was born. Charles could talk for an hour from memory on up to sixty historical topics. As a boy, Whitney occasionally accompanied his father on his lecture tours. And he pursued his father's interests in history and oratory.

Growing up in Madison, Wisconsin, Whitney liked to spend his weekends combing rural fields for arrowheads and gained so much expertise on Indian mounds that at age fifteen he wrote an article, "The Scientific and Correct Method of Opening Indian Mounds." He also absorbed lessons on labor and economic history from one of his neighbors, the progressive economist and historian John R. Commons. At age fifteen, Whitney entered the University of Wisconsin, earned tuition by working at the library three to four hours a day, and distinguished himself as a debater. Two years into college, his father died, in 1918, at age seventy-five. Inspired by his father's tales of the city, Seymour moved to New York City after graduating at age nineteen and enrolled at Columbia Law School.

At Columbia, Seymour got married and supported himself during his third year by teaching up to five classes a day as an associate professor at City College while attending law school full-time. He impressed the Columbia law dean, Harlan Fiske Stone, and became lifelong friends with the future United States attorney general and Supreme Court justice. It was Stone who had advised him to accept a job with Simpson, Thacher & Bartlett.

As a young lawyer at Simpson, Thacher, Seymour earned a reputation as an excellent trial lawyer and gained a new mentor in Thomas D. Thacher. The son of one of the firm's founding partners, Thacher had worked as an assistant U.S. Attorney for the Southern

District of New York and in 1925 became a federal trial judge. Five years later, Judge Thacher left the bench to become solicitor general, representing the Hoover administration before the Supreme Court. He tapped Seymour, who had made partner the previous year, to be his principal assistant.

During his final few months as assistant solicitor general, Seymour was arguing roughly two cases a week. His oral arguments impressed several of the Court's most esteemed justices. While living in Washington, he visited Louis Brandeis, Benjamin Cardozo, and Oliver Wendell Holmes Jr. at their homes. In his library, Seymour treasured books and letters signed by all three justices. Seymour greatly admired Holmes's and Brandeis's opinions defending the importance of free speech and assembly and insisting that criminalizing speech required a clear and present danger of an imminent threat of violence. An appeal argued during the 1932 term also inspired Seymour to represent Herndon. In October 1932, Seymour sat in the courtroom and watched with awe as his friend Walter H. Pollak, a noted New York civil liberties lawyer, argued *Powell v. Alabama* and won new trials for the Scottsboro defendants. In *Powell*, Pollak had shown Seymour that Herndon's case also could be won at the Supreme Court.

It was Gellhorn and possibly Wechsler who had suggested that Seymour argue Herndon's case. Gellhorn had worked for Seymour in the solicitor general's office. He and Wechsler admired Seymour as a Supreme Court advocate and for the way he supervised the solicitor general's office's skilled team of constitutional lawyers. Seymour, not Thacher, had run the solicitor general's office day to day before both men returned to Simpson, Thacher.

Carol Weiss King did not need to be persuaded to hire a former assistant solicitor general and a member of the Republican political establishment to represent Herndon. She had been angling for Seymour, who was friends with her brother Louis and had donated to the Scottsboro defense fund at her brother's request, to work on the ILD's cases and to join the International Juridical Association's national committee. She knew that Seymour offered the best chance of persuading five justices to reverse Herndon's conviction.

Eager to defend Herndon's right to free speech and assembly, Seymour very much wanted to take the case. But before he agreed to represent Herndon on appeal without collecting a fee, Seymour asked Thacher for permission, because defending a Black communist might reflect badly on the firm. Thacher encouraged him to take the case because of the important constitutional rights at stake. Seymour also informed the ILD that he would represent Herndon only if he had "complete control" of the legal strategy. Fortunately, he and King agreed to attack the insurrection law based on Herndon's rights to free speech and assembly. Seymour worried about the ILD's inclination to supplement their legal strategy with mass protest. He had been assistant solicitor general on November 7, 1932, when the Court was supposed to hand down its decision in *Powell v. Alabama*. An hour before the announcement, approximately 100 communists had picketed outside the Court in support of the Scottsboro defendants. The Capitol police had greeted the protesters with nightsticks and tear gas.

King tried to assuage Seymour's fears of representing a communist by sending him the guidelines for ILD attorneys and alerting him to the relevant pages about the organization's goal of providing "the best possible defense" even if the lawyer did not subscribe to the client's political views. In Herndon's case, Seymour and the ILD agreed on legal strategy. On August 30, 1934, the ILD announced that Seymour had volunteered to appeal Herndon's case without collecting a fee and to defend "the basic rights of free speech, assemblage and organization for the working class and the oppressed Negro people." At Seymour's request, Wechsler and Gellhorn agreed to write the briefs with King.

For the preceding month, Herndon's legal team had been trying to extricate the case from the Georgia courts. On August 2, Chief Justice Russell had refused to provide Herndon's lawyers with a certificate to appeal to the U.S. Supreme Court because they had not raised the free speech and assembly claims in the state trial court and supreme court. This was exactly the issue that concerned King and had prompted her to ask Wechsler to write a memorandum about it. Herndon's lawyers knew that Chief Justice Russell might refuse to certify the appeal, as required by the rules of the U.S. Supreme Court, and therefore sought a more definitive Georgia Supreme Court ruling on the free speech and assembly claims. On August 9, they attempted to file a petition for rehearing with the state supreme court. The clerk of the court refused to accept the petition without the permission of the chief justice. Initially, Russell denied the request, arguing that a petition for rehearing should have been filed within ten days of the state supreme court's decision. The Georgia Supreme Court's rules, however, said no such thing. Herndon's lawyers appealed to the entire court. On August 20, the state supreme court voted, 3–2, to allow Herndon to file a petition for rehearing.

The Georgia Supreme Court, King and Wechsler believed, had provided Herndon's legal team with an opening. According to several U.S. Supreme Court decisions beginning with Justice Holmes's opinion in 1919 upholding the Espionage Act conviction of Charles Schenck, a criminal conviction for incitement required proof of a clear and present danger of imminent violence. Consistent with those decisions, Herndon's lawyers argued, Judge Wyatt had instructed the jury at the end of Herndon's trial that "it must appear clearly by the evidence that immediate serious violence against the State of Georgia was to be expected or advocated." In its initial opinion, the Georgia Supreme Court had rejected Herndon's contention that the evidence at trial did not show that he had advocated "immediate serious violence." The court, moreover, insisted that it was not "necessary to guilt that the alleged offender should have intended that an insurrection should follow instantly or at any given time . . . as a result of his influence, by those whom he sought to incite." The state supreme court's emphasis on "at any given time," Herndon's lawyers argued, contradicted the U.S. Supreme Court's requirement of a clear and present danger. And several U.S. Supreme Court decisions, they contended, permitted defendants to raise free speech and assembly claims for the first time on appeal in light of an erroneous state supreme court decision.

In its September 28 opinion denying the petition for rehearing, the Georgia Supreme Court provided the Seymour-led defense team exactly what it needed—a ruling from a state court on the free speech and assembly claims. The court observed that Herndon's lawyers had neglected to object to the insurrection law on free speech and assembly grounds before, during, or after the trial or in their initial appeal. Yet the court attempted to explain its prior decision that the jury could have found Herndon guilty of attempting to incite an insurrection "at any time" in the future. The court claimed that the phrase "at any time" meant "within a reasonable time" or "within such time as one's persuasion or other adopted means might reasonably be expected to be directly operative in causing an insurrection." Justice R. C. Bell, writing separately, argued that Herndon's lawyers had not raised the free speech and assembly claims in state court and, even if they had, the insurrection law did not violate the U.S. Supreme Court's decisions requiring proof of "a clear and imminent danger." The insurrection law, Justice Bell concluded, also "does not fail for want of sufficient certainty. All men subject to its penalties may well know what acts it is their duty to avoid."

Pleasantly surprised by the state supreme court's ruling on the free speech and assembly claims, Seymour obtained an order from Chief Justice Russell permitting the appeal of Herndon's case to the U.S. Supreme Court. On December 26, Seymour filed a notice of appeal along with an assignment of twenty-one errors in the state supreme court's opinion. On January 19, 1935, he filed a statement of jurisdiction explaining that the Georgia Supreme Court's interpretation of the insurrection law violated Herndon's rights to free speech and assembly and that the insurrection law was unconstitutionally vague. The statement reviewed the charges and evidence against Herndon and Judge Wyatt's jury instructions. The state supreme court's rulings, Seymour argued, conflicted with the Court's requirement of an imminent threat of violence and therefore required U.S. Supreme Court review.

In his appeal to the U.S. Supreme Court, Seymour argued that the state supreme court had interpreted the Georgia law in a way that violated Herndon's Fourteenth Amendment right to due process of law. Since its 1925 decision in *Gitlow v. New York*, the Court subjected state laws to free speech and assembly challenges because they were fundamental liberties protected by the Fourteenth Amendment's Due Process Clause ("nor shall any State deprive any person of life, liberty, or property, without due process of law"). With Herndon's liberties of speech and assembly at stake, Seymour's jurisdictional statement concluded that the state supreme court's interpretation of the insurrection law had created "a substantial Federal question" requiring the Court to hear the case.

Though the Court agreed to hear Herndon's appeal, the justices indicated concern with whether his lawyers had raised free speech and assembly claims in state court before seeking relief in the U.S. Supreme Court. On February 11, the Court announced that it had put Herndon's case on its docket, but it reserved consideration whether his lawyers had properly raised free speech and assembly objections to the insurrection law in state court until after the justices had read the briefs and heard oral argument.

Seymour's team of Wechsler, Gellhorn, and King had a few months to write a brief explaining why the Georgia law as interpreted by the state supreme court violated Herndon's right to free speech and assembly, why the law was unconstitutionally vague, why the claims could be raised for the first time after the state supreme court's decision, and, ultimately, why Herndon should not have to return to Georgia to serve eighteen to twenty years on a chain gang.

■ ■ ■ ■

SINCE HIS TRIUMPHANT ARRIVAL at New York's Penn Station on
August 7, 1934, Angelo Herndon had emerged as a leading Black
public figure and spokesman for the communist cause. He lambasted
anticommunist Black columnist George Schuyler for predicting
that he would jump bail. Schuyler, Herndon wrote, "never missed"
an "opportunity to betray the struggles of the Negro people," and
"repeatedly knifed the Scottsboro boys, so you have attempted to
knife me also." Herndon denied that he would skip bail, vowed
to return to Georgia, and dismissed Schuyler as an "Uncle Tom."
In September, the ILD published a short pamphlet, *You Cannot Kill the Working Class*, embellishing Herndon's life story as a
Cincinnati-born coal miner and explaining why he joined the Communist Party and how he ended up sentenced to eighteen to twenty
years on a Georgia chain gang. A leading Black weekly newspaper,
the *Baltimore Afro-American*, serialized it in ten parts and gener-
ated more publicity about Herndon's pending Supreme Court case.

Herndon hit the lecture circuit in a way that would have made
Whitney North Seymour's father proud. Joined by Ida Norris,
the mother of imprisoned Scottsboro defendant Clarence Norris,
and Richard B. Moore, the national field organizer for the ILD,
Herndon sought to raise $15,000 for the Scottsboro-Herndon legal
defense fund on a speaking tour of northeastern, midwestern, and
western cities. At Pilgrim Baptist Church in Chicago, a crowd of
about 3000 people, "one of the most enthusiastic audiences ever
assembled in this city," crammed into the pews and stood in the
aisles. In a quiet voice, Herndon told the story of his arrest and
imprisonment and vowed: "the fight has just begun."

At the beginning of his West Coast tour in Los Angeles, about
2000 Black and white people packed the Mason Opera House to
hear Herndon's talk. Before an audience of roughly 500 people a
few days later, Herndon denounced the NAACP and its leaders, as
well as Schuyler, for pretending to be interested in the welfare of

working-class Black people. The NAACP, having been shunned by the Scottsboro defendants and their families in favor of the ILD's lawyers, refused to contribute to the Scottsboro-Herndon defense fund. A local Black minister at the second talk, outraged by Herndon's attack on the NAACP, accused him of spouting communist propaganda. A nonplussed Herndon insisted that his nineteen months in a Georgia jail could be called propaganda, but they reflected his real-life experiences. He asserted that only the ILD had fought for his freedom and the freedom of the Scottsboro defendants.

The most high-profile moment of Herndon's West Coast tour was his January 1935 visit to San Quentin Prison to see radical labor leader Tom Mooney. Mooney had been convicted and sentenced to death for the Preparedness Day parade bombing on July 22, 1916, in San Francisco, which killed ten people and injured forty-one. The chief eyewitness against him was a perjurer who was not permitted to testify against Mooney's alleged co-conspirators. Mooney's conviction, however, was allowed to stand. At the beginning of their one-hour meeting, Mooney, dressed in white prison garb, shook hands with Herndon over a wooden partition and described the visit as "a treat." Herndon asked him how the U.S. Supreme Court, which was also considering Mooney's appeal, would decide his case. Mooney had been imprisoned for eighteen years, and he harbored "no illusions" that the nine justices would set him free. Herndon told Mooney how the ILD had raised $15,000 to get him out of Fulton Tower and vowed to fight for Mooney's freedom. He was impressed that Mooney was "still determined to help carry on the struggle for the emancipation of the working-class."

During speaking engagements in California, Washington, and Oregon, Herndon was moved by the "militancy" of white and Black working-class people he met in small towns. He was impressed with how they "vehemently protested against the frame-up of the Scottsboro Boys, Herndon, Mooney, [convicted Oregon Communist Party leader Dirk] De Jonge and all class war prisoners."

Herndon's speaking tour had raised his national profile. In the *Daily Worker*, Anna Damon, the ILD's acting national secretary, observed that during the last eight months "hundreds of thousands from coast to coast have seen Angelo Herndon, have heard him speak, have pressed his hand. They know him for the courageous youthful leader that he is. And to these thousands, the thought that Herndon must go back to the chain gang, to torture and death is intolerable."

The ILD saw encouraging signs that the Supreme Court might rule in Herndon's favor. On April 1, 1935, the Court reversed the Alabama Supreme Court decision and remanded the cases of Clarence Norris and Haywood Patterson, two of the Scottsboro defendants, because qualified Black jurors had been systematically excluded from the jury rolls during their retrials (and because the justices saw for themselves that the state had forged the jury rolls to include the names of potential Black jurors after the retrials). This was the type of claim that Ben Davis Jr. and John Geer had tried to raise before Herndon's trial. The Georgia Supreme Court had already ruled that Herndon's trial counsel had not properly preserved objections to the jury issue and, even if they had, denied that Fulton County prosecutors had systematically excluded Black jurors.

With Herndon's appeal pending before the U.S. Supreme Court, Seymour, King, and the rest of the legal team decided to stay the course in attacking the insurrection law on free speech and assembly grounds. The state of Georgia had indicted eighteen communists, including the Atlanta Six, under the insurrection law. For the past year, Atlanta's radical left had faced a constant threat of harassment and arrest. In September 1934, police arrested two white women for distributing communist literature to striking textile workers. A month later, Assistant Solicitor John Hudson and other local police raided communist meetings in Fulton and DeKalb Counties, seizing radical literature and arresting six people. The raids soon extended to middle-class Black organizations, including the Urban League and the Butler Street YMCA. The future of interracial organizing in Georgia—by the Communist Party or civil rights groups—was at stake. "Not only are the rights of Negroes involved," a *New Masses* editorial observed, "but the basic rights of free speech, assemblage, and the right to organize and to demand relief."

. . . .

FOR SEVERAL MONTHS before the oral argument, Herndon's lawyers drafted his Supreme Court brief. Filed on March 16, 1935, signed by Seymour, and listing Wechsler, Gellhorn, and King as of counsel, the brief made four main arguments: 1) the Georgia insurrection law violated Herndon's liberty of speech and assembly; 2) the law did not a provide a definite enough standard of guilt; 3) the evidence failed to support the jury's verdict that Herndon had advocated the use of violence; and 4) Herndon's counsel had properly raised his speech and assembly claims in state court before appealing to the U.S. Supreme Court.

After reviewing the facts of Herndon's arrest and conviction, his lawyers argued that the Georgia Supreme Court's interpretation of the insurrection law violated his liberty of speech and assembly because it did not require proof of a clear and present danger of imminent violence. In a section of the brief drafted by Wechsler, Herndon's lawyers contended that the clear and present danger test—introduced in 1919 in Justice Oliver Wendell Holmes's opinion affirming the Espionage Act conviction of Socialist Party secretary Charles Schenck—represented the current state of the law. Herndon's lawyers quoted Justice Louis Brandeis's concurrence in *Whitney v. California*, the 1927 decision affirming Communist Labor Party member Charlotte Anita Whitney's conviction under a state syndicalism law, which described the requirement of a clear and present danger of imminent violence as a constitutional "command." Other Supreme Court decisions, Herndon's legal team conceded, had not always followed the clear and present danger test, yet had not overruled it.

In contrast to California and other state laws criminalizing specific threats of violence aimed at the state, Herndon's lawyers explained that Georgia had passed its initial insurrection law in 1804 because of fears of slave revolts. The Georgia law, revised in 1866 because of fears of Black violence during Reconstruction, did not refer to Blacks or slavery and, for the most part, had fallen into disuse. Herndon's lawyers argued that the Georgia insurrection law, unlike the syndicalism laws of other states making it illegal to advocate radical political and economic change by violent or criminal means, was not intended to be used against Communist Party members. The Communist Party, they argued, was not a threat to the state of Georgia. "The present record demonstrates," they concluded, "that the doctrine advocated in the Party literature did not give reasonable grounds to fear violent overthrow of the State."

In a section drafted by Gellhorn, Herndon's lawyers argued that the insurrection law was invalid because it failed to provide "sufficiently definite and certain standards of guilt." The vagueness of the law was another reason that it violated the Fourteenth Amendment's Due Process Clause. Herndon's lawyers reviewed several Supreme Court decisions invalidating state and federal criminal laws because they were unconstitutionally vague.

The insurrection law also was invalid as it applied to Herndon, his lawyers argued, because the evidence did not support his conviction for attempting to incite insurrection. The evidence presented at trial showed that Herndon had recruited a handful of Communist Party members, held a few meetings, and kept meeting minutes. The literature seized from him at the post office and from his room, moreover, did not advocate a violent insurrection. Specifically, Herndon's lawyers argued that literature discussing the Black Belt thesis—the Communist Party's idea of a Black majority expropriating white-owned land and creating their own sovereign nation in the South—did not advocate doing so by violence or force.

Finally, Herndon's counsel had "properly raised" his free speech and assembly claims, his lawyers argued, because the Georgia Supreme Court opinion interpreted the insurrection law as not requiring proof of a clear and present danger of imminent violence. Herndon's trial counsel could not have raised the issue earlier, his lawyers argued, because Judge Wyatt's jury instructions had correctly explained the law in requiring the jury to find a threat of imminent violence. The petition for rehearing was the first opportunity to raise the issue in state court, Herndon's lawyers argued, and, according to several U.S. Supreme Court decisions, satisfied the requirement of prior state review of federal constitutional claims.

In its response, filed on April 2, the state of Georgia argued that the Supreme Court should dismiss the appeal because Herndon's free speech and assembly claims could have been raised earlier in state court. On January 18, 1933, Herndon's trial counsel had moved to quash his indictment as a violation of Paragraph 15, Article I, of the Georgia Constitution, as well as of the U.S. Constitution. The motion to quash did not specify which part of the U.S. Constitution had been violated. Nor did the pretrial motion argue, as the Atlanta Six's counsel had at the time of their indictment, that the insurrection law violated freedom of speech and assembly. After the jury's verdict, Herndon's motion for a new trial did not raise any free speech and assembly objections to the insurrection law. Herndon's counsel, the state argued, should have raised these federal constitutional claims before Judge Wyatt, not on a motion for rehearing to the Georgia Supreme Court. The state supreme court's opinion interpreting the insurrection law as not requiring proof of a clear and present danger of imminent violence was not an "unanticipated ruling" permitting Herndon to raise the issue for the first time in a petition for rehearing. The state supreme court, the state contended, could not rule on the free speech and assembly claims. As a result, the state argued, the Georgia courts had never ruled on these claims—therefore denying the U.S. Supreme Court the ability to hear them for the first time on appeal.

Even if the U.S. Supreme Court could hear Herndon's constitutional claims, the state argued that the insurrection law did not violate his rights to free speech or assembly. The state supreme court's interpretation of the law as not requiring proof of a clear and present danger of imminent violence was consistent with the U.S. Supreme Court's decisions. Since 1919, the state argued, the Court had not required proof of a clear and present danger. It merely had required that the speech have a "dangerous tendency." Justices Brandeis and Holmes had advocated for the clear and present danger test, the state observed, but usually in dissent. The state rejected Herndon's argument that the insurrection law, because of its slavery and Reconstruction-era roots, could not be applied to the Communist Party. All criminal laws, the state argued, could be applied to new factual circumstances, such as the Party's idea that a Black majority take over the Black Belt. The Georgia insurrection law, the state argued, was no more vague or indefinite than other state syndicalism and insurrection laws upheld by the Court. Finally, the evidence— Herndon's admission that he was a Communist Party organizer and the Party's advocacy of Black self-determination in the Black Belt— supported his conviction for attempting to incite insurrection.

The oral argument set for April 12, 1935, offered both sides the opportunity to persuade the justices to rule for or against Herndon.

■　■　■　■

FOR ANGELO HERNDON, the most difficult part of the oral argument was gaining admission to the crowded courtroom. In the spring of 1935, the Supreme Court was still located in the basement of the Old Senate Chamber in the U.S. Capitol. When Herndon arrived there on the afternoon of April 12, there was a long line of sightseers and sympathizers, many of them Black, waiting for seats. It looked as if Herndon would not get a seat, not without some official help. Sasha Small, the editor of the *Labor Defender*, marched into the office of the marshal of the Court, Frank Key Green.

"Mr. Angelo Herndon whose case is coming up this afternoon is outside and cannot get into the courtroom because of the long line ahead of him," Small told Green.

Green, who was wearing "a stiff wing collar and starched shirt," had been the marshal since 1915 and apparently had never heard of a criminal defendant trying to attend his own argument. "Angelo Herndon?" Green replied. "Isn't he colored?"

"Yes," Small replied.

"But he's in jail," Green insisted.

"I beg your pardon," Small corrected him. "He is right outside your door. He has been out of jail, on bail, since last August."

Green handed a slip of paper to an assistant, who escorted Herndon into the courtroom. Herndon sat in the middle of the second row, immediately behind a brass railing separating spectators from the well of the semicircular courtroom. Seymour, accompanied by Wechsler, Gellhorn, and King, sat in front of Herndon waiting for the case to be called.

Almost immediately after Herndon took his seat at 2:30 p.m., the justices filed into the courtroom and stood behind a long desk covered with law books and briefs. Chief Justice Charles Evans Hughes, who "looked like god" with his prominent white beard and mustache and "talked like god" with his baritone voice, indicated for the justices to be seated and intoned: "Angelo Herndon versus the State of Georgia."

Seymour rose, approached the lectern, and immediately addressed the toughest question of whether Herndon's free speech and assembly claims had been raised properly in state court before they reached the U.S. Supreme Court. The state supreme court, he argued, had interpreted the insurrection law as not requiring a clear and present danger of imminent violence. The state's highest court, moreover, had not corrected the mistake in its opinion denying Herndon's petition for rehearing. It had erred in claiming that it was sufficient that the literature in Herndon's possession could cause violence "at any time in the future." Several justices revealed their skepticism about whether the speech and assembly claims had been raised in a timely fashion in state court. Willis Van Devanter, George Sutherland, and occasionally Hughes questioned Seymour about the state's contention that the speech and assembly claims should have been raised before Judge Wyatt.

After explaining that the issue was properly before the Court, Seymour framed the bigger issues at stake: "The basic constitutional rights to speak, assemble and petition for redress of grievance[s]." He highlighted how a former slave insurrection statute had been used to convict a law-abiding communist organizer. He argued that the state supreme court's interpretation of the insurrection law failed to require an immediate threat of violence and the wording of the law was so vague as to allow anyone who espoused unpopular political views to be convicted. The literature seized from Herndon, Seymour contended, did not support his conviction. Nor did the Party's idea of self-determination of the Black Belt at some hypothetical time in the future. Seymour spoke for an hour, patiently answered the few questions he received, and highlighted pertinent pages of the record as the justices followed along. Courtroom observers declared that Seymour's performance was "splendid." Herndon described it as "a brilliant and eloquent plea."

Tapped by Fulton County solicitor general John Boykin to argue the appeals in Herndon's case, Assistant Solicitor Walter LeCraw was making his first appearance before the U.S. Supreme Court. He made no apparent effort to temper his fiery personality or to avoid racially derogatory language. His argument reminded Herndon of the prosecutor's "ranting and raving and shouting" and "open call to race hatred" at the trial. LeCraw appealed to the justices' racial fears and harped on the Communist Party's idea of Black self-determination in the Black Belt. "Maybe when they say to seize the land and give it to the Niggers, maybe they don't mean force and violence," he yelled while holding up a copy of the pamphlet *The Communist Position on the Negro Question* and an issue of the *Daily Worker* whose front page called for self-determination in the Black Belt. "Can you confiscate this land without force?" he shouted. "Can this be political action—to take the land and turn it over to the Niggers?" he fumed. "We thought that was settled by the Civil War, but apparently the Communists don't admit that the question of secession is settled." LeCraw, perhaps sensing that racial epithets did not play well with the justices, may have switched to referring to Black people as "Nigras."

The New York–born Chief Justice Hughes was not persuaded and asked the state's lawyer to highlight evidence in the record where Herndon had advocated the use of force or violence. LeCraw pointed to the membership book seized from Herndon at the post office. "The membership book of the Communist Party," he said, "shows that a member of the Communist Party must abide by the decisions of the Russian branch." If his point was not clear enough, LeCraw returned to the Party's goal of self-determination in the Black Belt: "The idea of a separate country for the Niggers orig-inated in the Communist International, in Rooshia." LeCraw, according to a *Newsweek* reporter, "seemed to irritate the nine Jus-tices a bit."

As successful as Seymour's argument was compared with LeCraw's, it took the Court less than six weeks and only three and a half pages to dismiss Herndon's appeal. In a 6–3 opinion issued on May 20, 1935, Justice Sutherland ruled that Herndon's liberty of speech and assembly claims should have been raised earlier in state court. Sutherland faulted Herndon's trial counsel for raising only a general constitutional objection to the indictment before trial, not making free speech and assembly objections to the insurrection law, and not following state procedural rules in preserving those pretrial objections. Sutherland deferred to the Georgia Supreme Court's refusal to revisit the speech and assembly claims on a motion for rehearing. The state's highest court, Sutherland argued, had already rejected a free speech challenge to the section of the Georgia law about attempting to incite insurrection in a March 18, 1933, pretrial decision in the Atlanta Six cases. Herndon's trial lawyers, Suther-land insisted, should have known about that decision and should have objected to the insurrection law on free speech and assembly grounds in their new trial motion before Judge Wyatt and in the state supreme court before appealing to the U.S. Supreme Court. "It follows," Sutherland concluded, "that his contention that he raised the federal question at the first opportunity is without substance, and the appeal must be dismissed for want of jurisdiction."

Justice Cardozo, joined by Brandeis and Stone, wrote a dissent urging the Court to hear Herndon's speech and assembly claims on the merits. The former chief judge of the New York Court of Appeals, Cardozo was regarded as one of the most profound thinkers in American law when he had succeeded Justice Holmes on the Supreme Court three years earlier. Though often unhappy on the Court and plagued by ill health, the quiet, ascetic Cardozo had not lost his gifts as a literary stylist. In his dissent, Cardozo emphasized the differences between Judge Wyatt's jury instructions requiring a clear and present danger of imminent violence and the state supreme court's initial decision interpreting the insurrection law as requiring the possibility of violence at any time in the future. Because Herndon's lawyers had filed a motion for rehearing with the state supreme court, Cardozo argued that "the protection of the Constitution was seasonably invoked, and that the court should proceed to an adjudication of the merits." He pointed to the Court's decisions finding that when a constitutional violation occurred for the first time on appeal, the litigant could "challenge the unexpected ruling" on a motion for rehearing.

Though not resolving Herndon's speech and assembly claims, Cardozo argued that the requirement of a clear and present danger of imminent violence "has color of support in words uttered from this bench, and uttered with intense conviction." Requiring Herndon to object at trial, Cardozo wrote, seemed absurd in light of Judge Wyatt's jury instructions requiring a threat of imminent violence. Judge Wyatt could not have instructed the jury in light of the state supreme court's March 18, 1933, decision in the Atlanta Six case, Cardozo observed, because it was handed down nearly two months after Herndon's trial. The Georgia Supreme Court's decision on his motion for rehearing, Cardozo declared, was "an unequivocal rejection" of the clear and present danger test. "If the rejection of the test of clear and present danger was a denial of fundamental liberties," he wrote, "the path is clear for us to say so." In conclusion, he reminded the majority of the importance of "the questions that the defendant lays before us after conviction of a crime punishable by death in the discretion of the jury. I think he should receive an answer."

This was a Supreme Court at odds with a popular president and a Democratic majority in Congress. A week after its decision in Herndon's case, the Court invalidated the centerpiece of the Roosevelt administration's early New Deal programs—the National Industrial Recovery Act's codes of fair competition in numerous industries—as exceeding Congress's power to regulate interstate commerce and as delegating too much power to an administrative agency, the National Recovery Administration. Known as the "sick chicken case," the unanimous *Schechter Poultry* opinion sided with poultry processors who had violated the industry's fair competition code and allegedly had sold diseased chickens. That same day, the Court also invalidated a federal program providing a five-year mortgage moratorium for farmers. An infuriated President Roosevelt criticized the Court's "horse-and-buggy definition of interstate commerce."

Six justices—Van Devanter, James C. McReynolds, Sutherland, and Pierce Butler, as well as Chief Justice Hughes and Owen J. Roberts—voted to dismiss Herndon's appeal because his lawyers had not properly raised his free speech and assembly claims in state court. The 6–3 decision surprised some of the Court's most astute observers. Harvard law professor Felix Frankfurter praised Cardozo's dissent and confided to Brandeis: "The jurisdictional disposition by [the] majority is rather shocking. I hope Seymour did well." In the *Harvard Law Review*, Frankfurter and Henry M. Hart Jr. described the decision as "harsh."

The Court's decision prompted white daily newspapers, left-wing magazines, and the Black press to highlight the injustice of

Herndon's case. "All honor is due Justices Cardozo, Brandeis and Stone who dissented and upheld Herndon's right to a hearing," the *New York Post* editorial page declared. "But more honor to the young Georgia Negro, Herndon, who had the courage in the face of death and the chain gang to help organize the most miserable, the most divided, the most exploited workers in this country."

Herndon's communist supporters turned to mass protest. On June 3, 1935, the last day in the Court's old building, about a dozen people picketed in front of the Old Senate Chamber and carried signs that read, "Herndon Jailed for Demanding Bread; Demand His Freedom," "Free Angelo Herndon," "Abolish Vicious Anti-labor Laws," and "Unity of All Workers Will Free Angelo Herndon." Capitol Police and the "Red Squad" of the D.C. police department tore up the signs. Calling itself the Citizens Committee for the Defense of Angelo Herndon, the group featured prominent Washingtonians, including opera singer Lillian Evanti, journalist and recently fired Agricultural Adjustment Administration official Gardner Jackson, lawyer Belford Lawson Jr., and *Washington Afro-American* editor George Murphy Jr. Herndon's brother Milton protested along with several New York members of the committee. A delegation of seven or eight people tried to present Chief Justice Hughes with a request to rehear Herndon's case. Only two people were allowed to enter the anteroom of the marshal's office, where they presented the petition to the marshal. In their petition, they vowed to "bring to the attention of every justice-loving person in America the fact that the highest body of justice in the United States has taken such [an] attitude in the case of an innocent person."

Herndon, who had recently lectured at several northeastern colleges, did not join the protesters at the Court. Speaking at several New York area rallies, he did not hesitate to criticize the Court's decision. At a Communist Party rally of about 15,000 people at Madison Square Garden on May 27, he declared that "those ghostly-looking men did not dare go into the merits of my case, because they knew that the lynch masters of the South had put over one of the most vicious frame-ups in history." In the June issue of the *Labor Defender*, Herndon wrote: "What the Supreme Court has done by upholding the sentence against me, is to strike a blow at the whole working-class, at the Negro people, at all those who are hungry and demand bread, at all those who are homeless and demand a roof to sleep under." He accused the justices of hiding "behind long words and legal technicalities" to uphold the insurrection law. He compared the Court's decision in his case with its 1857 ruling in *Dred Scott v. Sandford*, declaring that Blacks were not citizens under the Constitution. Herndon vowed that this was not the end of his case and called his supporters to action: "Flood the Supreme Court at Washington with your protests. Demand a re-hearing of the case! . . . You can save me from the chain-gang and smash the lynchers' slave-law."

Mass protest alone was not going to free Herndon. Seymour planned to file an official petition for rehearing with the Court, if only to delay his client's return to Georgia until the fall. Herndon appealed for help from an unlikely source—the NAACP and its lead counsel, Charles Hamilton Houston.

CHAPTER SIX

THE CIVIL RIGHTS LAWYER

Charles Hamilton Houston

For several years, the NAACP had wanted nothing to do with Angelo Herndon's case. The organization refused to work with the ILD after the legal arm of the Communist Party had seized control of the Scottsboro appeals, and the NAACP disagreed with the ILD's legal strategy and publicity tactics. The two organizations clashed over the NAACP's failure to turn over $6000 it had raised for the Scottsboro defense team. The bad blood continued after Herndon's conviction. In a February 1933 letter from Chicago, Leroy Braxton appealed to NAACP executive secretary Walter White to aid in the efforts to secure his younger brother's release from Fulton Tower. White replied that the NAACP welcomed the opportunity to represent Herndon yet required "exclusive control of the case." He added that "the efforts should be conducted in the courts without the introduction of extraneous matter for propaganda purposes. The right of free speech is a fundamental one and should be fought vigorously but I frankly do not believe that the chances of success are very good if the Communists use it for the exploitation of their economic and political beliefs." The ILD accused White and the NAACP of employing the same "sabotaging maneuvers" in Herndon's case as in the Scottsboro case and decried the NAACP's "lying attack."

By 1935, however, the ILD's attitude toward the NAACP and other left-wing organizations had changed. The Communist Party USA responded to the rising threat of fascism in Nazi Germany by pursuing a united front—also known as the Popular Front—with other legal and political organizations. The Herndon case was Exhibit A. Four days after the U.S. Supreme Court's decision in May 1935, Herndon wrote a letter to Walter White explaining the ILD's intention to file a petition for rehearing and requesting a meeting "to discuss with you the basis for united action, involving your entire organization, in the struggle against this barbarous decision." White replied a few days later that the NAACP was "deeply interested in your case" and, though it was tied up with several other cases, he would refer Herndon's letter to the organization's National Legal Committee. The committee contacted Whitney North Seymour and received permission to file a friend-of-the-court brief supporting Herndon's petition for rehearing written by the NAACP's first full-time special counsel, Charles Hamilton Houston.

Privately, Houston informed White that Ben Davis Jr. and his co-counsel, John Geer, had created "a poor record" in Herndon's case. Houston knew it was their first criminal trial and that no experienced Atlanta lawyer was willing to take orders from the Communist Party about legal strategy. Nonetheless, Houston believed that "they have brought Herndon uncomfortably close to 18 years on the chain gang."

■ ■ ■ ■

ON THE SURFACE, Houston and Davis had grown up in the same milieu. Their fathers had been active in Republican Party politics and had served together on the Supreme Court of the Grand United Order of Odd Fellows. They were children of the Black middle class unafraid to compete against their white peers. Eight years older than Davis, Houston had inspired the younger man to attend Amherst College and Harvard Law School. And they socialized together as adults because of their family and school ties.

But whereas Davis was a tennis-playing bon vivant, Houston was intense, intellectually ambitious, and professionally driven. Pushed to succeed by his lawyer father, Houston had graduated from the nation's premier black public high school, M Street (later Dunbar) High School in Washington, D.C., at age fifteen. Four years later, he graduated from Amherst College magna cum laude and Phi Beta Kappa after writing an honors thesis on the poet Paul Laurence Dunbar, which earned plaudits from Dunbar's widow. For two years after graduation, Houston taught English as an instructor at Howard University, before he volunteered for the American Expeditionary Forces during the Great War.

The racially segregated U.S. Army exposed Houston to injustice and inspired him to become a civil rights lawyer. One of the army's few Black officers, he accepted a demotion from first lieutenant to second lieutenant so that he could participate in field artillery training. He never used his artillery skills in combat because the army relegated Blacks to service units. As a Black officer who had not yet gone to law school, he was forced to serve as the prosecutor in a court-martial of a Black sergeant accused of insubordination for trying to break up an alcohol-fueled dispute between two Black enlisted men. The sergeant was acquitted but sent to the stockade anyway. Houston vowed never again to be put in a situation where he did not know his rights as well as the rights of others. For Houston and other Black officers, army life became even more perilous when their unit was sent to France. White American soldiers brought their racist attitudes with them. When one of the Black officers tried to date a white Frenchwoman, he nearly got Houston and other Black officers in their unit lynched in retaliation.

After two years of army service, Houston could handle any challenges or obstacles he encountered at Harvard Law School. He earned several As on his exams at the end of his first year. As a second-year student, he improved his grades to four As and one B and qualified for membership on the *Harvard Law Review*. He was the *Review*'s first Black member. He knew that some of the other editors did not want him on the *Review*, yet paid them no mind. He started the Dunbar Law Club for Black and Jewish students after he was excluded from the all-white law clubs. Houston impressed leading members of the Harvard law faculty, including Dean Roscoe Pound and Felix Frankfurter, who believed that he had a future teaching law. The year after his graduation, Houston studied with Pound and Frankfurter and received his doctorate in law. He also won a Sheldon Traveling Fellowship and studied civil law for a year at the University of Madrid.

Upon his return to Washington, D.C., Houston passed the bar, joined his father's law practice, got married, and took on an ambitious project—transforming Howard's law school from an unaccredited night school into a fully accredited day program. In 1927, he studied and interviewed Black lawyers throughout the United States, concluded that no law school was educating Black lawyers the way Howard's could, and envisioned Howard-trained Black lawyers as "social engineers" who could use the law as a tool to fight racial injustice. By 1929, Houston was vice dean of the law school, had hired three full-time professors, and had applied for full accreditation. One of the new instructors he hired was William Hastie, an associate in the Houston firm, his second cousin, and the second Black member of the *Harvard Law Review*. During the early 1930s, Houston built up the student body and discovered a star protégé—a tall, thin, handsome, quick-witted Lincoln University graduate from Baltimore, Thurgood Marshall.

As vice dean at Howard, Houston worked on high-profile cases for the NAACP and showed Marshall and other aspiring Black lawyers the courage and self-control it took to defend Blacks on trial for their lives before all-white southern juries. To the NAACP's Walter White, Houston insisted on an all-Black defense team in agreeing to take on the capital murder case of George Crawford. Wanted for the January 1932 murder of a white Middleburg, Virginia, socialite and her elderly white maid, Crawford fled to Boston and lived there for a year before getting arrested for burglary. In April 1933, Houston succeeded in fighting the Massachusetts governor's extradition order by persuading Boston federal judge James A. Lowell to release Crawford because Loudoun County, Virginia, excluded Blacks from juries. Lowell's decision, however, was reversed on appeal on June 15, and Crawford was extradited to Loudoun County. Before and during the trial in Leesburg, Virginia, Houston repeatedly challenged the county's exclusion of Blacks from juries, the same issue initially raised in Herndon's case. Every day Houston and his Black legal team commuted to the trial from Washington, D.C., because no inn in Leesburg would rent them rooms. During his pretrial investigation and interviews with witnesses, Houston became convinced of Crawford's guilt. He succeeded in persuading the all-white jury to sentence Crawford to life in prison rather than the electric chair. The NAACP considered this outcome a partial victory. The Communist Party, however, charged that Houston betrayed Crawford by not proving his innocence.

Despite the Communist Party's criticism, Houston represented white ILD lawyer Bernard Ades in disbarment proceedings for zealously defending Euel Lee, the Black man convicted and executed for murdering a white family on Maryland's Eastern Shore. After Ades was found guilty in April 1934 of two ethical violations, Houston persuaded the judge to reprimand Ades rather than disbar him. But it wasn't good enough. Ades and other ILD lawyers voiced their displeasure with the reprimand. As a result, Houston declined to represent Ades in a subsequent bar grievance proceeding.

One prominent ILD lawyer, however, took Houston's side during the disputes over the Crawford and Ades cases—Carol Weiss King. King respected Houston as a pragmatic legal strategist who was more willing than other NAACP lawyers to work with the ILD on cases of mutual interest. In July 1933, Houston investigated Willie Peterson's death sentence for the kidnapping of three and murder of two white Birmingham women based on an erroneous eyewitness identification. He also co-authored a brief to the U.S. Attorney General about the lynching of the two young Black Tuscaloosa men, Dan Pippen Jr. and A. T. Harden, and recommended federal prosecution of the local sheriff. The Scottsboro and Peterson cases, Houston wrote, "must be won" because they "mark a social crisis which may determine future leadership of Negroes in the South."

Carol Weiss King also understood that, unlike other NAACP officials, Houston refused to let petty squabbles with the ILD over contributions to the Scottsboro legal defense fund prevent him from assisting in the defense of the wrongly convicted Black youths. During the winter of 1933, Houston offered words of encouragement to lead trial counsel Samuel Leibowitz. In May 1934, he advised King and other ILD attorneys about the appeals process. A month later, Houston accepted King's offer to join the International Juridical Association's executive committee and praised the *IJA Bulletin* as the only publication accurately reporting on civil rights cases. He made a fund-raising appeal for the Scottsboro legal defense team and offered to go to Alabama to work on the case. In February 1935, he appeared before the U.S. Supreme Court and successfully moved to change the lawyers arguing the Scottsboro appeal. On May 27, he made a similar appearance for Seymour and King to file notice of a petition for rehearing in the Herndon case. In short, Houston and King trusted each other. It was no surprise, then, that in June 1935, a month before he officially became the NAACP's new special counsel, he brought the organization into the Herndon case.

■ ■ ■ ■

WHITNEY NORTH SEYMOUR respected Charles Houston as one of the nation's leading civil rights lawyers. He wanted Houston and the NAACP to file a friend-of-the-court brief so that Herndon's case would look like more than a communist cause. Seymour and Houston viewed Herndon's case as not only about civil liberties but also about civil rights.

Houston quickly learned that the NAACP could not file a brief unless both Seymour and the state of Georgia consented. On June 8, Walter LeCraw, the assistant solicitor who had argued the case before the Supreme Court, and his boss, Solicitor General John Boykin, withheld consent to the NAACP's Atlanta counsel, A. T. Walden. Two white members of the NAACP's National Legal Committee, Arthur Spingarn and James Marshall, wanted to drop the matter. Houston and other organization officials prevailed in pressing forward.

On June 11, NAACP executive secretary Walter White wired Chief Justice Charles Evans Hughes alerting him that the organization was "deeply interested" in Herndon's case and that "the grave issues involved have vitally stirred our association and its members throughout the country." White explained the state of Georgia's refusal to consent to a friend-of-the-court brief and requested the chief justice's permission to file one anyway. The next day, Clerk of the Court Charles Elmore Cropley replied that Hughes was unavailable but that the rule on friend-of-the-court briefs was "strictly enforced." The only option was to file leave to submit the brief when the full Court reconvened on October 7.

Herndon's legal team was not optimistic that the Court would grant the petition for rehearing, but the process would delay his

return to Georgia authorities for three to four months and keep him
off the chain gang. Georgia prisoners, according to *Labor Defender*
editor Sasha Small, preferred the electric chair to the chain gang's
slow death. The prisoners, eyewitnesses reported, worked from
sunup to sundown with one hour for meals and rest, walked with
their ankles chained together twenty-one inches apart, and slept
chained and locked in steel cages. As Herndon argued to the press,
no one had survived more than ten years on a chain gang, much
less eighteen to twenty. He knew that on the chain gang he was a
dead man.

Fortunately for Herndon, the Court acceded to the delay. The
same day the NAACP wired Chief Justice Hughes, Justice Roberts granted Seymour's request to stay the execution of Herndon's
sentence until ten days after a decision on the petition for rehearing
in October.

In the meantime, Herndon embarked on a two-month speaking
tour of midwestern cities—beginning with the NAACP's annual
meeting in St. Louis. In his June 27 speech, Herndon called for a
united front among the ILD, NAACP, and other organizations as
"the only way that they will not only free me and the Scottsboro
boys, but the oppressed people of this country." Houston and his
NAACP colleagues White, assistant secretary Roy Wilkins, and
field secretary William Pickens signed the ILD's petition calling for
Herndon's freedom.

Houston's biggest challenge was finding the time to write the
friend-of-the-court brief for Herndon while embarking on the most
important legal campaign of his career. Based on a report by Nathan
Margold, a former Harvard Law School classmate, Houston pursued a strategy of attacking the Supreme Court's racially "separate but equal" doctrine by forcing states to provide Blacks with
equal schools, teacher salaries, and other funding sources. Houston began by suing states that provided law and graduate schools
for whites but not for Blacks. In June 1935, he and his former star
student Thurgood Marshall appeared in a Baltimore trial court to

argue for the admission of Donald Gaines Murray, a twenty-two-year-old Black Amherst College graduate, to the all-white University of Maryland Law School. In January, the university had denied Murray's application because of his race. On June 25, a Maryland trial judge ordered Murray's admission because the state had not established a law school for Black students. The university immediately appealed to the state's highest court, which affirmed the order admitting Murray. The Murray case represented the first victory in Houston and the NAACP's attack on racially segregated public schools.

In July, Houston took a sabbatical as vice dean of Howard Law School, moved to New York City, and assumed his full-time duties as the NAACP's special counsel. He immediately began traveling all over the South, working on cases and giving speeches to the organization's local chapters. He knew that the NAACP could not stay on the sidelines of Herndon's case because of the constitutional rights at stake.

By the end of the summer, Houston began writing the Herndon brief. In September, he asked Thurgood Marshall, by then a solo practitioner in Baltimore and frequent co-counsel with Houston and the NAACP, to help him coordinate with the all-Black National Bar Association and the cosponsors of the brief. King selected the other people and organizations, including Arthur Garfield Hays and Morris Ernst of the ACLU, and religious leaders, including Reverend Harry Emerson Fosdick and Rabbi Stephen S. Wise, to join the brief as friends of the court. George Lawrence of the National Bar Association and Thurgood Marshall and James Marshall of the NAACP put their names on the brief as of counsel.

October 7, 1935, was the first day of the Supreme Court's new term and the first day in its new nearly $10 million building, across First Street from the Old Senate Chamber. Many of the justices considered the marble palace designed by Cass Gilbert over the top. "I wonder," one of the justices quipped, "if we will look like nine black beetles in the Temple of Karnak."

At noon, the nine justices entered the crowded courtroom. Chief Justice Hughes admitted new candidates to the Supreme Court bar, then entertained a few motions. The NAACP's special counsel rose, moved to the lectern, and formally requested permission to file a friend-of-the-court brief in Herndon's case. In his motion to file the brief, Houston argued that he had received consent from Seymour and "tacit consent" from the state of Georgia. The latter was technically true. In fact, Houston had gone over the heads of Assistant Solicitor LeCraw and Solicitor General Boykin. On September 16, he had wired Georgia Attorney General M. J. Yeomans for consent for the NAACP to file a brief. Two days later, Yeomans replied that he was "without authority in this matter." Houston reprinted Yeomans's reply in a footnote for the benefit of the Court. The justices granted Houston's motion to file the brief.

In his brief, Houston argued that the Court's dismissal of Herndon's appeal for failing to raise the federal constitutional questions in state court was "wrong." Herndon could not have anticipated the Georgia Supreme Court's misinterpretation of the insurrection law in a way that violated his free speech and assembly rights. Judge Wyatt, who had instructed the jury to find proof of a threat of imminent violence, correctly interpreted the insurrection law and the U.S. Supreme Court's decisions. The first opportunity to challenge the state supreme court's misinterpretation of the law, therefore, was on a petition for rehearing with that court. Contrary to the state's contention, Houston argued that on rehearing, the state supreme court had ruled on the issue and had rejected Herndon's free speech and assembly claims. Herndon had "conclusively demonstrated," Houston concluded, that his lawyers had raised his constitutional claims in a timely fashion before the state supreme court and in his appeal to the U.S. Supreme Court.

As a practical matter, Houston predicted that the NAACP's brief would "not be of very great help on the law" in light of the thorough petition for rehearing filed on June 13 by Herndon's legal team. In eighteen pages written by Gellhorn, Wechsler, and

King and edited by Seymour, Herndon's lawyers argued that he could not have raised these issues any sooner. The state supreme court's pretrial decisions in 1932 and 1933 in the Atlanta Six cases did not address the constitutional questions in Herndon's case. In his instruction to the jury, Judge Wyatt had properly interpreted the insurrection law as requiring a threat of imminent violence. On appeal and rehearing to the state supreme court, Herndon's lawyers had argued that the insurrection law would violate his right to free speech and assembly if it did not require proof of a clear and present danger. The state supreme court, however, insisted that the danger of violence did not have to be imminent and could occur "at any time" in the future. The state supreme court's rulings, Herndon's lawyers argued, contravened the U.S. Supreme Court's free speech decisions and therefore raised important constitutional questions. The brief also included two appendices containing the Georgia law on criminal procedure and excerpts of Herndon's state supreme court briefs raising free speech and assembly claims.

Though his brief might not make a difference, Houston knew that Herndon's case was bigger than a communist cause or a Black cause—it was about free speech and assembly rights critical to the success of any political and social movement engaging in peaceful protest. The purpose of the brief filed by the NAACP, he wrote, was to demonstrate to the Supreme Court "the widespread interest felt by all classes of persons and organizations in this case and with the fundamental nature of the issues in the case as related to agitation for social reform."

■　　■　　■　　■

ON OCTOBER 14, Herndon was about to join a picket line in Harlem protesting the *Amsterdam News*'s decision to fire unionized employees when he heard the news: the U.S. Supreme Court had denied his petition for rehearing. He had ten days to turn himself in to Georgia authorities—or as soon as the U.S. Supreme Court sent the state supreme court its mandate ending the appeal. Herndon rejoined the picket line after briefly commenting on the Court's decision: "I haven't lost hope, because I haven't lost faith in the power of the workers of America to get me off. But I do want to say that there is not a moment to be lost."

The Supreme Court's refusal to rehear Herndon's case was front-page news in the Black press and sparked protests in New York City. The ILD called for two million people to sign a petition to Georgia governor Eugene Talmadge urging him to free Herndon and to request the repeal of the insurrection law. More than 400 Columbia law students met to criticize the Court's decision, with 200 of them signing the Talmadge petition. A small group of college newspaper editors protested in front of the White House and the Supreme Court and left a petition describing Herndon's sentence as "a shameful blow to our democracy."

During his final days of freedom, Herndon spoke at several ILD rallies in New York City. "I am not guilty of any crime," he told approximately 2000 people in Union Square on October 21, "but go to the chain gang because I challenged the right of the State of Georgia to prevent white and Negro workers from organizing." Two days later, at a rally of about 3000 people at the Manhattan Opera House, the ILD announced that Herndon would not be leaving for Atlanta that night because the Supreme Court mandate had not reached the Georgia Supreme Court. The meeting included numerous speakers. Herndon, however, was the headliner. Dressed in a dark suit and tie, he emphasized the importance of a united front: "Let us achieve the kind of united fighting alliance that would make Herndon cases impossible, that would be on guard against all reaction, against all manifestations of class oppression. Smash the insurrection law. Break the chains around my legs."

Two days before he had to turn himself in, Herndon boarded a train at New York's Penn Station bound for Atlanta. For 1000 miles, he and *New Masses* journalist Joseph North sat up all night and talked. They switched to a segregated railcar in Washington,

D.C., with North pulling up his collar and sitting near the window to avoid the prohibition against whites sitting in Black-only railroad cars. They arrived in Atlanta around midnight and stayed in the home of one of the Scottsboro mothers in the Black section of town. The family greeted him with hugs, fed him fried fish, and played blues records. Herndon sang a song he had learned inside Fulton Tower.

On the afternoon of October 28, Herndon prepared to turn himself in to Sheriff James I. Lowry at the same Fulton County courthouse where he had led a peaceful protest four years earlier. About a block from the courthouse, he turned to the journalist North and said: "You know, the nearer I get to the court, the nearer I feel freedom. I'm dead sure the united front'll get me out soon." Herndon entered the courthouse and looked for his lawyer waiting for him at the sheriff's office.

Back in New York, Herndon's legal team plotted how to set him free. Houston suggested that the ILD use the indictments of the Atlanta Six and other communists under the insurrection law to raise the same arguments in Herndon's brief to the U.S. Supreme Court. Winning their cases would make Herndon's confinement "morally and socially indefensible." Houston also proposed using the NAACP's southern contacts to submit a formal pardon request to Governor Talmadge.

Seymour, King, and the rest of Herndon's legal team could not wait that long, not with the chain gang looming. Instead, they lined up two prominent white Atlanta lawyers who knew a state trial judge with a guilty conscience.

CHAPTER SEVEN

THE GUILTY JUDGE

Elbert Parr Tuttle

A STERN-LOOKING WHITE LAWYER WITH BLUE EYES greeted Herndon at the sheriff's office and turned his new client over to Sheriff James Lowry. At first glance, Elbert Parr Tuttle seemed like any other young member of the Georgia legal establishment. The past president of the Lawyers Club of Atlanta and the commander of Fulton County's American Legion post, Tuttle cofounded one of the city's up-and-coming law firms—Sutherland, Tuttle, and Brennan—with his brother-in-law, William Sutherland.

In his role as lead counsel, Seymour enlisted Sutherland to serve as Herndon's new Georgia counsel. Ben Davis Jr. and John Geer, Herndon's former trial counsel, had left the state. Davis was in Harlem editing the *Negro Liberator* and engaged in communist political causes. Geer had moved to Louisville after getting married and causing quite a stir in Atlanta for agreeing to represent two white women charged under the insurrection law for distributing communist literature to striking textile workers.

A Georgia-born tax specialist, Sutherland possessed the pedigree, constitutional law background, and respect from the local bench and bar to win Herndon's case in the Georgia courts. He graduated from the University of Virginia at age seventeen, earned a master's in economics from the University of Wisconsin, and graduated from Harvard Law School by age twenty. After his law school graduation, he served for two years as the secretary (law clerk) to Justice Louis Brandeis. A visitor to Sutherland's office in 1935 described him as "a hard-boiled lawyer, who exhibits most of the stereotyped prejudices of the southern white man, but who, at the same time, is possessed by a kind of fanatical passion for freedom of speech. He has been influenced by John R. Commons at Wisconsin, Frankfurter and others at Harvard, and by association with Justice Brandeis at Washington. . . . I should say off hand that if there is any one man in Atlanta who could command the confidence of the Georgia courts and at the same time fight this case strictly on the grounds of the safeguarding of the Federal Constitution . . . Sutherland is the man."

Sutherland's partner, Tuttle, was just as capable and had none of his brother-in-law's "stereotyped prejudices of the southern white man." Born in Pasadena, California, and the son of a bookkeeper who worked for a Hawaii sugar plantation, Tuttle attended the Punahou School in Honolulu, grew up surfing, and joined his brother at Cornell University, where he was senior class president. Tuttle began training to be a pilot before the Great War ended. After the war, he wrote for several newspapers and enrolled at Cornell Law School. On vacation in Jacksonville, Florida, he met Sutherland's sister, Sara. They married in 1919 and, after Tuttle graduated from law school, joined her brother in Atlanta. Unlike Sutherland and most other white lawyers in Georgia, Tuttle belonged to the Republican Party.

Despite their different attitudes on race and politics, Tuttle and Sutherland shared a willingness to appeal cases of wrongly convicted Black criminal defendants. As a member of the Georgia National Guard in 1931, Tuttle was called to the Elbert County jail to protect two Black prisoners accused of raping a white woman from a mob of nearly 1000 white people. That night, Tuttle helped the sheriff hold off the mob and move the prisoners to Atlanta. One of the men, John Downer, had been convicted by an all-white jury after five minutes of deliberation and sentenced to death. Tuttle knew Downer's trial in Elberton had been a sham in light of the 200 National Guardsmen preventing the white mob outside the courthouse from lynching the defendant. Sutherland agreed to represent Downer on appeal along with Atlanta's leading Black lawyer, A. T. Walden. Two days before Downer's execution, they filed a petition for habeas corpus in federal court challenging the constitutionality of his conviction. Sutherland argued that a mob-dominated criminal trial, according to the U.S. Supreme Court's 1923 decision in *Moore v. Dempsey*, violated Downer's right to due process. The Macon-based federal judge denied the petition. The Fifth Circuit Court of Appeals in New Orleans, however, remanded the case for a new hearing. The second time, the federal trial judge granted the petition. Downer was retried in Augusta, convicted, and in March 1934 died in the electric chair. Tuttle harbored "serious doubt" about Downer's guilt.

More than experienced appellate lawyers willing to protect the constitutional rights of a Black defendant, Tuttle and Sutherland knew a Georgia trial judge with a guilty conscience.

Two decades earlier, Hugh M. Dorsey had risen to political power through his dogged prosecution of one of the state's most notorious criminal cases—the murder trial of Jewish Atlanta pencil factory superintendent Leo Frank. As Fulton County solicitor, Dorsey tried Frank for the rape and murder of a thirteen-year-old pencil factory worker, Mary Phagan. Dorsey's case against the Cornell-educated Frank hinged on the testimony of Jim Conley, a Black janitor with a checkered past and an unlikely story. Conley admitted carrying Phagan's lifeless body down the elevator, hiding it in the factory's basement, and writing two murder notes, supposedly at Frank's request, found near the body. Somehow, Dorsey believed Conley's story over Frank's—even though Conley's own lawyer doubted his client's story. At the end of a nearly monthlong trial in August 1913, Dorsey awed courtroom observers with an impassioned closing argument lasting nine hours over three days. The jury convicted Frank, who was not permitted to attend his capital sentencing the next day for fear of a lynching by the angry white mob outside the courthouse. In April 1915, the U.S. Supreme Court, by a 7–2 vote, denied Frank's claim that his mob-dominated trial violated his right to due process. On June 21, the day before Frank's scheduled execution, Governor John M. Slaton acknowledged the case had been "marked by doubt" and outraged many white Georgians by commuting Frank's sentence to life imprisonment. On August 16, prominent white citizens from Phagan's hometown of Marietta abducted Frank from the state prison in Milledgeville and lynched him. Postcards of the Leo Frank lynching were sold all over the South.

Buoyed by his fame as the Frank prosecutor and backed by Georgia populist Tom Watson, the thirty-five-year-old Dorsey successfully ran for governor of Georgia and won reelection two years later. During his second term, he took on the issue of race. On March 21, 1921, two Black foremen were charged with murdering eleven Black farmworkers held in peonage on the Jasper County plantation of John S. Williams. Dorsey deplored the murders and revealed they were not isolated incidents. On April 22, he called the first meeting of the newly created Committee on Race Relations at the Piedmont Hotel and read from a remarkable document. In *A Statement from Governor Hugh M. Dorsey as to the Negro in Georgia*, commonly known as *The Negro in Georgia*, Dorsey documented 135 instances of lynching, peonage, or other acts of cruelty against Black Georgians. "In some counties the negro is being driven out as though he were a wild beast," he wrote. "In others he is being held as a slave. In others, no negroes remain." Though he did not mention the names of the perpetrators, Dorsey revealed that only 2 of the 135 cases involved accusations of rape against white women. "To me," he wrote, "it seems that we stand indicted as a people before the world. If the conditions indicated by these charges should continue, both God and man would justly condemn Georgia more severely than man and God have condemned Belgium and Leopold for the Congo atrocities. But worse than that condemnation would be the destruction of our civilization by the continued toleration of such cruelties in Georgia."

Released a few days later to the press, Dorsey's report prompted cries for his impeachment. Incoming governor Thomas Hardwick described it as a "slander on the state." Even without impeachment, Dorsey's career in elected politics was essentially over. Watson had already defeated him in a run for the U.S. Senate. Dorsey seemed to draw strength from calling attention to racial injustice. During his final gubernatorial address to the general assembly on June 25, 1921, he documented the fifty-eight Black men and women lynched since he had taken office in 1917 and lamented that "the hands of those who participated in taking the lives of several negroes are stained with the blood of men innocent of any crime." After leaving office, he returned to his family's law practice until September 1926, when he was named a city court judge. In May 1935, he was appointed a Fulton County superior court judge.

Dorsey apparently held Tuttle in high regard. On September 20, four months into his term as a superior court judge, he appointed Tuttle solicitor pro tem to conduct a grand jury investigation of perjury allegations against Solicitor General John Boykin. The principal witness, a convicted perjurer sentenced to eight to twelve years in prison for his part in a fake damages claim racket, was far from reliable. But additional evidence of corruption by county officials prompted the appointment of an independent committee. As a result of his grand jury investigation, Tuttle declined to present an indictment against Boykin. In the process, Tuttle gained a valuable ally in Dorsey as well as insight into the judge's mind. Tuttle believed that Dorsey wanted to make amends for his dogged prosecution of Leo Frank—and the Herndon case was the perfect opportunity.

As soon as Tuttle turned Herndon over to Sheriff Lowry, he and Sutherland filed a petition for habeas corpus with Judge Dorsey arguing that the constitutional questions about Herndon's conviction had never been ruled on by the Georgia courts. Dorsey signed the petition and scheduled a hearing for November 12. Until then, Herndon returned to Fulton Tower, the same jail that had housed Leo Frank during his trial and Herndon during his trial and first round of appeals.

■　■　■　■

AT FULTON TOWER, Herndon occupied a cell with nearly thirty Black inmates, including some condemned to die. The inmates usually greeted a newcomer by holding a kangaroo court and fining the person $1.50 for "breaking into jail." They made an exception for the man who traveled 1000 miles by train to turn himself in to Sheriff Lowry. One of the inmates had heard Herndon speak in California and informed the others that Herndon had stood up for the common man.

Herndon and his new cellmates slept in bunk beds for two men. A third person slept beneath them on the floor. They spent most of their days and nights playing cards. In fact, Herndon played cards so much that he dreamed about it. There was not much for him to do. Initially, he was denied his books and magazines and was limited to reading local newspapers and to writing communist colleagues. They wrote him back and enclosed the air mail stamps and small amounts of cash he requested.

Herndon's first few days in prison did not trigger flashbacks to the painful nineteen months he had endured in Fulton Tower. Prison conditions, due to the negative national publicity about Herndon's case, had improved dramatically. The inmates slept on mattresses, showered twice a week, and ate edible food. Herndon did not feel like he had been "re-incarcerated." In his mind, he was a free man. He simply waited for the courts to agree with him.

A petition for habeas corpus is a civil lawsuit challenging the legality of a person's criminal conviction and confinement and requires that the state "produce the body." Seymour, therefore, asked the sheriff to bring Herndon to the hearing. On the afternoon of November 12, 1935, Herndon arrived in Judge Dorsey's eighth-floor courtroom dressed like "a youthful college student" with his "tailored oxford grey suit, brown shoes, white shirt and red tie." As he sat down next to Seymour and the other lawyers, Herndon put two books on the table so that everyone in the courtroom could see them. One of the books, *The Letters of Sacco and Vanzetti*, was a visible reminder of his communist sympathies and the radical left's unsuccessful efforts to save the two Italian anarchists from the electric chair. Judge Dorsey's courtroom was packed with so many Black spectators that some of them sat in the whites-only section. They had come to see Herndon and whether his lawyers Whitney North Seymour and William Sutherland could persuade Judge Dorsey to set him free.

Seymour made two main arguments why Judge Dorsey should overturn Herndon's conviction. First, he argued that the Georgia insurrection law violated Herndon's right to free speech and assembly as applied to the states by the Fourteenth Amendment's Due

Process Clause. Second, he argued that the Georgia insurrection law was unconstitutionally vague in failing to define what constitutes "attempting to incite insurrection." Herndon could not be convicted under the law, Seymour argued, for simply trying to organize Black and white unemployed workers. None of the literature seized from Herndon, Seymour contended, advocated inciting insurrection. And even if it had, Herndon could not be convicted for trying to overthrow the government by "force" because only twenty-three people voted for the Communist Party in the entire state. Seymour argued, the *Daily Worker* declared, "with the same brilliant forcefulness which characterized his splendid presentation of the Herndon appeal to the United States Supreme Court." During his argument before Judge Dorsey, Seymour read from Holmes's dissent in *Abrams v. United States* and Brandeis's concurring opinion in *Whitney v. California* warning against the criminalization of free speech absent a "clear and present danger" of imminent violence. In a birthday note to Brandeis, Seymour described the "very noticeable effect upon almost everyone in the courtroom" of reading "such magnificent lines" but feared it was "only temporary."

Assistant Solicitor Walter LeCraw, however, was impressed by Seymour's "fine and powerful" argument and worried about its effect on Judge Dorsey. The next morning in Dorsey's courtroom, LeCraw responded by focusing on one of the pamphlets seized from Herndon, *The Communist Position on the Negro Question*, and its advocacy of self-determination in the Black Belt. For nearly three hours, the prosecutor argued that Herndon was convicted of trying to implement the Black Belt thesis. "Herndon," LeCraw insisted, "sought to foster the aims of the Red Committee at Moscow advocating the confiscation of the property of white landlords for the use of Negro farmers." He also claimed that Herndon "advocat[ed] the overthrow of republican government to set up a Negro government in the so-called Black Belt in the South."

To rebut LeCraw's argument, Sutherland spoke to Judge Dorsey white southerner to white southerner. "This idea of a 19-year-old

Negro boy seizing the property of all these states and setting up a Black republic as argued by Mr. LeCraw is so fanciful, and so absurd, that it becomes almost ridiculous for us to stand before Your Honor and argue about it," he told the judge. Sutherland did not stop there. He revealed how strongly he felt about Herndon's First Amendment right to read what he wanted and to his political beliefs. "I now have an altogether different light on this case after listening to Brother LeCraw's argument," Sutherland said. "I thought the state was charging this boy with distributing this literature, but I notice that he does not even mention that. He wants to make him serve that ungodly sentence merely because he had that reading material. It's almost unbelievable. I can't imagine such a ridiculous thing."

Finally, Sutherland appealed to the judge who wrote *The Negro in Georgia*: "It is unusual that Georgia, where good relations exist between the Negro and white man, and where the Negro has played no part in our political life, should single out a Negro boy for its first victim under the Insurrection statu[t]e."

The well-dressed Herndon, with a persistent cough that worried his supporters, listened attentively to the entire proceedings. He was "not optimistic" that the judge would set him free. Shortly after noon on November 13, Judge Dorsey took the case under advisement. Based on the local newspapers, Herndon expected the decision would come in a matter of days. Instead, it took weeks. The wait, exacerbated by a bout with tonsilitis, weighed on him. The only thing keeping him sane were letters from his communist allies. Ben Davis Jr., his former trial counsel turned communist writer and activist, promised to send him cigarettes, money, or anything else he needed and vowed: "I shall be in the front line of every single effort to hasten your freedom."

On December 7, Herndon's forty-first day in Fulton Tower, Judge Dorsey finally issued his decision. The judge agreed with Seymour's second argument that Georgia's insurrection law was "too vague and indefinite to provide a sufficiently ascertainable standard of guilt" and therefore violated the Fourteenth Amendment's Due Process Clause. A few newspapers connected Dorsey's decision to the Leo Frank case and to his racial progressivism as governor. In a separate statement, Dorsey reminded the people of Georgia and their elected officials that many "states have laws that have been upheld by the Supreme Court of the United States, which give ample protection against doctrines such as Herndon was advocating." The judge gave the state twenty days to appeal and ordered Herndon released on $8000 bond.

A little before noon that day, Herndon was reading *Sawdust Caesar*, an antifascist book about Mussolini, when a reporter burst into the cell block during visiting hours and informed him of Judge Dorsey's order. A turnkey told Herndon to gather his things. Fellow inmates began helping him pack his books. Shortly before 1:00 p.m., he waited in Sheriff Lowry's office, accompanied by two deputies. Badly in need of a haircut, he was wearing a clean shirt, new shoes, and a faded overcoat. He was carrying his belongings in a paper bag and a stack of books wrapped in a bath towel. He took out a cigarette from his socks. One of the deputies ordered him to take off his hat.

Herndon's lawyer Elbert Tuttle entered the sheriff's office with the clerk of court and paid bail with eight $1000 Treasury bonds (Sheriff Lowry had returned the $15,000 bond the ILD had raised the last time). A smiling Herndon signed the release form. "You can go now," the deputy sheriff said.

Out on the street, Tuttle handed him some money. Herndon headed for Auburn Avenue, Atlanta's Black commercial district, to get something to eat. A Black man stopped him and asked, "Excuse me, aren't you Mr. Herndon?" After his meal, Herndon watched a Tarzan movie with a friend and got a haircut before boarding a northbound train. Edward R. Kane, a young lawyer in Sutherland and Tuttle's office, accompanied him on a segregated railcar to Washington.

At Washington's Union Station, Herndon ate with *Labor*

Defender associate editor Louis Colman and *Daily Worker* reporter Marguerite Young at the station's lunch counter before boarding a train for New York City. In Philadelphia, ILD acting national secretary Anna Damon joined him on the train. In Newark, forty members of a voluntary committee boarded Herndon's car. He told them he had already wired the Scottsboro defendants at the Jefferson County jail to raise their spirits.

Around 4:10 p.m., nearly 3000 people greeted Herndon at the Thirty-First Street entrance of New York's Penn Station. Damon and a few Communist Party officials escorted him to the waiting area. The crowd picked him up, carried him up the steps, and sang "The Internationale." They marched down Thirty-First Street to Seventh Avenue. Herndon and the committee celebrated that night at the Harlem headquarters of the Communist Party. Herndon credited the united front for his release. "This must, this will mean a broader campaign for the Scottsboro boys," he said. "It will mean more and stronger united-front actions against anti-union legislation, against war, in defense of civil rights and labor standards wherever they are attacked."

Herndon's release thrilled Black people in Harlem and inspired its leading writers and artists. The poet Langston Hughes wrote a one-act play, *Angelo Herndon Jones,* for the New Theatre League. In early January 1936, Hughes saw Herndon at the Third U.S. Congress Against War and Fascism in Cleveland. Less than a month later, Hughes published one of his most famous poems, "Kids Who Die," in the *Daily Worker.* Hughes's poem warned that "the old and rich . . . / Don't want the people to get wise to their own power, / To believe an Angelo Herndon, or even get together."

The nation's leading civil rights lawyer, Charles Hamilton Houston, knew that Seymour deserved tremendous credit and congratulated him on his "stirring and challenging victory." Houston believed that "it is going to be the means of great advances on the liberal front. We are deeply indebted to you and your associates."

Seymour had been smart enough to request the "assistance"

of two of Atlanta's most respected lawyers, Sutherland and Tuttle. Tuttle knew the ideal judge to hear Herndon's habeas petition, and Sutherland knew what to say to him. Seymour also knew he needed their continued help when the case returned to the Georgia Supreme Court.

The state wasted no time appealing Judge Dorsey's decision. On December 11, 1935, the state objected on evidentiary grounds and disagreed that the insurrection law was unconstitutionally vague. Three days later, Herndon's lawyers filed counter objections to preserve their arguments about the law violating his rights to free speech and assembly. Both sides wrote their briefs and prepared for oral argument at the end of January before the Georgia Supreme Court.

On January 25 and 26, 1936, the justices of the Georgia Supreme Court heard arguments from both sides. Solicitor General John Boykin, making his first appearance in the case, declared that "the doctrine of violence is inculcated in the mind of every communist." He urged the justices to reverse Judge Dorsey and to uphold Herndon's conviction under the insurrection law because he advocated the Communist Party line of establishing a "black belt republic." Boykin observed that "the communist party interlocks with the soviet republic of Russia" and "the American branch preaches overthrow of the government by force and violence."

Sutherland appealed to the justices' southern sensibilities. "This case has been used as a spearhead for the liberals throughout the country," he said, "when you limit freedom of speech, you invite violence." He seemed to be belittling his own client: "When a man like Herndon is made a martyr, there is real danger to democracy." Finally, he predicted that "if this case doesn't go to the supreme court of the United States, some other will."

Seymour, taking over for Sutherland, recounted how Herndon had been arrested after conducting a peaceful protest of 600 whites and 400 Blacks for unemployment relief and for the communist literature found in his room. Backed by Judge Dorsey's decision, he argued that the insurrection law was too vague to be applied to those facts. The facts, Seymour contended, did not support Herndon's conviction for attempting to incite an insurrection. "We think," Seymour remarked, "in 1932 the state was secure because the communists only polled 28 [*sic*] votes."

Assistant Solicitor LeCraw reminded the justices that they had already ruled that the law was not unconstitutional because of vagueness.

Rather than rule quickly, the Georgia Supreme Court sat on the case for nearly six months. Still awaiting the decision in May, Seymour was holed up in Greenwich Hospital in Connecticut after an emergency appendectomy. He was "especially touched" by a get-well note from his client Herndon. Instructed by his doctor to rest for most of the summer, Seymour soon left for Bermuda for two months and advised Sutherland to contact Walter Gellhorn in the event of an adverse ruling.

On June 13, Justice Samuel C. Atkinson issued a unanimous two-page opinion reversing Judge Dorsey's decision. Chief Justice Russell did not participate. Justice Marcus W. Beck merely concurred in the judgment. Quoting at length from the Georgia Supreme Court's rejection of Herndon's petition for rehearing, Justice Atkinson reiterated that the attempt to incite insurrection did not have to result in imminent violence and that the violence did not actually have to happen. He also rejected the arguments that the insurrection law violated Herndon's rights to free speech and assembly or that the law was unconstitutionally vague. "The foregoing provisions of the Constitutions," he wrote of the federal and state constitutions, "do not guarantee freedom of speech or the right of assembly in the perpetration of a crime."

In remarks so important that the conservative New York *Herald Tribune* reprinted them, Anna Damon, the acting national secretary of the ILD, revealed the stakes in Herndon's case: "The decision of the Georgia Supreme Court is a challenge to all American labor. . . . The decision is at the same time a challenge to the Negro people of the country, whose liberties are particularly threatened under this law and who have already rallied in hundreds of thousands to fight to free Angelo Herndon." She also observed that eighteen other Black and white suspected communists had been arrested and charged under the Georgia insurrection law. She urged a united front opposing the decision: "we are calling upon all trade unions, all progressive-minded people and organizations to join with us in this fight against reaction."

The NAACP's special counsel, Charles Houston, heard Damon's message loud and clear. On July 20, he wrote a memorandum to the civil rights organization's board of directors urging them to join the Herndon defense committee rather than continue to write friend-of-the-court briefs on its own. The Georgia Supreme Court's decision in the Herndon case, Houston wrote, "marks a crisis in the development of civil rights in the South. The Herndon case may affect much of our own work. I feel sure that the Herndon case is just as important as the Scottsboro case in the long run and that there is no more danger of the Association being compromised in the Herndon case than in the Scottsboro case. I believe that our participation in the Scottsboro case has been decidedly to our advantage and I think our participation in the Herndon case will go down likewise." The NAACP heeded Houston's warning. That fall, the board of directors agreed to join other organizations on the Joint Committee to Aid the Herndon Defense.

Herndon, in a bylined article in the *Labor Defender*, put it even more bluntly: "The decision of the State Supreme Court of Georgia was no surprise or shock to me. I know Georgia justice. I have felt its sting for the last four years and I know that it will stop at nothing in its determined effort to crush the organized labor movement and the Negro people."

The Georgia Supreme Court stayed the execution of Herndon's sentence for sixty days, until August 17, so that his lawyers could appeal to the U.S. Supreme Court. The U.S. Supreme Court, however, was a backward-looking institution hostile to the interests of organized labor. It had scarcely protected the rights of African Americans. It was on the brink of a showdown over the constitutionality of the New Deal. And the Supreme Court justice who had provided the fifth vote to invalidate a New York minimum wage law for women was under fire.

CHAPTER EIGHT

THE JUSTICE
UNDER FIRE

Justice Owen J. Roberts

O N JUNE 1, 1936, TWELVE DAYS BEFORE THE GEORGIA
Supreme Court reversed Judge Dorsey's ruling for Herndon, the
U.S. Supreme Court had shocked lawyers and politicians seeking to
help the nation recover from the Great Depression. In a 5–4 decision in *Morehead v. Tipaldo*, the Court invalidated New York's
minimum wage law for women as violating the Fourteenth Amendment's "freedom of contract." Progressives had drafted the New
York law—which established an industrial commission to set minimum wages based on the industry in question—to comply with the

Court's 1923 decision in *Adkins v. Children's Hospital* invalidating a Washington, D.C., minimum wage law for women. The D.C. law had established the same minimum wage for women across all industries. The Court, however, dismissed the factual differences between the two laws. The majority opinion by Justice Pierce Butler held that *Adkins* controlled, reaffirmed that "[f]reedom of contract is the general rule and restraint the exception," and declared the New York minimum wage law unconstitutional.

For President Roosevelt, the Court's decision in *Tipaldo* was the final straw. On May 27, 1935, a day known as Black Monday, the Court had struck down two of his New Deal programs and ruled that he had unlawfully removed a Federal Trade commissioner. At the time, Roosevelt had vented to the press about the Court's "horse-and-buggy definition of interstate commerce." Still fuming over the Court's 1935 decisions and three more in 1936 striking down other New Deal programs, Roosevelt did not mention the *Tipaldo* decision by name. Yet when asked about it by reporters on June 2, he observed that the Court had created a "No Man's Land" where neither the states nor the federal government could pass economic legislation. Roosevelt's comments made front-page news.

The fifth and deciding vote in *Morehead v. Tipaldo* had come from one of the Court's newer justices, Owen Roberts. Roberts joined the Court's 5–4 majority opinion striking down the New York law without comment. Roberts's votes on economic regulation puzzled progressives who had praised his Supreme Court nomination six years earlier. Felix Frankfurter, however, had been warned by a friend that Roberts was "an ingrained conservative" and that "we'd be fooled by him."

Owen Josephus Roberts was a product of the Philadelphia business and legal establishment. The son of a wagonmaker and hardware store owner, he graduated from the private Germantown Academy as the class salutatorian at age fifteen and the University of Pennsylvania as class valedictorian at age nineteen. Three years

Herndon declared victory in this July 1932 leaflet after a peaceful interracial protest at the Fulton County courthouse forced county officials to increase unemployment relief by $6000.

OUR DEMONSTRATION GOT US $6,000. FROM THE COUNTY

WORKERS OF ATLANTA!

EMPLOYED AND UNEMPLOYED!   NEGRO AND WHITE!

The County Commissioners voted $6,000. to continue our relief, because Thursday, hundreds of us, Negro and white, went to the Court House, showed the bosses there was plenty of starvation in Atlanta, and DEMANDED RELIEF. We crammed that liedown the throat of Commissioner Hendricks who said there were no starving families- but this gentleman was not present Thursday morning. While we have gained something by showing the bosses we will not starve peacefully, this is not enough! The County and City say they have no money. Where is the $470,000.00 that was saved by cutting the salaries of the county officials? Why cant this money be given for relief? WE CAN FORCE THESE FAKERS TO GIVE US MORE RELIEF IF WE ORGANIZE AND FIGHT FOR IT!

THEY ARE STILL TALKING ABOUT SENDING US TO THE FARMS TO WORK FOR NOTHING. THE BOSSES WILL USE ANY TRICK TO KEEP US FROM GETTING THE RELIEF WE ARE ENTITLED TO. DONT BE FOOLED BY THIS TALK ABOUT GOOD TIMES ON THE FARMS! THE FARMERS ARE STARVING AND AS RAGGED AS WE ARE!

BOSSES SHOCKED BY UNITY OF NEGRO AND WHITE

The biggest surprize handed the bosses who have been starving us out was when they saw Negro and white workers come down together to fight for relief. For many years they have handed us a lot of bunk about not having anything to do with the Negroes, and at the same time, STARVING BOTH OF US. WE WHITE WORKERS SHOULD NOT HAVE ALLOWED COMMISSIONER STEWART AND THOSE OTHER FAKERS TO SEPARATE US FROM THE NEGROES WHO CAME THERE WITH US. IF WE ALLOW THE BOSSES TO DIVIDE US THEY WILL KEEP US BOTH STARVING. WE NEGRO AND WHITE WORKERS MUST STICK TOGETHER BECAUSE THAT IS THE ONLY WAY WE CAN WIN. The bosses know this; that is why they work so hard to separate us. The privelege of starving separately dont mean anything to any sensible worker these days. The ex-servicemen in Washington know this, and Negro and white ex-servicemen are sticking together until they get their Back Pay- called the Bonus.

WE MUST ORGANIZE

Every day the bosses and landlords cut off our water and throw us out on the streets, both Negro and white. They dont care how many of us starve, white or black. WE WONT STARVE IF WE ORGANIZE! The UNEMPLOYED COMMITTEE calls on the workers of every neighborhood to get together, organize your committees and see that no worker is evicted because he cant pay the rent. WE MUST SEE THAT EVERY RELIEF STATION STAYS OPEN AND ALL OF US AND OUR KIDS ARE FED! THERE IS NO REASON FOR ANY WORKER TO STARVE IN THE MIDST OF PLENTY! THE UNEMPLOYED COMMITTEE WILL CALL A MEETING IN THE NEAR FUTURE OF ALL WORKERS, NEGRO AND WHITE, TO GET TOGETHER AND MAKE UP OUR PROGRAM OF DEMANDS THAT WE WILL ORGANIZE AND FIGHT FOR.

WATCH FOR OUR NEXT CIRCULAR!

For information, write to C. Jones, Chairman Box 339, Atlanta, Ga.

Unemployed Committee of Atlanta

Ben Davis Jr. (*right*) and Herndon, the client who inspired him to join the Communist Party.

Herndon languished in Fulton Tower, the county jail known for its 100-foot granite tower and nicknamed Big Rock.

Citizens Meeting
— ON THE —
Angelo Herndon Case

SPEAKERS:

MRS. M. RAOUL MILLIS
Sociologist and Writer

REV. J. A. MARTIN
Editor, Sunday School Periodicals, C. M. E. Church

MR. VAN WOODWARD
Professor, Georgia School of Technology

MR. BENJAMIN J. DAVIS, JR.
Defense Attorney, Herndon Case

And Other Prominent Public Citizens

FOR FREE SPEECH, ASSEMBLY, AND PRESS
AS GUARANTED BY THE
CONSTITUTION OF THE STATE OF GEORGIA

EVERYBODY IS WELCOME

SUNDAY, MAY 7th — 5:00 P. M.
AT TAFT HALL — Auditorium Armory

AUSPICES: PROVISIONAL COMMITTEE FOR THE
DEFENSE OF ANGELO HERNDON

This committee is composed of representative citizens and organizations of the community.

ADMISSION FREE

C. Vann Woodward, a Georgia Tech English instructor, spoke at the May 7, 1933, Provisional Committee meeting at Atlanta's Taft Hall.

Black protesters marched down Pennsylvania Avenue on May 8, 1933, calling on Congress and President Franklin D. Roosevelt to free the Scottsboro defendants and Angelo Herndon.

Herndon's brother Milton (*left*) greeted him at Penn Station on August 7, 1934, along with former Scottsboro accuser Ruby Bates (*center*) and several Communist Party leaders (*right*).

James W. Ford and another Communist Party leader carried Herndon up the stairs of Penn Station.

A cheering throng at Penn Station awaited Herndon.

Columbia law professors Walter Gellhorn (*left*) and Herbert Wechsler (*right*) worked with Carol Weiss King and drafted the Supreme Court briefs on appeal.

"I am not guilty of any crime," Herndon declared at an International Labor Defense rally in New York City in late October 1935, before his return to Fulton Tower jail.

Judge Hugh Dorsey, the former Georgia governor who had prosecuted Leo Frank, was Tuttle's choice to hear the challenge to Herndon's conviction.

At the request of his lawyer, Whitney North Seymour, Herndon attended the November 12, 1935, habeas corpus hearing before Judge Dorsey.

The International Labor Defense produced this pamphlet in 1935 to raise money and publicity for Herndon's appeals.

Herndon standing on the front portico of the Supreme Court with ILD leaders Anna Damon (*center*) and Joseph Gelders (*right*) after the April 12, 1935, oral argument in his case.

The front pages of the *Baltimore Afro-American* and *Daily Worker* hailing Herndon's Supreme Court victory.

Ralph Ellison quit his job with the Federal Writers' Project to join Herndon as the managing editor of the *Negro Quarterly*.

The second issue of the *Negro Quarterly*, edited by Herndon and Ellison.

THE NEGRO QUARTERLY

A REVIEW OF NEGRO LIFE AND CULTURE

INDIA AND THE PEOPLES' WAR
KUMAR GOSHAL

MEN IN THE MAKING
RICHARD WRIGHT

ANTI-NEGROISM AMONG JEWS
LOUIS HARAP

ANTI-SEMITISM AMONG NEGROES
L. D. REDDICK

BANQUET IN HONOR
LANGSTON HUGHES

2 SUMMER 1942

50 CENTS

later, he graduated from the University of Pennsylvania Law School with the highest honors. The fall after his law school graduation, he returned as an instructor, and after three years, the law school made him an assistant professor.

Roberts did not just teach law. He also distinguished himself in private practice and in Philadelphia courtrooms. In 1902, he was named the city's assistant district attorney. Tall, imposing, and with an intense gaze, he commanded the courtroom and did not mince words in prosecuting criminals. After a few years in the district attorney's office, he returned to private practice and in 1912 founded the firm Roberts, Montgomery, and McKeehan. He represented the city's leading corporations and showed little interest in protecting the powerless. As a special federal prosecutor in 1918, he successfully prosecuted two editors and three publishers of a Philadelphia German-language newspaper for violating the Espionage Act because of seditious statements attempting to undermine the draft and the war effort. A few years later, he railed against the federal government's efforts to regulate the coal industry. Yet he also contributed to civic causes and in 1929 joined the board of trustees of a historically Black college, Lincoln University. He and his family lived in a mansion in Philadelphia's tony Rittenhouse Square neighborhood and owned a 700-acre dairy farm in nearby Chester County.

Roberts rose to national prominence in 1924 when President Calvin Coolidge named him the special prosecutor to investigate the Teapot Dome scandal. Appointed on the recommendation of U.S. Senator George Wharton Pepper, Roberts prosecuted Harding administration officials and private businessmen for their roles in a bribery scandal over the sale of government-owned oil reserves. Several leading figures were acquitted of criminal charges. Roberts, however, succeeded in convicting Harding's interior secretary, Albert B. Fall, of bribery and in recovering the Teapot Dome oil reserve in Wyoming from a private corporation.

Known as a prosecutor rather than an expert on constitutional law, Roberts was an unlikely and unexpected Supreme Court nominee. On March 21, 1930, after the death of Justice Edward T. Sanford, President Hoover nominated North Carolina federal Court of Appeals judge John J. Parker. The Parker nomination outraged leading progressive organizations. The American Federation of Labor objected to Parker's 1927 Court of Appeals decision upholding yellow dog contracts that forbade union membership as a condition of employment. The NAACP, opposing a Supreme Court nominee for the first time in its history, revealed Parker's comments as a 1920 gubernatorial candidate supporting Black disenfranchisement. The Senate defeated Parker's nomination, 41–39. Parker's loss was Roberts's gain.

At the time, Harvard law professor Felix Frankfurter and other progressives hailed Hoover's nomination of Roberts. They did not know much about him besides his Teapot Dome prosecutions. An overjoyed Frankfurter wrote the Court's newest justice: "There is a good deal of talk about 'conservative' and 'liberal.' The characterizations hardly describe anybody since we are all a compound of both. What divides men much more decisively is the extent to which they are free—free from a dogmatic outlook on life, free from fears. And that is what cheers me so about your appointment. For you have, I believe, no skeletons in the closet of your mind, and are a servant neither of a blind traditionalism nor of blind indifference to historic wisdom."

During his first five years on the Court, Roberts wrote opinions and voted in ways that puzzled legal observers. Black commentators objected to his 1935 majority opinion in *Grovey v. Townsend* upholding Texas's all-white primary scheme as proof of his unwillingness to protect their rights under the Fourteenth Amendment. Frankfurter and other progressives abhorred Roberts's 5–4 majority opinion in 1935 invalidating the Railroad Retirement Act's pension system and his three votes against the Roosevelt administration on Black Monday. After the railroad pension decision, the press declared that Roberts had thrown his lot with the justices opposed to the New Deal and other forms of economic regulation. Roberts, however, was hard to peg. In 1934, he wrote the majority opinion in *Nebbia v. New York* upholding a state law fixing minimum milk prices because the dairy industry was "in the public interest." Two years later, however, he wrote the majority opinion in *United States v. Butler* striking down the Agricultural Adjustment Act's payments to encourage farmers to reduce their acreage or production as exceeding Congress's power and infringing on the power of the states. And six months later, he voted with the majority in *Morehead v. Tipaldo*—for reasons unknown at the time—to invalidate New York's minimum wage law for women.

"Roberts is dejected—the gay, charming, refreshing youthful fellow of six years ago is gone," Brandeis confided to Frankfurter on May 20, 1936. "He is in terror—he fears dictatorship and all that." Roberts may have feared that the Roosevelt administration, backed by a Democratic majority in Congress, was expanding federal power beyond its limits and into the realm of "local activities." But a fear of a Roosevelt dictatorship or of too much federal power fails to explain Roberts's vote to strike down a state minimum wage law. Either way, his anti–New Deal decisions in 1935 prompted some Republicans to consider Roberts as a possible "strict constructionist" presidential nominee to challenge Roosevelt.

If the Supreme Court was going to overturn Herndon's conviction after a second oral argument, Herndon needed Roberts's vote. Roberts had voted with the majority to dismiss Herndon's first Supreme Court appeal. Then, on June 11, 1935, he had granted a stay of Herndon's sentence so that his lawyers could file a petition for rehearing with the Supreme Court—delaying Herndon's return to Georgia.

Owen Roberts was a more likely vote for Herndon the second time than some of his colleagues in the initial 6–3 majority. Van Devanter, McReynolds, Butler, and Sutherland—labeled by their critics as the Four Horsemen—often voted to strike down economic legislation in 1935 and 1936, especially if it benefited organized labor. Despite sometimes voting to protect civil liberties, they were unlikely to vote for Herndon.

Willis Van Devanter, a seventy-seven-year-old former Wyoming railroad lawyer, was the Court's longest-serving justice. A stickler about the Court's jurisdiction to hear state and federal cases, he probably made the strongest case for the dismissal of Herndon's first Supreme Court appeal during the justices' private conference discussions. Though he played an instrumental role in the Court's deliberations, Van Devanter was a painfully slow writer and rarely authored majority opinions.

James McReynolds, a seventy-four-year-old Kentuckian raised in Tennessee, was the Court's most openly racist and antisemitic justice. He publicly referred to a Black person as a "darky" and turned his back on Black advocates before the Court. He refused to speak to the Court's two Jewish justices, Brandeis and Cardozo. He made no secret of his dislike of Roosevelt and the New Deal, publicly referring to the President in announcing a 1935 dissent as "Nero at his worst." He was the least likely vote for Herndon, having joined Butler's dissent from Sutherland's majority opinion in *Powell v. Alabama* in favor of the Scottsboro defendants.

George Sutherland, a bearded, bespectacled, English-born, seventy-four-year-old former Utah congressman and senator, joined the Court in 1922 and prized individual liberty over economic regulation—especially if the regulation benefited workers or organized labor. He wrote the 1923 majority opinion in *Adkins v. Children's Hospital*, invalidating the D.C. minimum wage law for women, and the 1936 majority opinion in *Carter v. Carter Coal*, striking down the Bituminous Coal Conservation Act's attempt to set minimum wages and maximum hours and to promote unionization. Although his 1932 majority opinion in *Powell v. Alabama* showed that he cared about civil liberties, he was unlikely to vote for a communist labor organizer.

Pierce Butler, the seventy-year-old former Minneapolis railroad lawyer, joined the Court in 1923. Progressives objected to him in part because as a member of the University of Minnesota board of regents he had voted to oust radical professors. The only Catholic justice, he dissented in the 1927 decision of *Buck v. Bell*, which upheld the state of Virginia's compulsory sterilization of Carrie Buck and a year later in *Olmstead v. United States*, permitting federal agents to use wiretapped phone conversations. Yet he also dissented in *Powell v. Alabama*. Finally, he wrote the majority opinion denying Herndon's first appeal and was unlikely to change his vote the second time around.

Besides Roberts, the other possible vote for Herndon was Chief Justice Charles Evans Hughes. The former governor of New York, the seventy-four-year-old Hughes was in his second go-round on the Supreme Court. He had resigned as an associate justice in 1916 to accept the Republican nomination for president and nearly defeated incumbent Woodrow Wilson. After serving as Harding and Coolidge's secretary of state, he returned to the bench in 1930 as Hoover's surprising choice for chief justice. Hughes cared deeply about the Court as an institution. Of late, however, he had sided with Roberts and the Four Horsemen against the New Deal. He joined Roberts's opinion in the 1935 Railroad Retirement Act case, authored the 1935 majority opinion in *Schechter Poultry* striking down the National Industrial Recovery Act, wrote a concurring opinion in 1936 in *Carter Coal* against the Bituminous Coal Conservation Act, and joined Roberts's majority opinion in *United States v. Butler* invalidating the Agricultural Adjustment Act. Yet he dissented in *Morehead v. Tipaldo* because of factual distinctions between the D.C. and New York minimum wage laws for women. Though he joined the majority in Herndon's first appeal, Hughes was an independent thinker who had voted to uphold the rights of African Americans and had joined Holmes's dissent in the Leo Frank case. He was also a canny politician who understood the rising public frustration with the Court's anti–New Deal decisions.

Most important of all, Hughes had written several groundbreaking opinions for the Court on free speech and free press. In a 7–2 decision in May 1931, he wrote the majority opinion overturning the conviction of the communist Yetta Stromberg for violating a California law prohibiting the public display of a red flag. Over dissents by Butler and McReynolds, Hughes declared that the California law was unconstitutionally "vague and indefinite" and violated Stromberg's right to free speech. In a 5–4 decision in June 1931, Hughes vacated court-ordered injunctions against Jay Near and Howard Guilford, the owners of a Minneapolis newspaper, *The Saturday Press*, for accusing local officials of being in cahoots with gangsters. Hughes's opinion invalidated the Minnesota public nuisance law as violating the rule against prepublication censorship and recognized the freedom of the press to write about the conduct of public officials. Owen Roberts joined Hughes's decisions in *Stromberg* and *Near*.

It was possible that Hughes and Roberts, who had been sympathetic to free speech and press claims, might vote in Herndon's favor because of their shared concerns about the Court's institutional standing. During the summer of 1936, Hughes and his wife visited the Robertses at their Pennsylvania farm. The two justices apparently walked up and down the terrace and discussed their work at the Court for hours. Mrs. Roberts, who knew her husband was not a walker, tried to call them back to the house for tea. Instead, the two justices just kept walking and talking. After dinner, they continued their discussion in Roberts's library.

Despite their votes in free speech and free press cases, Hughes and Roberts often found themselves in cases about economic regulation caught between the anti–New Deal Four Horsemen and the three justices who had dissented in Herndon's initial appeal—Brandeis, Stone, and Cardozo.

Louis Brandeis, the seventy-nine-year-old justice Roosevelt nicknamed Isaiah because he looked like an Old Testament prophet (his angular features reminded others of Abraham Lincoln), was the Court's champion of free speech. The first Jewish justice, he joined the Court in 1916 after a contentious confirmation process because of antisemitism and his progressive economic views. In April 1919, Brandeis joined Holmes's opinions affirming the Espionage Act convictions of radicals Charles Schenck, Jacob Frohwerk, and Eugene Debs because it had been wartime. After the war, however, Brandeis began to rethink his views on free speech. In November 1919, he joined Holmes's dissent in the case of anarchist Jacob Abrams about the importance of free speech in the marketplace of ideas. During the 1920s, Brandeis developed his own theory of free speech in dissenting and concurring opinions from the Court's decisions upholding the criminal convictions of radical speakers. He highlighted the importance of protecting unpopular speech as essential to a functioning democracy. "It is the function of speech to free men from the bondage of irrational fears," he wrote in his 1927 concurrence in *Whitney v. California*. "To justify suppression of free speech there must be reasonable ground to fear that serious evil will result if free speech is practiced. There must be reasonable ground to believe that the danger apprehended is imminent." This was the language that Seymour had invoked in Judge Dorsey's courtroom in arguing that there must be an "imminent" threat of violence to abridge the right to free speech and assembly.

The second dissenter in Herndon's appeal, sixty-three-year-old Harlan Fiske Stone, joined the Court in 1925 after serving as Coolidge's attorney general. The former dean of Columbia Law School, he had graduated from Amherst College a year ahead of Coolidge and as attorney general had been tasked with cleaning up a Justice Department rife with corruption and mismanagement under Harding. During his early years on the Court, Stone often joined majority opinions invalidating economic legislation and ruling against radical speakers. By the late 1920s and early 1930s, however, he gravitated to the dissents of Holmes and Brandeis defending economic regulation and civil liberties. During the New Deal constitutional crisis of 1935 and 1936, he had lost all respect for Chief Justice Hughes because of the Court's hostility to regulation. Prior to the justices' private conferences, Stone met privately with Roberts, Brandeis, and Cardozo to discuss votes on pending cases.

The author of the *Herndon* dissent, sixty-six-year-old Benjamin Cardozo, was dismayed by the Court's decisions striking down federal and state economic legislation. The son of a corrupt former New York trial judge, he restored the family name by writing groundbreaking opinions about the law of accidents and products liability as a judge and chief judge on the New York Court of Appeals. He also published a series of lectures in an influential book about judging, *The Nature of the Judicial Process*. Nominated to the Supreme Court in 1932 to replace Holmes, the white-haired, beetle-browed Cardozo battled health problems and longed to be back on the New York Court of Appeals. Gentle and soft-spoken, he confided to Frankfurter that "we here have really ceased to be a Court."

One of the people most eager to change the makeup of the Court, Franklin Roosevelt, was running for a second term. Though the country had not fully recovered from the Great Depression, Roosevelt had assuaged the fears of the American people during "fireside chat" evening radio addresses and had delivered on his promise of a New Deal—federal programs, public works projects, and economic regulation. He and leading members of Congress expressed frustration with the Court's willingness to strike down their New Deal programs. Roosevelt's Republican opponent in the general election, Kansas governor Alf Landon, was backed by the pro-business and anti–New Deal group the Liberty League. At 10:00 p.m. on June 26, 1936, Roosevelt accepted his party's presidential nomination at the Democratic convention in Philadelphia. He had initially included criticism of the Court in early drafts of his acceptance speech but left them on the cutting room floor. Instead, he focused on the "economic tyranny" of monopolists and big businessmen, their exploitation of working people, and their objections to New Deal legislation: "These economic royalists complain that we seek to overthrow the institutions of America. What they really complain of is that we seek to take away their power. Our allegiance to American institutions requires the overthrow of this kind of power. In vain they seek to hide behind the Flag and the Constitution. In their blindness they forget what the Flag and the Constitution stand for. Now, as always, for over a century and a half, the Flag, the Constitution, stand against a dictatorship by mob rule and the over-privileged alike, and the Flag and the Constitution stand for democracy, not tyranny; for freedom, but not subjection."

Similarly, the Democratic Party platform was devoid of criticism of the Court despite the efforts of Roosevelt adviser Felix Frankfurter to include some. Instead, the platform attacked the Republican Party platform's pledge to leave the nation's economic problems to the states. "We have sought," the Democratic platform said, "and will continue to seek to meet these problems through legislation within the Constitution." If legislation did not work, the platform vowed to seek amendments to the Constitution "in order adequately to regulate commerce, protect public health and safety and safeguard economic security." And on the topic of civil liberties, the platform declared: "We shall continue to guard the freedom of speech, press, radio, religion and assembly which our Constitution guarantees; with equal rights to all and special privileges to none."

■ ■ ■ ■

AS ONE OF THE MOST visible symbols of the fight for free speech and assembly, Angelo Herndon was as outspoken as ever. At the communist-backed American Youth Conference in Cleveland on July 6, Herndon called for unity among the young delegates or else "the forces of reaction and fascism will sweep all of us away. . . . I know from experience what unity means. Even my freedom depends on unity." More than five months earlier, on January 25, leaders of the radical American Youth Congress had accepted an invitation for tea at the White House with Eleanor Roosevelt. They had tried to convince her that democracy was in decline, pointing to the Herndon and Scottsboro cases as prime examples. The First Lady replied that "when things like that happen, we must make it our business to really try and see that justice is done."

For his part, Herndon waded into domestic and international political disputes and highlighted acts of injustice. On August 21, 1936, he decried the discrimination America's Black athletes faced at the 1936 Summer Olympics in Berlin. "The Nazi Olympics have given American Negro youth a picture of what they may expect in the United States if the reactionary forces represented by the Liberty-League-Hearst-Landon combination triumph," he said. He praised four-time gold-medal-winning track star Jesse Owens and other Black athletes and observed how Nazi leader Adolf Hitler had snubbed them by declining to shake their hands like he did with victorious white athletes. Herndon also predicted what would happen if Nazi-style fascism flourished in America. "The triumph of fascism in the United States," he said, "would mean that the persecution and discrimination suffered by the Negroes in certain Southern states would be intensified many times."

After Owens's triumphant return home, Herndon wrote the track star praising him for agreeing not to stump for Republican Alf Landon. The party of Abraham Lincoln was hoping to use Black celebrities, including heavyweight boxer Joe Louis, to influence Black voters to vote for the Republican nominee. Herndon opposed Landon because of the danger the Republican candidate posed toward efforts to feed, to house, and to find jobs for unemployed workers. He considered Roosevelt to be indecisive on the unemployment issue but was willing to work with pro-Roosevelt groups—unlike some of his communist colleagues. At the conference of the communist-backed Workers Alliance of America on September 17, Herndon saw his resolution to work with pro-Roosevelt labor groups defeated.

Despite his support for a united front, Herndon steadfastly supported the Communist Party during the 1936 election and toured the country to campaign for the Party's presidential ticket of Earl Browder and James Ford. Having established residency in New

York, Herndon ran for the state assembly in the Twenty-First District on the communist-backed Harlem All People's Party ticket. "Keep Herndon Off the Chain Gang," a *Daily Worker* editorial declared, "by Sending Him to Albany." On October 26, Herndon appeared alongside Ford, the Communist Party's African American candidate for vice president, at a rally in Harlem and received "a rousing reception." The day before the election, Herndon "spoke calmly and clearly" at a rally headlined by Browder before about 20,000 people at Madison Square Garden. Herndon's speech "was frequently interrupted by spontaneous applause."

Like his fellow Communist Party candidates, Herndon lost badly but managed to raise public awareness about his case and his appeal to the Supreme Court. "Sometimes I wonder what went on in the minds of those nine old men in Washington when my case was brought before them for the second time in less than two years," he wrote in a bylined article in the *Labor Defender*. Herndon connected his case to the Court's rejection of Roosevelt's New Deal programs: "because today the battle between reaction and progress, democracy and fascism is so sharp, the Herndon case is more important than it has ever been before. The Liberty League is out to 'defend the constitution' by plunging this country into blackest reaction. Most of the recent decisions of the United States Supreme Court seem to indicate that they have ideas not very different from the Liberty League as to how the Constitution must be defended."

In the presidential race, the American people rejected the pro-business Liberty League and the Supreme Court's anti–New Deal decisions by reelecting Roosevelt in a landslide. Roosevelt won 523 electoral votes to 8 for Landon and carried forty-six of the forty-eight states. With a massive mandate, Roosevelt set his sights on the Supreme Court. He quietly asked a few legal advisers to generate ideas about what he could do about the Court and its opposition to his New Deal programs. Roosevelt's landslide victory put Roberts, Hughes, and the Four Horsemen on notice just as Herndon's case returned to their docket.

On September 11, 1936, Herndon's lawyers had filed a notice of appeal with the Supreme Court after obtaining an order to do so from Georgia Chief Justice Richard Russell Sr. They also filed a statement of jurisdiction. In a twenty-three-page document drafted by Herbert Wechsler and filed on October 11, Herndon's lawyers explained how Judge Dorsey had granted Herndon's petition for habeas corpus because of the unconstitutional vagueness of the Georgia insurrection law. The Georgia Supreme Court, in overruling Judge Dorsey's decision, upheld the state insurrection law and denied Herndon's claims that the law violated his rights to free speech and assembly or that it was so vague as to violate his right to due process. Thus, his lawyers argued, the state's highest court had ruled on Herndon's constitutional claims and had made those claims ripe for review by the U.S. Supreme Court. This time, Georgia officials did not contest that Herndon's constitutional claims had been properly raised in state court.

As the Court opened its new term on the first Monday in October, the ILD tried to raise money for Herndon's appeal by describing it as "the most important case from the point of view of the rights of labor and of the Negro people." Herndon proclaimed "that there would be no Herndon case today if it were not for the Prisoners Relief work of the ILD. Its work of solidarity kept me alive those many months in Fulton Tower jail."

On November 23, the Supreme Court officially noted its intention to hear the case. Herndon was in Milwaukee to speak to the Workers Alliance when he heard the news. "The name of Angelo Herndon has gone 'round the world," a *Daily Worker* editorial declared. "This heroic young Negro Communist has become the symbol of the struggle of 14,000,000 Negroes against the shameful lynch-rule . . . in the South. . . . More, Angelo Herndon is the symbol of the fight of the whole American people, white as well as black, for the preservation of their civil liberties. For the statute under which he was convicted is a flagrant violation of the Bill of Rights." The ILD proclaimed November 30 "National Herndon

Day" and aspired to hold "Herndon Defense Meetings" in more than 500 cities. Ben Davis Jr. wrote a *Daily Worker* column rebutting claims in the *California Eagle* that Herndon, his former client, was "contemplating suicide" if the Supreme Court ruled against him and sent him to the chain gang. The stakes, however, remained high for Herndon and the eighteen other communists charged under the insurrection law. On December 16, the Supreme Court delayed oral argument from December to February, which gave his lawyers more time to work on his brief to the Court—and more time for Herndon to be a free man.

In the meantime, Herndon embarked on another nationwide speaking tour. In San Francisco, he again met with jailed labor leader Tom Mooney and with fellow communists imprisoned under a California criminal syndicalism law. Upon arriving home in Harlem at the end of December, Herndon found a letter with a Brooklyn postmark and a sticker on the back of a hooded Klansman on a horse holding a "fiery-cross." Inside the envelope, a small note in red and black ink warned him: "Communism must be destroyed."

At the end of the year, a few lawyers in Roosevelt's Justice Department quietly worked on the issue of judicial reform by drafting a bill to increase the number of Supreme Court justices. Attorney General Homer Cummings, Solicitor General Stanley Reed, and their aides drafted the bill in secret. Roosevelt's closest advisers knew nothing about it. They understood the frustration of the President, members of Congress, and the American people with the nine, unelected justices striking down New Deal programs and state minimum wage laws.

Unbeknownst to Roosevelt and his small team of Justice Department lawyers, change—thanks to Owen Roberts—was on its way. On December 16 and 17, the justices heard oral argument in a case challenging the constitutionality of a Washington State minimum wage law for women. Elsie Parrish, a chambermaid at the Cascadian Hotel in Wenatchee, sued for back pay under the state minimum wage law. The owner of the hotel asserted that the law was unconstitutional. At their private conference on December 19, Roberts and Hughes voted with Brandeis and Cardozo to uphold the law and to overrule the Court's 1923 decision in *Adkins v. Children's Hospital* holding that minimum wage laws violated freedom of contract. A decision in *West Coast Hotel v. Parrish*, however, was delayed by Stone's absence from the Court because of illness.

A few weeks later, on January 5, 1937, the Supreme Court gave Herndon's appeal a major boost by overturning the conviction of Communist Party member and longshoreman Dirk De Jonge. On July 27, 1934, De Jonge had spoken at a public meeting of about 150 to 300 people at the Unemployed Unity Center in Portland, Oregon, to protest the police shooting of four striking longshoremen and the raids of workers' homes and halls. At the end of the meeting, the police arrested De Jonge and a few other Party leaders. De Jonge was tried and convicted under an Oregon criminal syndicalism law for advocating "crime, physical violence, sabotage or any unlawful acts or methods as a means of accomplishing or effecting industrial or political change or revolution." Even though the Communist Party meeting was "public and orderly and was held for a lawful purpose," De Jonge was sentenced to seven years in prison. Like Herndon, he was free on bail raised by the ILD and ACLU.

In an 8–0 opinion by Chief Justice Hughes (Stone took no part in the case because of his illness), the Court reversed De Jonge's conviction and protected the right to protest in a peaceful way. "Freedom of speech and of the press are fundamental rights which are safeguarded by the due process clause of the Fourteenth Amendment of the Federal Constitution," Hughes wrote, adding that the "right of peaceable assembly" was "equally fundamental." In reversing De Jonge's conviction, Hughes distinguished between constitutionally protected peaceable assembly and unlawful incitement to violence: "peaceable assembly for lawful discussion cannot be made a crime. The holding of meetings for peaceable political action cannot be proscribed. Those who assist in the conduct of such meetings cannot be branded as criminals on that score."

On January 21, sixteen days after the *De Jonge* decision, Herndon's lawyers—Seymour, Sutherland, Wechsler, Gellhorn, and King—submitted their brief to the Supreme Court arguing that the Georgia insurrection law had violated his right to free speech and peaceable assembly. It was narrowly drafted to attract the votes of Roberts and Hughes. Building on the Court's decision in *De Jonge*, Herndon's lawyers argued that the state may not "penalize the advocacy of political, social or economic change to be achieved by lawful means or the organization of a group to further such advocacy." Nor may the state "make the act of conducting, attending or speaking at a peaceful meeting . . . a crime." The state of Georgia, Herndon's lawyers contended, had not produced any evidence that Herndon "had personally advocated forcible overthrow of the State Government or other acts of violence." All Herndon had done, his lawyers observed, was hold meetings for prospective communist members and successfully advocated for $6000 more in relief for unemployed workers.

Herndon could not be convicted, his lawyers contended, solely for possessing radical literature such as *The Communist Position on the Negro Question*. Herndon's conviction, his lawyers argued, "can no more be sustained because [he] had in his possession a book of this character, than if it were based upon his possession of a copy of the Encyclopedia Britannica, which contains many descriptions of revolution and economic and political doctrine. It is not to be inferred that men advocated violence because they read, or because their reading includes modern equivalents of the radicalism of Thomas Paine."

In their brief, Herndon's lawyers argued that the Georgia law, as construed by the state supreme court, violated their client's rights to free speech and peaceable assembly because the law did not require proof of an imminent threat of violence or a "clear and present danger." In acknowledging the rights of states to protect themselves from threats of violence, Herndon's lawyers quoted *De Jonge*: "The greater the importance of safeguarding the community from incitements to the overthrow of our institutions by force and violence, the more imperative is the need to preserve inviolate the constitutional rights of free speech, free press and free assembly in order to maintain the opportunity for free political discussion, to the end that government may be responsive to the will of the people and that changes, if desired, may be obtained by peaceful means." They also extensively quoted from Brandeis's concurrence in *Whitney v. California* about the importance of free speech in a democracy.

As a practical matter, Herndon's lawyers distinguished the New York and California syndicalism laws passed to stop radicals and anarchists from advocating violent political and economic change from the Georgia law based on an 1804 slave insurrection statute and revised in 1866 because of fears of Black violence during Reconstruction. The Communist Party, Herndon's lawyers argued, was not a threat to the state of Georgia—not with only five or six members in Atlanta, sixty-four Georgia votes for the Communist Party in the 1928 presidential election, and only twenty-three Georgia votes for the Communist Party in 1932. Finally, echoing Judge Dorsey's decision, Herndon's lawyers argued that the insurrection law's standard of guilt was "so vague and indefinite" as to violate Herndon's right to due process. Herndon's brief observed that the Georgia courts—referring to Judge Wyatt's jury instructions and the two Georgia Supreme Court decisions in Herndon's case—had interpreted the law in "three different and inconsistent ways." The Georgia insurrection law, Herndon's lawyers argued, was a trap for unpopular political speakers and violated First Amendment rights protected in *De Jonge*: "This Court has recently said that upon the preservation of the rights of free speech, free press and free assembly 'lies the security of the Republic, the very foundation of constitutional government.'" Aside from *De Jonge*'s protection of the right to speak at a public meeting and a few other First Amendment decisions, Herndon's lawyers knew that the Court's precedents largely cut against them. "I'm kind of struck with how little we had," Wechsler recalled. "But I do think that the De Jonge case just preceding us indicated that the wind was blowing a bit our way."

About two weeks later, the state of Georgia—in a brief signed by Attorney General M. J. Yeomans, Solicitor General Boykin, and Assistant Solicitor LeCraw—argued that the evidence supported Herndon's conviction for attempting to incite insurrection. Herndon was not convicted for a particular speech at a particular meeting. He was convicted, the state argued, because he admitted coming to Georgia as a paid organizer for the Communist Party and took orders from an international organization that sought to overthrow the government. He was arrested, the state observed, with radical literature including *The Communist Position on the Negro Question*, a pamphlet advocating self-determination in the Black Belt by confiscating white property for Black farmers and by seizing control of the government. Herndon also attempted to distribute copies of the *Daily Worker* and its call for equal rights and Black self-determination. Those objectives, the state contended, "could not be accomplished by peaceful means." The communist materials seized from Herndon, the state argued, "set forth an unquestioned plan of force and violence against the lawfully constituted government, and that Herndon therefore was an accomplice in this attempt to incite an insurrection."

The state distinguished the De Jonge case because Dirk De Jonge was not arrested for joining the Communist Party or for Party organizing but for speaking at a peaceful public meeting. In contrast to De Jonge, the state argued, Herndon was arrested for holding Communist Party meetings, soliciting members, and circulating radical literature. Herndon, the indictment alleged, was "part of a conspiracy to organize, establish and set up a group of persons for the purpose of overthrowing the lawful authority of the State by force and violence."

The Georgia law, the state insisted, did not violate Herndon's right to free speech or assembly. The state interpreted the Supreme Court's decisions as requiring proof of a "dangerous tendency."

A "clear and present danger of success," the state argued, was not required by the Court in upholding Charlotte Anita Whitney's conviction under the California criminal syndicalism law. Whitney was convicted, the state contended, for joining the Communist Labor Party, participating in its convention, and agreeing to the Party's platform of violent overthrow of the government. The origin of the Georgia insurrection law, according to the state, was irrelevant as to whether Herndon had been lawfully convicted. A "dangerous tendency," not a "clear and present danger," was the only thing that the state was required to prove. The Georgia law, moreover, was "sufficiently definite and certain" and no more vague than other state and federal criminal laws upheld by the Supreme Court. Georgia officials concluded by reminding the Court that state criminal laws are "presumed to be constitutional." Herndon, the state argued, had not "overcome this presumption of constitutionality." The state asked the justices to affirm the Georgia Supreme Court's decision.

Early on the morning of February 8, Angelo Herndon, his former trial counsel Ben Davis Jr., and several ILD officials left New York by train for Washington, D.C., to attend the Supreme Court oral argument that day in Herndon's case. Shortly before noon, Herndon arrived at the Court and sat in the center of the courtroom. He was joined by ILD officials Anna Damon, Sasha Small, Rose Baron, and Frank Griffin. Davis, a new staff writer for the *Daily Worker*, covered the argument for the newspaper. Herndon's counsel, Whitney North Seymour, William Sutherland, Herbert Wechsler, Walter Gellhorn, and Carol Weiss King, sat at counsel's table in the lawyer's section.

There was a tension and uneasiness in the crowded courtroom— with good reason. Three days earlier, President Roosevelt had shocked his closest advisers, members of Congress, and the nation by announcing what his select team of Justice Department lawyers had been working on for several months—the Judicial Procedures Reform Bill of 1937. Known as the "court-packing plan," the bill proposed to add a federal judge for every one older than seventy years, six months, who had chosen not to retire—including up to six new Supreme Court justices. In announcing the bill, the President claimed that older federal judges and justices had fallen behind on their work. In truth, Roosevelt and his allies in Congress wanted to change the composition of the Supreme Court and not have to worry whether nine, unelected justices would uphold his New Deal programs such as the National Labor Relations Act and Social Security Act.

The morning of February 5, when Roosevelt unveiled his court-packing plan, Seymour and his co-counsel had sat in the Supreme Court courtroom waiting to see if Herndon's case would be called. The justices had received a copy of Roosevelt's bill and were reading it while sitting on the bench. It was just as well that the preoccupied justices did not hear Herndon's case until the following Monday.

The day of the oral argument, the atmosphere was still tense as talk swirled in Congress and in the press about Roosevelt's attempt to add up to six new justices. Around noon, the people in the court-room rose as the court crier, Thomas E. Waggaman, announced: "The Chief Justice and the Associate Justices of the Supreme Court." Justice Brandeis, for some reason, entered prematurely through the red velvet curtains behind the bench. When he realized that he had jumped the gun, he turned around and waited for Chief Justice Hughes and his colleagues to join him. After the justices took their seats, the crier continued: "Oyez! Oyez! God save the United States and this honorable Court."

In the Court's first item of business, Chief Justice Hughes admitted Wechsler and several other new members to the Supreme Court bar. Legal observers packed the courtroom. They were expecting an announcement in the Washington State minimum wage case, *West Coast Hotel v. Parrish*, because Stone was back on the bench. None was forthcoming.

At 12:27 p.m., the chief justice called for the case of *Angelo Herndon v. Sheriff James I. Lowry*. Seymour stepped to the lectern located a few feet in front of the bench. A few months earlier, William Sutherland had requested that he and Seymour split the argument. As a former Brandeis clerk who had appealed to the southern sensibilities of the justices on the Georgia Supreme Court, Sutherland felt that he deserved half the oral argument. Seymour, however, had worked on Herndon's case as lead counsel for nearly two years without collecting a fee. He knew many of the justices personally. The day before the argument, he had visited with Brandeis and other "old friends" on the Court, presumably Stone and Cardozo. Seymour also could have visited with Roberts. In 1931, with Roberts new to Washington and Seymour serving as assistant solicitor general, they had lived in the same Georgetown neighborhood and had met while walking their dogs. "Our dogs," Seymour recalled, "used to be great friends. We saw a lot of him. Those really were our dearest friends and gave rise to the most treasured memories." Seymour did not need any inside information from the justices, nor would he have asked for any. This case was his to win or lose. He turned down Sutherland's request. An experienced advocate, Seymour identified Roberts and Hughes as the key votes he needed to win Herndon's appeal. Seymour believed that he could convince them that the Georgia insurrection law violated Herndon's rights to free speech and assembly—especially after the Court's decision in favor of Dirk De Jonge.

Seymour began by asserting that the state's evidence against Herndon did not support his conviction for attempting to incite insurrection. The testimony of law enforcement officials about Herndon's Communist Party organizing and the radical literature seized from him had not proven that he advocated the overthrow of the government or incited acts of violence. Herndon, Seymour argued, "was engaged in lawful political activity . . . there was no danger to the State in the activities of Herndon." The law, moreover, violated his rights to free speech and assembly because it did not require an imminent threat of violence to the state. Finally, he contended that the law was unconstitutionally vague, as Judge

Dorsey had found in granting Herndon habeas corpus, because there was no clear standard of guilt of what it meant to attempt to incite insurrection.

Assistant Solicitor LeCraw, appearing for the second time before the U.S. Supreme Court in this case, attempted to rebut Seymour's argument that the evidence did not support Herndon's conviction. Herndon, LeCraw argued, had been working in Georgia for several months organizing for the Communist Party. LeCraw spent nearly three-quarters of his argument discussing *The Communist Position on the Negro Question* and its calls for self-determination in the Black Belt. The pamphlet, LeCraw insisted, "advocated taking the land from the white folks and giving it to the Negroes."

Waving copies of the *Daily Worker*, LeCraw argued that Herndon's conviction was lawful because he was taking orders from the Communist Party in Russia to start a revolution in the American South. "Yessir, Herndon is working for this 'Communist International thing' with headquarters in Moscow. And he wants to take the land from the rich white landowners—think of it, the white landowners—and give it to Negroes."

Chief Justice Hughes asked whether the invalidity of the insurrection law was properly before the Court. LeCraw conceded that whether the law was "void" had been raised in the Georgia courts. Hughes replied that whether the law was "invalid" or "void" was the same thing. The audience laughed. Stone asked whether the radical literature LeCraw waved before the justices had been seized from Herndon. LeCraw said yes. McReynolds, Van Devanter, and Sutherland also asked questions. Roberts did not say a word.

In a brief rebuttal, Seymour concluded by quoting from the Court's *De Jonge* decision and arguing that it "required a reversal of the Georgia Supreme Court's decision." Seymour, Ben Davis Jr. wrote in the *Daily Worker*, spoke "with dignity and eloquence" and "answered every issue arising in the famous case."

People in attendance for Herndon's argument remarked how tense it was in the courtroom. It was the first Supreme Court session since the public announcement of the court-packing plan. And it was the same day that Senator Henry F. Ashurst of Arizona, the chair of the Senate Judiciary Committee, introduced the court reform bill after conferring with the President. Roosevelt faced fierce opposition to the bill from members of his own party. The court-packing plan was the talk of the town. The justices may have been stunned into silence.

The justices and the lawyers sitting in the courtroom also may have been anticipating the next case. After the Court's half-hour lunch recess, lawyers for the Virginia Railway Company challenged the constitutionality of the Railway Labor Act's requirement that railroad companies collectively bargain with unions. It was the first of five days of argument about similar provisions in the National Labor Relations Act. Everyone wanted to know whether the Court, faced with the possible increase in the number of justices, would strike down another signature piece of New Deal legislation and whether it would continue to favor big business over the rights of workers.

On Saturday, February 13, five days after they heard Herndon's case, the justices met in their private conference room to discuss and vote on the cases argued that week. As always, only the nine justices sat around the conference table. No law clerks or staff were permitted in the room. The conference discussions are secret. Pierce Butler's shorthand conference notes are the best surviving evidence of what happened that day.

Chief Justice Hughes obsessively prepared for the Court's Saturday conferences, extensively reviewing each case, and as a result excelled at framing the discussion and identifying the most important issues. By custom, the chief justice spoke first. Hughes talked at length about *Herndon v. Lowry*. He began by observing that Judge Wyatt had required the jury to find proof of an "immediate" threat of violence. The chief justice was troubled that there was "no evidence of any advocacy" of violence by Herndon. The only evidence, Hughes continued, was that Herndon had "circulated unemployment documents." Nor did the evidence show that he had advocated the "tenets" of the Communist Party. Hughes, according to Butler's notes, then "listed a lot" of Herndon's constitutional rights, presumably including free speech and peaceable assembly. Although the state did not have to wait for violence to occur before prosecuting someone and may criminalize the "advocacy of violence," Hughes differentiated between "party" doctrine and what "Herndon did." Hughes concluded that the Georgia insurrection law was "a dragnet" and was too "vague and indefinite." He voted to reverse Herndon's conviction.

The other justices, beginning with Willis Van Devanter, spoke in order of seniority. A stickler about procedure and a formidable voice at conference, Van Devanter disagreed with Hughes. Questions "of fact" in the indictment, Van Devanter argued, were not before the Court at this stage of the appeal. The facts, as in most appeals of a habeas corpus petition, had been decided at Herndon's trial. According to those "established facts," Herndon was a Party "member" who was soliciting new members and was sent to Atlanta "to get members." The evidence, Van Devanter argued, revealed the "principles" of the "Communist Party." Van Devanter, therefore, voted to affirm Herndon's conviction. McReynolds also voted to affirm. Brandeis voted with the chief justice to reverse. Sutherland and Butler voted to affirm. Stone, Roberts, and Cardozo voted to reverse. It is unclear what, if anything, Roberts said to his colleagues that day. As the chief justice in a 5–4 majority, Hughes retained the power to assign the opinion in Herndon's case. Hughes, who prided himself in taking great care in this "most delicate task," assigned *Herndon v. Lowry* to the other justice who had voted to dismiss Herndon's initial appeal—Owen Roberts.

In the meantime, people speculated about what the justices had decided. One of the observers at the oral argument, Joseph S. Gelders of the National Committee for the Defense of Political Prisoners, linked the Court's deliberations in Herndon's case with its anti–New Deal decisions. "In the Herndon case," Gelders wrote, "the United States Supreme Court is again on trial before the people of the United States, this time on a question involving the basic constitutional rights of freedom of speech, press, and assembly, rights cherished by all working people, and by political, national, racial, and religious minorities. Its recent decisions against progressive New Deal legislation have led many people to characterize the court as the defender of special privilege. . . . If, on the other hand, the court interprets the constitutional provisions guaranteeing personal rights so loosely as to uphold this ancient and notorious Georgia insurrection law, while interpreting the guarantees of property rights so strictly as to prevent the readjustments attempted by the New Deal we will then know that it is not conservative but reactionary."

A few weeks later in Washington, Herndon met the person who, as a result of the court-packing plan, wielded the most influence over the Court—President Roosevelt. As one of 4500 delegates to the American Youth Congress, Herndon marched down Pennsylvania Avenue to the White House on February 20 to urge the President to pass the American Youth Act to provide $500 million for jobs and education for unemployed young people between ages sixteen and twenty-five. At 4:30 p.m., Herndon was one of seven delegates, including future Roosevelt biographer Joseph P. Lash, who met for twenty-five minutes with the President. Roosevelt asked the group of young leaders their opinions on the court reform bill. "Well, Mr. President," Herndon replied, "that all depends on how the Supreme Court decides my case." Roosevelt looked surprised and inquired about the case. To which the young man replied: "I am Angelo Herndon." The exchange made the front page of the *New York Times*.

Herndon's star rose even higher on March 1, when Random House published his autobiography, *Let Me Live*. The social-realist cover by illustrator, muralist, and Communist Party member Hugo Gellert features a striking illustration of a shirtless Black man with his hands aloft in blue chains. An embellished account of Herndon's life, the book conveniently erases his identity as Eugene Braxton and how he grew up the son of sharecroppers in Bullock, County, Alabama. Instead, *Let Me Live* begins with his father's death in the coal mines near Cincinnati and vividly recounts his transformation from thirteen-year-old coal miner to Communist Party activist to nineteen-year-old political prisoner sentenced to the chain gang. The second half of the book chronicles his legal odyssey through his pending appeal to the Supreme Court.

Some reviewers refused to believe that someone who had left school after the sixth grade could have written *Let Me Live*. "Although it has come out as his autobiography," the New York *Herald Tribune* reviewer wrote, "it is clear that while the material is his, the writing was done by another hand." The writer Dorothy Parker disagreed. In her review in *The Atlantic Monthly*, Parker insisted that "no seasoned ghost came between the young man and his book," compared its style to that of a Horatio Alger novel, and declared that "the innocence of his hard-labored phrases, like a good boy writing home, attains a most competent result of tearing out the heart." The *New York Times* reviewer was also sympathetic: "He tells his story simply. And of course it is a one-sided story, full of bitterness and suffering; the story of an extremist and of how he became one. Much of it is dreadful. Much of it is heart-rending. But if it is simple and direct as one human being's life story, its tragic implications are complex. And no sentient and patriotic American can read it without a new emphasis of conviction, a hope burning anew, that the conditions which breed misery and desperation must be uprooted."

Let Me Live is a gripping story of a young Black man's life during the Great Depression, what it meant to be the "last hired, first fired," to receive less unemployment relief than whites did, to expect little help from Roosevelt's New Deal because it was not intended to help poor Black people in the South, and to look to the U.S. Supreme Court as the only place to achieve some measure of justice. Whether Herndon wrote *Let Me Live* is an open question. The Communist

Party USA in the mid-1930s contained a stable of talented writers, several of whom published accounts of Herndon's life. Herndon, however, insisted that he had written the book and compared himself with Frederick Douglass and other self-educated men who had penned autobiographical works. Herndon's extant papers contain a typewritten draft of 347 pages with handwritten corrections. His "tentative outline" and correspondence with Random House executives Donald S. Klopfer and Robert K. Haas indicate that he responded to their editorial changes and replied with some of his own. Herndon received a $1000 advance and viewed the book as the beginning of his career as a writer. He soon signed another contract with Random House for a book about sharecroppers.

With his case in legal limbo, Herndon sent signed copies of *Let Me Live* to his New York lawyers Whitney North Seymour, Herbert Wechsler, and Walter Gellhorn. They separately thanked him and praised the book. In his thank-you note, Seymour indicated he had already bought a copy and read it. "It is a fine and moving book," Seymour wrote Herndon on March 15. "I had rather hoped that the Court would decide your case by this time, but I do not think the delay need concern you. It has been a great pleasure to represent you in the case, and I hope the outcome is what we all hope it will be."

In the meantime, Roosevelt's court-packing plan continued to dominate the news. During debates in the Senate, the bill's opponents attacked the administration's disingenuous argument that older federal judges and Supreme Court justices had fallen behind on their work. On March 22, Senator Burton K. Wheeler of Montana began his testimony against the bill by introducing a letter signed by Chief Justice Hughes and Justices Brandeis and Van Devanter insisting that the Court was "fully abreast of its work" and arguing that additional justices would only create more inefficiency.

Five days later, the chief justice dealt another blow to the court bill. On March 27, Hughes announced the Court's 5–4 decision in *West Coast Hotel v. Parrish* upholding the constitutionality of

Washington State's minimum wage law for women, overruling the Court's 1923 decision in *Adkins v. Children's Hospital*, and rejecting the idea that the Fourteenth Amendment's Due Process Clause contained a "freedom of contract."

The decisive fifth vote in *West Coast Hotel v. Parrish* came from Owen Roberts. Once again, Roberts did not write an opinion explaining why he had voted to invalidate the New York law in June 1936 only to turn around and uphold the Washington State law in March 1937. Court observers assumed that Roberts had switched his vote in response to Roosevelt's court-packing plan. The press dubbed Roberts's vote the "switch in time that saved nine."

Legal cognoscenti and the press had no idea that Roberts had voted at the justices' private conference to uphold the Washington State law on December 19, 1936, nearly two months before Roosevelt announced the court bill. After he retired from the Court, Roberts claimed that he had switched his vote because the lawyers defending the New York law, unlike the lawyers defending the Washington State law, had not asked the Court to overrule *Adkins v. Children's Hospital*. At the time, however, Roberts's switch was deemed a purely political act of self-preservation.

The timing and reasoning behind Roberts's votes in the minimum wage cases do not explain why he also voted to uphold the National Labor Relations Act. On April 12, Hughes announced *NLRB v. Jones & Laughlin Steel*, a 5–4 decision upholding the law establishing the National Labor Relations Board and guaranteeing workers the right to unionize. Once again, Roberts simply joined Hughes's majority opinion and did not write a separate opinion explaining his vote.

The Court's two-week recess immediately after its decision in *NLRB v. Jones & Laughlin Steel* left Herndon's case in doubt and his supporters fearing the worst. Anna Damon, the ILD's acting national secretary, wondered why the Court had not handed down its decision in his case. She prepared his supporters for the possibility that Herndon would be forced to submit to a Georgia chain gang within ten days of the Court's decision. "In those ten days," Damon wrote, "nationwide support which has already registered its willingness to fight in his behalf must be mobilized. This means that everyone must stand ready, and we must not allow the stalling and delay of the United States Supreme Court to weaken the fight to free Herndon."

On the morning of Monday, April 26, the Supreme Court released fifteen opinions, led by its 5–4 decision overturning Angelo Herndon's conviction on free speech and assembly grounds. Writing for a five-justice majority, Owen Roberts methodically laid out the facts of Herndon's case, the materials seized during his arrest, the text of the insurrection law, and the state supreme court's interpretation of the law as not requiring an imminent threat of violence. In his opinion, Roberts observed that the state of Georgia "especially relies" on *The Communist Position on the Negro Question*'s advocating self-determination in the Black Belt. Yet he also observed that Herndon did not distribute any materials "advocating forcible subversion of governmental authority." Herndon's conviction, Roberts concluded, "must rest upon his procuring members for the Communist Party and his possession of that party's literature when he was arrested."

Before reviewing the Court's free speech decisions, Roberts put the states on notice about prosecuting unpopular political groups for a peaceful meeting or protest: "The power of a state to abridge freedom of speech and of assembly is the exception rather than the rule and the penalizing even of utterances of a defined character must find its justification in a reasonable apprehension of danger to organized government. The judgment of the legislature is not unfettered. The limitation upon individual liberty must have appropriate relation to the safety of the state. Legislation which goes beyond this need violates the principle of the Constitution. If, therefore, a state statute penalize[s] innocent participation in a meeting held with an innocent purpose merely because the meeting was held under the auspices of an organization membership in which, or the advocacy of whose principles, is also denounced as criminal, the law, so construed and applied, goes beyond the power to restrict abuses of freedom of speech and arbitrarily denies that freedom."

Herndon, Roberts wrote, "had a constitutional right to address meetings and organize parties" unless he violated a valid state law. Of Georgia's decision to charge Herndon with insurrection or attempting to incite insurrection, Roberts observed: "If the evidence fails to show that he did so incite, then, as applied to him, the statute unreasonably limits freedom of speech and freedom of assembly and violates the Fourteenth Amendment. We are of opinion that the requisite proof is lacking." The state of Georgia did not have a law on the books making it illegal to be a member of the Communist Party. The evidence, Roberts wrote, revealed that the only political objectives Herndon pursued were "unemployment and emergency relief which are void of criminality. His membership in the Communist Party and his solicitation of a few members wholly fails to establish an attempt to incite others to insurrection."

Roberts also agreed with Judge Dorsey that the insurrection law did "not furnish a sufficiently ascertainable standard of guilt." In his opinion, Roberts rejected the Georgia Supreme Court's conclusion that the law did not require proof of a clear and present danger of imminent violence and that it was sufficient that the advocacy of political change might produce "forcible resistance to the State" at any time "in the distant future."

Roberts dismissed the state supreme court's reliance on the "dangerous tendency" of the Communist Party's ideas potentially to lead to violence sometime in the future and concluded: "The statute, as construed and applied, amounts merely to a dragnet which may enmesh any one who agitates for a change of government if a jury can be persuaded that he ought to have foreseen his words would have some effect in the future conduct of others. No reasonably ascertainable standard of guilt is prescribed. So vague and indeterminate are the boundaries thus set to the freedom of speech and assembly that the law necessarily violates the guarantees of liberty embodied in the Fourteenth Amendment."

In a lengthy dissent joined by McReynolds, Sutherland, and Butler, Willis Van Devanter contended that the Georgia insurrection law provided "a reasonably definite and ascertainable standard by which to determine the guilt or innocence of the accused, and does not encroach on his right of freedom of speech or of assembly." Herndon, Van Devanter argued, was properly charged with "attempting to induce and incite others to join in combined *forcible* resistance to the lawful authority of the State." Van Devanter quoted several paragraphs from the Georgia Supreme Court's decisions and painstakingly reviewed the communist literature found in Herndon's possession. After his lengthy recitation of *The Communist Position on the Negro Question* and its call for self-determination in the Black Belt, Van Devanter noted: "It should not be overlooked that Herndon was a negro member and organizer in the Communist Party and was engaged actively in inducing others, chiefly southern negroes, to become members of the party and participate in effecting its purposes and program." It was the second time in the opinion that he had mentioned that Herndon was "a negro and a member of the Communist Party."

The opinion turned out to be one of Van Devanter's last. On March 13, Congress had passed a law restoring the justices' pensions to their full annual salaries after cutting their pensions in half in 1932 as a Depression-era measure. The seventy-eight-year-old Van Devanter had been hoping to retire to his 778-acre Maryland farm for the past two years but wanted to do so with a full pension. With his pension now secure, he announced on May 18 that he was retiring at the end of the term. Van Devanter's retirement provided Roosevelt with his first Supreme Court vacancy.

Yet before Van Devanter announced his retirement, the Court's decision on April 26 to free Angelo Herndon grabbed front-page headlines in the *New York Times*, New York *Herald Tribune*, *Washington Post*, and the Black press. It was the subject of numerous editorials and proved to be fodder for opinion columnists—especially in light of the constitutional showdown between Roosevelt and the Supreme Court, the congressional debates over the President's court-packing bill, and Roberts's "switch in time" on the constitutionality of minimum wage laws and vote to uphold the National Labor Relations Act.

"The man who set Angelo Herndon free was Franklin D. Roosevelt," the *New York Post* declared. "The Herndon decision yesterday was a clear reversal of the Supreme Court's past decisions on—and against—civil liberties. It represents as complete an about-face as the minimum-wage and Wagner [National Labor Relations] act rulings.

"Mr. Justice Roberts has again, by changing his mind, changed 'the Constitution' as interpreted and applied in the past by the Supreme Court," the *Post's* editorial concluded. "We congratulate Justice Roberts and his four concurring colleagues on this fine liberal decision BUT—We'd feel more comfortable if Congress, by enlarging and liberalizing the Court, will make it unnecessary to depend on whether the changeable Mr. Justice Roberts again changes his mind."

For Carol Weiss King, the ILD's strategist who had constructed the legal team of Gellhorn, Wechsler, and Seymour and who had worked with the NAACP's Charles Hamilton Houston, Roberts's opinion was a mixed bag. On the one hand, it required states to prove a clear and present danger of imminent violence in order to abridge freedom of speech and assembly. It saved Herndon from the chain gang and eventually ended the prosecution of eighteen other suspected communists charged under the Georgia insurrection law. On the other hand, it was unclear whether it invalidated the Georgia law or ruled only that the state had failed to produce enough evidence to convict Herndon. In an article in the *Labor Defender*, she described Roberts's opinion as "confused and difficult to understand" and "full of contradictions." She also pilloried Van Devanter's dissent for insisting that "Herndon should by all means be tortured on the Georgia chain-gang for the greater glory of the Constitution," for the four dissenters' willingness to invoke the Constitution to strike down Roosevelt's New Deal programs but not to recognize Herndon's rights to free speech and assembly, and for twice mentioning that Herndon was "a Negro and an organizer for the Communist Party."

Ultimately, King believed that they won Herndon's case because of Roosevelt's court-packing bill: "The close division of the court, the lines of reasoning on which the judges split, and the obvious relation between the social and economic views of some of the justices and the sides on which they voted, serve as another indication of how little importance legalistic authorities have as compared with living factors and prejudices. One of the factors in the Herndon case was the President's proposal for reform of the court, announced to the world three days before the argument in the case, helping to bludgeon it into a more decent point of view at the time of the decision."

Other Supreme Court insiders agreed with King's analysis. Felix Frankfurter told one of his protégés, Charles E. Wyzanski Jr., a young Justice Department lawyer who had defended the Social Security Act during oral argument on April 8 and 9 in *Stewart Machine Company v. Davis*: "I do not want to minimize the incentive for your zealous work on the Davis case, but I should like to bet you 10 to 1 that for the rest of the term the Court will sustain everything that should be sustained and invalidate, as in the Herndon case, everything that will vindicate the Court as the unflagging guardian of our liberties!!!" Likewise, Justice Stone confided to his former law clerk Herbert Wechsler that the court-packing bill "may have done your client a lot more good than anything you filed, Wechsler."

These contemporaneous comments about the court-packing bill are telling. They reflect anger with Hughes and Roberts for joining Van Devanter, McReynolds, Sutherland, and Butler to strike down Roosevelt's New Deal programs in 1935 and 1936. They ignore

Roberts's vote to uphold the Washington State minimum wage law six weeks before Roosevelt announced the court-packing bill. They also fail to differentiate between Roberts's votes on cases involving economic regulation and the First Amendment. In 1931, Roberts had joined Hughes's 5–4 decisions in two key First Amendment cases, Yetta Stromberg's right to fly a red flag and Jay Near and *The Saturday Press*'s right to accuse public officials of corruption. The Court's 8–0 decision in January 1937 in favor of Dirk De Jonge's right to speak at a Communist Party meeting also increased Herndon's chances of winning. *Herndon v. Lowry*, as indicated by the four dissenters, was more contentious than De Jonge's case but no less important. Herndon's victory revealed that the New Deal constitutional crisis was not only about the constitutionality of federal and state economic regulation but also about the importance of protecting civil rights and civil liberties during the rise of fascism. Raymond Clapper, one of the nation's most astute syndicated columnists, praised the five justices in the *Herndon* majority for "rebuilding the prestige of the court after its recent nose dive. They have come forward to vindicate the underlying principles on which this democracy was founded. They have in effect said that the United States is not Germany, Italy or Russia."

Owen Roberts—the justice most famous for his "switch in time"—deserves credit for his majority opinion defending Angelo Herndon's rights to free speech and peaceable assembly and establishing the right to protest as an essential component of American democracy.

CHAPTER NINE

THE HARLEM LITERARY HERO

Let Me Live by Angelo Herndon

ANGELO HERNDON WAS A FREE MAN. THE DAY THE Supreme Court announced its decision in his case, he impressed reporters at an informal press conference at the Young Communist League's offices. "I was prepared for the worst, but hoped for the best," he said, admitting that it "felt funny" to be truly free for the first time since his arrest on July 11, 1932. He described the Court's decision as a "decisive victory for progressive forces in this country" which dealt "another blow at the Jim Crow oppression of the Negro people." Asked why these things happened in the South, Herndon replied: "It is done to keep Negroes in the peon class. They are barred from voting and other constitutional rights; they are oppressed in every possible way so that they can be exploited more thoroughly. Racial discrimination is due to the economic situation." He hailed the ILD-led united front of left-wing organizations that helped set him free. Yet he understood that the decision in his favor was only 5–4 and believed that the best way "to preserve democracy and basic constitutional rights is through the President's Supreme Court reorganization proposal." He aspired to return to the South to fight for the rights of sharecroppers and believed that the Court's decision in his case "gives southern labor the right to participate more freely in necessary struggles. And it thus ensures more concessions to the workers and sharecroppers from landowners, textile manufacturers, etc."

A *New York Times* reporter was struck by the "marked transformation" in "his appearance and bearing" from five years earlier. Herndon was no longer the scared eighteen-year-old charged with attempting to incite insurrection. He was a confident twenty-three-year-old Young Communist League official completely at ease discussing his case as well as American politics.

A dynamic young Communist Party leader, a published author admired by other aspiring Black writers, and a rising force on the American political scene, Herndon was Harlem's hero. "Harlem is happy again," the *Daily Worker* declared. "Have you heard?" people asked on the streets. "Herndon's free." Black Americans, whether Communist or not, celebrated his freedom. "Herndon's victory," Harlem civil rights leader Adam Clayton Powell Jr. declared in his New York *Amsterdam News* column, "is a victory of the masses by the masses."

"I am free and I am happy," Herndon told a cheering crowd of about 20,000 people at Madison Square Garden on May 3 at the eighth Young Communist League convention. The national chairman of the convention, Herndon presided over the meeting's opening session. At a subsequent session on "Negro work," he proposed a national celebration of the emancipation from slavery as a way of drawing attention to the economic plight of Black people. Though his idea did not gain traction, the Young Communist League elected Herndon its vice president.

During the late spring and summer of 1937, Herndon emerged as a national spokesman for the rights of Black people. Before an interracial gathering of Washington's leading citizens at an American Civil Liberties Union dinner on May 20 at the National Press Club, Herndon encouraged the Senate to pass a federal antilynching law. "Of course it will not do the entire job," he told the audience, "but it will at least show that there is sufficient Federal recognition of the problem to start a concerted campaign against mob rule." He also sought federal aid for sharecroppers in light of the dispossession of 40,000 families the previous year.

A month later, Herndon returned to Washington, D.C., and spoke at the ILD's three-day national conference at the Hotel Washington along with his former trial counsel Ben Davis Jr.; Ada Wright, mother of two of the Scottsboro defendants, Roy and Andy Wright; and John P. Davis of the National Negro Congress. The Scottsboro case topped the ILD's agenda. On June 14, the Alabama Supreme Court affirmed defendant Haywood Patterson's fourth conviction and seventy-five-year-sentence. Several of Patterson's codefendants faced new trials after the U.S. Supreme Court had reversed their convictions in 1935 in *Norris v. Alabama* and *Patterson v. Alabama* because Blacks had been systematically excluded from their juries. The ILD vowed to appeal Patterson's case to the U.S. Supreme Court and to fight the cases "to the end."

In the *Daily Worker*, Herndon found his voice on another important issue and one with a personal connection—the Spanish Civil War. Members of the Communist Party USA and "fellow travelers" were volunteering for military service to fight Spain's fascist insurgents led by General Francisco Franco and aided by Hitler and Mussolini. In June 1937, Herndon's older brother Milton joined the Abraham Lincoln Brigade, a left-leaning group of American volunteers fighting on the side of Spain's Republican government. It was the culmination of several years of Milton's Communist Party activism. During Angelo's imprisonment, Milton had moved to Harlem and had been arrested during a protest at a white-owned lunch counter on Lenox Avenue. In Spain, he joined an interracial coalition of American volunteers to fight for democracy. Angelo published one of his brother's letters in the *Daily Worker* describing "thousands of heroic defenders of Spanish democracy . . . driven from their homes" and the fight against fascist forces as "not a national fight, but a fight of the people the world over to defend democracy and defeat fascism." Milton had not yet seen action on the front lines, but he was headed there soon.

At home in Harlem, Herndon championed the cause of Spain's Republican government in the *Daily Worker* and at public events. Two days before the one-year anniversary of the fascist insurrection in Spain, he wrote a *Daily Worker* article on behalf of the Young Communist League calling on people to picket and protest at the German and Italian consulates. On the night of the one-year anniversary, he spoke at a rally of about 20,000 people at Madison Square Garden along with other prominent left-wing leaders and helped raise $8500 for medical aid. A month later, he wrote a series of articles for the *Daily Worker* about the International Youth Commission for Aid to Republican Spain, organized in Paris.

Herndon's political activism and literary success inspired a new staff writer in the *Daily Worker*'s Harlem bureau, Richard Wright. The twenty-eight-year-old Wright's life story was eerily similar to Herndon's. Born on a plantation in rural Mississippi, Wright was the son of sharecroppers. He grew up in grinding poverty. His father left the family when Wright was six, and his mother fell ill. For the next few years, Wright and his brother lived with relatives in different southern cities. He graduated valedictorian of his junior high school class in Jackson, Mississippi, but never finished high school before he moved to Memphis and eventually settled in Chicago. During the Great Depression, Wright lost his job as a postal clerk, joined the leftist John Reed Club, and tried to make a living as a freelance poet and writer. He needed a new start in a new city.

New York City offered Wright more literary opportunities than Chicago, a paying gig with the *Daily Worker*, and a benevolent boss in Ben Davis Jr.

In early 1937, Herndon befriended the short, heavyset Wright and gave him a copy of *Let Me Live*. Wright devoured the book. *Let Me Live* predated Wright's own autobiographical sketch published in August 1937 in a Federal Writers' Project anthology and eventually inspired Wright's classic autobiographical work, *Black Boy*. Herndon was not the writer Wright was, yet *Let Me Live* explored themes that dominated Wright's thoughts. "Wright," the scholar Frederick T. Griffiths observed, "had to write his way out of Herndon's shadow."

In January 1937, Wright submitted an article to *New Masses*, "The Way of Herndon" arguing that Black writers should be more like the activists in the Herndon and Scottsboro campaigns, but the editor rejected it and encouraged him to submit a poem about Herndon. "So far as we are aware," Loren Miller, a Black editor and lawyer, wrote Wright, "Herndon has not called forth the poetic treatment to which his case is entitled."

Instead, Wright wrote admiringly about Herndon in a *Daily Worker* article featuring Hattie Holmes, a Black woman living on West 153rd Street, who persuaded her twenty-year-old daughter Artie May, on a holiday break from a Florida convent, to join the Communist Party.

DAUGHTER: Mother, who's [sic] picture is that you've hung on your wall since I've been away to school?
MOTHER: That's Angelo Herndon, darling.
DAUGHTER: Who's he?
MOTHER: A Communist.
DAUGHTER : Oh, he's what the Sisters at the Convent called hell-raisers.
MOTHER: He's a Communist hero, darling.
DAUGHTER: What did he do?
MOTHER: Well, that's a long story.

DAUGHTER: Well, tell me about it, Mother!

MOTHER: Angelo Herndon went to jail in Georgia because he led a demonstration of Negro and white to demand bread to eat. He stood up in a Southern court room and told the landlords of the South that they could not kill the working class.

Wright's article explained how the unemployed Hattie had met a member of the Communist Party who provided her with food, medical care, and a sense of self-worth. Hattie succeeded in persuading her daughter to join the Party. Artie May, Wright explained, "read Angelo Herndon's 'Let Me Live' and she wept over it."

By the end of 1937, Wright quit the *Daily Worker* and began to devote himself full-time to writing fiction. He had been disenchanted with the Communist Party since his days in Chicago because of the Party's distrust of Black intellectuals for promoting a bourgeois Black nationalism at odds with class-based orthodoxy. He and Herndon remained friends. Herndon's ties to the Party, however, were stronger than Wright's—so Herndon promoted Black political and economic equality as part of the larger communist cause.

Since his early days in the Party, Herndon had been advocating for the freedom of the Scottsboro defendants. On July 24, 1937, Alabama authorities dropped rape charges against four defendants—Olen Montgomery, Willie Roberson, Eugene Williams, and Roy Wright. Five days after their release, Herndon greeted them on the stage of New York's Hippodrome Theatre and told the press: "Let this victory and great cause for jubilation hasten on the struggle for the freedom of the other five boys." In "The Shame of America," in the October issue of the *Labor Defender*, Herndon wrote that "the whole world knows that the Scottsboro boys are not guilty. Nobody will be fooled by the insidious move of releasing four in order to murder the other five." Herndon called on people to raise money for the Scottsboro Defense Committee by referring to his own case: "It can be done. My freedom is proof of it, the freedom of four of the Scottsboro Boys is further proof."

Herndon returned to the public eye because of a family tragedy—friends of the Abraham Lincoln Brigade received a wire that his brother Milton was dead. The leader of a machine gun brigade that he named after Frederick Douglass, Milton was ordered to move a machine gun to support the advance of his battalion in a battle in Zaragoza, Spain. Based on an early account, he was positioning the machine gun on a hill on October 13 and died instantly from a bullet in the heart. According to another report six weeks later, he died trying to rescue a wounded man and was shot in the head and mouth. Either way, he died a hero and was buried near the battlefield in Fuentes. The same day the news broke about Milton's death, the ILD's Anna Damon received a letter from him about how American troops had informed their Spanish counterparts about the need to free the five imprisoned Scottsboro defendants. "Any victory that can be won from the reactionary fascist forces, whether in Spain or America," Milton wrote, "can only be realized by the organized determination of the liberty-loving masses."

Herndon's mother, Hattie, was living in Detroit and unaware that one of her sons had been fighting in Spain. The task of informing her of twenty-nine-year-old Milton's death fell to Angelo. He also wrote and spoke publicly about Milton's sacrifice and activism. "My brother's death is significant," he told the *Daily Worker*, "because it shows that the Negro people are realizing more and more that only through uniting with the whole of the progressive people can they win their own freedom against Jim Crowism and lynch terror."

Milton's death resonated with several of Harlem's promising young Black writers who traveled in communist circles. Richard Wright wrote several *Daily Worker* articles about Milton's memorial service at Harlem's St. James Presbyterian Church. Langston Hughes covered the Spanish Civil War for the *Baltimore Afro-*

American and interviewed members of Milton's company about how he had died saving a wounded member of his brigade.

In the *Sunday Worker*, Angelo eulogized his brother. He explained how Milton had been a steelworker in Detroit and Chicago, had been laid off in Chicago during the Depression, and had joined the Young Communist League in Harlem. Milton had dedicated himself to the Black freedom struggle and had volunteered in Spain because a victory over fascism would "be a decisive victory for the Negro people in their fight against fascist lynch terror in the United States." Milton, Angelo explained, "always wanted to be in the thick of the fight for Negro rights." Angelo revealed the shock and sadness he felt when he heard the news about his brother. Rather than yield to despair, he was inspired by his brother's sacrifice: "His death will forever remain a guide for me in the struggle about lynch terror, jim-crowism and persecution of the Negro people by the reactionary Bourbons of the South. . . . Milton's unselfish example will stand out in history as a beacon light . . . and a call to action."

After Milton's death, Angelo made more calls for a united front to help Black people rather than to pursue the Communist Party's political agenda. The Party wanted to free Herndon and to challenge the capitalist system. Herndon for a while wanted to challenge the capitalist system but he also wanted to advance the struggle for racial equality—whether it was antilynching legislation, aid for sharecroppers, or freeing the last five Scottsboro defendants.

An incident at the William Penn Hotel in Pittsburgh revealed the fissures between Herndon's interest in Black empowerment and Party politics. He agreed to serve as a delegate at a communist conference, the People's Congress for Democracy and Peace. Upon his arrival on November 24, however, he and other Black delegates were denied rooms both at the William Penn and another hotel in violation of Pennsylvania's equal rights law. Speaking at his brother's memorial service a few days later, Herndon recounted the incident and criticized several white colleagues who had begun picketing and confronting hotel management on their own rather than agreeing to a unified plan of action. His comments ignited so much controversy that he clarified them in the *Daily Worker*. "What I actually said was that the more group action among Negroes themselves as a component part of the growing People's Front," he wrote, "the more justice, respect and human recognition could they command from their oppressors."

Enjoying his new life in Harlem, Herndon made front-page news in the Black press in early March 1938 for a happy occasion—he had married twenty-three-year-old Joyce M. Chellis. Angelo and Joyce both came from big families with Alabama roots and fathers who died when their children were young. The youngest of six children, Joyce was born in Gadsden, Alabama, to a butcher and a maternity nurse. Her father died when she was nine. Her mother moved the family to Youngstown, Ohio. In the mid-1920s, Joyce left to live in Yonkers, New York, with an older brother and his wife. A popular fixture in the local Black society pages, she was voted "most attractive" by her peers. By 1938, she was living about ten blocks away from Angelo in Harlem and working as a stenographer. On February 18, they were married at the city clerk's office with Henry Winston, the national administrative secretary of the Young Communist League, serving as one of the witnesses. They moved into Angelo's small apartment at 42 West 120th Street.

After getting married, Herndon continued to work for the Communist Party and championed Black political and social causes. In April, he spoke at a Union Square rally of 8000 people urging Congress to pass antilynching legislation. A month later, he and other members of the Young Communist League joined the NAACP and other organizations in protesting the opening of Oscar Micheaux's film *God's Step Children* at the RKO Theatre in New York City because of the film's negative portrayal of Black people; the film closed after two days. He wrote about the Alabama Supreme Court's latest decision affirming the third rape conviction of Clarence Norris, one of the five still-imprisoned Scottsboro defendants, arguing that "the voice of every progressive American who believes in our ideal of democracy and justice for all, must now rally to the defense of the Scottsboro boys" just as they did in his case.

As an active Communist Party member and Black activist, Herndon earned the scrutiny and surveillance of law enforcement. The Federal Bureau of Investigation (FBI) kept tabs on him and his party activities. According to one of the Bureau's reports, Herndon was elected a member of the National Committee at the Communist Party USA's Tenth National Convention in May 1938 and that same year attended a communist school in Beacon, New York. The public also identified him as a communist. In August, when John P. Frey, the president of the Metal Trades Department of the American Federation of Labor, testified before the House Un-American Activities Committee, he named Herndon as a communist delegate to the convention of the Workers Alliance of America. Of Herndon, Frey remarked: "There is no doubt about that, is there?"

During the early part of 1939, Herndon visited southern cities to research the book he was writing about sharecroppers. He shared an outline of the book with Langston Hughes and asked to use Hughes's name as a reference to apply for a grant from the Rosenwald Fund. In late April, Herndon attended the All-Southern Negro Youth Conference in Birmingham—where he had discovered the Communist Party while working in TCI's coal mines and had been beaten and wrongly accused of rape and murder by the local police. He was no longer an obscure communist known as Eugene Braxton. He returned to Birmingham eight years later known by one and all as Angelo Herndon. The *Daily Worker* identified him as one of many "nationally known figures" at the conference and as a "young Communist leader." In June, he was named vice president of the Young Communist League.

What he needed from the Party was a paying, full-time job, and he found one a month later on the staff of the *Daily Worker*. Despite his sixth-grade education, he had proven himself as a writer. He collected an annual salary of $1200 from the *Daily Worker*, where his friend and former trial counsel Ben Davis Jr. was his boss. Herndon and Davis were the only two Black staff writers on any of the New York City daily newspapers. The only other bylined Black reporter, Ted Poston, was a contributor but not a staff writer for the *New York Post*.

Herndon took over his friend Richard Wright's role as the voice of Harlem's Black masses. He wrote about how Harlem came to a standstill, then erupted after heavyweight champion Joe Louis knocked out Tony Galento at Yankee Stadium; a job campaign in the New York area against racial bias and discrimination; the housing and employment problems facing Harlem's Black residents; the lives of four Scottsboro defendants after their release from prison; suicides among Harlem's Works Progress Administration workers; NAACP executive secretary Walter White's speech assailing southern members of Congress for neglecting the plight of Black farmers; and the Negro Actors Guild.

Herndon's emphasis on the Black freedom struggle made his employment more precarious. The Communist Party USA discouraged its Black members from engaging in Black nationalism and from pursuing race-based policies and goals at cross-purposes with the Party's class-driven political orthodoxy. Ex-Communist leader turned informant George Hewitt (aka Timothy Holmes) testified that Party officials instructed Ben Davis Jr. to "do everything in his power to break Angelo." Davis and other Party leaders, Hewitt alleged, tried to freeze Herndon out of the Young Communist League. Herndon regularly visited Hewitt's office and told him about receiving "the silent treatment." Hewitt, however, was charged with but not convicted of perjury for accusing University of Washington professor Melvin Rader of being a communist.

Regardless of the veracity of Hewitt's testimony, Herndon's relationship with the Communist Party must have been tested by the Nazi-Soviet Pact. On August 23, 1939, the Soviet Union entered into an alliance with Nazi Germany—undermining the Communist Party's fight against fascism in Italy, Germany, Spain, and

Italian-occupied Ethiopia. Three days later, Herndon wrote about the response of members of the Party's Bronx chapter to the Nazi-Soviet alliance but kept his personal views out of the article. Less than two years removed from Milton's death fighting fascists in Spain, the turn of events must have been painful.

To make matters worse, the Communist Party USA and its prominent Black members had supported the Soviet Union's show trials and executions from 1936 to 1938 of Trotskyite opponents of Soviet leader Joseph Stalin. The trials constituted a small part of Stalin's massive purge of his political enemies. In 1938 and 1939, Langston Hughes and other leading American writers and intellectuals endorsed the show trials after opposing the one that Herndon had endured six years earlier before an all-white Fulton County jury.

Though the show trials and the Nazi-Soviet Pact had undermined the Communist Party's credible commitment to opposing fascism, Herndon kept writing for the *Daily Worker* in 1939 and early 1940. He skewered Pierce Butler upon the justice's death in November 1939 as "a valiant fighter, who twisted the Constitution in so many ways to protect the rights of Big Business. This he did up to the very time of his death." A month later, he objected to the movie *Gone with the Wind* because of its denial of the "great sacrifice, courage and heroism" of Union soldiers and its stereotypical portrayal of Black people as lazy. He exposed its "true intent and purpose" to disrupt "the growing unity of Negro and white labor in the South which is challenging the feudalistic manors of the Southern slave lords." Herndon concluded: "The American people will not permit the noble deeds of Lincoln, Frederick Douglass, Wendell Phillips, William Lloyd Garrison, John Brown and other real Americans who gave their lives in the fight for the destruction of slavery to be cast down into oblivion by the new traitors and secessionists of our times." A *Washington Post* editorial mocked Herndon's *Daily Worker* article for "opening our eyes" about the movie's purpose and accused "Communist critics" of "substituting Hollywood for Russian gold."

Since the publication of *Let Me Live*, Herndon had transformed himself from a Communist Party symbol of oppression into one of Harlem's emerging literary figures. He had attended the June 1939 American Writers' Congress, a Communist-backed annual gathering of prominent left-wing writers; had befriended Langston Hughes, Richard Wright, and other aspiring Black authors; and had regularly published articles in the *Daily Worker* and Black newspapers. As a staff writer at the *Worker*, he had chronicled Black life and culture and joined a burgeoning Black literary scene.

Thanks to the publication of Richard Wright's novel *Native Son*, 1940 was a watershed year for Black literature. Two years earlier, Wright had published a collection of stories, *Uncle Tom's Children*, where he had improved upon anecdotes from Herndon's *Let Me Live*—including the beating of a Black criminal suspect chained to a tree, a Black reverend informing on a Black labor organizer to white authorities, and an interracial demonstration of Black and white workers for unemployment relief. In a June 1938 review in the *Young Communist Review*, Herndon praised *Uncle Tom's Children* as an "exposé of what it means to be a Negro" and "a challenge to the southern system of feudalism." *Native Son* shocked the American public. The first novel by a Black writer to be a Book-of-the-Month Club selection, *Native Son* features one of the most polarizing characters in American literature—Bigger Thomas. Bigger migrates from the Black Belt South to urban life on the South Side of Chicago, accidentally suffocates to death a well-to-do white woman, Mary Dalton, and is sentenced to death for her rape and murder. Bigger tries to pin Dalton's murder on Communist Party members by planting in his own bedroom the same radical literature found on Herndon at the time of his Atlanta arrest. Bigger's defense lawyer's closing argument echoes Ben Davis Jr.'s argument to Herndon's Fulton County jury. The novel outraged whites, middle-class Blacks, and the Harlem branch of the Communist Party. Ben Davis Jr. criticized *Native Son* because Bigger was an exaggerated "symbol of the whole Negro people" and objected that the ILD defense attorney instructs Bigger to plead guilty rather than try to acquit him of accidental murder. Wright learned from a mutual friend that Herndon was "horrified by the murder of Mary!"

With Wright on top of Harlem's literary world, Herndon reinvented himself as a publisher. In February 1940, he cofounded a Communist-backed outlet for Black history, Pathway Press. His partner, longtime Party member Richard Moore, had traveled the country with Herndon in 1934 publicizing the Scottsboro defendants' wrongful convictions. Born in Barbados in 1893, Moore had moved to the United States when he was sixteen and had distinguished himself in Harlem as a self-educated Black intellectual and as an orator. He and Herndon shared a mutual interest in African American history and in publishing Black authors. Moore was the president of Pathway Press. Herndon was the treasurer.

Their initial major offering was the reissue of one of Frederick Douglass's autobiographies, *Life and Times of Frederick Douglass*. It was the first time in nearly fifty years anyone had published a new edition. Herndon and Moore clashed from the outset. Moore, who was also the executive director of the Frederick Douglass Historical and Cultural League, charged that Herndon had misused the press's meager funds, had mangled the editor's note and removed Moore's name as the sole editor, and had pushed Moore aside and stolen all the credit for the book. Indeed, the acknowledgments assert that Herndon, "more than any other single individual, gave of his all, to insure the publication." At a public event on March 10, Herndon presented the first copy of the book to Lawrence D. Reddick, the head of the Schomburg Collection of Negro Literature; Moore was one of several speakers. In his review of the book in *New Masses*, Marxist historian Herbert Aptheker concluded: "All who yearn for a decent, creative life are heavily in debt to the worthy successors of Frederick Douglass—Angelo Herndon, Richard B. Moore, Paul Robeson, and Dr. Lawrence D. Reddick, whose vision and perseverance made possible the publication of this book."

Unlike Moore, who was drummed out of the Party for his Black nationalism, Herndon managed to stay in the Communist Party's good graces. In November 1941, Herndon chaired the committee to free Party general secretary Earl Browder, who had been convicted and sentenced to four years in prison for traveling abroad under false passports. The Browder-led Communist Party had worked hard to free Herndon and the Scottsboro defendants. As a result, Herndon and other Black leaders lobbied for Browder's release. "He is the most outstanding white American," Herndon said at a meeting of seventy-five Black leaders at Harlem's Hotel Theresa. "He is the one who has fought hardest not only in the interest of Negro people, but in behalf of the broader interests of the entire American people." The lobbying efforts and the U.S.-Soviet alliance following Germany's invasion of the Soviet Union led to Browder's release in May 1942, after fourteen months in federal prison.

After their disagreements over the publication of *Life and Times of Frederick Douglass*, Herndon split with Moore and Pathway Press and cofounded a new publishing company—the Negro Publication Society of America. Moore protested to Party officials that Herndon had misappropriated funds and produced records to support his claims. Herndon, however, managed to avoid Party discipline and forged ahead with his new publishing venture. Herndon was listed as the secretary of the nonprofit literary society with a board of directors including white and Black writers Alain Locke, Theodore Dreiser, Dashiell Hammett, and Henrietta Buckmaster. The society initially reissued an 1856 book, *The Kidnapped and the Ransomed* by Kate E. R. Pickard, a nonfiction account of enslaved person Peter Still and how he purchased his freedom and the freedom of his wife and children. "Now is the time for us to have books like this book of the real, strong, courageous Negro," Herndon told the Black press. " 'Old Black Joe' and 'Uncle Tom' have had their day." The society also distributed *The Negro Caravan*, an anthology of African American literature from poet Phillis Wheatley to Richard Wright, edited by Black scholars Sterling Brown, Arthur P. Davis, and Ulysses Lee.

The Negro Publication Society's most ambitious project was a new, Herndon-edited journal, the *Negro Quarterly: A Review of Negro Life and Culture*. On February 17, 1942, he published the first issue of "a review of Negro thought and opinion" and pledged to "strive to reflect the true aspirations of the Negro people and their traditions of struggle for freedom." In introducing the magazine, Herndon acknowledged how the U.S. entry into World War II had changed the contours of the Black freedom struggle and highlighted "the need of reflecting upon the genuine attitudes, thoughts and opinions of Negroes." He vowed to "devote space and time to research into the history of the Negro people" and recognized that "[t]he literary and artistic talents of Negro writers have for too long a time lain dormant."

The *Negro Quarterly*'s first issue featured a who's who of Black and white literary and political thinkers. Black poet Sterling Brown wrote about "The Negro Author and His Publisher"; Langston Hughes contributed two poems; Herbert Aptheker explored "Slavocracy's System of Control." The issue also included reviews of Black literature by Aptheker, Lawrence Reddick, and Herndon. In his review of Richard Wright's nonfiction book *12 Million Black Voices*, Herndon highlighted how Wright "disposes of the idyllic and romantic South of Margaret Mitchell, Thomas Dixon, and others, as an historic fraud fashioned into a legend by the representatives of plantation owners and whip-wielders and perpetuated by our 'historians.'" He praised Wright for not giving in to despair about the insoluble problem of American race relations and highlighted how "Wright replies in the voice of twelve million black Americans, who despite the thorny path they have had to tread, and the obstacles still to be removed, are rapidly coming into their own."

In editing the first issue, Herndon impressed a promising young Black literary critic—Ralph Ellison. On November 25, 1941, Herndon had written "Mr. Ralph Ellerson" to solicit an article for the *Quarterly*'s first issue on "the Negro in the war." Instead, Ellison published a lengthy review of William Attaway's novel *Blood on the Forge*. Herndon invited Ellison to the *Quarterly*'s launch party on March 8, 1942, at the Gramercy Park home of Harry Levine, one of the journal's financial backers. Herndon spoke at the event along with several others and listed Ellison as one of the event's sponsors. Ellison liked the first issue so much that he quit his job with the Federal Writers' Project to accept Herndon's offer to be the *Quarterly*'s managing editor.

With a name like Ralph Waldo Ellison, he was destined to be a writer. Born in Oklahoma City on March 1, 1913, Ellison lost his father at age three, developed a passion for jazz and classical music, and played the trumpet. Desperate to escape Oklahoma City, the twenty-year-old Ellison rode the rails to Alabama to attend Tuskegee Institute's music school on a scholarship. His interests at Tuskegee expanded to literature after he read T. S. Eliot's *The Waste Land*. The summer after his junior year, Ellison lived at the Harlem YMCA, befriended Black writers Alain Locke and Langston Hughes, and decided not to return to Tuskegee for his senior year. In 1937, the dapper, slender Ellison met Richard Wright through Hughes and published a book review in Wright's short-lived journal, *New Challenge*. Wright encouraged Ellison to write fiction, praised Ellison's first short story, yet criticized the second one for imitating Wright's own style. Ellison, who moved to Dayton, Ohio, to be with his ill mother before she died, ended up staying for seven months and returned to Harlem with several short stories. By 1938, he frequently contributed book reviews and fiction to *New Masses* and other publications, worked for the Federal Writers' Project, and, like Wright, dabbled in Communist Party politics. Ellison fiercely defended Wright's novel *Native Son*, describing it as "the first philosophical novel by an American Negro" and a work that "possesses an artistry, penetration of thought, and sheer emotional power that places it into the front rank of American fiction." Like Wright, Ellison incorporated anecdotes from *Let Me Live* into his own fiction, was inspired by Herndon's life story and leadership skills, and wrote for communist and other radical publications more out of economic and literary necessity than deep political conviction.

Initially, the Communist Party supported Herndon's new publishing venture. In March 1942, the *Daily Worker* praised Herndon for organizing the Negro Publication Society, for raising money to fund the *Quarterly*, and for starting the nation's only magazine "devoted entirely to the review of Negro life and culture." The Party tolerated Herndon's focus on Black nationalism, at least for now, as long as the magazine did not criticize the Allies' war effort. After the German invasion of the Soviet Union, the Communist Party pledged its full support for the Allies and lobbied them to start a second front to save the Soviet army.

The war's impact on the Black freedom struggle was foremost on Herndon's mind. He echoed the themes of the *Pittsburgh Courier*'s "Double Victory" campaign—victory against racist enemies at home and against Hitler and fascist enemies abroad. "We've got to lick Jim Crow in order to lick Hitler," Herndon told the *Daily Worker.* He rejected the notion that Black people did not support the war effort or could be influenced by Japanese propaganda. "Negroes, you see, love freedom perhaps even more than most other people. Our people have fought for freedom with their lives and they know what it means to live in slavery. A Hitler victory would return them and all mankind to that slavery. They know what is at stake." Herndon hinted that the magazine was his contribution to the war effort: "The Quarterly sprang into being to help the Negro people 'do their part.'"

With Ellison as managing editor, Herndon produced a second issue of the *Quarterly* twice the size of the first one. Ellison wrote the lead editorial arguing that "the Four Freedoms" must apply to African Americans and people of color all over the world if the Allies hoped to prevail against the Axis powers. Ellison also solicited excerpts of *12 Million Black Voices* from Richard Wright as well as submissions from white writers. The Jewish scholar Louis Harap wrote about "Anti-Negroism Among Jews" and Reddick about "Anti-Semitism Among Negroes." Langston Hughes contributed a short story, "Banquet in Honor." The issue included articles about life in India and Africa as well as about Black life in America. Dressed in dark suits and ties to promote the second issue with members of the Black press, Herndon and Ellison connected the Black freedom struggle in America with the struggles of people of color all over the world. "What we are doing is attempting to project a consciousness about these problems," Herndon told the New York *Amsterdam News*, "to bring influence to bear not only upon our own national problems, but also upon the co-related problems of the Indians, the Chinese, etc."

As one of the more prominent young Black leaders in America, Herndon attempted to raise funds for the Negro Publication Society and the *Quarterly* by holding two star-studded live performances. On June 26, 1942, musicians including Lead Belly, Brownie McGhee, and Woody Guthrie played at the Third Cavalcade of Folk Music at Town Hall. A few months later, the *Quarterly* cosponsored an event dramatizing the Four Freedoms produced by Orson Welles at Harlem's Golden Gate Ballroom. The second event evidently lost money. With their remaining funds, Herndon and Ellison published a series of pamphlets, including one by Herndon on Frederick Douglass.

The financial troubles and political tension with the Communist Party weighed on Herndon. In April 1943, he traveled to Philadelphia to set up a temporary office for the *Negro Quarterly* in the same building as a Black newspaper, the *Philadelphia Tribune*. He confided to someone who turned out to be an FBI informant about the lack of support for the *Quarterly* from Harlem's Black political leaders and from the Communist Party. Herndon, according to the informant, was "getting considerable criticism from all sides relative to The Negro Quarterly. The Party members say that it is far too intellectual and for that reason lack[s] popular appeal. He deplored this criticism." Herndon, who worked out of the *Quarterly*'s Harlem office at 308 Lenox Avenue, struggled to keep the magazine afloat. The *Quarterly*'s third issue, published in the fall of 1943, was the last one for more than a year.

The *Quarterly*'s lack of funds and delay in publishing another issue led to a parting of ways with his managing editor Ellison. Ellison's weekly paychecks had often failed to materialize. Herndon disappeared as the *Quarterly*'s creditors came calling and its checks bounced. "Herndon's job was to get the money," Ellison wrote a fellow writer, "and perhaps you've heard about Herndon." In May 1943, Herndon tried to reach Ellison by phone. Ellison, whose health and first marriage were failing, had moved to Vermont before joining the merchant marine. Herndon and Ellison, despite the collapse of their joint enterprise, stayed on good terms.

The same could not be said of Herndon and the Communist Party. A public controversy over Herndon's draft status was the final straw. On May 2, Herndon requested and received a six-month deferment arguing that he was essential to the war effort as the editor of the *Negro Quarterly*. Incensed over Herndon's "self-serving statement," the colonel in charge of the New York City draft board successfully appealed in August, reclassifying Herndon from a 2-A deferral for occupational purposes to 1-A as available for military service. Herndon replied that he was "not fighting the draft" and was "merely protecting my rights provided by the regulations of the draft law." He insisted that the *Negro Quarterly* was "not a Communist magazine nor does it have any connection whatever with any political organization." He argued that his "deferment . . . is provided by law" and "is enjoyed by hundreds of other editors throughout the country." On August 5, Frederick Woltman, an anticommunist reporter for the *New York World-Telegram*, broke the story and portrayed Herndon as a "dyed-in-the-wool Communist" and the *Negro Quarterly* as "an unofficial Communist literary magazine." Two days later, Herndon defended himself in the *Daily Worker*. Speaking to the press, he regarded "my contribution as important as a military victory" after riots in Harlem a week earlier and considered his editorial duties "essential in

the sense that we are concerned with many of the problems confronting Negroes as a result of the war, such as morale among the
armed forces and civilians." Herndon appealed because he had not
received an opportunity to contest the board's decision. He received
a deferment until the spring and was reclassified 2-A. The colonel,
however, was not giving up. During a final appeal, Herndon lost
and again was reclassified 1-A—making him immediately eligible
for military service—because the *Negro Quarterly* had published
only three issues and had not produced an issue in nearly a year.
The bespectacled, five-foot-ten, 165-pound Herndon never made
it to his induction ceremony. On October 25, he failed his selective
service physical—perhaps because of poor eyesight from months of
reading by candlelight in prison—and was permanently reclassified
4-F as unfit for military service.

Soon after the initial story broke, the Communist Party began to
sever ties with Herndon. On August 10, the Party withdrew its support for the *Negro Quarterly* and "charge[d] him with nationalism."
Herndon believed that the Party, which had informed him of his
changed draft status, had leaked the story to Woltman and the *World-
Telegram*. Herndon, though he had not been formally expelled from
the Communist Party, was "very bitter agianst [*sic*] them."

In early September 1943, the Communist Party formally distanced itself from Herndon upon learning that he was trying to
raise money for the *Quarterly* on the West Coast. The Party dis-
avowed Herndon and the *Negro Quarterly* and claimed "no responsibility for either its editorial or business policies, or for the actions
of Angelo Herndon in this or any other connection." The order
was drafted by New York Communist Party executive secretary
Gil Green, approved by general secretary Earl Browder, and signed
by several Party officials, including Herndon's former lawyer and
boss, Ben Davis Jr.

The Party was upset about the draft controversy as undermining
its support for a second front against the Nazis to save the Soviet
army, Herndon's mismanagement of the *Negro Quarterly* funds,

and his emphasis on Black nationalism. For his part, Herndon had been distancing himself from the Party for months because it was "neglecting the cause of the American Negro" to focus on its all-consuming effort to lobby for a second front. Herndon, according to an FBI informant, wanted the Party to sponsor a test case to challenge racial segregation in the U.S. armed forces. The Party, however, refused because a test case would have compromised communist support for the Allies. Herndon, according to the informant, was one of many Black members who believed that the Party had "side tracked the struggle for Negro rights."

By the end of September, Herndon moved to San Francisco, where he persisted in publishing the *Negro Quarterly*. The issue's lead editorial, probably written by Ellison, counseled Black people to engage in "critical participation" in the war effort and the freedom struggle: "Thus, while affirming the justice of the Allies' cause, it never loses sight of the Negro peoples' stake in the struggle."

Herndon contributed the issue's lead essay, "Frederick Douglass: Negro Leadership and War," some of which had appeared in *There Were Giants in the Land*, an edited volume published in 1942 about twenty-eight historic Americans. Addressing Black attitudes toward the war, he viewed it as a global struggle against the subjugation of people of color: "We are fighting for the freedom of the enslaved peoples of the world without regard to race or color, or we are just simply expending men, material and energy for the perpetuation of the evils of the 'Old World.'" He described Frederick Douglass's evolution as a spokesman for the abolitionist movement, publisher of the *North Star* and facilitator of the Underground Railroad to Canada, as well as Douglass's insistence on the abolition of slavery as a central aim of the Civil War. Likewise, Herndon wanted to use World War II to fight for racial justice at home and abroad. He agreed with A. Philip Randolph and other Black leaders who wanted organized labor to use its clout to lobby for integrated military units and to end racial discrimination in war industries. He called on people of color around the world to insist upon their freedom: "Our conception of freedom envisions the millions of non-English speaking peoples everywhere marching in their majesty out of the present hell of slavery into the dawn of a new world. That is the meaning of this war to us." He rejected the argument that the freedom struggle might hurt the war effort and insisted not on failed promises but on real progress: "What we need is more deeds and less words!"

The final issue of the *Negro Quarterly*, published in February 1944 and titled "The South Moves West," spanned ninety-two pages about "the West" as a "testing ground for post-war racial adjustment in America." With the Black population increasing in West Coast cities from about 134,000 to 500,000 since 1940, the editor's note declared: "This westward shift of large numbers of Negroes marked the closing of the last frontier in racial adjustment in America." The issue featured excerpts from Fair Employment Practices Committee hearings about racial discrimination by unions in the shipbuilding industry. It also included testimony by Black workers, several articles about Black life on the West Coast, and a poem by Gwendolyn Brooks.

Herndon's innovative attempt to revive the *Quarterly* on the West Coast ultimately failed. One of the magazine's influential contributors, Black literary critic J. Saunders Redding, blamed its demise on "the rumor that [the Negro Publication Society of America] was a Communist front organization. It was a particularly hard rumor to kill because one of the organization's officers, Angelo Herndon, had once been a very active Communist. But just as the [society] was getting going again, America entered the war, paper for publishers became scarce and more expensive, and [the society] was forced to shut up shop." Assessing his experiences editing the journal, Ellison reported that he liked working with Herndon, "tried to translate Negro life in terms of Marxist terminology," and insisted "there was never anything like it before in Negro journalism." Decades later, Ellison recalled that the *Quarterly* was "Herndon's attempt to become something more than a Communist figurehead."

Herndon was not content to let his publishing dreams die with the *Negro Quarterly*, even if it meant reestablishing his Communist Party ties. He informed Bay Area members that he had not been expelled from the Party—which was technically true. He then borrowed money from several Party members and never repaid it. He raised funds to start a Black newspaper and described San Francisco as "a center of a new era for the Negro" and "a chance to set a new pat[t]ern for inter-racial living."

In January 1944, Herndon launched a bimonthly Black newspaper in San Francisco, the *People's Advocate*. Founded by the Negro Publication Society and "not financed or subsidized by any partisan group, organization or individual," the newspaper pledged to "base our whole program on the goal of equality of opportunity for Negroes to share fully in the political, economic and public life of the country, without discrimination or segregation. . . . We have confidence in the ability of America to solve the conflict of race, and to realize a genuine democracy which discriminates against no man or woman because of color." In the January 24 issue, Herndon wrote a full-page editorial praising the Black press for its role in the freedom struggle. Funded by subscriptions, the *People's Advocate* reprinted articles from the *Negro Quarterly* and the Black press.

For its part, the Communist Party wanted nothing to do with Herndon or his literary enterprises. On March 16, California Party leaders issued a statement that Herndon "was dropped from the Party in New York some time ago" and had given some San Francisco communists the mistaken impression that he was still working with the Party. The statement accused Herndon of "developing a nationalist line in his activities among the Negro people" and of "financial irresponsibility in his efforts to finance his paper."

Herndon was coediting the *People's Advocate* with William Henry McClendon, the Black editor and publisher of the *People's Observer* in Portland, Oregon. The *People's Advocate* struggled to gain traction in San Francisco and stopped publishing in May. Herndon moved to Portland in August 1944 to work with McClen-

don on the *People's Observer*. Like Herndon, McClendon was disenchanted with the Communist Party's stance toward the fight
for racial equality. Party officials warned its Portland members to
beware of Herndon and his efforts to raise money.

The Communist Party USA was in turmoil. In February, General Secretary Earl Browder had proposed changing the name of
the organization to the Communist Political Association to work
within the American political system. William Foster and other
Party loyalists, who wanted the organization to keep its name and
emphasis on the class struggle and to take its orders from Moscow,
succeeded in ousting Browder. Some people lost faith in the Party
altogether. On May 18, the eve of the Communist Party Congress
in which Browder unsuccessfully proposed to dissolve the old
organization, Anna Damon leapt to her death from her fifteenth-
floor Gramercy Park apartment. As the acting national secretary of
the ILD, she had championed Herndon's fight for freedom and had
frequently corresponded with him while he was in Fulton Tower.

Wright, Ellison, Herndon, and many other Black writers and
intellectuals had already broken with or distanced themselves from
the Communist Party. After Wright published the first of two
Atlantic Monthly articles in August 1944 about his negative experiences in the Party, Herndon congratulated him. And of Party loy-
alist Ben Davis Jr.'s attempt to rebut Wright's article in the *Daily
Worker*, Herndon was dismissive: "he's to be pitied." Writing to
Wright from Portland, Herndon indicated that he planned to return
to California: "You'll hear from me again."

Free from the Communist Party line, Herndon reestablished
contact with Ellison, his former managing editor at the *Negro
Quarterly*. During the summer of 1944, Herndon briefly returned
to New York City—presumably to see his wife and to raise money
for the Negro Publication Society—but missed Ellison. "Sorry I
did not get a chance to see you before leaving New York," Herndon
wrote. "It was a sort of a flying trip that kept me busy while there."
He left his wife, Joyce, back in New York. In February 1945, she

reported to mutual friends that "she had not seen her husband nor heard from him in months." By August, she had gotten a divorce— presumably because of his prolonged absences but possibly because of other reasons—and remarried.

Despite his estrangement from the Communist Party, Herndon refused to sacrifice his belief in civil rights and civil liberties or to be exploited as a stool pigeon to persecute loyal Party members. In the fall of 1948, the federal government tried to deport Black communist Claudia Jones. Born in Trinidad and raised in Harlem, Jones had joined the Young Communist League in February 1936 and was inspired by the Party's defense of the Scottsboro case. By 1937, she was writing for the *Daily Worker* and quickly emerged as one of the leading young Black members of the Party. During her deportation hearings, she was represented by Herndon's radical New York lawyer, Carol Weiss King. The federal government sub-poenaed Herndon, one of King's most prominent former clients, to testify against Jones.

Obeying the subpoena and appearing at the September 30 hear-ing, Herndon read a long statement that compared his trial for attempting to incite insurrection in Atlanta with Claudia Jones's deportation hearing over her political beliefs. He refused to tes-tify against her on moral grounds: "I have never in the past, and I cannot now allow myself to be used as a robot, a cog in the wheel of a machine that will grind people to death." Herndon, however, emphasized his break with the Communist Party and his turn to Black nationalism: "The accused is a Negro and a Communist. I am a Negro and not a Communist. . . . I can not ever forget that I am a Negro. No Negro can ever forget that he is a Negro as long as America remembers it." With his remarks reprinted in the *Daily Worker* and by the leftist Civil Rights Congress, Herndon reminded people of how hard Jones and other Party members had fought for his freedom: "As the symbol of man's struggle for freedom sixteen years ago in Georgia, the highest point in my life, I cannot and will not permit this moment to become the lowest, most tragic point of my life."

But with his first act as a young Communist Party leader and his second act as an emerging Black writer and publisher effectively over, Herndon was completely adrift. Sometime in 1945 or early 1946, he had moved in with his brother Leroy on the South Side of Chicago and had eschewed politics for business. The last time Ellison saw Herndon was in 1946 in New York City. Herndon boasted to the Ellisons about the money he made selling fur coats on installment plans to poor women. "He looks well, is off of politics and has become a rather cynical businessman—insurance brokerage and women's clothing," Ellison wrote Richard Wright's wife, Ellen. Herndon expressed no desire to return to political or literary endeavors. "But for the cynicism spawned by his disillusionment with the Party," Ellison lamented to Henry Louis Gates Jr. years later, "Herndon might have turned into an effective leader. Neither of us was much of an editor, but under the circumstances—the war atmosphere, the lack of a group of supporting writers, etc.—we did the best we could."

Ellison's fascination with Herndon endured. During the 1950s, Ellison once saw Ben Davis Jr. at a drugstore lunch counter and Davis exclaimed: "Why there's Ralph Ellison!" Davis had criticized Ellison's 1952 novel, *Invisible Man*—which won the National Book Award and made Ellison, like his erstwhile mentor Richard Wright, one of America's foremost literary figures. At the lunch counter, Ellison walked over to Davis and wanted to know one thing: Did he have any news about Angelo Herndon?

Like Ellison's protagonist in *Invisible Man*, Herndon had disappeared underground.

HOME SWEET HOME

Last known photograph of Angelo Herndon
at June 9, 1969, appearance in Harlem

RALPH ELLISON AND THE REST OF BLACK AMERICA READ
about what happened to Angelo Herndon in the April 29, 1954, issue
of *Jet* magazine. Herndon's days of playing fast and loose with other
people's money finally caught up with him. Communist Party members in Chicago had been warned not to trust him "with any large

sums of money." Herndon, who had opened a real estate business
with Black communist Ishmael Flory, managed to find unsuspect-
ing victims. Herndon had taken $25,000 from five different potential
buyers, including an unemployed autoworker who was a father of
four, to sell them the same South Side Chicago apartment building.
His victims recalled his intellect and his penchant for quoting Aris-
totle. Herndon was arrested at a rooming house where he had been
hiding out, held on $30,000 bail in the Cook County jail, and charged
with embezzlement, larceny, and running a confidence game. The
headline of the *Jet* article blared in red ink: "Swindle Suspect Identified as Ex-Red Angelo Herndon." The magazine's reporters discovered him in jail under his birth name, Gene Braxton.

At his arraignment, Herndon pleaded not guilty and insisted
that he wanted to go to trial. During the summer of 1954, his trial
was postponed until September 9. On the day of the trial, he was
transferred from the Cook County jail to an anteroom near the
judge's chambers. His lawyer, Gloria E. Wilson, one of the first
Black women graduates of John Marshall Law School, advised him
to plead guilty. She had conferred with the prosecutor and judge
and informed the forty-year-old Herndon that the judge offered to
sentence him to two to seven years in prison if he pleaded guilty.
Herndon refused. Wilson spoke with the prosecutor and judge
again and, according to Herndon, counseled him that the judge
equated the crime to armed robbery and offered to sentence him to
one to ten years in prison. Herndon refused. She returned to con-
fer with the prosecutor and judge once more and, again according
to Herndon, the judge vowed to sentence him to eight to ten years
in prison if he decided to proceed with a jury trial. Herndon again
refused. She spoke with the judge and prosecutor a fourth time.
They were willing to sentence him to two to six years in prison if
he pleaded guilty. Herndon finally agreed.

Accompanied by his lawyer, Herndon was ushered into the courtroom of newly elected Judge Leslie E. Salter. The prosecutor, John
Gutknecht, reviewed the witness testimony in the indictment. Hern-

don agreed to waive his right to a jury trial and to change his plea to
guilty. Judge Salter sentenced him to two to six years for running a
confidence game. Herndon was transferred to Joliet State Prison.

More than two years into his sentence, on October 22, 1956,
inmate #35956 at Joliet Prison, known as Gene Braxton, filed a
federal lawsuit alleging that the prosecutor, Gutknecht, and Judge
Salter had conspired to violate his constitutional rights and several federal civil rights laws. He charged that the prosecutor and
judge had coerced him to plead guilty, denying him the right to a
jury trial and violating his Fourteenth Amendment rights to equal
protection and due process. In his complaint, he detailed the four
meetings between "his disloyal counsel" and the prosecutor and
the judge on the day of his trial and described "the use of intimidation, threats, coercion, trickery and promise of less time for a plea
of guilty and waiver of trial by jury." He claimed that the plea bar-
gaining was "a trial conducted in secrecy and without the presence
of the accused to testify freely and give evidence and personally
defend his interests." He sought $200,000 in compensatory dam-
ages because he was "deprived of his constitutional liberty and suffered great humiliation, the loss of his business, [and] physical and
mental distress." He also requested $50,000 in punitive damages
and a $150,000 judgment against each defendant. Herndon was rep-
resenting himself.

This time, the Fourteenth Amendment did not set Angelo Herndon free. After granting him leave to file the complaint as an indigent person, Judge Michael L. Igoe heard a motion to dismiss the
complaint for failing to state a claim. Gutknecht's counsel argued
that the judge and prosecutor could not be sued for actions taken
pursuant to their official duties and that the complaint's assertions
were conclusory. On November 20, the same day as the hearing,
Judge Igoe dismissed Herndon's lawsuit.

With no lawyer willing to plead his case, Herndon attempted to
vindicate his own constitutional rights on appeal. On December 4,
Herndon moved to certify the case for an appeal and to transmit the

record to the Seventh Circuit Court of Appeals. Judge Igoe, however, denied Herndon's motion to file his appeal as an indigent—forcing him to pay transcript and other filing fees. Earlier that year, the U.S. Supreme Court had ruled in *Griffin v. Illinois* that the state of Illinois could not force indigent defendants to pay transcript fees in order to file appeals. It is unclear whether Herndon, unable to file as an indigent or to obtain a fee waiver, pursued a federal appeal. He lacked funds, legal counsel, and a viable constitutional claim. Nor was a national legal and political campaign trying to set him free.

■ ■ ■ ■

THE LAWYER HERNDON RECRUITED into the Communist Party, Ben Davis Jr., experienced his own dramatic rise and fall. In November 1943, Davis was elected to Adam Clayton Powell Jr.'s former seat on the New York City Council. His father, Ben Sr., the powerful former Georgia Republican national committeeman, died at age seventy-five on October 28, 1945, in Harlem Hospital while visiting his son in New York City and witnessing his ascent to political power. Known as Harlem's councilman, Davis was reelected in November 1945 to a full four-year term on the city council and emerged as the nation's highest-profile communist elected official.

The federal government took notice. During an interrogation of Communist Party leaders in October 1945 before the House Un-American Activities Committee, John E. Rankin (D-Miss.), the chair, threatened Davis with contempt for criticizing the committee's failure to call him to the witness stand in a timely fashion and for pulling him away from his reelection campaign. A defiant Davis retorted: "I certainly do not expect Mr. Rankin to give any consideration to a Negro in this House. . . . You can do one good thing; just end this witch hunt." The *Daily Worker* played up Davis's remarks. But the FBI and other federal authorities were watching Davis. In July 1948—fifteen years after Davis's defense of Herndon in Atlanta against similar state charges—Davis and eleven other

Communist Party leaders were charged under the Smith Act with conspiring to teach and advocate the overthrow of the U.S. government by force and violence.

The Herndon case was front and center during Davis's Smith Act trial. Judge Harold Medina and the federal prosecutor repeatedly interrupted Davis as he sought to testify about his formative experiences in 1933 as Herndon's defense counsel. Davis attempted to explain how the communist literature he had read in preparation for the trial had inspired him to join the Party, how one of the prosecution's witnesses had used racial slurs, and how Judge Lee Wyatt had failed to sustain Davis's objections to those epithets. In addition to his persistent objections to the testimony, the prosecutor attempted to impeach Davis by pointing out the absence of some of those epithets in the trial record. As he had at the time, Davis insisted that Wyatt and the court reporter had created a "crooked record" for the appeal (in 1943, Wyatt had been appointed to the Georgia Supreme Court, and in 1947 he served for five months as a judge at the Nuremberg tribunal of Nazi war criminals). During the closing arguments at the trial of the communist leaders, the prosecutor accused Davis and his alleged co-conspirators of using the Party's literature as weapons by teaching people to overthrow the government.

At the end of the nine-month trial, Judge Medina refused to allow Davis to represent himself and to present his own closing argument to the jury. Instead, no closing argument was made on Davis's behalf. On October 14, 1949, the jury convicted Davis and ten others. A week later, Medina sentenced Davis to five years in federal prison. Before his sentencing, Davis unloaded on the judge: "I will not be intimidated. I was not intimidated by the lynchers' court in Georgia, and I will not be intimidated by any court, by any forces of reaction anywhere . . . , and neither will my people and my party."

A month after his conviction, Davis lost his reelection bid. His fellow city council members voted to expel him with a month left in his term. For three years, Davis and his codefendants appealed their convictions. In a 6–2 decision on June 4, 1951, in *Dennis v. United States*, the Supreme Court—at the height of the perceived threat of communism to U.S. national security—affirmed their convictions and rejected a free speech challenge to the Smith Act.

In July 1951, a federal judge ordered Davis to begin serving his five-year sentence. Davis, seizing another opportunity to speak, declared: "Why, I think the sentence should be reduced and abolished. It's a crime against the people—the Negro people, too. I'm about to lose my freedom." The judge disagreed that Davis had been convicted "because you are a Negro" and threatened him with contempt. Four deputies led him off to jail. On July 10, the forty-seven-year-old Davis was separated from his communist colleagues and transferred to a federal prison in Terre Haute, Indiana. During his incarceration, he wrote a memoir in longhand (which prison officials confiscated and refused to return until after his death), sued over his racially segregated cell block, and suffered from chronic back pain. On March 1, 1955, he was released after three years and four months—but not for long. He was immediately transferred to a state prison in Allegheny, Pennsylvania, to serve a sixty-day sentence for contempt of court for refusing to testify about other suspected communists. At a Smith Act trial in Pittsburgh in August 1953, a tired and drawn-looking Davis had declined to identify people who had been involved in the National Negro Commission of the Communist Party.

Back in Harlem after serving his second prison sentence, Davis started a family and resumed his life as a Communist Party leader and activist. He refused, unlike many other American members, to break with the Party in 1956 after the Soviet Union's invasion of Hungary. An ally of William Foster and supporter of Foster's pro-Soviet position, Davis was elected national secretary of the Communist Party USA in December 1959 yet never attained its top position of general secretary.

The federal government pursued Davis until the end. In March

1962, he was charged with violating the McCarran Internal Security Act for refusing to register as a member of the Communist Party. A popular lecturer on college campuses, he spoke at Harvard Law School about the McCarran Act—recounting how defending Herndon had turned him into a communist and extolling the virtues of the Communist Party in front of 600 students and faculty, including a former law school classmate, Dean Erwin Griswold. "I leave Harvard, after seeing my old classmate, and the thoughtful, probing democratic-minded students, with greater confidence in the future of democracy in our country," Davis said. "In extending me the right to be heard, Harvard has made a contribution in defense of constitutional liberties." He was not as sanguine about the Kennedy administration and its decision to prosecute him under the McCarran Act. Davis died of lung cancer at age sixty on August 22, 1964—a few months before the scheduled date of his McCarran Act trial.

Davis's biggest legal triumph—indeed the single most important episode of his life because it led to his decision to join the Communist Party—was his defense of Angelo Herndon. In Herndon's case but not Davis's own, the Court vindicated Davis's argument that "you can't kill a man because of the books he reads."

■ ■ ■ ■

DAVIS'S WHITE SOUTHERN ALLY on the Provisional Committee for the Defense of Angelo Herndon fared much better. Getting fired as an English instructor at Georgia Tech nudged C. Vann Woodward into the profession he was made for—a historian of the American South. He entered the PhD program in history at the University of North Carolina and in 1938 published his dissertation about the Georgia populist Tom Watson as a critically acclaimed book. In Woodward's telling, the southern ruling class employed racial discrimination and prejudice to crush the young Watson's vision of interracial populism and turned Watson into a racist, demagogic politician. Climbing the academic ladder by attacking the idea of a post-Reconstruction New South, Woodward published two ground-breaking books in 1951—*Reunion and Reaction*, a National Book Award finalist about the contested presidential election of 1876, and *Origins of the New South*, a Bancroft Prize–winning history of the American South from 1877 to 1913.

The idealistic young professor who had attempted to rally fellow white southerners to Herndon's cause could not escape the pull of current events. As the program chair of the Southern Historical Association's annual meeting in 1949 in Williamsburg, Virginia, he challenged racial norms by inviting John Hope Franklin to be the first African American historian to deliver a paper. Four years later, Woodward joined Franklin and other historians in advising Thurgood Marshall and the NAACP Legal Defense Fund about drafting a Supreme Court brief about the history of the Fourteenth Amendment and Reconstruction in preparation for oral argument in the landmark cases outlawing racially segregated schools known as *Brown v. Board of Education*. Inspired by his research for Marshall and the Legal Defense Fund and encouraged by Franklin, Woodward prepared a series of lectures for the University of Virginia about the history of racial segregation in the South and initially published them in 1955 as *The Strange Career of Jim Crow*. Historians continue to debate Woodward's thesis that racial segregation was not a timeless southern phenomenon but arose out of political and economic conflict in the 1890s. The book sold more than 800,000 copies in Woodward's lifetime. Woodward joined other historians at the historic voting rights march from Selma to Montgomery on March 25, 1965, and heard Martin Luther King Jr. praise *Strange Career* and invoke its arguments to attack the idea that racial segregation was an inherent part of the southern way of life.

At the top of his profession, Woodward could not escape his involvement, however tangential, in the Herndon case. In 1951, a colleague recommended him to be a historical adviser to the Joint Chiefs of Staff. A Defense Department background check revealed his involvement in the Herndon case and alleged "communist influence." John Hudson, the former assistant solicitor who had prosecuted Herndon and other communists, claimed to have heard Woodward describe himself as "a Socialist" who believed that every American had "the right to revolt."

If anything, Woodward drifted rightward during the late 1960s after he joined the Yale faculty. He successfully blocked Marxist historian Herbert Aptheker from teaching a Yale class on W. E. B. Du Bois, opposed multiculturalism and Black studies, and accepted an award from the conservative National Association of Scholars. And yet, at the request of Yale's president, he wrote a prominent report in 1974 championing free speech on college campuses. He periodically fielded questions about his involvement in the Herndon case and believed that the Communist Party had exploited Herndon for publicity purposes. C. Vann Woodward died in 1999 in Hamden, Connecticut, at age ninety-one, hailed as one of America's preeminent historians.

■　■　■　■

THE RADICAL LAWYER who had assembled the legal team that freed Angelo Herndon dedicated her life to defending the persecuted and the powerless as one of the nation's leading immigration lawyers. Carol Weiss King cofounded the National Lawyers Guild and served as general counsel of the American Committee for Protection of Foreign Born. She recruited lawyers, plotted strategy, and drafted briefs to prevent the federal government from deporting radicals and union leaders because they were suspected communists.

In 1938, she joined the defense team for Harry Bridges, the head of the San Francisco–based International Longshoremen's and Warehousemen's Union, in a series of deportation proceedings because of allegations that he belonged to the Communist Party. The Australian-born Bridges became a naturalized U.S. citizen after the Supreme Court ruled in 1945 that the evidence did not support allegations of Party membership. King also prevented the deportation of William Schneiderman, the secretary of the California Communist Party and a naturalized U.S. citizen, by recruiting former Republican presidential nominee Wendell Willkie to argue Schneiderman's case before the Supreme Court. The federal government continued to pursue Bridges and Schneiderman—and their lawyer as well. Because of her work on the initial Bridges case in 1938, the FBI opened an investigation into King's ties to the Communist Party and other radical groups and created a file that spanned more than 1400 pages.

During the rise of McCarthyism and the second Red Scare in the late 1940s, King represented scores of clients and juggled appearances in deportation hearings and federal courtrooms, at Ellis Island, before the U.S. Congress, and at the Supreme Court. At the deportation hearing of Black communist Claudia Jones, King came face-to-face with Angelo Herndon for the last time. Jones was eventually deported, but not because of the testimony of King's former client.

Throughout her career, King deferred to her male colleagues in arguing cases in court. In November 1951, however, King finally argued her first Supreme Court case because she could not find anyone else to do it. She contested the federal government's decision to deny bail to John Zydok, a Russian-born member of the Communist Party. In failing health at the time of the argument, King did not live to see the outcome—a 5–4 defeat for her client. She died of cancer on January 22, 1952, at age fifty-six. Her editorship of the *IJA Bulletin*, her recruitment of talented defense lawyers, and her brief writing and strategic skill saved hundreds of people who had faced deportation or death for espousing unpopular beliefs or because of the color of their skin. Less than a year before her death, the *Saturday Evening Post* claimed that King had "probably defended more Reds than any other lawyer in the U.S." She went to her grave denying that she was a member of the Communist Party yet devoted her life to defending communists and protecting their rights. Few people today know the name Carol Weiss King. Her legacy, however,

lies in fighting for the constitutional rights of Angelo Herndon and
so many other people who were politically powerless.

■ ■ ■ ■

THE HERNDON CASE inspired the two lawyers who briefed and
argued his appeal, Whitney North Seymour and Herbert Wechsler.
Less than two years after they won a Supreme Court victory for
Herndon, King enlisted them to brief and argue the Supreme Court
case of Joseph George Strecker. An Austrian-born restaurateur in
Hot Springs, Arkansas, Strecker admitted that he had joined the
Communist Party in 1932 but insisted that he was no longer a member. The federal government tried to deport him anyway. Based on
a brief written by Wechsler and King and an argument by Seymour,
the Supreme Court—in a 5–4 opinion written by none other than
Justice Owen Roberts—ruled in 1939 that the Anarchist Exclusion
Act excluded deportation based on past Communist Party membership. The victory saved Strecker from deportation and aided King's
efforts to do the same for labor leader Harry Bridges.

Though he never teamed up again with King, Whitney North
Seymour advised lawyers to help the less fortunate and to serve
the public good. He joined the board of the ACLU a year after the
Herndon case and served for the next fifteen years. At the height
of McCarthyism, he chaired an American Bar Association special
committee recommending a model code of fair procedures for congressional investigations of suspected communists, and he decried
the persecution of lawyers who agreed to represent them. And in
1965, he cochaired the Lawyers' Committee for Civil Rights Under
Law, established two years earlier by President John F. Kennedy.
Seymour viewed lawyers not simply as corporate mouthpieces but
as public servants.

An eminent member of the New York bar, Seymour worked
his entire career at Simpson, Thacher & Bartlett yet found time to
serve as president of the Association of the Bar of the City of New

York, the American Bar Association, and the Legal Aid Society. He threw himself into civic and social causes in New York City. Like his father, the itinerant lecturer, he was a gifted raconteur and after-dinner speaker. "I've tried to recognize," he often said, "that one owes the community a debt which he could spend a lifetime paying." His children took those lessons to heart. His son Whitney North Seymour Jr. joined him at Simpson, Thacher and served from 1970 to 1973 as U.S. Attorney for the Southern District of New York and in 1986 as independent counsel investigating former Reagan White House aide Michael Deaver for perjury and lying to Congress. A lifetime away from the young boy in Madison, Wisconsin, hunting arrowheads, Whitney North Seymour Sr. died on May 21, 1983, at age eighty-two—celebrated in New York City for his public service.

Seymour's brief writer in the Herndon case, Herbert Wechsler, enjoyed a similarly long and illustrious career. Early on, he was not always on the side of the politically powerless. As an assistant attorney general in the Justice Department's war division during World War II, he played a key role in editing the government's brief in the case of Fred Korematsu challenging the internment of Japanese Americans. In fact, Wechsler eliminated part of a footnote casting doubt on the government's evidence of a security threat. The Supreme Court upheld Korematsu's conviction for refusing to report to a relocation center pursuant to Roosevelt's executive order removing all Japanese Americans from the West Coast. Wechsler, however, made more positive public contributions to the law. After the war, he assisted U.S. Judge Francis Biddle at the Nuremberg trials of Nazi war criminals. In 1964, Wechsler briefed and argued the Supreme Court case of *New York Times v. Sullivan* defending the newspaper—as well as Martin Luther King Jr. and three other Alabama ministers—against charges that they had libeled a Montgomery, Alabama, police commissioner in an advertisement. The Court ruled 9–0 in Wechsler's favor and established the "actual malice" standard of knowing falsehood or reckless disregard for the truth in all libel lawsuits brought by public officials. A landmark First Amendment decision, *New York Times v. Sullivan* established breathing room for people to criticize public officials without fear of civil lawsuits or criminal prosecution.

A professor at Columbia Law School for nearly sixty years, Wechsler believed that his work on the Herndon and Strecker cases tarred him as a radical and prevented him from having a longer career in public life. Nonetheless, Wechsler made major legal contributions as an expert on constitutional law, federal courts, and criminal law. In 1959, he wrote a groundbreaking article calling for "neutral principles" in constitutional law and criticizing the reasoning of the *Brown v. Board of Education* school desegregation decision. In the article, he defended his racial bona fides by referring to his work with the NAACP's Charles Hamilton Houston. Wechsler's greatest contribution to American law may have been his work from 1952 to 1962 in drafting the American Law Institute's Model Penal Code. The code was designed to assist states in updating and standardizing their criminal laws and to avoid the type of dragnets such as the Georgia insurrection law that had ensnared Angelo Herndon and other people with unpopular beliefs or the wrong skin color. Herbert Wechsler died on April 26, 2000, at age ninety. By 2007, thirty-seven states had adopted part of the Model Penal Code. And his casebook with Henry Hart, which redefined the study of federal courts, is still widely assigned in American law schools today.

■ ■ ■ ■

CHARLES HAMILTON HOUSTON'S LIFE was as short as Seymour's and Wechsler's were long—yet just as pathbreaking. He had been adamant in insisting that NAACP officials during the mid-1930s put aside their reservations about the communist-backed ILD and join the Herndon defense committee because the case represented "a crisis in the development of civil rights in the South" and "may affect much of our own work." His 1935 brief urging the Supreme Court to rehear Herndon's case represented a united front across racial and political lines. He was one of the few NAACP lawyers willing to collaborate with the ILD, and he worked closely with Carol Weiss King, Seymour, and Wechsler on legal strategy in a number of cases, including Herndon's.

Soon after the Herndon victory, Houston stepped up his legal assault on the Supreme Court's cases permitting racial segregation and discrimination. He challenged what was deemed "equal" under *Plessy v. Ferguson*'s racially "separate but equal" doctrine by targeting states with graduate schools for whites but not for Blacks. Two years after winning Black Amherst graduate Donald Murray's admission to the all-white University of Maryland Law School in state court, he took a similar case to the U.S. Supreme Court. In 1938, Houston argued and won Black student Lloyd Gaines's case against the all-white University of Missouri Law School. Six years later, Houston won a Supreme Court ruling that a railroad union had violated federal law by refusing to represent Black railroad workers. In 1948, he argued and won another Supreme Court decision in *Hurd v. Hodge*, a companion case to the landmark decision in *Shelley v. Kraemer*, that racially restrictive covenants in his hometown of Washington, D.C., could not be enforced in court. At the end of his oral argument in the restrictive covenant case, Houston declared: "Racism must go."

Fighting racism in state and federal courts took its toll on Houston's health. Despite a failing heart, Houston never stopped fighting injustice—whether it involved suspected communists or African Americans. He represented screenwriters John Howard Lawson and Dalton Trumbo of the Hollywood Ten, who had been convicted of contempt for refusing to identify members of the Communist Party before the House Un-American Activities Committee. Houston unsuccessfully petitioned the Supreme Court to hear their case. He also returned to the site of his first major victory—the University of Maryland. Eleven years after winning Donald Murray's admission to the state's all-white law school, Houston challenged the university's refusal to admit Black student Esther McCready to its all-white nursing school. Just as it did in the Murray case, the state's highest court ordered McCready's admission. Houston heard the news from his hospital bed. Shortly thereafter, he died of heart disease, on April 22, 1950, at age fifty-four.

Sadly, Houston did not live to see Marshall's landmark Supreme Court victory nearly four years later in *Brown v. Board of Education*. Thurgood Marshall is the name everyone remembers today—and rightly so. Yet Marshall always gave credit where it was due—to his teacher and mentor Charles Hamilton Houston, the greatest civil rights lawyer of his generation. Houston showed Marshall the courage it took to represent a Black criminal defendant in an all-white southern courtroom and the strategic blueprint to attack the racially separate but equal doctrine. Throughout his career, Houston rose above petty turf wars between the ILD and NAACP, in Herndon's case and others, discovered inventive ways to challenge Supreme Court precedents stacked against him, and fought for the constitutional rights of communists and African Americans with equal fervor.

■ ■ ■ ■

THE WHITE ATLANTA LAWYER who helped revive Herndon's constitutional claims in the Georgia court system, Elbert Parr Tuttle, played a major role in implementing Houston's and Marshall's efforts to desegregate southern schools. Tuttle had revealed his interest in fighting racial injustice in the early 1930s while trying to save John Downer from a lynching and an execution for the alleged rape of a white woman. At the most perilous moment in the Herndon case—after the Supreme Court had dismissed it in 1935 for failing to raise free speech and assembly claims in state court—Tuttle understood that Judge Hugh Dorsey, the former Leo Frank prosecutor and racially progressive governor, might rule in Herndon's favor. Dorsey's ruling granting Herndon habeas corpus propelled the case back to the state supreme court and the U.S. Supreme Court (Dorsey survived a 1936 reelection challenge from Herndon prosecutor John Hudson and served as a superior court judge until 1948, the year he died).

The Herndon case spurred Tuttle's efforts to protect civil rights and civil liberties. Based on Whitney North Seymour's recommendation, Tuttle appealed the case of Monroe Bridwell and John Johnson, who had been tried and convicted in federal court, without the benefit of a lawyer, of spending and possessing counterfeit twenty-dollar bills. Tuttle felt so strongly about the case that he paid the court costs out of his own pocket. In a 6–2 decision in *Johnson v. Zerbst*, the Supreme Court held that a person charged with a federal crime has a right to counsel. In the majority opinion, Justice Hugo L. Black quoted the Court's decision in *Powell v. Alabama* about the trials of the Scottsboro defendants that the "right to be heard would be, in many cases, of little avail if it did not comprehend the right to be heard by counsel."

During World War II, Tuttle volunteered for combat duty in his midforties, was wounded on an island near Okinawa, and received the Purple Heart, Bronze Star, and other military honors. After the war, he threw himself into Republican Party politics. Dwight D. Eisenhower, the 1952 Republican presidential candidate, took notice of Tuttle, the chair of the Georgia Republican Party and of Eisenhower's Georgia campaign. From 1953 to 1954, Tuttle served as general counsel of the Treasury Department and was preparing to return to his Atlanta law firm when Attorney General Herbert Brownell Jr. and Deputy Attorney General William P. Rogers persuaded him to accept a federal appeals court judgeship. On July 6, 1954, a few months after *Brown v. Board of Education*, Eisenhower nominated Tuttle to serve on the Fifth Circuit Court of Appeals.

Unlike Eisenhower, who was ambivalent at best about the *Brown* decision, Tuttle played a leading role in enforcing it. As the chief judge of the New Orleans–based Fifth Circuit from 1960 to 1967,

Tuttle, assisted by several like-minded colleagues, enforced school desegregation throughout the Deep South. In 1961, he ordered the admission of Hamilton Holmes and Charlayne Hunter to the University of Georgia and wielded the court's power to issue injunctions to force southern school districts to desegregate. Those decisions exposed Tuttle and his fellow judges to death threats and social ostracism and, in places such as New Orleans and Birmingham, triggered white backlash and violence. As Herndon's former local counsel, Tuttle must have relished his role in preventing the state of Georgia from employing its insurrection law to harass civil rights activists. In 1963, Tuttle and two other federal judges declared the insurrection law "unconstitutional and void." Three years later, they prevented the state from invoking the law to prosecute Stokely Carmichael and other members of the Student Nonviolent Coordinating Committee. In 1981, Tuttle received the Presidential Medal of Freedom. Eight years later, the United States Court of Appeals building in Atlanta was named in his honor. Tuttle, proud of his small role in the Herndon case, died on June 23, 1996, at age ninety-eight.

■ ■ ■ ■

AS ESTEEMED AS ELBERT TUTTLE WAS in legal circles, Justice Owen Josephus Roberts has been portrayed as one of the Supreme Court's lesser lights. The "switch in time that saved nine"—his votes to overturn and then uphold state minimum wage laws in 1936 and 1937—suggests that he was a weak-willed justice who bowed to the political pressure of Franklin Roosevelt's court-packing plan. Yet as Roberts revealed eight years later to his colleague Felix Frankfurter, the second vote on the Washington State minimum wage law had occurred on December 19, 1936, six weeks before FDR announced his judicial reform bill. Either way, Roberts never found happiness on the Court. In 1945, after only fifteen years on the bench, he resigned in disgust with his colleagues. Hugo Black was so at odds with Roberts that Black and the other justices could not agree on the wording of a congratulatory letter. Even Frankfurter, one of his closest friends on the Court, believed that Roberts lacked the intellectual equipment to be a great justice.

Whatever he lacked in judicial imagination, Roberts compensated for with an innate sense of right and wrong and a willingness to side with minorities. In 1944, with Hugo Black writing the majority opinion, William O. Douglas joining it, and Frankfurter writing a concurrence, Roberts dissented from the Court's notorious decision upholding the conviction of Fred Korematsu for refusing to obey the government's wartime relocation and internment of Japanese Americans. In his *Korematsu* dissent, Roberts argued that "the indisputable facts exhibit a clear violation of Constitutional rights" because "it is the case of convicting a citizen as a punishment for not submitting to imprisonment in a concentration camp, based on his ancestry, and solely because of his ancestry, without evidence or inquiry concerning his loyalty and good disposition towards the United States."

As his *Korematsu* dissent revealed, Roberts's majority opinion in Herndon's case was the product of someone with an ingrained sense of injustice. It is no accident that he wrote 5–4 opinions in Herndon's case as well as in Joseph Strecker's deportation case two years later. Upon his retirement from the Court, Roberts served as the dean of his alma mater, University of Pennsylvania Law School, from 1948 to 1951. He died on May 17, 1955, at age eighty at his Chester County, Pennsylvania, farm.

Owen Roberts was not a deep constitutional thinker. Driven by facts, he wrote narrow opinions without memorable language. With the notable exception of the all-white primary cases, he often landed on the side of minority rights. He also understood basic truths about America's democracy. "The power of a state to abridge freedom of speech and of assembly is the exception rather than the rule," he wrote in *Herndon v. Lowry*. Indeed, of all the lawyers connected to the Herndon case, Roberts deserves credit as the justice who protected the rights to free speech and peaceable assembly and who saved Herndon from the chain gang.

■ ■ ■ ■

THE PERSON WHO SUFFERED THE MOST during the five years of litigation of Herndon's case was Angelo Herndon himself. He spent nearly three years in prison for a crime he did not commit at an age when most people were finding jobs, getting married, and starting families. After his release in 1937, Herndon overcame his sixth-grade education and transformed himself into a political leader and a young Black writer in Harlem. To Ralph Ellison and others, Herndon exhibited undeniable leadership potential—whether as a Communist Party orator, a Black journalist and editor, or a civil rights activist. During the 1930s and early 1940s, everyone in Black America knew his name. "I remembered Angelo Herndon and wondered, again," James Baldwin wrote in 1961, "whatever had become of him." The failure of the *Negro Quarterly* and the *People's Advocate* robbed Herndon of his idealism and growing sense of Black empowerment. Undone by his willingness to engage in financial impropriety, he bragged about making money in Chicago by preying on poor South Side residents. He was not, however, willing to sell out his former Communist Party colleagues—to make a buck from a national magazine article or to testify against them in a deportation hearing.

Transferred to the Cook County jail in December 1956 and released no later than December 15, 1958, Herndon (or Gene Braxton) kept a low profile. The FBI considered the Black communist a security threat and kept close tabs on him—especially when he reconnected with other Black communists in Chicago. During the late 1950s, he attended several Communist Party social events. In 1962, he was living at the Indiana farm of Black communist Claude Lightfoot and working as a cook. A year later, he recited a poem during the West Side community of Lawndale's celebration of Negro history week.

In May 1967, Herndon returned to the only organization where he had achieved sustained success and officially rejoined the Communist Party in Chicago. He was assigned to the South Central Freedom of the Press Committee and worked at the Afro-American Book Store operated by his former real estate partner, Ishmael Flory. At one of the committee's meetings, Herndon was introduced and told the members: "I realize that the Communist Party has the answers to the many problems facing all of mankind. The time is right for the Party to move ahead to improve the social and political conditions and eventually lead the working class to socialism." The national party leadership welcomed Herndon back into the fold. At another event that May, Henry Winston, the Communist Party USA national chairman, warmly reunited with Herndon for the first time in decades. Herndon continued to attend committee meetings until August 1967, when he vanished. Flory said Herndon had gone "on a trip but would be coming back soon." The FBI could not find him. The Bureau's informants described Herndon as a "drifter" who had a "mental problem" and often disappeared for long stretches of time. He was eventually spotted at a supermarket on Chicago's West Side and claimed to be writing a book on "the history of the Negro."

In June 1969, Herndon triumphantly returned to Harlem to honor his former trial counsel, Ben Davis Jr. Louise Thompson Patterson, a longtime left-wing activist and the wife of former ILD national secretary William Patterson, asked Herndon to speak at a celebration of the posthumous publication of Davis's memoir. She urged Herndon "to relate the present-day struggles to the past" because "too many of the young militants don't know anything of the history of the liberation struggle, nor of the people like you and Ben and Pat and many, many others who paved the way." She promised him airfare and invited him to stay at her apartment. Herndon agreed. For days, the *Daily Worker* hyped Herndon's appearance as the keynote speaker.

At the Adam Clayton Powell Auditorium on West 138th Street,

Herndon told the story of his arrest for organizing Black and white unemployed workers, his indictment for attempting to incite insurrection, and his trial before an all-white jury—and the courage Davis had shown in defending him. "You've got to fight, black and white together," Herndon told the cheering crowd of about 325 people. "This is the greatest monument you can erect to Ben Davis. You've got to tell them what Ben Davis did." After the speech, about fifty people gathered at the Patterson apartment for a small reception to honor Herndon. It was his final public appearance.

Herndon never again spoke about his life. During the late 1960s and early 1970s, he declined interview requests from two historians, including one who had contacted Vann Woodward, Thurgood Marshall, and FBI director J. Edgar Hoover regarding Herndon's whereabouts. Herndon's former communist colleagues thought he was living in Chicago. He told people in Chicago that he was living in New York and writing a book. The FBI lost track of him and, after thirty-eight years, finally stopped surveilling him in 1972. Herndon lived in the Midwest, residing in Milwaukee during the 1980s. He chose to spend the final years of his life in the South and died on December 9, 1997, at age eighty-three in Sweet Home, Arkansas. Not a single newspaper published an obituary.

For years, historians and writers took for granted that Herndon had been born into a coal-mining family in Cincinnati, Ohio, rather than a sharecropping family in Bullock County, Alabama. The truth was that Herndon had grown up in rural poverty with minimal education and little hope of a better life. Besides embellishing his origin story to protect his relatives, most of his anecdotes in *Let Me Live* about his experiences as a young communist in his teens and early twenties in Birmingham, New Orleans, and Atlanta have been corroborated by newspapers and other primary sources. He narrowly escaped the brutality of Birmingham police officers intent on pinning the murder of two white women and the shooting of a third on a Black suspect. He survived several years inside Fulton Tower and avoided a certain death on the chain gang.

The son of sharecroppers overcame long odds to transform himself into a Harlem success story.

As inspiring as Herndon's life story was to his literary friends Richard Wright and Ralph Ellison, Herndon's legacy is written not in *Let Me Live* but in the Supreme Court's majority opinion in *Herndon v. Lowry*. A year after the decision, Justice Harlan Fiske Stone wrote an opinion known as *Carolene Products* pledging that the Supreme Court would defer to the political process when it came to economic regulation. But in a famous footnote, he vowed that the judiciary would intervene to protect free speech and peaceable assembly and other rights essential to a democracy—and referred to *Herndon v. Lowry* as a prime example. The violation of the most basic rights of democratic citizenship is what drew people as diverse as Ben Davis Jr., C. Vann Woodward, Carol Weiss King, Charles Hamilton Houston, Whitney North Seymour, Herbert Wechsler, Elbert Tuttle, and Owen Roberts to Herndon's cause. A Black person cannot be convicted and sentenced to eighteen to twenty years on a chain gang by an all-white jury for organizing a peaceful, interracial demonstration outside a county courthouse, for reading radical books and literature espousing unpopular political ideas, or for attempting to recruit people to join his cause.

America is a nation founded on political disagreement; the Constitution safeguards it; and, indeed, the history books often celebrate it. The American people are free to question their government without fear of retribution, to call for political, social, and economic change as long as they do so peacefully rather than encouraging or participating in acts of violence. Generations of protesters from opposite sides of the political spectrum—civil rights activists and white supremacists, abortion rights and pro-life advocates, the Tea Party and Black Lives Matter, and pro-Israeli and pro-Palestinian demonstrators—stand on the shoulders of Angelo Herndon.

Herndon and his legal team forced the Supreme Court to differentiate between a peaceful protest and an imminent threat of violence, as well as to establish free speech and peaceable assembly as essential to a functioning democracy. They entrenched Brandeis's idea that "fear of serious injury cannot alone justify suppression of free speech and assembly" and "it is the function of speech to free men from the bondage of irrational fears." In saving Herndon from a slow death on the chain gang, they prevented the state of Georgia from killing "a man because of the books he reads."

ACKNOWLEDGMENTS

For more than twenty years, I have wanted to write a book about Angelo Herndon. Two excellent books—Herndon's 1937 autobiography, *Let Me Live,* and Charles Martin's 1976 monograph, *The Angelo Herndon Case and Southern Justice*—left me with several lingering questions. What led a Black man reportedly born in Cincinnati to risk his life as a Communist Party activist in the Deep South and an organizer of Atlanta's unemployed white and Black workers during the Great Depression? What inspired prominent lawyers, writers, and intellectuals from all walks of life to rally to his cause? What prompted the Supreme Court, at the height of a constitutional crisis in 1937, to use Herndon's case to safeguard the rights of free speech and peaceable assembly? What happened to Herndon, an emerging Harlem literary star who inspired Langston Hughes, Richard Wright, and Ralph Ellison, and why did Herndon die in obscurity in 1997?

As usual, I'm indebted to dozens of talented librarians and archivists across the country starting with my home institution, Georgetown Law. The Georgetown Law Library staff past and present, including Jennifer Krombach, Valerie Larrieu, Hannah Miller-Kim, Maureen Moran, Thanh Nguyen, Leah Prescott, Carole Prietto, Yelena Rodriguez, Erie Taniuchi, and Austin Williams, never tired of my persistent requests for books, microfilm, digitization, electronic database access, or genealogical research assistance. They went above and beyond for me and never said no.

The historians, librarians, and archivists at the Library of Congress Manuscript Division are so friendly and knowledgeable about their collections. Barbara Bair, Adrienne Cannon, Loretta Deaver, Patrick Kerwin, Bruce Kirby, Mutahara Mobashar, Ryan Reft, Kristen Reichenbach, Edith Sandler, Lara Szypszak, Kerrie Williams, and Lewis Wyman helped me with the NAACP Papers, Ralph Ellison Papers, and the papers of numerous Supreme Court justices. At the Harvard Law School Historical and Special Collections Library, Lesley Schoenfeld helped me access a small collection of Ben Davis Jr.'s papers. At the Supreme Court of the United States, curator Matthew Hofstedt provided me with copies of the justices' docket books from several cases from the 1930s, including Herndon's.

One of the joys of this project was visiting archives I had never been to, learning about historical figures through collections I had never seen, and meeting librarians and archivists I had never met. At the Schomburg Center for Research in Black Culture, associate chief librarian Maira Liriano, Bridgett Pride, and the staff ably assisted me with the International Labor Defense Papers, Herndon Papers and Collection, Ben Davis Jr. Papers, Gerald Horne Papers on Ben Davis Jr., Richard Moore Papers, and several other collections and documents, including the only extant copy of the final volume of the *Negro Quarterly*. At the Tamiment Library and Wagner Labor Archives at New York University, Peter Filardo, Malia Guyer-Stevens, Michael Koncewicz, and their colleagues repeatedly helped me with the *Daily Worker* Collection, Carol Weiss King FOIA Collection, and the papers of other members of the radical left. At the Stuart A. Rose Manuscript, Archives and Rare Book Library at Emory University, Kathleen E. Shoemaker and her colleagues assisted me with the Louise Thompson Patterson Papers, Glenn W. Rainey Papers, and Raoul Family Papers. At the Yale Manuscripts and Archives at Sterling and Beinecke libraries, my friend Michelle Light and the staff assisted me with the C. Vann Woodward Papers, Langston Hughes Papers, and Richard Wright

Papers. The New York Public Library Manuscripts, Archives, and Rare Books Division staff helped me access the papers of Whitney North Seymour Sr.

Numerous other archivists, librarians, and private individuals helped me access collections and photographs, including Richard Peuser at the National Archives II in Greenbelt, Maryland; archivists at National Archives I in Washington, D.C., for the Supreme Court clerk's office files; Glenn Longacre at the National Archives in Chicago for finding Herndon's federal civil lawsuit; Julius Machnikowski of the Cook County Criminal Archives for finding Herndon's criminal trial records; Kirsten Carter, Virginia Lewick, and Kevin R. Thomas at the FDR Library; Paul Crater, Jena Jones, Serena McCracken, and the Atlanta History Center staff; Irina Kandarasheva at the Columbia Law Library; Tara Craig and the staff at the Columbia University Manuscripts and Archives for access to the Herbert Wechsler Papers and Walter Gellhorn Papers; Tim Hodgdon and the staff at the University of North Carolina's Wilson Library for access to interviews with C. Vann Woodward and a master's thesis on Herndon; Brea Johnson at the Moorland-Spingarn Research Center at Howard University for access and scans from the Charles Hamilton Houston Papers; Rachel Minetti of the Georgia Historical Society; Hendry Miller at the State of Georgia Archives for access to the Herndon trial transcripts; David A. Olson at the Columbia Oral History office; Allison Reynolds of the Georgia Tech Library Archives; Billie Jo Kaufman and John M. Perkins at Mercer Law School; the Rubenstein Library at Duke University; Linda M. Evans at the Henderson State University Archives; Derek Gray at the D.C. Public Library; Mary Linnemann of the Hargrett Rare Book and Manuscript Library at the University of Georgia; Jill Severn of the Richard B. Russell Library for Political Research and Studies at the University of Georgia; Oyinda Omoloja of the *Baltimore Afro-American* Archives; Tony Pecinovsky at the *People's World*; Michelle Victoria Asci at the Georgia State University Special Collections and Archives; Christiana Newton at Getty Images; Tricia Gesner at AP Images; Roon Brown for permission to publish her grandfather Robert Disraeli's photograph of Herndon and Ben Davis Jr.; Alison Jakobovic at Random House; Donn Zaretsky representing the estate of Ralph and Fanny Ellison; and Abigail, Liz, and Sam Seymour for information about Whitney North Seymour Sr.

My brilliant and talented Georgetown Law students assisted me with research and fact-checking. Some even visited archives in Atlanta, New York, and Washington, D.C. Thanks to Aaron Cheese, Juli Dajci, Lilly Gaines, Josh Goode, Oge Maduike, Nat Sherrick, Jordan Michael Terry, and Tinesha Zandamela for all their hard work and dedication to this project.

Betsy Kuhn, Georgetown Law's secret weapon, edited this manuscript prior to submission and proofread it prior to publication. The book is better because of Betsy's discerning edits, gift for narrative storytelling, and requests for more historical and legal context. Special thanks to John Barrett, Ben Kerschberg, Linda Snyder, and Kyu Ho Youm for proofreading the book.

My colleague David Vladeck is the best FOIA lawyer an author could ever have. He successfully sued the National Archives and Federal Bureau of Investigation to gain access to Angelo Herndon's rich, multivolume FBI file. Vladeck and members of Georgetown Law's Civil Litigation Clinic spent hundreds of hours on my case. Special thanks to scholars and journalists, including Adam Goldman of the *New York Times*, Peniel E. Joseph of the University of Texas, and Nedra Rhone of the *Atlanta Journal-Constitution*, for submitting affidavits and writing about the historical importance of the FBI's surveillance of Herndon from the 1930s until 1972. At this writing, litigation is still pending over the redaction of the names of confidential FBI informants who in the early 1940s revealed Herndon's disagreements with the Communist Party over his publication of the *Negro Quarterly* and his draft status. Thanks again, David, for all the time you've spent on this litigation.

I am indebted to several members of the Braxton family for generously sharing their time and memories. Angelo P. Braxton, Herndon's eighty-six-year-old nephew and namesake and the son of Leroy Braxton, spoke with me on several occasions and recalled distant memories of his uncle and grandmother. Angelo P. Braxton's daughter, Eva Braxton, connected me with family historian Wilma Braxton. Wilma Braxton, Herndon's niece and Leo Braxton's daughter, provided me with insights into her father's relationship with Herndon.

Several scholars shared source material with me. No one was more generous than historian Charles H. Martin, author of *Angelo Herndon and Southern Justice*. Professor Martin spoke with me several times; shared his typewritten notes of interviews with Whitney North Seymour, Walter Gellhorn, and prosecutor Walter LeCraw; and alerted me to files he had donated to Georgia State University. I am so grateful for the well-documented research in Professor Martin's book and for his willingness to help me. Esteemed southern historian James C. Cobb, author of the 2022 biography *C. Vann Woodward: America's Historian*, shared with me a copy of Woodward's 1951 Naval Criminal Investigatory Service File. Historian Robin D. G. Kelley, author of the groundbreaking book *Hammer and Hoe*, encouraged me to write about Herndon; Kelley's more recent writings confirmed for me that Herndon was the product of Alabama sharecroppers and was not born in Cincinnati. Other scholars provided advice and expertise, including John Callahan on the Ralph Ellison Papers, Anne S. Emanuel on Elbert Parr Tuttle, Robert Goldstein, Gerald Horne on Ben Davis Jr., Maurice Isserman on the Communist Party USA, Lawrence Jackson on Ralph Ellison and the *Negro Quarterly*, Erik S. McDuffie, Neil Skene, Robert Thompson, and Anders Walker on Herbert Wechsler.

Two legendary historians sparked my interest in writing about Angelo Herndon. As a sophomore in the late Raymond Gavins's introductory Afro-American History class at Duke University, I read eminent southern historian Dan T. Carter's book *Scottsboro: A*

Tragedy of the American South. Originally published in 1970, Carter's book chronicled infighting between lawyers for the NAACP and the communist-backed ILD during the decades-long efforts to overturn the wrongful convictions of the nine black youths falsely accused of raping two white women on an Alabama train. James Goodman's 1994 book, *Stories of Scottsboro*, showed me a new way of writing narrative history and inspired me to structure the chapters of my book around the life stories of the people who fought to overturn Herndon's conviction. Both Carter and Goodman read my entire manuscript and offered valuable insights and feedback. I am so honored that they took the time to make me a better historian.

In addition to Dan Carter and Jim Goodman, I thank my dream team of Steve Bright, Dan Ernst, Laura Kalman, Mike Klarman, Mike Seidman, and Mark Tushnet for reading every word of the book and for providing detailed criticism. Your willingness to "be honest and unmerciful," in the words of Philip Seymour Hoffman's character Lester Bangs in the movie *Almost Famous*, means so much to me. Georgetown Law's dean, Bill Treanor, a talented historian in his own right, provided generous financial support for my research. Melanie Hudgens helped all along the way, and Whitney Carr processed numerous reimbursement requests. My friends and colleagues at Georgetown Law offered encouragement and friendship that sustains me.

My agent, Flip Brophy of Sterling Lord Literistic, has championed my work for more than twenty years. I am fortunate to be Flip's client but more important to be her friend. Flip, Jessica Friedman, and their colleagues at Sterling Lord have been incredibly helpful and supportive of my career.

John Glusman is the editor every writer dreams of having. He fights for my work, tells me hard truths, laughs with me about life's absurdities, and, most important of all, makes my books better. What more could a writer ask for? Huge thanks to John, his talented colleague Helen Thomaides, copy editor Trent Duffy, project editor Robert Byrne, and everyone at W. W. Norton for publishing this book.

My family pays the biggest price for my obsessive work on my books. My amazing wife, Shelby, and my joyful children, Lily and Max, are the loves of my life. Thanks for putting up with me even when it is not always easy. Special thanks to the rest of my cheering section: my parents, Linda and Harry Snyder; in-laws, Jack and Donna Hunt; my brother, Ivan (the American history buff to whom this book is dedicated), his wife, Tamara, and my nieces, Maya and Elana; and my sister-in-law, Beth, and her husband, Darren.

Finally, to Angelo Herndon. Thank you for your courage in fighting for your rights to free speech and peaceable assembly and for protecting essential aspects of American democracy. I hope I have done your story justice.

Brad Snyder
Washington, D.C.
March 24, 2024

NOTES

ABBREVIATIONS

AC	*Atlanta Constitution*
ACLUP	American Civil Liberties Union Papers, Princeton University
ADW	*Atlanta Daily World*
AH	Angelo Herndon
AHP	Angelo Herndon Papers
AJ	*Atlanta Journal*
BAA	*Baltimore Afro-American*
BaltSun	*Baltimore Sun*
BJD	Benjamin J. Davis Jr.
BN	*Birmingham News*
BP	*Birmingham Post*
CCFH	*Communist Councilman from Harlem*, by Benjamin J. Davis (1969)
CDef	*Chicago Defender*
CHH	Charles Hamilton Houston
CHHP	Charles Hamilton Houston Papers, Howard University
CICP	Commission for Interracial Cooperation Papers
COH	Columbia Oral History
CT	*Chicago Tribune*
CVW	C. Vann Woodward
CVWL	*The Letters of C. Vann Woodward*, edited by Michael O'Brien (2013)
CVWP	C. Vann Woodward Papers, Yale University Papers
CWK	Carol Weiss King
DW	*Daily Worker*
FF	Felix Frankfurter
FFLC	Felix Frankfurter Papers, Library of Congress
HFS	Harlan Fiske Stone

ILDP   International Labor Defense Papers, Schomburg Center for Research in
              Black Culture
Int.   Interview
LDB   Louis D. Brandeis
LML   *Let Me Live*, by Angelo Herndon (1937)
NAACPP   NAACP Papers, Library of Congress
NARA   National Archives and Records Administration
NJG   *Norfolk Journal and Guide*
NM   *New Masses*
NYA   *New York Age*
NYAN   New York *Amsterdam News*
NYHT   New York *Herald Tribune*
NYT   *New York Times*
NYWT   *New York World-Telegram*
OH   Oral history
PC   *Pittsburgh Courier*
PI   *Philadelphia Inquirer*
PT   *Philadelphia Tribune*
RE   Ralph Ellison
REP   Ralph Ellison Papers, Library of Congress
RGASPI   Russian State Archive of Social and Political History, Files of the Com-
              munist Party of the USA in the Comintern Archives
RNB   Roger Nash Baldwin
SA; SAC   Special Agent; Special Agent in Charge
SW   *Southern Worker*
WashTrib   *Washington Tribune*
WES   *Washington Evening Star*
WLHP   William LePre Houston Papers, Library of Congress
WNS   Whitney North Seymour Sr.
WNSP   Whitney North Seymour Papers, New York Public Library
WP   *Washington Post*
YCKWC   *You Cannot Kill the Working Class*, by Angelo Herndon (1934)

Introduction

xi   The stench of feces: *LML*, 200–201. AH is commonly referred to as a nineteen-year-
     old, but he was born in 1914, not 1913. See note to chapter 1, "May 6, 1914."
xii "without bread" & "Hunger and misery": *AC*, 6/19/1932, 1A. See *AC*, 6/21/1932,
     1, 2.
xii days of rumors: *AJ*, 6/5/1932, 1, 11; *AC*, 6/5/1932, 3A; *AJ*, 6/9/1932, 27; *AJ*, 6/12/1932,
     3; *AC*, 6/12/1932, 3C; *AC*, 6/17/1932, 1, 8.

xii   "Thousands of us" & "no starving families" & "show this faker": Document no. 30, October Term 1934 U.S. Supreme Court Record, 123–24. See Otto Hall, "Report on the Situation in Atlanta," n.d., pp. 1–4, RGASPI, fond 515, reel 255, delo 3311.

xii   about 150 white and Black: Document no. 31, October Term 1934 U.S. Supreme Court Record, 124. Sources vary on the size of the crowd: *AC*, 7/1/1932, 3 (150); *AC*, 7/2/1932, 2 (300); *DW*, 7/9/1932, 6, and *YCKWC*, 24 (both about 1000); Nanny Washburn, *75 Years of Struggle! The Life of Nanny Washburn* (1975), 9.

xii   "They had come to town": Washburn, *75 Years of Struggle!*, 9. See Nanny L. Washburn Int. by Clifford M. Kuhn, 12/8/1978, Atlanta History Center; Clifford M. Kuhn, Harlon E. Joye, and E. Bernard West, *Living Atlanta: An Oral History of the City, 1914–1948* (Athens: University of Georgia Press, 1990), 206–7.

xiii   white protesters & no money: *DW*, 7/9/1932, 6; *AC*, 7/2/1932, 2; *AJ*, 6/30/1932, 8.

xiii   The police stood nearby: *DW*, 7/9/1932, 6; *AC*, 7/10/1932, 27.

xiii $6000: *AC*, 7/2/1932, 1.

xiii   "While we have gained" & "The biggest surprise": Document No. 31, October Term 1934 U.S. Supreme Court Record, 124–26.

xiii   Two police officers & John A. Boykin & they searched: *LML*, 193; *YCKWC*, 24; October Term 1934 U.S. Supreme Court Record, 56–60, 64–68.

xiv   small, unlit room: *LML*, 194–96; *YCKWC*, 25; *DW*, 5/6/1933, 3. The arresting officer denied AH's account of the interrogation: October Term 1934 U.S. Supreme Court Record, 57–59.

Chapter One: The Coal Miner

1   Georgia prosecutors: The Fulton County assistant solicitor testified at trial that AH claimed to have worked in a Lexington coal mine before coming to Atlanta: *ADW*, 7/14/1932, 1; October Term 1934 U.S. Supreme Court Record, 61.

2   "Cincinnati Negro": *WP*, 1/18/1933, 3. In autobiographical accounts, AH erases his family's sharecropping roots in Bullock County, changes names of relatives and friends, and misdates important events: *YCKWC*, 5–6; *LML*. Many details have been corroborated by newspaper and other primary sources. Some, however, are unconfirmable. I have provided as much documentation as possible and have added to the standard account of AH's early life: Charles H. Martin, *The Angelo Herndon Case and Southern Justice* (1976), 8–9. But see Robin D. G. Kelley, "The Great Depression," in *Four Hundred Souls*, ed. Ibram X. Kendi and Keisha N. Blain (2021), 293 (recognizing AH's Alabama roots and questionable Cincinnati origin story).

2   Bullock County: 1910 Census, Alabama, Union Church, Bullock County, E.D. 43, p. 10B, 5/7/1910, 8251, line 98 (listing Paul and Hattie Braxton as farmers).

2   vote in 1867: Return of Qualified Voters, Alabama, Bullock County, 1867, Precinct 6, line 5 (listing Paul Braxton).

2   children's children: 1870 Census, Alabama, Bullock County, Union Church, Roll M5_4, p. 118A, line 32 (Paul Braxton); 1880 Census, Alabama, Bullock County, Bruceville, E.D. 31, p. 34B, line 40 (Paul's son Hilliard); 1880 Census, Alabama, Bullock County, Union Church, Non-Population Schedule 2, E.D. 1149, p. 14B, line 3 (listing Bird H. Braxsam as a corn tenant farmer of thirty acres); 1900 Census, Alabama, Bullock County, Union Church, E.D. 40, p. 2B, line 67 (Hilliard's son Paul); 1880 Census, Alabama, Bullock County, Union Church, E.D. 31, p. 21a,

line 49 (Frank Herndon as farmer); 1880 Census, Alabama, Bullock County, Union Church, Non-Population Schedule 2, E.D. 1159, p. 13A, line 4 (thirty acres); 1900 Census, Alabama, Bullock County, Union Church, E.D. 40, p. 5B, line 54 (thirty acres); *CDef*, 9/22/1934, 4 (discussing life of Black Bullock County sharecroppers and tenant farmers).

2   **December 26, 1905:** Alabama Marriage Record, 12/26/1905, Bullock County, Alabama.

2   **"high cheekbones" & "a Black Cherokee":** Herndon's nephew Angelo P. Braxton Int. by author, 6/21/2023. *LML*, 3 (describing her as having Native American and white ancestry).

2   **May 6, 1914:** AH claimed he was born in Cincinnati on May 6, 1913, based on his family Bible: *YCKWC*, 6; *LML*, 3. But Alabama birth records list a son as born in Union Church, Alabama, to Paul and Hattie Braxton on May 6, 1914: Alabama Birth Certificate, 5/6/1914, Alabama Births and Christenings, 1881–1930; 1920 Census, Alabama, Bullock County, Union Church, E.D. 44, p. 1A, line 6 (confirming Alabama birth and 1914 birth year of "Inglo Braxton").

In 1937, AH applied for a passport and told the passport office that he had been born in Cincinnati at 304 Cutter Street and included a sworn statement from his mother, Harriet, and a first cousin, James Green: SAC WFO to FBI Dir., 7/1/1968, Herndon FBI File, 100-WFO-47734, 4.

In 1956, however, the Immigration and Naturalization Service (INS) investigated whether AH was an American citizen and concluded that he had been born in Bullock County, Alabama. The INS interviewed AH's older brother Leo, who showed the INS investigator his own Bullock County birth certificate from July 15, 1912. Leo swore under oath that Angelo was born there two years later (confirming the 5/6/1914 birth record from Bullock County), and that the midwife was a woman named Linda Baltimore. Herndon's mother, Harriet, also told the INS that Herndon had been born in Bullock County, but not under oath: INS Investigative Report of Angelo Herndon, 2/7/1956, 2–3, Herndon FBI File, 100-HQ-18143, vol. 1, 87–88.

2   **mother's narrow eyes:** *LML*, 37.

2   **six days later:** Paul Braxton, Death Certificate, 3/8/1917, Hamilton County, file 18421, Ohio Death Records, 1908–57. The burial was listed as taking place in Milstead, Alabama, on 3/14/1917.

2   **the train to take his father's body:** *LML*, 26–34.

2   **religious family & baptized at age twelve:** *LML*, 4–11, 20–25.

3   **might be able to stay in school:** *LML*, 12–16, 36–37. Leo Braxton recalled they attended the Oak Grove School: INS Investigative Report of Angelo Herndon, 2/7/1956, 3 (based on interview with Leo Braxton).

3   **Angelo ran away & Lexington, Kentucky, mine:** *YCKWC*, 6–9; *LML*, 38–48; October Term 1934 U.S. Supreme Court Record, 61.

3   **DeBardeleben Coal and Iron Company:** Robert H. Woodrum, *"Everybody Was Black Down There"* (2007), 16, 53.

3   **company town in Sipsey:** Brian Kelly, *Race, Class, and Power in the Alabama Coalfields, 1908–1921* (2001), 62, 138.

3   **live with an aunt and uncle:** 1930 Census, Alabama, Jefferson County, Birmingham, E.D. 37-2, p. 41B, line 55 (listing fifteen-year-old Eugene Braxton as a coal miner living with Sallie Herndon); 1928 Birmingham City Directory, 560, and 1930 Birmingham City Directory, 418 (Alex and Sallie Herndon). Herndon's account refers to Aunt Catherine; it was Aunt Sallie: *LML*, 48. Angelo's mother moved to

Birmingham, worked as a laundress, and soon lived next door: 1929 Birmingham City Directory, 245, and 1930 Birmingham City Directory, 125, 1124.

3   **Blacks made up a majority of Birmingham's unskilled workforce:** Robin D. G. Kelley, *Hammer and Hoe: Alabama Communists During the Great Depression* (1990), 1–10; Woodrum, *"Everybody Was Black Down There,"* 27–28.

3   **Leo found work:** *LML*, 48.

3   **life of peonage & Lock 18 & Goodyear Rubber Company:** *LML*, 49–56; *YCKWC*, 9. Herndon's account refers to Lock 18 on the Alabama River: *LML*, 51. It was in fact the Coosa River: *Dothan (AL) Eagle*, 3/18/1927, 1; *Dothan (AL) Eagle*, 5/11/1927, 4.

4   **The Depression cost American workers:** David M. Kennedy, *Freedom from Fear: The American People in Depression and War, 1929* (1999), 10–42.

4   **hit Birmingham's mines:** Kelley, *Hammer and Hoe*, 9–10.

4   **Tennessee Coal, Iron, and Railroad Company:** Ronald L. Lewis, *Black Coal Miners in America: Race, Class, and Community Conflict, 1780–1980* (Lexington: University Press of Kentucky, 1987), 69; Woodrum, *"Everybody Was Black Down There,"* 27–29; Kelley, *Hammer and Hoe*, 5.

4   **Docena mine & Jimmy was electrocuted:** *LML*, 57–64; *YCKWC*, 9–11. It is difficult to pinpoint the exact date of the electrocution in the records of Alabama mining deaths. AH often changed the names of friends and relatives, and his timeline was off by a few years. At the Docena mine, a Black miner, loader C. D. Reed, was electrocuted on October 3, 1929. From 1925 to 1930, twenty-nine Black Alabama miners died of electrocution: Alabama Coal Mine Fatalities, 1898–1938, Birmingham Public Library.

4   **"Would you rather fight":** *LML*, 73; *YCKWC*, 12. The handbill slogan was usually "Fellow workers, fight—don't starve": Nell Irvin Painter, *The Narrative of Hosea Hudson: His Life as a Negro Communist in the South* (1979), 373.

5   **Unemployed Councils:** Harvey Klehr, *The Heyday of American Communism: The Depression Decade* (1984), 49–68; Daniel J. Leab, "'United We Eat': The Creation and Organization of the Unemployed Councils in 1930," *Labor History*, 8, no. 3 (Fall 1967): 300–15.

5   **Founded in 1919 & factions and approximately 15,000 members:** Klehr, *The Heyday of American Communism*, 3–10.

5   **Sixth World Congress:** Jay Lovestone, "The Sixth World Congress of Communist International," *The Communist*, 11/1928, pp. 659–75; Kelley, *Hammer and Hoe*, 13–14.

5   **headquarters of District 17:** Kelley, *Hammer and Hoe*, 14–15.

5   **May 22, 1930, & "industrial and economical equality":** *BN*, 5/23/1930, 28; Kelley, *Hammer and Hoe*, 239n6 (identifying May 22 as first meeting and with pseudonyms "Frank Williams" for Frank Burns, "Tom Wilson" for Tom Johnson, and "John Lindley" for Walter Lewis, from *LML*, 75–78); *LML*, 73–80; *YCKWC*, 11–12.

6   **Tom Johnson:** Tom Johnson, *"The Reds in Dixie": Who Are the Communists and What Do They Fight for in the South?* (New York: Workers Library Publishers, 1935); Kelley, *Hammer and Hoe*, 14–15; John Haynes, "What Became of Tom Johnson?," H-Net, 5/16/2022, https://networks.h-net.org/node/6077/discussions/10256791/what-became-tom-johnson.

6   **follow-up meeting, and began immersing himself:** *BN*, 5/28/1930, 17; *LML*, 81–83.

6   **the devil's work:** *LML*, 80.

6   **his first peaceful protest:** *Investigation of Communist Propaganda: Hearings Before a Special Committee to Investigate Communist Activities in the United States of the*

House of Representatives, 71st Cong., 2nd sess., pt. 6, vol. 1 (1930), p. 92 (700 to 800 people); *BP*, 5/30/1930, in ibid., p. 171 (300 people); *LML*, 83–86 (500 people).

6   Oscar W. Adams: *BP*, 5/30/1930; *LML*, 85–86.

6   burned in effigy: *BN*, 6/20/1930, 1.

7   criminal anarchy law: *BP*, 6/19/1930, and *BN*, 6/19/1930, both in *Investigation of Communist Propaganda*, pt. 6, vol. 1, pp. 163–65.

7   declared the speeches "harmless": *BP*, 6/24/1930, in *Investigation of Communist Propaganda*, pt. 6, vol. 1, pp. 162–63.

7   two whites and three Blacks: *BN*, 6/29/1930, 1.

7   "Red hoodlums" & "Communism must be wiped out": *LML*, 92; ibid., 92–95; *YCKWC*, 16–17; *DW*, 7/5/1930, 1, 5.

7   Trade Union Unity League: Kelley, *Hammer and Hoe*, 60; Painter, *Narrative of Hosea Hudson*, 372–74.

7   the city's Black and white miners: Woodrum, *"Everybody Was Black Down There,"* 27–29, 56–57, 60–61.

8   On July 24: *Investigation of Communist Propaganda*, pt. 6, vol. 1, pp. 96–97; Tom Johnson to Secretariat, 7/27/1930, pp. 6–7, in RGASPI, fond 515, reel 151, delo 1960; Tom Johnson to Sam Darcy, 7/27/1930, p. 1, in ibid., reel 162, delo 2150; Tom Johnson to Sam Darcy, 7/30/1930, in ibid.; *DW*, 8/1/1930, 2; *DW*, 8/2/1930, 1; *SW*, 8/16/1930, 1, 3 (placing the arrest with Carr on July 26 near Ensley); Crusader News Agency Press Release, 8/9/1930, in ACLUP, vol. 405, p. 3; *PC*, 8/23/1930, 5; *LML*, 96–102.

8   his conviction was dismissed: *SW*, 1/17/1931, 2; Rosenthal and Rosenthal to Kathryn Fenn, 3/13/1931, in ACLUP, vol. 450, p. 65.

8   September 1: *Investigation of Communist Propaganda*, pt. 6, vol.1, pp. 97–98; Hyman Gordon to Secretariat, 9/1/1930, pp. 1–2, in RGASPI, fond 515, reel 154, delo 1996; Tom Johnson to [William] Weiner, 9/2/1930, p. 1, in ibid.; Tom Johnson to Sam Darcy, 9/4/1930, in ibid.; Tom Johnson to Secretariat, 9/15/1930, p. 3, in ibid., fond 515, reel 151, delo 1960; *DW*, 9/3/1930, 2; *DW*, 9/4/1930, 2; *SW*, 9/6/1930, 4; Crusader News Agency Press Release, 9/8/1930, p. 4, in ACLUP, vol. 405, p. 9; *SW*, 9/13/1930, 1; Herndon FBI record, 3/4/1968, Herndon FBI File, 100-HQ-18143, vol. 1, 196–97 (listing Braxton as arrested in Birmingham on 9/2/1930 and released from city jail).

8   "it is feared": *SW*, 9/6/1930, 1.

8   "dog house": *LML*, 110. See ibid., 105–13.

8   "Dear Sir": *SW*, 9/27/1930, 1. In his autobiography, AH misremembered it as the *Daily Worker*: *LML*, 113.

9   "Eugene Braxton, colored": *Investigation of Communist Propaganda*, pt. 6, vol. 1, p. 198.

9   Chattanooga getting indoctrinated: *Investigation of Communist Propaganda*, pt. 6, vol. 1, p. 98; District 17 Minutes, 9/29/1930, p. 3, RGASPI, fond 515, reel 162, delo 2149.

9   February 5: Tom Johnson to Earl Browder, 2/7/1931, pp. 1–2, in RGASPI, fond 515, reel 176, delo 2322; Tom Johnson to Rudy Baker, 2/12/1931, in ibid.; Tom Johnson to Rudy Baker, 2/18/1931, p. 2, in ibid.; *SW*, 2/14/1931, 1.

9   Camden, Alabama: *LML*, 129–47. AH's memoir mistakenly says Camden County. It's probably Camden, Alabama, which he describes as Governor Meek Miller's hometown, in Wilcox County. See *SW*, 3/7/1931, 1 (article by "E. Braxton" reporting on Feb. 28 meeting with sharecroppers in Alberta, Alabama); Kelley, *Hammer and Hoe*, 247–48n13.

9   "He is a fine boy": Johnson to Baker, 2/18/1931, p. 2.

9   Angelo to New Orleans: *SW*, 5/16/1931, 1; *SW*, 5/23/1931, 1 (naming both Hern-
        don and Braxton); *LML*, 115–18; Herndon FBI record, 3/4/1968 (listing Herndon as
        arrested on 5/8/1931, held as a "suspicious person," residing at 308 Chartres Street);
        SW, 2/14/1931, 1 (listing 308 Chartres Street as the union hall and site of Unem-
        ployed Council meetings).

10   nine Black youths: James Goodman, *Stories of Scottsboro* (1994), 3–18; Dan T. Car-
        ter, *Scottsboro: A Tragedy of the American South* (1979), 3–50.

10   International Labor Defense: Charles H. Martin, "Communists and Blacks: The
        ILD and the Angelo Herndon Case," *Journal of Negro History* 64, no. 2 (Spring
        1979): 131–41; Goodman, *Stories of Scottsboro*, 24–31.

11   In 1909, a coalition of Black activists: Patricia Sullivan, *Lift Every Voice: The
        NAACP and the Making of the Civil Rights Movement* (2009), 1–24; Susan D.
        Carle, *Defining the Struggle: National Organizing for Racial Justice, 1880–1915*
        (2013), 249–86; Susan D. Carle, "Race, Class, and Legal Ethics in the Early NAACP
        (1910–1920)," *Law and History Review* 20, no. 1 (2002): 97–146.

11   *Moore v. Dempsey*: 261 U.S. 86 (1923); Brad Snyder, *The House of Truth: A Washing-
        ton Political Salon and the Foundations of American Liberalism* (2017), 353–54.

11   White believed that the ILD had duped: Walter White to Robert W. Bagnall and
        Herbert J. Seligman, 5/3/1931, pp. 1, 4–5, in NAACPP, I-D-68, reel 2, pp. 825, 826–
        27; Walter White to Clarence Darrow, 4/10/1931, in ibid., p. 620; Walter White, "The
        Negro and the Communists," *Harper's Magazine*, 12/1931, pp. 12–13, in NAACPP,
        I-D-71, reel 5, p. 131; Goodman, *Stories of Scottsboro*, 32–38; Carter, *Scottsboro*,
        51–103.

11   In New Orleans, he attended: Tom Johnson to Rudy [Baker], 6/4/1931, in RGASPI,
        fond 515, reel 176, delo 2322; *LML*, 118–24.

12   "You say you will let me": *DW*, 6/9/1931, 1. See *LML*, 124–27; Harry Haywood,
        Black Bolshevik: Autobiography of an Afro-American Communist (1978), 362–63;
        Sheldon Avery, *Up from Washington: William Pickens and the Negro Struggle for
        Equality, 1900–1954* (Newark: University of Delaware Press, 1989), 126–28.

12   Shades Mountain: *BN*, 8/5/1931, 1–2; Melanie S. Morrison, *Murder on Shades
        Mountain: The Legal Lynching of Willie Peterson and the Struggle for Justice in Jim
        Crow Birmingham* (2018), 15–18; Kelley, *Hammer and Hoe*, 82–90.

12   "reign of terror": *SW*, 8/15/1931, 1.

13   Within three days of the shootings: *LML*, 148–64; *YCKWC*, 20–21; *BN*, 8/6/1931,
        1; *DW*, 8/10/1934, 3; *DW*, 8/11/1931, 1; *DW*, 8/12/1931, 3; *DW*, 8/15/31, 5; *SW*,
        8/15/1931, 2; *PC*, 8/15/1931, 16; *NM*, 8/21/1934, 12.

13   vagrancy. He was fined $25: *SW*, 8/22/1931, 1; *SW*, 8/29/1931, 1; *SW*, 9/5/1931, 1.

13   Willie Peterson: Morrison, *Murder on Shades Mountain*, 20–22, 55–59, 70, 178–79,
        189–92.

13   It took Angelo several weeks: *LML*, 165.

13   In September 1931: Harris Gilbert to Tom Johnson, 9/21/1931, in RGASPI, fond
        515, reel 176, delo 2322 ("Gene's address is—Angelo Herndon [name he is using]
        Box 339 Atlanta").

13   focal point of civil rights activism: Tomiko Brown-Nagin, *Courage to Dissent:
        Atlanta and the Long History of the Civil Rights Movement* (2011); Glenda Eliza-
        beth Gilmore, *Defying Dixie: The Radical Roots of Civil Rights, 1919–1950* (2008);
        Karen Ferguson, *Black Politics in New Deal Atlanta* (2002).

13   Black Shirts: "The Black Shirts Meet Defeat (A Confidential Statement)," 1930, pp.
        1–8, CICP, reel 4, folder 70; John Hammond Moore, "Communists and Fascists in a

Southern City: Atlanta," *South Atlantic Quarterly* 67, no. 3 (Summer 1968): 437–54; *LML*, 165–67.

14   an old slave insurrection law: 1816 Ga. Code, Fourth Division, §§1, 4, at 146; 1817 Ga. Code, Third Division, §§1, 4, at 94–95; 1833 Ga. Code, Third Division, §4, at 147.

14   John T. Gibson & failed to specify: Gibson v. State, 38 Ga. 571, 571–73 (1869); *AC*, 7/1/1869, 4; Martin, *The Angelo Herndon Case*, 21; Maryan Soliman, "Inciting Free Speech and Racial Equality: The Communist Party and Georgia's Insurrection Statute in the 1930s" (PhD diss., University of Pennsylvania, 2014), 38–40.

14   Georgia legislators revised the law: 1866 Ga. Code, §§3–4, at 152–53; 1871 Ga. Code, at 19–20.

14   Corday Harris: *AC*, 9/1/1875, 1; *Georgia Weekly Telegraph*, 9/7/1875, 1; *Augusta Chronicle*, 9/11/1875, 1; *AC*, 9/12/1875, 2.

14   William Pollard: *Macon News*, 11/18/1916, 1; *AC*, 11/25/1916, 5; *AC*, 11/29/1916, 9; *AC*, 12/2/1916, 1; *AC*, 12/5/1916, 1; *AC*, 3/16/1917, 9; *AC*, 5/1/1917, 4; Charles H. Martin, "The Angelo Herndon Case and Southern Justice," in *American Political Trials*, ed. Michal R. Belknap (1994), 162.

14   Atlanta Six: Martin, *The Angelo Herndon Case*, 19–29; Gilmore, *Defying Dixie*, 115–17; Soliman, "Inciting Free Speech and Racial Equality," 28–70; Charles Henry Martin, "The Angelo Herndon Case and Georgia Justice, 1930–1937" (PhD diss., Tulane University, 1972), 1–38.

14   circulating insurrectionary papers: 1866 Ga. Code, Art. 3, §58.

15   "the terror": Hall, "Report on the Situation in Atlanta," 1.

15   attacking one another: Hall, "Report on the Situation in Atlanta," 2; Sol Harper to Robert Minor, 4/16/1932, pp. 1–3, in RGASPI, fond 515, reel 225, delo 2927; AH to Clarence Hathaway, 5/12/1932, in ibid.; AH to Clarence Hathaway, 5/25/1932, in ibid.

15   "very lazy streak": Harry Jackson to Clarence Hathaway, 5/23/1932, p. 2, in RGASPI, fond 515, reel 225, delo 2927.

15   charges of his own: AH to Earl Browder, 6/5/1932, in RGASPI, fond 515, reel 225, delo 2927.

15   William Z. Foster: Edward P. Johanningsmeier, *Forging American Communism: The Life of William Z. Foster* (1994), 261–66.

15   first mass interracial demonstration: *DW*, 7/9/1932, 6; Hall, "Report on the Situation in Atlanta," 3.

15   distributed the leaflets: *DW*, 7/9/1932, 6; *LML*, 188–90.

15   could not sleep & an hour early: *LML*, 190–92.

16   hundreds of Black and white workers: Document No. 31, October Term 1934 U.S. Supreme Court Record, 124. Sources vary on the size of the crowd: *AC*, 7/1/1932, 3 (150); *AC*, 7/2/1932, 2 (300); *DW*, 7/9/1932, 6, and *YCKWC*, 24 (both 1000); Nanny Washburn, *75 Years of Struggle! The Life of Nanny Washburn* (1975), 9.

16   the peacefulness of the protest: *LML*, 190–92.

16   reversed their decision: *AC*, 7/2/1932, 1, 2.

16   "considerable prestige" from its "partial victory": *DW*, 7/9/1932, 6.

16   communists should have been more aware: *DW*, 7/9/1932, 6; Hall, "Report on the Situation in Atlanta," 3–4; *LML*, 193.

16   P.O. Box 339: October Term 1934 U.S. Supreme Court Record, 56–59. See *AC*, 7/12/1932, 5.

16   fake electric chair: *DW*, 5/6/1933, 3; *LML*, 195–96; *YCKWC*, 25. The officers denied the use of an electric chair: October Term 1934 U.S. Supreme Court Record, 56–59.

16   John A. Boykin: *LML*, 193.
16   "C-O-M-M-U-N-I-S-T": John Hammond Moore, "The Angelo Herndon Case, 1932–1937," *Phylon* 32, no. 1 (1971): 62.
16   For eleven days: October Term 1934 U.S. Supreme Court Record, 73–74; *AC*, 7/21/1932, 14.
16   He smuggled a letter: *LML*, 201; *YCKWC*, 25; *DW*, 7/15/1932, 32.
16   Oliver C. Hancock: Otto Hall to Earl Browder, 7/21/1932, p. 1, in RGASPI, fond 515, reel 225, delo 2928; Hall, "Report on the Situation in Atlanta," 4.
16   2:30 p.m.: *AC*, 7/21/1932, 14; *ADW*, 7/23/1932, 1A.
16   An all-white grand jury indicted: *LML*, 337–41; October Term 1934 U.S. Supreme Court Record, 5–9.

Chapter Two: Atlanta's Prince

19   On July 12: *AC*, 7/12/1932, 5; *Harlem Liberator*, 5/27/1933, 5; *CCFH*, 53 (misremembering it as June).
19   They talked for two hours: *CCFH*, 53–55.
19   a Black lawyer on the case: William L. Patterson to Charles H. Martin, 5/25/1970, p. 1, in Charles H. Martin Papers (on file with author); Charles H. Martin, *The Angelo Herndon Case and Southern Justice* (1976), 11 (citing 5/25/1970 Patterson letter); Patterson OH, 2/28/1970, 17–18, Ralph J. Bunche OH Collection. On Patterson, see Gerald Horne, *Black Revolutionary: William Patterson and the Globalization of the African American Freedom Struggle* (2013).
20   willing to work for free: Otto Hall to Earl Browder, 7/21/1932, p. 1, in AHP, box 1, folder 1.
20   sat at counsel's table: *ADW*, 7/21/1932, 1.
20   "fire-ball" serves: *ADW*, 1/15/1932, 5.
20   reached the semifinals: *AC*, 7/31/1933, 7.
20   "Atlanta's prince of the Clay Courts": *ADW*, 7/26/1932, 5A.
20   A virtuoso violinist: *Atlanta Independent*, 12/29/1917, 7; *NYAN*, 10/30/1943, A12.
20   society pages: *PC*, 7/10/1926, 6; *CDef*, 4/12/1930, 11; *BAA*, 9/6/1930, A12.
20   He favored tailored suits & took pride & "a gold-headed cane": *BAA*, 11/23/1935, 6.
20   "Fighting Ben" & bricklayer before becoming: *Atlanta Independent*, 12/15/1917, 8; *PC*, 12/8/1928, 5; *CCFH*, 21–30.
20   oust him as national committeeman: *PC*, 2/13/1932, 1; *NYAN*, 6/30/1934, 9; Gerald Horne, *Black Liberation/Red Scare: Ben Davis and the Communist Party* (2021), 18–26.
20   Ben Jr.'s mind: *Harlem Liberator*, 5/27/1933, 5; Horne, *Black Liberation/Red Scare*, 26.
20   Morehouse, he balked at singing Negro spirituals: *DW*, 6/23/1934, 7; *NYAN*, 6/30/1934, 9; *NYAN*, 11/20/1943, 7; *CCFH*, 31–39; Ridgely Torrence, *The Story of John Hope* (New York: Arno, 1969), 238–39; Horne, *Black Liberation/Red Scare*, 28.
21   applied to Amherst: *Atlanta Independent*, 12/6/1923, 7; Ben Davis Jr. Amherst Admission Application, pp. 2–3, Gerald Horne Papers, box 36; Horne, *Black Liberation/Red Scare*, 29–30.
21   C and D grades & only A: Amherst College, Grades, Benjamin J. Davis Jr., Small Materials Collection, Harvard Law School (also in Gerald Horne Papers, box 36); 1925 Amherst College *Olio*, p. 200; Horne, *Black Liberation/Red Scare*, 29.

21   northern racism: *NYAN*, 6/30/1934, 9.

21   Charles Drew & Paul Robeson: *PC*, 10/4/1924, 6; Horne, *Black Liberation/Red Scare*, 30.

21   music club & game at Princeton: *DW*, 8/4/1953, 6; *PC*, 10/4/1924, 6.

21   trolley car: *CCFH*, 40–42; Horne, *Black Liberation/Red Scare*, 29–30.

21   an elite college & one-third: Bruce A. Kimball and Daniel R. Coquillette, *The Intellectual Sword: Harvard Law School, the Second Century* (2020), 160. The admissions policy changed in fall 1927, when undergraduate students at first-tier colleges had to finish in the top third of their class: ibid.

21   lowest passing grade & barely survived: Davis Harvard Law School grades, Gerald Horne Papers, box 36; Horne, *Black Liberation/Red Scare*, 30–31; Erwin N. Griswold, *Ould Fields, New Corne* (1992), 233 (recalling his classmate Davis and admiring his "considerable ability").

21   All male and almost all white: Kimball and Coquillette, *The Intellectual Sword*, 178–89; Kenneth W. Mack, *Representing the Race: The Creation of the Civil Rights Lawyer* (2012), 34–36, 165.

21   Dean Roscoe Pound: *CCFH*, 90–91; Horne, *Black Liberation/Red Scare*, 31. On Pound's deanship at Harvard Law School, see Kimball and Coquillette, *The Intellectual Sword*, 157–63. On the Dunbar Club started by Charles Hamilton Houston, see ibid., 184.

22   an indifferent law student: *CCFH*, 40.

22   retake his trusts exam: BJD to Guy H. Holliday, 5/7/1929, and Guy H. Holliday to BJD, 5/9/1929. Both in Benjamin J. Davis Jr., Small Materials Collection. His original grade in trusts was a 53 (below the D passing grade of 55).

22   *Illustrated Feature Section*: *PC*, 2/18/1933, 10; *CCFH*, 43–44; Horne, *Black Liberation/Red Scare*, 32.

22   January 1932: *AJ*, 1/5/1932, 25; *AC*, 1/6/1932, 17; *PC*, 1/30/1932, A3; *CCFH*, 44.

22   John H. Geer: John Geer Kentucky Death Certificate, 11/12/1946; Will W. Alexander to RNB, 1/24/1933, in ACLUP, vol. 654; *CCFH*, 47–49; Martin, *The Angelo Herndon Case*, 38, 38n5 (based on 3/14/1975 letter from Geer's wife, Mary V. Bennett).

22   smoking a cigar: *AJ*, 4/14/1932, 25; *AC*, 4/15/1932, 14; *ADW*, 4/15/1932, 1; *BAA*, 4/23/1932, 2; *CCFH*, 49–50.

22   stop sign: *ADW*, 8/19/1932, 6A.

22   unhappy with Hancock's strategy: Hall to Browder, 7/21/1932, p. 1 (relaying that Hancock "isn't worth a damn"); Joan Barbour to Acting ILD National Secretary Carl Hacker, 7/26/1932, in RGASPI, fond 515, reel 225, delo 2928, and also in Clarina Michaelson Papers, box 1, folder 13 (describing Hancock's "stupidity or sabotage" in forfeiting the bail money and "laughing about the Herndon case with the judge"); RNB to Will Alexander, 8/1/1932, in CICP, reel 7, folder 143 (describing Hancock as "not competent"); Otto Hall, "Report on the Situation in Atlanta," n.d., pp. 4–5, RGASPI, fond 515, reel 255, delo 3311.

22   H. A. Allen & in late November withdrew: Barbour to Hacker, 7/26/1932 (remarking Allen "seems good" and enclosing "Lawyers in Atlanta, Georgia," with comments); Oliver C. Hancock to Abraham Isserman, 7/27/1932, p. 2, in ACLUP, vol. 564; Clarina Michaelson to Communist Party USA (CPUSA) Secretariat, 8/19/1932, p. 1, in Michaelson Papers, box 1, folder 13 (urging ILD to hire Allen "AT ONCE"); "Political Prisoner, ANGELO HERNDON, 19 years old," p. 1, AHP, box 1, folder 1 (noting Allen off case on Nov. 26); Hall, "Report on the Situation in Atlanta," 6–7;

LML, 215–17; *CCFH*, 55–57; *ADW*, 8/30/1932, 5A; *ADW*, 9/14/1932, 6A; *ADW*, 11/27/1932, 1. On Allen, see Anne Westbrook Green, "H. A. Allen: The Lawyer and the Man," *Journal of Southern Legal History* 16, no. 1 and 2 (2008): 119; Mack, *Representing the Race*, 171.

23   **Equal Protection Clause:** Strauder v. West Virginia, 100 U.S. 303, 310 (1880). But the states could exclude Blacks by establishing other qualifications for jury service: see Benno C. Schmidt Jr., "Juries, Jurisdiction, and Race Discrimination: The Lost Promise of *Strauder v. West Virginia*," *Texas Law Review* 61, no. 8 (1983): 1401.

23   **Maryland's highest court:** Lee v. State, 161 A. 284 (Md. 1932).

23   **$100 retainer:** "Expense Account—Angelo Herndon Case," ca. 9/1933, ACLUP, vol. 654; Hall, "Report on the Situation in Atlanta," 6. ILD national secretary William Patterson claimed that the white lawyer he retained for $800 was fired for refusing to work with Davis: William Patterson to Charles Martin, 5/25/1970, p. 1; Patterson OH, 2/28/1970, 17–18; William L. Patterson, *Ben Davis: Crusader for Freedom and Socialism* (1967), 19, 21. Patterson, however, was referring to Macon lawyer W. A. McClellan, who refused to work with Davis and Geer on the Atlanta Six cases: W. A. McClellan to ACLU, 1/24/1933, pp. 1–2, in ACLUP, vol. 654.

23   **Davis's suggestion & scoring political points:** BJD to RNB, 5/11/1933, p. 1, in ACLUP, vol. 654. Cf. Will Alexander to RNB, 5/1/1933, in ibid. (relaying that Walden denied having been offered the job as Herndon's counsel). Davis, however, heard the story from Walden firsthand: see "Lawyers in Atlanta, Georgia," enclosed in Barbour to Hacker, 7/26/1932, p. 2 (describing Walden as "very able" but "might be in play with bourgeois elements"); NAACP regional field secretary Daisy E. Lampkin to NAACP assistant secretary Roy Wilkins, 2/4/1933, p. 1, in NAACPP, Atlanta Branch Files Apr.–Dec. 1933, reel 10, p. 277.

000   **A. T. Walden & paid Davis's five-dollar fine:** *PC*, 1/30/1932, A3; *ADW*, 4/15/1932, 1; *CCFH*, 45, 49–50. On Walden, see Funeral Program, 7/7/1965, Austen T. Walden Papers, sect. 2, box 2, folder 1; *ADW*, 1/1/1961, 1, 3; J. Clay Smith Jr., *Emancipation: The Making of the Black Lawyer, 1844–1944* (1993), 198–99; Tomiko Brown-Nagin, *Courage to Dissent: Atlanta and the Long History of the Civil Rights Movement* (2011), 1–2; Mack, *Representing the Race*, 154, 166–67, 170–71; David Kenneth Pye, "Complex Relations: An African American Attorney Navigates Jim Crow Atlanta," *Georgia Historical Quarterly* 91, no. 4 (Winter 2007): 453–77.

23   **Atlanta's NAACP branch:** *ADW*, 3/4/1932, 1.

23   **the state's law library:** *ADW*, 9/30/1932, 1A.

24   **27 Club, a private organization:** *ADW*, 10/25/1932, 1. On the 27 Club, see Jesse O. Thomas, *My Story in Black and White* (1967), 114–15.

24   **"a raw deal" & "no isolated case" & "starving":** *Harlem Liberator*, 5/27/1933, 5.

24   **read the communist literature seized:** *DW*, 6/23/1934, 7; *CCFH*, 57–59.

24   **Charles Hamilton Houston:** BJD to CHH, 6/12/1933, in CHHP, box 163-26, folder 9; Mack, *Representing the Race*, 171, 302.

24   **"I think I can handle":** BJD to William Patterson, 10/20/1932, p. 2, in RGASPI, fond 515, reel 226, delo 2929.

24   **Davis prioritized:** BJD to Patterson, 10/20/1932, p. 2.

24   **filthy, inhumane conditions:** *Labor Defender*, 3/1933, 25.

24   **food—peas and bacon & smuggled in medicine:** October Term 1934 U.S. Supreme Court Record, 74–76; AH to William Patterson, 12/16/1932, p. 4, in AHP, box 1, folder 1; *LML*, 205–14.

24   **yearned to leave:** AH to Patterson, 12/16/1932, pp. 1–2.

25   increased to $5000: *ADW*, 11/27/1932, 1; October Term 1934 U.S. Supreme Court Record, 76.

25   filed a writ of habeas corpus: ILD Press Release, 12/5/1932, in ILDP, reel 17, p. 611; *AC*, 12/3/1932, 3; *AC*, 12/4/1932, 22.

25   the prosecution, over the defense's objection: ILD Press Releases, 12/12/1932 and 12/13/1932, in ILDP, reel 17, pp. 612–13; *ADW*, 12/11/1932, pp. 1, 6, in ILDP, reel 16, pp. 903–4; *AC*, 12/11/1932, 14A; *AC*, 12/13/1932, 7; *AC*, 12/14/1932, 15.

25   "Negroes have been systematically": ILD Press Release, 12/15/1932, p. 1, in ILDP, reel 17, p. 615; *BAA*, 12/24/1932, 18; *CDef*, 12/24/1932, 2.

25   "important victory": ILD Press Release, 12/15/1932. See *BAA*, 12/24/1932, 18.

25   seized during raids & "same thing as treason": *Investigation of Communist Propaganda: Hearings Before a Special Committee to Investigate Communist Activities in the United States of the House of Representatives*, 71st Cong., 2nd sess., pt. 6, vol. 1 (1930), pp. 206–7, 210.

25   six foot three and 200 pounds: *CCFH*, 64. On Hudson, see *LML*, 222–23; Sasha Small, "Way Down South," *NM*, 8/20/1935, 12; *AC*, 1/15/1936, 1, 2.

25   "partially bald": *LML*, 222.

26   "flailing his arms": *CCFH*, 66 See *LML*, 222 (describing Hudson was "stretching out his long arms like the blades of a windmill").

26   "one of the most consummate hypocrites": *CCFH*, 64.

26   reduce Herndon's bail to $2500: ILD Press Release, 12/13/1932; *AC*, 12/14/1932, 15; *BAA*, 12/24/1932, 18.

26    $25,000 "so that damn Red": *LML*, 220. See *DW*, 12/26/1932, 1.

26   Herndon was released: *DW*, 12/26/1932, 1; *AC*, 12/29/1932, 3.

26   Two Black Atlanta pharmacists: *LML*, 220; "Political Prisoner, ANGELO HERNDON," p. 1.

26   Davis was impressed: *CCFH*, 57.

26   "The Klan Rides Again": *CCFH*, 62. See "Political Prisoner, ANGELO HERNDON," p. 2 (noting threats to Davis and Geer on 12/10/1932 from seven or eight white men).

26   two Black men & declared another partial victory: October Term 1934 U.S. Supreme Court Record, 55; *ADW*, 1/4/1933, in ILDP, reel 16, p. 926 (first time since 1862); *DW*, 1/4/1933, 1; *DW*, 1/10/1933, 2 (first time since 1872); *BAA*, 1/14/1933, 19 (first time since 1862); *NJG*, 1/21/1933, 14; Martin, *The Angelo Herndon Case*, 36–37.

26   the state's move as a "sham": *ADW*, 1/4/1933; *BAA*, 1/14/1933, 19.

26   packed with more than 100 people: *CCFH*, 62.

26   Viola Montgomery: *DW*, 1/23/1933, 3.

27   lawyers-only railing & Curious white members: *CCFH*, 62.

27   red striped tie: October Term 1934 U.S. Supreme Court Record, 60.

27   Davis knew he was in trouble & successfully prevailed: *CCFH*, 64–65.

27   motion to quash: October Term 1934 U.S. Supreme Court Record, 9–10, 12. Davis and Geer also moved for a plea in abatement for excluding Blacks from the grand and trial juries and for indicting Herndon based on an insurrection law "in direct violation of the Constitution of the United States and the state of Georgia": ibid., 11. See *LML*, 223; *YCKWC*, 26; *CCFH*, 64.

27   Mercer Law School graduate: Wyatt graduated from Mercer in 1914; Hudson graduated in 1916. They did not overlap because, at the time, the law school was a two-year program: *The Cauldron*, vols. 4 (1914) and 6 (1916).

27   twelve witnesses: October Term 1934 U.S. Supreme Court Record, 41–55.

27 **conceded that no Black man:** October Term 1934 U.S. Supreme Court Record, 43–44 (jury commissioners A. S. Nance and George Sims); ibid., 47 (deputy sheriffs A. Gordon Hardy and R. B. Gaines); ibid., 48 (tax collector W. S. Richardson); ibid. (clerk of Fulton County Superior Court J. W. Simmons).

27 **"the most intelligent":** October Term 1934 U.S. Supreme Court Record, 44 (jury commissioner A. S. Nance). See ibid., 43 (jury commissioner Oscar Palmour describing the 4000 potential grand jurors as "the most upright men"); ibid., 46 (jury commissioner F. J. Paxon describing grand jurors as "the most intelligent, the best qualified").

28 **white cards:** October Term 1934 U.S. Supreme Court Record, 54 (jury commissioner F. J. Paxon). In 1953, the Supreme Court declared Georgia's practice of using white and pinks cards unconstitutional. See Avery v. Georgia, 345 U.S. 559, 562 (1953).

28 **attempt to seat two Black men:** October Term 1934 U.S. Supreme Court Record, 55 (assistant solicitor John H. Hudson).

28 **David T. Howard & R. L. Craddock:** Martin, *The Angelo Herndon Case*, 39–40. Charles H. Martin observed that Howard's and Craddock's testimony had been omitted from the trial record but that an objection to Craddock's testimony had been included in Ground No. 13 of Herndon's amended new trial motion: ibid., 40n9; October Term 1934 U.S. Supreme Court Record, 27. See *LML*, 224 (referring to Craddock's testimony); *CCFH*, 65 (referring to Howard's testimony). It is possible that they could have testified at the December 15 pretrial hearing in the judge's chambers.

28 **also conveniently excluded from the trial record:** The ILD charged that the record had been falsified shortly after the trial: ILD Press Release, 7/29/1933, in ILDP, reel 17, p. 635; *DW*, 7/29/1933, in ibid., reel 16, p. 992; *CCFH*, 92 (recalling "the state had cut the guts of the transcript" and describing it as a "crooked record").

28 **"It ain't clear" & "unjudicial" & "the same courtesy" & "That's enough" & "contemptuous" & "I'll handle this!":** *CCFH*, 67.

28 **Denying Davis's motions:** October Term 1934 U.S. Supreme Court Record, 10, 12; *AC*, 1/17/1933, 5; *AJ*, 1/17/1933, 5.

28 **"Watch yourself" & "Leave the Klan" & "We'll be here tomorrow":** *CCFH*, 68–71. This intimidation by seven or eight white men may have occurred after the December 10, 1932, hearing—though the dates are off in the timeline in AH's papers. See "Political Prisoner, ANGELO HERNDON," 2.

29 **Reverend J. A. Martin:** *CCFH*, 68–71. See *CDef*, 2/4/1933, 4; *ADW*, 3/31/1934, 1.

29 **"The Klan Rides Again" & pulled the cross & escorted by Reverend Martin:** *CCFH*, 71. See Painter, *Narrative of Hosea Hudson*, 226 (recalling that Reverend Martin and his deacons hid pistols in their overalls to protect BJD at the courthouse).

29 **member of the Klan:** *CCFH*, 72.

29 **"I expect you to inflict":** *AJ*, 1/17/1933, 5. See James H. Street, *Look Away!: A Dixie Notebook* (1936), 147–48 ("The subject of communism came up right at the beginning when the state charged that Herndon was a dangerous radical and should be killed. He was pictured as advocate of a black republic and the prosecutor inflamed the injury by reading snatches of literature form communist pamphlets which mentioned social equality between whites and blacks"). Hudson's opening statement was not included in the trial record.

29 **F. B. Watson & "paste-board box":** October Term 1934 U.S. Supreme Court Record, 56–57, 59.

30 **On cross-examination:** October Term 1934 U.S. Supreme Court Record, 57–59.

30 "a certain scurrilous letter": October Term 1934 U.S. Supreme Court Record, 60.
Cf. *ADW*, 11/27/1932, 1 (Solicitor General Boykin purportedly told the grand jury
that AH had sent him "several letters of a threatening nature").

30 referred to him as a "nigger": *CCFH*, 73. Newspaper and eyewitness accounts
confirmed that Watson used both slurs: *Macon Telegraph*, 1/18/1933, 12; New York
Daily News, 1/18/1933, 7; *DW*, 1/20/1933, 3; *Richmond Planet*, 1/28/1933, in ILDP,
reel 16, p. 920; *DW*, 2/4/1933, 4. Cf. Street, *Look Away!*, 146–47 (the white Associated Press reporter at the trial recalled that Davis objected to the prosecutor calling
Herndon a "niggah"). See David Entin, "Angelo Herndon" (master's thesis, University of North Carolina–Chapel Hill, 1963), 30n20 (quoting 4/2/1963 letter from
Atlanta Daily World reporter Cliff W. Mackay that witnesses, the prosecutor, and
Judge Wyatt used the word "nigger"). Davis remembered the racist testimony coming from the first witness, but it was the third witness, Assistant Solicitor Stephens:
CCFH, 73; Martin, *The Angelo Herndon Case*, 48n28.

30 "darkey" & "prejudicial to our case" & "nigger" or "darkey": October Term 1934
U.S. Supreme Court Record, 60–61. See *CCFH*, 92 (recalling omission of "nigger"
from transcript); Mack, *Representing the Race*, 86 (exploring the "fine line" Black
lawyers "walked" in southern courtrooms and quoting Davis).

30 "revolutionary material" & "irrelevant and immaterial" & "If Emory University": October Term 1934 U.S. Supreme Court Record, 68–69.

31 "Equal Rights for Negroes" & "You understand that to mean" & "irrelevant
and immaterial" & objected again that the question was "irrelevant": October
Term 1934 U.S. Supreme Court Record, 80–82. See *AC*, 1/18/1933, 4; *CCFH*, 74–75
(recalling the questions came from Hudson, not LeCraw).

31 Under Georgia law at the time: Ga. Code 1866 Ga. Laws 138 (not competent to tes-
tifying under oath); 1879 Ga. Laws 53 (unsworn statement). See Ferguson v. Georgia, 365 U.S. 570, 570–71, 596 (1961) (declaring the Georgia code provision denied
the defendant the right to counsel and violated the Fourteenth Amendment's Due
Process Clause).

31 "calm and collected": *LML*, 235.

31 "impassioned" fifteen-minute speech: *PC*, 1/28/1933, 8A.

31 he explained & He described: October Term 1934 U.S. Supreme Court Record,
70–78.

32 county jailers and prison doctor: October Term 1934 U.S. Supreme Court Record,
82–92 (testimony of W. T. Turner, R. N. Holland, and Dr. J. C. Blalock).

32 "they can hold" & "collapse": October Term 1934 U.S. Supreme Court Record,
76–78. The official trial record differs from AH's speech printed in autographical
accounts: cf. *LML*, app. 3, 342–48; *YCKWC*, 27 (adding "You may succeed in killing
one, two, even a score of working-class organizers. But you cannot kill the working
class"). At the time, the ILD charged that the official record omitted key portions of
AH's speech and other parts of the trial. See note above from this chapter, "also conveniently excluded from the trial record." Therefore, I quote from the transcript, the
published speech, and eyewitness accounts.

32 "no matter what you do": *LML*, 348.

32 "Do with me" & "unique in the annals": "Death of Herndon Is Asked by State,"
AC, 1/18/1933, 1.

32 "really talked himself into jail": Street, *Look Away!*, 149. Only three reporters covered the trial: Street for the Associated Press, Foster Eaton for United Press International, and Cliff W. Mackay for the *Atlanta Daily World* (ibid., 147).

32   "a turning point": Patterson, *Ben Davis*, 21.

33   had advised the ILD's William Patterson: BJD to Patterson, 10/20/1932, pp. 1–2.
      See Entin, "Angelo Herndon," 37*n*44 (suggesting BJD had been a communist at the
      time of AH's trial, based on interviews with CVW, 2/25/1963, and Assistant Solici-
      tor Hudson, 1/31/1963).

33   "political mentor": Patterson, *Ben Davis*, 23.

33   Communist Party membership application: *Harlem Liberator*, 5/27/1933, 5;
      CCFH, 75–76; Benjamin J. Davis, "Why I Am a Communist," *Phylon* 8, no. 2
      (1947): 108–9.

33   "flailed his arms": CCFH, 76. The official transcript omitted the opening and clos-
      ing arguments, over Davis's objections.

33   "fiery speech": *AJ*. 1/18/1933, 22.

33   *The Life and Struggles of Negro Toilers* & "Stamp this thing": *BaltSun*, 1/19/1033,
      1, 5. See George Padmore, *The Life and Struggles of Negro Toilers* (London: R.I.L.U.
      magazine for the International Trade Union Committee of Negro Workers, 1931);
      Harvey Klehr, *The Heyday of American Communism: The Depression Decade*
      (1984), 340.

33   fifteen minutes. Surprised by the brevity: CCFH, 76.

34   portrayed Hudson: *LML*, app. 5, 351–54; CCFH, 76–79.

34   "This book should have been": *BAA*, 1/28/1933, 9.

34   Davis's invocation of lynching: *Macon News*, 1/19/1933, 5.

34   "small, chalk-white, wizened": CCFH, 64.

34   "If you don't send": *DW*, 2/4/1933, 4. See CCFH, 79–80.

34   insurrectionary literature & "mere acts" & "the advocacy" & "immediate seri-
      ous violence": October Term 1934 U.S. Supreme Court Record, 132–33. See *AC*,
      1/19/1933, 1.

35   All twelve jurors: Martin, *The Angelo Herndon Case*, 61*n*55 (describing the jury
      votes, based on Miscellaneous Documents at the Fulton County Courthouse).

35   The foreman read the verdict: *LML*, 239.

35   "Nothing in particular" & "Under the circumstances": *Macon News*, 1/19/1933,
      5. See *AC*, 1/19/1933, 1; *ADW*, 1/20/1933, in ILDP, reel 16, p. 936; October Term
      1934 U.S. Supreme Court Record, 139.

35   "a Christmas present": *LML*, 239.

35   journalist John L. Spivak: John L. Spivak, *Georgia Nigger* (New York: Brewer,
      Warren, and Putnam, 1932); John L. Spivak, *On the Chain Gang* (1932).

35   Robert Burns published: Robert E. Burns, *I Am a Fugitive from a Georgia Chain
      Gang!* (New York: Vanguard, 1932).

36   northern falsehoods: *AJ*, 1/19/1933, 2.

36   "certain death": *NJG*, 7/21/1934, in ILDP, reel 16, p. 1005.

36   March 11: *ADW*, 1/20/1933; *NYHT*, 1/20/1933, 30.

36   "There wasn't one iota": *ADW*, 1/20/1933.

36   national newspapers: *NYT*, 1/19/1933, 1; *NYHT*, 1/19/1933, 1; *BaltSun*, 1/19/1933, 1.

36   "shameful verdict": *Macon Telegraph*, 1/20/1933, 4.

36   "a shameful proceeding": *Macon Telegraph*, 1/23/1933, 4 (reprinting *St. Louis Post-
      Dispatch* editorial).

36   Black press sided with Herndon: *Richmond Planet*, 1/28/1933, in ILDP, reel 16,
      p. 918; *NJG*, 1/28/1933, in ibid.; *NYA*, 1/28/1933, in ibid., p. 920; *PT*, 1/26/1933, in
      ibid., p. 937; *St. Louis Argus*, 1/27/1933, in ibid., p. 939; *WashTrib*, 1/27/1933, in ibid.;
      CDef, 2/3/1933, in ibid., p. 951.

36   "tears away the last shred": *NYAN*, 1/25/1933, 1.

36   "callously sending": *PC*, 2/4/1933, 10.

36   "unnecessarily harsh" and "extremely stupid": *NYHT*, 1/23/1933, 12.

37   "Angelo Herndon must not die": *DW*, 1/26/1933, 3. See ILD Press Release, 1/20/1933, in ILDP, reel 17, p. 617.

37   jailhouse letter: *DW*, 1/26/1933, 1, 3. See ILD Press Release, 1/26/1933, in ILDP, reel 17, pp. 618–19.

37   opened an Atlanta office & fifty Black leaders & adopted a resolution: *AC*, 1/29/1933, 7; *DW*, 1/30/1933, 1; *DW* 2/1/1933, 1.

37   habeas corpus hearing: *AJ*, 2/2/1933, in ILDP, reel 16, p. 946; *AC*, 2/3/1933, 19; *AC*, 2/5/1933, 5C.

37   handcuffed to the other prisoner on a back bench & "full of errors": *BAA*, 2/11/1933, 13.

38   he "threatened" Herndon: *DW*, 2/6/1933, 3.

38   February 16 & solitary confinement: *DW*, 2/27/1933, 3. See AH to William Patterson, 2/19/1933, pp. 1–3, in AHP, box 1, folder 1; ILD Press Release, 2/25/1933, in ILDP, reel 17, p. 625; *AC*, 2/18/1933, 4.

38   going to be lynched & forced the county council: *BAA*, 3/4/1933, 13; *LML*, 245–47.

38   Davis worried: *CCFH*, 87.

38   "stale bread and foul water": *LML*, 248.

39   "You are too smart" & promised "trouble": *DW*, 2/14/1933, in ILDP, reel 16, p. 959. See *BAA*, 2/18/1933, 5; *WashTrib*, 2/24/1933, 3; *Harlem Liberator*, 5/27/1933, 5.

39   "The Ku Klux Klan rides": *CCFH*, 95. See *WashTrib*, 2/24/1933, 3; *Harlem Liberator*, 5/27/1933, 5; Harry Haywood, *Black Bolshevik: Autobiography of an Afro-American Communist* (1978), 404–5.

39   showed the note to his father: *CCFH*, 96.

39   prowess on the tennis court: *AC*, 7/31/1933, 7.

Chapter Three: The Son of the South

41   about 700 people: *Paducah (KY) Lighthouse*, 5/12/1933, 1, 5, in ILDP, reel 16, pp. 975–76, 978; *DW*, 5/11/1933, in ibid., p. 978 (over 400 people); *Labor Defender*, 6/1933, 75 (over 400 people); *CCFH*, 82–83 (almost 1000 people); *ADW*, 5/3/1933, in ILDP, reel 16, p. 973; *AC*, 5/7/1933, 19.

41   "citizens meeting": Handbill, n.d., Glenn W. Rainey Papers, box 19, folder 3. The ILD announced the formation of the Provisional Committee in early March: " 'Provisional Committee for Freedom of Angelo Herndon' Formed" (press release), 3/18/1933, in ILDP, reel 18, p. 230; *DW*, 3/21/1933, 2.

42   six feet tall: CVW, World War II Draft Card, p. 2, World War II U.S. Draft Cards for Young Men, 1940–1947, California, p. 1605.

42   deep southern accent: CVW, *Thinking Back: The Perils of Writing History* (1986), 86.

42   insurance salesman: The observation was Albert Murray's: Albert Murray, *South to a Very Old Place* (New York: McGraw-Hill, 1971), 16; John Herbert Roper, *C. Vann Woodward, Southerner* (1987), 273.

42   his uncle Comer: CVW Int. by John Herbert Roper, 7/18/1978, pp. 1–2, John Herbert Roper Papers, folder 10; CVW Int. by Roper, 4/13/1979, p. 3, ibid.; Roger Adel-

son, "Interview with C. Vann Woodward," *The Historian* 54, no. 1 (Autumn 1991): 3, 5, in CVWP, box 94, folder 33; James C. Cobb, *C. Vann Woodward: America's Historian* (2022), 14–16; Roper, *C. Vann Woodward, Southerner,* 16–17, 19–21; John Herbert Roper, "C. Vann Woodward's Early Career: The Historian as Dissident Youth," *Georgia Historical Quarterly* 64, no. 1 (Spring 1980): 8–9; James Green, "Rewriting Southern History: An Interview with C. Vann Woodward," *Southern Exposure* 12 (1984): 87–88; James Green, "Past and Present in Southern History," *Radical History Review* 36 (1986): 83.

42   **organize a student strike:** Cobb, *C. Vann Woodward: America's Historian,* 13; Roper, *C. Vann Woodward, Southerner,* 25–29; David Sesser, "'A Spirit of Unrest': The 1928 Student Strike at Henderson-Brown College," *Pulaski County Historical Review* 64 (Summer 2016): 50–68.

42   **transferred to Emory University:** Cobb, *C. Vann Woodward: America's Historian,* 14–15, 17–19; Roper, *C. Vann Woodward, Southerner,* 31–39; Emory *Campus* 1930, p. 44.

42   **John Hope:** CVW to David M. Potter, 6/23/1967, p. 1, in CVWP, box 44, folder 521; CVW Int. by Roper, 4/13/1979, p. 3; CVW, *Thinking Back,* 85; David M. Potter, "C. Vann Woodward," in *Pastmasters: Some Essays on American Historians,* ed. Marcus Cunliffe and Robin W. Winks (1969), 376; Roper, "C. Vann Woodward's Early Career," 9.

42   **Glenn W. Rainey and Ernest Hartsock:** *AJ,* 11/17/1933, 7; Adelson, "Interview with C. Vann Woodward," 5; Potter, "C. Vann Woodward," 376; Cobb, *C. Vann Woodward: America's Historian,* 19–23; Roper, *C. Vann Woodward, Southerner,* 39–42.

43   **Georgia Tech:** CVW to Hugh Woodward, ca. 1930, in CVWP, box 60, folder 732; *Technique (Atlanta, GA),* 10/3/1930, 1; Roper, *C. Vann Woodward, Southerner,* 48–49.

43   **J. Saunders Redding:** CVW, *Thinking Back,* 85; Larry Van Dyne, "Vann Woodward: Penetrating the Romantic Haze," *Chronicle of Higher Education,* 5/8/1978, pp. 13–14, in CVWP, box 94, folder 33; Adelson, "Interview with C. Vann Woodward," 6; Roper, *C. Vann Woodward, Southerner,* 49–51; Roper, "C. Vann Woodward's Early Career," 9–10; Cobb, *C. Vann Woodward: America's Historian,* 27.

43   **"exchanged views as an equal":** CVW, *Thinking Back,* 85.

43   **free speech and assembly:** *AJ,* 8/3/1930, 11A.

43   **Rosenwald Fellowship:** CVW to Glenn W. Rainey, 5/11/1931, *CVWL,* 11–13; *Technique (Atlanta, GA),* 5/22/1931, 1; Cobb, *C. Vann Woodward: America's Historian,* 23–24.

43   **Columbia University & J. Thomas Heflin:** CVW to Glenn Rainey, 10/20/1931, *CVWL,* 15–17; CVW to Glenn Rainey, ca. 4/1932, ibid., 21; CVW Int. by Roper, 4/13/1979, pp. 5–6; Roper, *C. Vann Woodward,* 51–52; Cobb, *C. Vann Woodward: America's Historian,* 24–26.

43   **Langston Hughes & acted in *Underground* & W. E. B. Du Bois:** CVW to Glenn Rainey, 9/17/1931, *CVWL,* 15; CVW to Glenn Rainey, 10/20/1931, ibid., 17; CVW to Rainey, ca. 4/1932, 20–21; *ADW,* 4/12/1932, 6; Adelson, "Interview with C. Vann Woodward," 6; CVW, *Thinking Back,* 85–86; Roper, *C. Vann Woodward, Southerner,* 52–53; Cobb, *C. Vann Woodward: America's Historian,* 27.

43   **Woodward traveled & injustice of the Scottsboro case:** CVW to Glenn Rainey, 8/11/1932, *CVWL,* 22–23; CVW Int. by Roper, 4/13/1979, pp. 4–5; Roper, "C. Vann Woodward's Early Career," 10; CVW, *Thinking Back,* 86; Roper, *C. Vann Woodward, Southerner,* 53–55; Cobb, *C. Vann Woodward: America's Historian,* 28–29.

44 **the ILD had been organizing:** ILD organizing secretary Bess Schwartz to Glenn Rainey, 2/9/1933, Rainey Papers, box 11, folder 10.

44 **"We must draw":** *DW*, 3/21/1933, 2.

44 **Martin and other Black ministers:** *AC*, 1/26/1933, 13; *ADW*, 1/29/1933, in ILDP, reel 16, p. 916; *ADW*, 2/2/1933, in ibid., p. 942; *CDef*, 2/4/1933, 4; *AC*, 3/1/1933, 12.

44 **27 Club adopted its resolution:** *ADW*, 1/29/1933; *DW*, 1/30/1933, 1; *ADW*, 1/31/1933, in ILDP, reel 16, p. 911; *DW*, 2/1/1933, 1; *DW*, 2/10/1933, 3.

44 **The Provisional Committee met:** *DW*, 3/21/1933, 2; *CDef*, 3/25/1933, 2.

45 **"with absolutely no segregation"** & **"Can't Live on Corn Bread":** *DW*, 5/13/1933, 2. See *ADW*, 5/3/1933, in ILDP, reel 16, p. 973; Don West, Southern OH Program Collection, 1/22/1975, at 00:48:29–00:54:17; Patrick Huber, *Linthead Stomp: The Creation of Country Music in the Piedmont South* (Chapel Hill: University of North Carolina Press, 2008), 94.

45 *Powell v. Alabama*: 287 U.S. 45, 71–72 (1932).

45 **Haywood Patterson & Ruby Bates:** James Goodman, *Stories of Scottsboro* (1994), 118–54; Dan T. Carter, *Scottsboro: A Tragedy of the American South* (1979), 192–242.

45 **triggered massive protests:** *NYT*, 4/11/1933, 1; *NYAN*, 4/12/1933, 1; *CDef*, 4/22/1933, 4.

45 **protesters held signs that read:** Photo of march, 5/8/1933, Getty Images, https://www.gettyimages.com/detail/news-photo/long-line-of-marchers-paraded-through-the-streets-of-news-photo/514901756.

45 **Roosevelt was too "busy"** & **Louis H. Howe:** *DW*, 5/9/1933, 1, 3. See *NYAN*, 5/10/1933, 1, 2; *BAA*, 5/13/1933, 1, 2; *NYT*, 5/9/1933, 38; *NYHT*, 5/9/1933, 16; *WP*, 5/9/1933, 18; *Labor Defender*, 6/1933, 65; Carter, *Scottsboro*, 248–51.

46 **From his cell in Fulton Tower:** *DW*, 5/6/1933, 3.

46 **The May 7 meeting:** *AC*, 5/7/1933, 5B; *AC*, 5/8/1933, 3; CVW to Wilma Dykeman Stokely, 12/1/1959, *CVWL*, 200; CVW to David Entin, 2/25/1963, ibid., 234; CVW Int. by Roper, 7/18/1978, pp. 3–4; Kevin Walker, "Comer Vann Woodward," 11/14/1980, p. 8 (based on 10/15/1980 Int. with CVW), in CVWP, box 90, folder 7; CVW, *Thinking Back*, 86; Adelson, "Interview with C. Vann Woodward," pp. 7–8; Glenda Elizabeth Gilmore, *Defying Dixie: The Radical Roots of Civil Rights, 1919–1950* (2008), 173–74. CVW conflated several committee meetings and mistakenly recalled that he was the vice chairman at the May 7 meeting. On May 7, however, Reverend J. A. Martin was vice chairman: *AC*, 5/8/1933, 3.

46 **Mary Raoul Millis:** Sarah H. Case, "Biography of Mary Raoul Millis, 1870–1958," Biographical Database of NAWSA Suffragists, 1890–1920, https://documents.alexanderstreet.com/d/1011147524; Mary Raoul Millis, *The Family of Raoul: A Memoir* (Asheville, NC: Privately printed, 1943), 152–56.

46 **Socialist Party of America & attracted new members:** Jack Ross, *The Socialist Party of America* (Lincoln, NE: Potomac Books, 2015), 306–33.

46 **Southern League for People's Rights:** *Harlem Liberator*, 6/10/1933, 5.

47 **"a dear, sweet old man":** CVW Int. by Roper, 7/18/1978, p. 4. See CVW to Stokely, 12/1/1959, 200–201; Green, "Past and Present in Southern History," 85–86; Charles H. Martin, *The Angelo Herndon Case and Southern Justice* (1976), 78, 78n45 (based on 11/8/1973 interview with CVW); Potter, "C. Vann Woodward," 376–77; Roper, *C. Vann Woodward, Southerner*, 57–58; Cobb, *C. Vann Woodward: America's Historian*, 29–30.

47 **A longtime mentor to Woodward:** Arthur F. Raper of Commission on Interracial Cooperation to John D. Black of Harvard University, 6/22/1931, in CVWP, box 90, folder 3 (extolling CVW's virtues as future expert on southern race relations).

47   **He disapproved:** CVW to Will Alexander, 10/12/1931, in CICP, reel 7, folder 149. The case was John Downer, who was sentenced to death for allegedly raping a white woman in Elberton, Georgia. Alexander worked with the Atlanta attorneys on Downer's appeal because they were not affiliated with the Communist Party: Will Alexander to CVW, 10/17/1931, ibid.

47   **"the cuts of a friend":** CVW Int. by Roper, 7/18/1978, p. 4. See CVW to Stokely, 12/1/1959, 200; Wilma Dykeman and James Stokely, *Seeds of Southern Change: The Life of Will Alexander* (Chicago: University of Chicago Press, 1962), 155–56; *Labor Defender,* 7/1/1933, 8 (Taub criticizing Alexander for describing AH as a "fanatic"). The article with CVW's remarks has not been found.

47   **"interested in the class struggle":** Will Alexander to Katherine Gardner, 10/26/1933, p. 1, in CICP, reel 7, folder 165. But see Helen Smith to acting ILD general secretary Carl Hacker, 8/3/1932, in Clarina Michaelson Papers, box 1, folder 13 (offering a more collaborative version of the meeting with Alexander and suggesting he approved of the reputation of H. A. Allen, the white criminal lawyer); Clarina Michaelson to CPUSA Secretariat, 8/19/1932, p. 1, in ibid. (urging them to hire Allen).

47   **Leonard Haas:** Smith to Hacker, 8/3/1932.

47   **Davis had not graduated:** Will Alexander to RNB, 1/24/1933, in ACLUP, vol. 654.

47   **A. T. Walden had declined:** Will Alexander to RNB, 5/1/1933, in ACLUP, vol. 654; RNB to Will Alexander, 5/13/1933, in ibid; Will Alexander to BJD, 5/17/1933, in ibid.

47   **"an argument"** & **"by a competent":** Alexander to RNB, 1/24/1933.

48   **"fed up with the cowardice":** *Harlem Liberator,* 5/27/1933, 5; William Patterson to RNB, 2/7/1933, in ACLUP, vol. 654 (rebutting Alexander's charges after RNB showed him Alexander's 1/24/1933 letter).

48   **Davis and ILD officials pleaded for financial support:** William Patterson to RNB, 5/6/1933, in ACLUP, vol. 654; RNB to BJD, 5/8/1933, in ibid.; BJD to RNB, 5/11/1933, pp. 1–2, in ibid.

48   **Founded by Baldwin:** Laura Weinrib, *The Taming of Free Speech: America's Civil Liberties Compromise* (Cambridge, MA: Harvard University Press, 2016); Robert C. Cottrell, *Roger Nash Baldwin and the American Civil Liberties Union* (New York: Columbia University Press, 2001); Samuel Walker, *In Defense of American Liberties: A History of the ACLU* (New York: Oxford University Press, 1990).

48   **American Fund for Public Service:** John Fabian Witt, "Garland's Million; or, the Tragedy and Triumph of Legal History," *Law and History Review* 40, no. 1 (2022): 123; Megan Ming Francis and John Fabian Witt, "Movement Capture or Movement Strategy? A Critical Race History Exchange on the Beginnings of *Brown v. Board,*" *Yale Journal of Law and the Humanities* 31, no. 2 (2021): 520.

49   **caught Baldwin and the ACLU off guard:** Oliver C. Hancock to ACLU, 12/16/1932, in ACLUP, vol. 564; Oliver C. Hancock to ACLU, 12/19/1932, in ibid.; RNB, Memo, 12/29/1932, ibid.

49   **Arthur Garfield Hays:** RNB to William Patterson, 1/24/1933, in ACLUP, vol. 654 (including RNB note of 2/14/1933, after phone call with Patterson declining Hays's offer); RNB to William Patterson, 1/26/1933, in ibid. See Arthur Garfield Hays, *Trial by Prejudice* (New York: Covici, Friede, 1933), 299–302.

49   **"our weakness was not Geer":** Patterson to RNB, 2/7/1933.

49   **$250 to appeal Herndon's case:** BJD to RNB, 6/26/1933, in ACLUP, vol. 654.

49   *Twenty Years for Free Speech!:* *Twenty Years for Free Speech!* (New York: American Civil Liberties Union, May 1933). See *BAA,* 5/27/1933, 3; *CDef,* 5/27/1933, 4.

49   **sent Davis only $100:** ACLU to John Geer and BJD, 6/15/1933, in ACLUP, vol. 654; BJD to ACLU, 6/16/1933, in ibid.

49   **nasty letters:** *Atlanta Georgian*, 6/13/1933, in ILDP, reel 16, p. 982; *AC*, 6/14/1933, 1; *NYT*, 6/14/1933, 6; *NYAN*, 6/21/1933, in ILDP, reel 16, p. 983.

49   **state highway board:** *NYT*, 6/18/1933, E1.

49   **In his new trial motion:** 1934 October Term U.S. Supreme Court Record, 14–40.

50   **"the right of free speech":** BJD to RNB, 6/26/1933, in ACLUP, vol. 654.

50   **a crime that "warranted death":** *DW*, 6/27/1933, 1.

50   **"emaciated, tired" & "I know I'm coming out":** *DW*, 6/23/1933, 2; *CDef*, 7/1/1933, 11. See ILD Press Release, 5/25/1933, in ILDP, reel 17, p. 626.

50   **He wrote his friends at the ILD:** AH to William Patterson, 6/1/1933, pp. 1–3, in AHP, box 1, folder 1.

50   **Judge Wyatt denied:** 1934 October Term U.S. Supreme Court Record, 40–41.

50   **"expected" & "The case will be carried":** *ADW*, 7/7/1933, 1, 4.

51   **Atlanta Six:** Carr v. State, 166 S.E. 827, 828–30 (Ga. 1932) (Carr I) (a Nov. 21, 1932, decision about §58 of the insurrection law about circulating insurrectionary literature); Dalton v. State, 169 S.E. 198, 199–200 (Ga. 1933) (a Feb. 28, 1933, decision about §58 about circulating insurrectionary literature); Carr v. State, 169 S.E. 201, 201–2 (Ga. 1933) (Carr II) (a March 18, 1933, decision about §56 about attempting to incite insurrection).

51   **Charles Schenck:** Schenck v. United States, 249 U.S. 47 (1919); Frohwerk v. United States, 249 U.S. 204 (1919); Debs v. United States, 249 U.S. 211 (1919).

51   **"clear and imminent danger" & "free trade in ideas":** Abrams v. United States, 250 U.S. 616, 627, 630 (1919) (Holmes, J., dissenting). On Holmes's *Abrams* dissent, see Brad Snyder, *The House of Truth: A Washington Political Salon and the Foundation of American Liberalism* (2017), 274–304; Thomas Healy, *The Great Dissent: How Oliver Wendell Holmes Changed His Mind—and Changed the History of Free Speech in America* (New York: Henry Holt, 2013); Geoffrey R. Stone, *Perilous Times: Free Speech in Wartime from the Sedition Act of 1798 to the War on Terrorism* (New York: W. W. Norton, 2004), 192–208; Richard Polenberg, *Fighting Faiths: The Abrams Case, the Supreme Court, and Free Speech* (New York: Viking, 1987); G. Edward White, *Justice Oliver Wendell Holmes: Law and the Inner Self* (New York: Oxford University Press, 1993), 420–36; David M. Rabban, *Free Speech in Its Forgotten Years* (New York: Cambridge University Press, 1997), 342–55.

52   **Benjamin Gitlow:** Gitlow v. New York, 268 U.S. 652, 666 (1925); Snyder, *The House of Truth*, 386–89; Marc Lendler, *Gitlow v. New York: Every Idea an Incitement* (Lawrence: University Press of Kansas, 2012).

52   **Harold B. Fiske:** Fiske v. Kansas, 274 U.S. 380, 387 (1927).

52   **"clear and present danger" & "Fear of serious injury":** Whitney v. California, 274 U.S. 357, 376 (1927) (Brandeis, J., concurring). On *Whitney*, see Snyder, *The House of Truth*, 460–61; Philippa Strum, *Speaking Freely: Whitney v. California and American Speech Law* (Lawrence: University Press of Kansas, 2015); Haig Bosmajian, *Anita Whitney, Louis Brandeis, and the First Amendment* (Madison, NJ: Fairleigh Dickinson University Press, 2010).

52   **"To justify suppression":** Whitney, 274 U.S. at 376 (Brandeis, J., concurring).

53   **"as a sign, symbol or emblem":** Stromberg v. California, 283 U.S. 359, 369–70 (1931).

53   **Either way, they objected:** October Term 1934 U.S. Supreme Court Record, 1–4; *DW*, 7/13/1933, in ILDP, reel 16, p. 991; *AC*, 7/16/1933, 8A.

53   had been "falsified": *DW*, 7/29/1933, in ILDP, reel 16, p. 992; *Harlem Liberator*, 7/29/1933, 7; *DW*, 8/1/1933, 3. See ILD Press Release, 7/29/1933, 1, in ILDP, reel 17, p. 635; *CCFH*, 92.

53   attempted to raise $1000: BJD to RNB, 7/18/1933, in ACLUP, vol. 654.

53   The ACLU reached out: RNB to BJD, 7/20/1933, in ACLUP, vol. 654; ACLU solic- itation letter, 8/7/1933, in ibid.; RNB to BJD, 8/25/1933, in ibid.

53   "Herndon Day Celebration": *ADW*, 7/6/1933, 1; *ADW*, 7/7/1933, 1; *ADW*, 7/12/1933, 1; *ADW*, 7/14/1933, 6; *ADW*, 7/21/1933, 1, 4; *ADW*, 7/23/1933, 1; *ADW*, 7/24/1933, 1, 4; *Harlem Liberator*, 7/29/1933, 1.

53   netted only $100: BJD to RNB, 9/6/1933, in ACLUP, vol. 654.

53   Ku Klux Klan burned a cross: *Harlem Liberator*, 8/12/1933, 7; *SW*, 8/15/1933, 2.

53   secretary of the local electrician's union: 1933 Atlanta City Directory, 1064.

54   Brittain gave him a "talking to": Roper, *C. Vann Woodward Southerner*, 58. See Green, "Past and Present in Southern History," 86; Green, "Rewriting Southern History," 88; CVW, *Thinking Back*, 86.

54   Depression-era budget cuts: CVW to Entin, 2/25/1963; CVW Int. by Roper, 7/18/1978, p. 4; Green, "Past and Present in Southern History," 86; Green, "Rewriting Southern History," 88; Glenn W. Rainey Int. by Charles H. Martin, 8/26/1970, p. 1, Charles H. Martin Papers; CVW, *Thinking Back*, 86; Roper, *C. Vann Woodward: Southerner*, 58–59; Cobb, *C. Vann Woodward: America's His- torian*, 30. At times, CVW intimated that there "may have been" a causal con- nection between his support for AH and getting fired: Green, "Past and Present in Southern History," 86. Mostly, however, Woodward attributed his firing to budget cuts and to his being the junior member of the English department. He made $1800 out of $25,430 budgeted for the English department in 1932–1933; the English Department's budget was reduced to $21,000 in 1933–1934: Georgia Institute of Technology Budget, 1932–33, group 4, p. 10, and Georgia Institute of Technology Budget, 1933–34, group 4, p. 10, Early Presidents Collection, box 6, folders 20–21.

54    $300 in back pay: Regents v. Woodward, 176 S.E. 677 (Ga. Ct. App. 1932); *AJ*, 9/22/1934, 10.

54   two Black Tuscaloosa teenagers: *BN*, 11/3/1933, 1–2; *Huntsville Times*, 11/3/1933, 8; *DW*, 11/8/1933, 1; *Montgomery Advertiser*, 11/9/1933, 1–2, 4; *The Plight of Tusca- loosa: Mob Murders, Communist Hysteria, Official Incompetence*, 10–24 (Atlanta: Southern Commission on the Study of Lynching, 1933).

54   "wrong crowd": CVW, *Thinking Back*, 17–18. In later life, CVW downplayed his youthful radicalism and questioned the Communist Party's motives in fighting for AH's freedom: CVW to Entin, 2/25/1963; Green, "Past and Present in South- ern History," 86; CVW Int. by Roper, 7/18/1978, p. 4; Roper, *C. Vann Woodward: Southerner*, 59.

54   Don West & Burlington textile workers: CVW to Glenn Rainey, 9/24/1934, p. 1, in Rainey Papers, box 6, folder 8; Cobb, *C. Vann Woodward: America's Historian*, 47. Woodward also established a committee in support of workers charged in a dyna- mite plot. CVW to Glenn Rainey, 3/3/1935, p. 1, in Rainey Papers, box 6, folder 8; *Daily Tar Heel*, 2/26/1935, 2; John A. Salmond, " 'The Burlington Dynamite Plot': The 1934 Textile Strike and Its Aftermath in Burlington, North Carolina," *North Carolina Historical Review* 75, no. 4 (Oct. 1998): 426.

54   "plot to murder him": *Harlem Liberator*, 8/5/1933, 8. See ILD Press Release, 8/3/1933, in ILDP, reel 17, p. 639.

54   three men about to be executed: *Harlem Liberator*, 6/17/1933, 1, 8; *AC*, 8/12/1933, 12; *Labor Defender*, 12/1/1933, 76; *LML*, 251–57, 260–61.

54   Glover Davis: *AJ*, 8/23/1933, 8; *ADW*, 8/24/1933, 1, 4; *ADW*, 8/25/1933, 1; *ADW*, 8/26/1933, 1; *ADW*, 8/29/1933, 1, 4; *ADW*, 9/2/1933, 1; *DW*, 9/4/1933, 4; *ADW*, 9/5/1933, 1, 4; *AC*, 9/5/1933, 2; *AJ*, 9/5/1933, 5; *DW*, 9/6/1933, 2.

55   "The funeral of Glover Davis": *ADW*, 9/5/1933, 4.

55   responsible for "any disorder": *CCFH*, 85. See *DW*, 9/8/1933, 2; *Harlem Liberator*, 9/9/1933, 6; *SW*, 9/20/1933, 2; Kansas City (KS) *Wyandotte Echo*, 9/22/1933, 1; *WashTrib*, 9/28/1933, 9; *CCFH*, 84–85; Martin, *The Angelo Herndon Case*, 91–93. BJD also represented Glover Davis's brother in an unsuccessful effort to prosecute the white officer: *ADW*, 9/17/1933, 1, 6; *ADW*, 9/19/1933, 1, 4; *AC*, 9/19/1933, 18; *DW*, 9/21/1933, 2.

55   "Perhaps so": BJD, "Raid on I.L.D. Headquarters, 141½ Auburn Avenue, Atlanta Georgia, 9/7/1933," ACLUP, vol. 654. See ILD Press Release, 9/9/1933, in ILDP, reel 17, p. 641; *AC*, 9/8/1933, 7; *ADW*, 9/8/1933, 1; *DW*, 9/8/1933, 2; *ADW*, 9/9/1933, 1; *BAA*, 9/16/1933, 3; *ADW*, 9/16/1933, 1, 4; *PC*, 9/23/1933, 5; *CDef*, 9/23/1933, 3; *CCFH*, 85–87.

55   struggling to pay the rent: BJD to RNB, 10/12/1933, p. 1, in ACLUP, vol. 654.

56   Will Alexander: BJD to RNB, 9/6/1933, in ACLUP, vol. 654.

56   "Whatever may be" & "rubber stamp": BJD to Will Alexander, 9/9/1933, pp. 1–2, in CICP, reel 7, folder 165. See BJD to Will Alexander, 9/21/1933, in ibid.

56   "a check for a small amount": Will Alexander to BJD, 9/28/1933, in CICP, reel 7, folder 165.

56   "wholly immersed": *CCFH*, 90.

56   rallies in Harlem and Birmingham: *DW*, 4/17/1933, 1; *DW*, 4/19/1933, 2; *DW*, 4/22/1933, 3; *DW*, 6/22/1933, 3.

56   ten days in September: *CCFH*, 91.

56   September 26: BJD to RNB, 9/21/1933, in ACLUP, vol. 654.

Chapter Four: The Radical Lawyer

57   cared little about her clothes: Ann Fagan Ginger, *Carol Weiss King: Human Rights Lawyer, 1895–1952* (1993), 49, 126, 180, 271, 395, 438.

57   never argued in court: Ginger, *Carol Weiss King*, 51–53.

58   Paul, Weiss: Ginger, *Carol Weiss King*, 38, 53, 79; Arthur L. Liman, *Lawyer: A Life of Counsel and Controversy* (New York: Public Affairs, 1998), 17–19; https://www.paulweiss.com/about-the-firm/history.

58   Palmer Raids & Hale, Nelles & Shorr: Ginger, *Carol Weiss King*, 6–22. Although Harvard and Columbia barred women, Yale admitted five in 1919 and Shirley M. Moore was the first to graduate, in 1920: Frederick C. Hicks, *History of the Yale Law School to 1915* (Union, NJ: Lawbook Exchange, 2001), 188–92.

58   Max Lowenthal: Ginger, *Carol Weiss King*, 6, 20–21; *Hearings Before the Committee on Un-American Activities*, 81st Cong., 2nd sess., 2980–82 (1950) (9/15/1950 testimony of Max Lowenthal).

58   By 1925 & Joseph R. Brodsky: Craig Thompson, "The Communist's Dearest Friend," *Saturday Evening Post*, 2/17/1951, 91; Ginger, *Carol Weiss King*, 11, 37–38, 68–69, 72–75.

58   death sentences of the Scottsboro defendants: *DW*, 3/8/1933, 1; Ginger, *Carol Weiss King*, 111–13; Powell v. Alabama, 287 U.S. 45, 71–72 (1932).

58   became the secretary and cofounder: Ann Fagan Ginger, "The Founding of the International Juridical Association: American Section," *Guild Practitioner* 41, no. 3 (1984): 73–79; Ann Fagan Ginger, "Workers' Self-Defense in the Courts," *Science and Society* 47, no. 3 (Fall 1983): 261; Ginger, *Carol Weiss King*, 115–20.

58   Gordon King: Ginger, *Carol Weiss King*, 100–103.

58   her brusque charm: Walter Gellhorn Int. by Charles H. Martin, 9/10/1970, p. 2, Charles H. Martin Papers (on file with author); Roger Nash Baldwin 1954 COH, pp. 139–40; Ginger, *Carol Weiss King*, 148–49, 180.

59   Whitehorn had taken it with him to Atlantic City & "Jewish or Christian?": CWK to Jay Leyda, 9/24/1933, pp. 1–4, in Jay and Si-Lan Chen Leyda Papers, box 5, folder 2. See CWK to Lucille B. Milner, 10/2/1933, in ACLUP, vol. 654; Ginger, *Carol Weiss King*, 177–78.

59   coffee, cigarettes & At 4:30 a.m. & "not a perfect job": CWK to Leyda, 9/24/1933, p. 4; Ginger, *Carol Weiss King*, 178.

59   copies and a few minor corrections: BJD to RNB, 10/12/1933, p. 1, in ACLUP, vol. 654; Isadore (Shad) Polier to RNB, 10/18/1933, in ibid.

59   King primarily argued: Herndon Merits Brief, Georgia Supreme Court, 9/26/1933, at 1–29, in ACLUP, vol. 654. See *IJA Bulletin*, 5/1934, 1.

60   In a reply brief: Herndon Reply Brief, Georgia Supreme Court, at 1–24, in ACLUP, vol. 654.

60   "indefatigable" work ethic & "into presentable" & Georgia Supreme Court bar: *CCFH*, 91.

60   law students & "utter contempt": *CCFH*, 92. See *AC*, 10/6/1933, 24.

61   accused him of pouring water: ILD Press Releases, 12/8/1933 and 12/13/1933, in ILDP, reel 17, pp. 642–43; *DW*, 12/11/1933, 2; *BAA*, 12/23/1933, 23; *CDef*, 12/23/1933, 13; *ADW*, 12/31/1933, 1.

61   alarmingly ill health: AH to Comrade Frieda, 10/12/1933, pp. 1–2, in ACLUP, vol. 742; *Labor Defender*, 12/1/1933, 76; AH to Comrade Frieda, 12/27/1933, p. 1, in AHP, box 1, folder 1; AH to William Patterson, 1/28/1934, p. 1, in ibid.; AH to William Patterson, 2/14/1934, pp. 1–2, in ibid.

61   "sexual perverts": *Labor Defender*, 4/1/1934, 22. See *DW*, 3/13/1934, 5; *DW*, 3/21/1934 3; *NM*, 3/27/1934, 4.

61   At Herndon's request: AH to Patterson, 1/28/1934, p. 1. See ILD Press Release, 3/5/1934, in ILDP, reel 17, p. 646; *DW*, 3/7/1934, 2; *DW*, 3/14/1934, 3; *CDef*, 3/17/1934, 4; *LML*, 269.

61   an independent medical examination: AH to William Patterson, 2/1/1934, pp. 1–2, in AHP, box 1, folder 1; AH to Patterson, 2/14/1934, pp. 1–2; AH to William Patterson, 2/27/1934, p. 1, in AHP, box 1, folder 1.

61   ordering meals from outside the prison: Laurence Emery to ILD, 3/3/1934, in ACLUP, vol. 754; Laurence Emery to RNB, 3/9/1934, in ibid.

61   "dying by inches": Laurence Emery to RNB, 3/3/1954, in ACLUP, vol. 742. See RNB to Laurence Emery, 3/5/1934, in ibid.

61   The publicity: *BAA*, 3/24/1934, 13; *LML*, 269–70.

62   The leaky pipe: *Harlem Liberator*, 3/31/1934, 1; *CDef*, 3/31/1934, 2.

62   Two doctors: *DW*, 4/27/1934, 3; *LML*, 273.

62   "the beginning of a break": Report of Dr. C. W. Powell, n.d., p. 2, AHP, box 1, folder 1. See BJD, "Note re: Examination," n.d., ibid.

62   A white woman doctor: *DW*, 4/21/1934, 5; *DW*, 4/24/1934, 3; *LML*, 273–75.

62   admitted to Grady Hospital: *ADW*, 5/3/1934, 1. See *ADW*, 4/28/1934, 1, 3; ILD
      Press Release, 5/7/1934, in ILDP, reel 17, p. 649; *LML*, 275.

62   Mary Raoul Millis: Edgar Watkins Sr. to Mary Raoul Millis, 3/10/1934, pp. 1–3,
      in ACLUP, vol. 754; Mary Raoul Millis to RNB, 3/13/1934, in ibid.; Edgar Wat-
      kins Sr. to RNB, 3/22/1934, pp. 1–2, in ibid.; RNB to Laurence Emery, 3/24/1934,
      in ibid.; RNB to Mary Raoul Millis, 5/1/1934, in ibid.; Mary Raoul Millis to RNB,
      6/22/1934, in ibid.; *Opportunity: A Journal of Negro Life*, 8/1934, 253, 256.

62   point by point: BJD to Laurence Emery, 4/13/1934, pp. 1–4, in ILDP, reel 18, pp.
      528–31.

62   "misleaders of the NAACP": *ADW*, 3/31/1934, 1. See *ADW*, 3/24/1934, 1; *ADW*,
      3/31/1934, 1, 5; *DW*, 4/3/1934, 3.

62   "negroes were merely" & "not opprobrious" & "the right of self-determination":
      Herndon v. State, 174 S.E. 597, 601, 609, 613 (Ga. 1934).

63   "at any time" & "a single revolutionary spark": Herndon v. State, 174 S.E. at 610,
      616 (quoting Gitlow v. New York, 268 U.S. 652, 669 [1925]).

63   "in the North" & "if we do not go up": William Patterson to RNB, 6/1/1934, in
      ACLUP, vol. 742.

63   On June 2: Exhibit C: Notice of Intent to Certiorari and Supersedeas, 6/2/1934,
      Angelo Herndon Collection, reel 22, p. 888.

63   he would have dissented: *SW*, 7/34, 4 (article by Geer quoting Russell).

64   for fifty days: Clerk to John Geer, 6/4/1934, Georgia Supreme Court Record, no.
      9871, p. 1176; Exhibit D, Chief Justice Russell Order, 6/14/1934, Herndon Collec-
      tion, reel 22, p. 889.

64   "never refer contemptuously": *CCFH*, 92.

64   "Georgia . . . intends to rid itself": *Harlem Liberator*, 6/2/1934, 1.

64   Ansel Morrison & Don West & claimed to have a warrant: Ansel Morrison
      to Don West, 5/29/1934, pp. 1–4, in ACLUP, vol. 742; *ADW*, 5/29/1934, 1; *DW*,
      5/30/1934, 3; *AC*, 6/3/1934, 1A; *DW*, 6/4/1934, 2; *Harlem Liberator*, 6/9/1934, 5;
      DW, 6/11/1934, 1–2. See Don West, Southern OH Program Collection, 1/22/1975, at
      00:48:29–00:54:17, 01:15:11–01:21:17; Don West, "georgia wanted me dead or alive"
      (1934), in *No Lonesome Road: Selected Prose and Poems*, ed. Jeff Biggers and George
      Brosi (Urbana: University of Illinois Press, 2004), 30–33; James J. Lorence, *A Hard
      Journey: The Life of Don West* (2007), 48–49; Glenda Elizabeth Gilmore, *Defying
      Dixie: The Radical Roots of Civil Rights, 1919–1950* (2008), 174–75.

64   "pure bluff": *DW*, 6/5/1934, 1.

64   Herndon encouraged Davis: AH to Comrade Frieda, 6/1/1934, in ILDP, reel 18, p.
      834; "My Treatment Since the Supreme Court Ruling," n.d., ibid., 775–80.

64   "one of the most remarkable": *DW*, 6/27/1934, 5. See *Harlem Liberator*, 5/4/1934, 4;
      ILD Press Release, 6/11/1934, in ILDP, reel 18, p. 781; *DW*, 6/26/1934, 5.

65   *Harlem Liberator*: *DW*, 6/23/1934, 7.

65   Don West & Ted Poston: *DW*, 6/23/1934, 7; *NYAN*, 6/30/1934, 9.

65   banquet at Lido Hall: *DW*, 6/30/1934, 4.

65   "literary prostitutes" & "keeping them from fighting": *NJG*, 7/7/1934, 4. See
      BAA, 6/30/1934, 13; *Negro Liberator*, 8/18/1934, 2.

65   Geer had been negotiating: *ADW*, 6/17/1934, 1.

65   bail at $15,000: *AC*, 6/21/1934, 3; *ADW*, 6/21/1934, 1; *DW*, 6/29/1934, 3; *DW*,
      6/30/1934, 1; *SW*, 7/34, 4.

65   A "confident" Herndon: AH to William Patterson, 6/24/1934, in AHP, box 1,
      folder 1. See AH to Comrade Al, 6/24/1934, in ibid.

65 began packing: *LML*, 287–90.

65 John Howard Lawson: *DW*, 6/23/1934, 5. See Gerald Horne, *The Final Victim of the Blacklist: John Howard Lawson, Dean of the Hollywood Ten* (2006), 84–85.

66 "lousy bums": John Howard Lawson, "A Southern Welcome (in Georgia and Alabama)," p. 10 (1934), in ACLUP, vol. 742. See *AC*, 7/3/1934, 2; *DW*, 7/5/1934, 1, 6; *CCFH*, 87–90.

66 "cordial and friendly": *AC*, 7/3/1934, 2. See Lawson, "A Southern Welcome," 12.

66 "You boys with them?": *CCFH*, 88–89.

66 "humble as the lowest farmer": Lawson, "A Southern Welcome," 12. See *DW*, 7/5/1934, 6; *BAA*, 7/21/1934, 23.

66 "Ben, you've been" & "What about you, Reverend?": *CCFH*, 88–89.

66 prisoner was "uppity": *DW*, 7/17/1934, 2. See Lawson, "A Southern Welcome," 4.

66 censoring any reading material: *AC*, 7/3/1934, 2; *DW*, 7/5/1934, 1, 6; Lawson, "A Southern Welcome," 4–6.

67 relaxed the restrictions: BJD to Louis Colman, 7/14/1934, p. 1, in AHP, box 1, folder 1.

67 "big-shot nigger" & "fascist dogs": BJD to Colman, 7/14/1934, pp. 1–3. See *DW*, 7/20/1934, 3; *Negro Liberator*, 7/28/1934, 1; *LML*, 293–94.

67 articles in *The New Republic*: *The New Republic*, 7/18/1934, 266; *NM*, 7/24/1934, 6; *The Nation*, 8/1/1934, 127–28.

67 and in the Black press: *PC*, 7/14/34, 4; *PT*, 7/19/1934, 5; *NJG*, 7/21/1934, 8; *PC*, 7/21/1934, 2.

67 The NAACP, still unwilling: *DW*, 7/3/1934, 2, 6.

67 "Free Angelo Herndon": *BAA*, 7/14/1934, 1.

67 small loans from hundreds: *DW*, 7/16/1934, 4; ILD Press Release, 8/11/1934, pp. 1–3, in ILDP, reel 17, pp. 667–69; *DW*, 8/15/1934, 3; *LML*, 290–93; *YCKWC*, 28–29.

67 only $5000: *DW*, 7/27/1934, 2.

67 $7000 short: *DW*, 7/30/1934, 3.

67 then $4000: *DW*, 7/31/1934, 3.

67 then $2400: *DW*, 8/1/1934, 3.

67 still needed $1149: *DW*, 8/2/1934, 1.

67 with the fund oversubscribed: *DW*, 8/3/1934, 2 (oversubscribed by $1324); ILD Press Release, 8/3/1934, pp. 1–2, in ILDP, reel 17, pp. 658–59 (oversubscribed by $3429.35); Corliss Lamont to A. L. Wirin, 8/23/1934, in ACLUP, vol. 742 (handwritten; oversubscribed by $4000).

67 a white turnkey: *LML*, 294–95.

67 "planned attack": ILD Press Release, 8/9/1934, pp. 1–2, in ILDP, reel 17, pp. 664–65.

67 The ACLU wired & Theodore Dreiser: ACLU to Eugene Talmadge, 8/3/1934, tel., ACLUP, vol. 742; Dreiser-Talmadge conversation, 8/3/1934, ibid.; National Committee for the Defense of Political Prisoners Press Release, 8/4/1934, pp. 1–2, in ILDP, reel 17, pp. 660–61; *LML*, 295–96.

68 flew to Atlanta: Joseph Brodsky, "Special to the Daily Worker," 8/5/1934 tel., pp. 1–2, in ILDP, reel 18, pp. 511–12; *DW*, 8/6/1934, 2.

68 no formal order: Brodsky, "Special to the Daily Worker," 8/5/1934 tel., p. 2; *DW*, 8/6/1934, 2; *ADW*, 8/5/1934, 1, 8; *AC*, 8/5/1934, 5A.

68 "Hope to see you back": *DW*, 8/6/1934, 1. See Brodsky, "Special to the Daily Worker," 8/5/1934 tel., p. 1; *LML*, 299.

68 At 5:00 p.m. & Two railway detectives & "circuitous route": *DW*, 8/6/1934, 1. See *ADW*, 8/5/1934, 8; *DW*, 8/6/1934, 1–2; *LML*, 298–301.

68 6:35 p.m.: *DW*, 8/6/1934, 1.

68 forming in Washington & a brown suit and vest: *Washington Afro-American*, n.d., in ILDP, reel 17, p. 72. See *BAA*, 8/11/1934, 1.

68 the cheering crowds: *PT*, 8/16/1934, 9; *PC*, 8/11/1934, 1, 4; *LML*, 304–5.

68 "Hurrah for Herndon": *PT*, 8/9/1934, 1.

69 "It was hell": *NYAN*, 8/11/1934, 1.

69 A delegation: *NYAN*, 8/11/1934, 16. Anna Damon, acting national secretary of the ILD, was quoted ten years later as saying, "It's a pity he isn't blacker!" The quote comes from ex–Communist Party official Timothy Holmes (aka George Hewitt), who claimed he heard it from AH: *NYWT*, 3/22/1944, 1. Less than two months later, Damon leapt to her death: *DW*, 5/19/1944, 5. Five years later, the quotation was widely circulated by historian Arthur Schlesinger Jr. in his *The Vital Center: The Politics of Freedom* (1949), 121. During his 1948 testimony before a Washington State Un-American Activities Committee, Holmes/Hewitt alleged that Ben Davis Jr. tried to run Herndon out of the Party: see note to chapter 9, "do everything in his power" & "the silent treatment."

69 500 more people & Black porter & a large bouquet & "Free Angelo Herndon": *DW*, 8/9/1934, 2 (Robert Minor and Milton Herndon hoisted him). See *Negro Liberator*, 8/11/1934, 1 (Clarence Hathaway, Minor, Ford, and Davis hoisted him); *LML*, 305 (Minor and Davis hoisted him); *YCKWC*, 28–29.

70 "quite tense" and "frail" & "Southern ruling class" & "They can send me": *NYAN*, 8/18/1934, 1.

70 misleaders: *NYAN*, 8/18/1934, 1; *DW*, 8/17/1934, 2; *Negro Liberator*, 8/25/1934, 2, 6.

70 "the only party": *DW*, 8/24/1934, at 2. See *Negro Liberator*, 9/1/1934, 5–6.

70 free the Scottsboro defendants & hands on a newspaper: *DW*, 8/18/1934, 8.

70 Ted Poston, who had covered: *NYAN*, 8/11/1934, 16.

70 Haywood Patterson and Clarence Norris: *DW*, 8/14/1934, 5.

71 As the point person: CWK to Deputy Clerk, 7/27/1934, Georgia Supreme Court Record, no. 9871, p. 01778.

71 freedom of speech and assembly: *IJA Bulletin*, 6/1934, 7.

71 Herndon's lawyers had not raised: *IJA Bulletin*, 8/1934, 3.

71 King consulted: Walter Gellhorn to Charles H. Martin, 5/6/1970, p. 1, Martin Papers (on file with author); Gellhorn Int. by Martin, 9/10/1970, p. 1, ibid. (on file with author); Gellhorn COH 1955, pp. 283–84, 286–89; Wechsler COH, pp. 125–27; William A. Sutherland to Walter Gellhorn, 8/24/1934, in Walter Gellhorn Papers, box 123 (confirming receipt of $100 check from Michael); Herbert Wechsler, "Jerome Michael, 1890–1953," *Columbia Law Review* 53, no. 3 (1953): 301.

71 Walter Gellhorn: Gellhorn COH 1955, pp. 159–92, 199–208 (Stone), 209–16 (solicitor general's office). See Jerome R. Hellerstein, chairman of IJA research committee, to Walter Gellhorn, 11/6/1933, in Gellhorn Papers, box 118 (asking Gellhorn for assistance in preparing a civil rights manual on behalf of CWK and the IJA); Charles H. Martin, *The Angelo Herndon Case and Southern Justice* (1976), 140 (suggesting King may have approached Gellhorn directly, based on 9/10/1970 Int. with Gellhorn); Herbert Wechsler to Charles H. Martin, 6/15/1970, Herbert Wechsler Papers, box 94 (recalling that Seymour brought him into the case).

71 friend and colleague Wechsler: Gellhorn COH 1955, p. 230; Wechsler COH, pp. 124–26.

71 winter of 1930: HFS to Walter Gellhorn, 1/5/1931, in Harlan Fiske Stone Papers, box 14, folder 3; Walter Gellhorn to HFS, 1/7/1933, in ibid.; HFS to Herbert Wechsler, 1/5/1931, in ibid., box 30, folder 3; Wechsler COH, pp. 53–54.

71   **the tall, fair-haired Gellhorn:** 1931 *Columbia Law Review* photograph;
      Wechsler COH, p. 60 (describing the partially Jewish Gellhorn as one of the
      "white-haired boys").

71   **top student in his class:** Wechsler COH, pp. 42, 54.

71   **Jewish-run firms:** Emory Buckner to Herbert Wechsler, 1/1/1931, in Wechsler
      Papers, box 90; Wechsler COH, pp. 54–55.

71   **assistant in law & succeeded Gellhorn:** HFS to Columbia Law School Dean
      Young B. Smith, 12/31/1931, in Stone Papers, box 30, folder 3; Herbert Wechsler to
      HFS, 1/3/1932, in ibid.; Walter Gellhorn to Herbert Wechsler, 12/19/1931, 1–2, in
      Wechsler Papers, box 4; Walter Gellhorn to Herbert Wechsler, ca. 12/1931, in ibid.;
      "Friday," pp. 1–6, ibid.; HFS to Herbert Wechsler, 12/31/1931, in ibid.; Wechsler
      COH, pp. 55–58.

72   **convictions of the Scottsboro defendants:** Herbert Wechsler to FF, 7/22/1946, p. 3,
      in Wechsler Papers, box 94; Anders Walker, "'Neutral' Principles: Rethinking the
      Legal History of Civil Rights, 1934–1964," *Loyola University Chicago Law Jour-
      nal* 40, no. 3 (2009): 385, 391. Wechsler's younger brother, James, was an aspiring
      journalist, a Columbia University student, and a member of the Young Communist
      League: Wechsler COH, pp. 27–28; James A. Wechsler, *The Age of Suspicion* (1953),
      33–98. James Wechsler became the editor of the *New York Post* and an influential
      columnist.

72   **joined the executive committee:** *IJA Bulletin*, 12/1933, 3; Ginger, "The Founding
      of the International Juridical Association," 75.

72   **Wechsler drafted a memorandum:** Ginger, *Carol Weiss King*, 179–80. See "Points
      for Letter to Chief Justice Russell," n.d., pp. 1–7, Angelo Herndon Collection, reel
      22, pp. 900–906; "Herndon Case—Notes," n.d., pp. 1–4, ibid., pp. 908–11.

Chapter Five: The Wall Street Lawyer

73   **the youngest partner:** *Newsweek*, 4/20/1935, 25.

73   **exclusive private clubs:** WNS COH, 3/22/1977, pp. 67–68; Eleanor M. Fox, ed., *A
      Visit with Whitney North Seymour* (1984), 28–29.

73   **thirty-five Supreme Court cases:** WNS COH, 3/22/1977, p. 26; Fox, *Visit with
      Whitney North Seymour*, 10. Cf. *Newsweek*, 4/20/1935, 25 (claiming Seymour made
      his twenty-first appearance before the Court in the first Herndon argument). A
      Westlaw search revealed Seymour on the briefs in forty-nine cases between May
      1931 and May 1933.

74   **Tacoma, Washington:** WNS COH, 3/22/1977, pp. 1–3; Fox, *Visit with Whitney
      North Seymour*, 4. See *Wisconsin State Journal*, 8/2/1918, 3; Williams College, Class
      of 1863, Fortieth Year Report (1903), 154; https://www.theoldcuriosityshop.net/
      charles-walton-seymour.

74   **sixty historical topics & accompanied his father:** WNS COH, 3/22/1977, pp. 4–5;
      Fox, *Visit with Whitney North Seymour*, 6; *Muscatine (IA) News Tribune*, 5/3/1904,
      1; *Minneapolis Journal*, 3/11/1903, 5.

74   **rural fields for arrowheads:** WNS COH, 3/22/1977, pp. 3–4; Fox, *Visit with Whit-
      ney North Seymour*, 5; *Wisconsin State Journal*, 8/22/1916, 5.

74   **Indian mounds & working at the library:** WNS COH, 3/22/1977, pp. 6–7; Fox,
      Visit with Whitney North Seymour, 6–7.

74   **John R. Commons:** WNS to John R. Commons, 2/6/1935, p. 1, in WNSP, box 2.
      On Commons at the University of Wisconsin, see John R. Commons, *Myself* (New
      York: Macmillan, 1934), 95–201.

74   **distinguished himself as a debater:** WNS COH, 3/22/1977, pp. 8–9; *Wisconsin State
      Journal*, 2/14/1917, 5; *Capitol Times* (Madison, WI), 10/17/1919, 4; 1921 University
      of Wisconsin *Badger*, 144; *Capitol Times* (Madison, WI), 4/25/1935, in WNSP, box
      117, folder "Angelo Herndon Material."

74   **his father died:** *Wisconsin State Journal*, 8/2/1918, 3.

74   **associate professor at City College:** WNS COH, 3/22/1977, pp. 9–10; Fox, *Visit
      with Whitney North Seymour*, 8–9; *The Brief* 21, no. 4 (1922): 290.

74   **Harlan Fiske Stone:** WNS COH, 3/22/1977, pp. 9, 24–25; Fox, *Visit with Whitney
      North Seymour*, 8–9; WNS to HFS, 10/31/1933, in WNSP, box 1, folder "WNS 1930–
      1937"; WNS to HFS, 10/10/1934, in ibid.; WNS to HFS, 10/19/1936, in ibid.; WNS
      to HFS, 10/10/1941, in ibid., folder "WNS 1941–1944"; WNS to HFS, 10/8/1943, in
      ibid.; WNS to HFS, 10/9/1944, in ibid.

74   **young lawyer at Simpson, Thacher:** WNS COH, 3/22/1977, pp. 14–16; Fox, *Visit
      with Whitney North Seymour*, 9–11, 15–16.

75   **two cases a week:** WNS COH, 3/22/1977, pp. 26–27; Fox, *Visit with Whitney North
      Seymour*, 10–11.

75   **at their homes:** WNS to Commons, 2/6/1935, p. 1.

75   **Seymour treasured books:** WNS to Lewis Merriam Wiggin, 6/10/1937, in WNSP,
      box 2; list of books, n.d., 1–2, (including signed copy of Cardozo's *The Nature of the
      Judicial Process*; signed copy of Holmes's *Collected Legal Papers, Representative
      Opinions of Mr. Justice Holmes,* and two signed Holmes letters; and *The Social and
      Economic Views of Mr. Justice Brandeis* and three signed Brandeis letters), in ibid.

75   **Walter H. Pollak:** WP, 12/20/1932, 16. See WNS, "The October, 1932, Term of the
      United States Supreme Court (Part I)," *Federal Bar Association* 1, no. 4 (1933): 37,
      39–40 (discussing *Powell v. Alabama*); Bethuel M. Webster, "A Memorial for the
      1984 Yearbook of the Century Association," in Fox, *Visit with Whitney North Sey-
      mour*, 96 (recalling that the Seymours celebrated the victory in *Powell v. Alabama*
      with the Pollaks at the Savoy Ballroom in Harlem).

75   **won new trials for the Scottsboro defendants:** Powell v. Alabama, 287 U.S. 45, 71–
      73 (1932).

75   **suggested that Seymour argue:** WNS COH, 3/22/1977, p. 29; Fox, *Visit with Whit-
      ney North Seymour*, 12; WNS Int. by Charles H. Martin, 9/8/1970, p. 1, Charles H.
      Martin Papers (on file with author). Others recalled Gellhorn alone asking WNS:
      Gellhorn 1955 COH, p. 289; Wechsler COH, pp. 97, 126–27; Gellhorn Int. by Mar-
      tin, 9/10/1970, p. 2; Walter Gellhorn to Charles H. Martin, 5/6/1970, p. 2, in Mar-
      tin Papers (on file with author); Charles H. Martin, *The Angelo Herndon Case
      and Southern Justice* (1976), 140; Ann Fagan Ginger, *Carol Weiss King: Human
      Rights Lawyer, 1895–1952* (1993), 179–80. Gellhorn conceded that his recollection
      of the sequence of events was not "fresh in my mind": Gellhorn Int. by Martin,
      9/10/1970, p. 2.

75   **She had been angling:** CWK to WNS, 12/18/1934, in WNSP, box 2; CWK to WNS,
      12/4/1934, in ibid.; WNS to CWK, 1/16/1935, in ibid. (declining to be on ILD's
      national committee).

75   **donated to the Scottsboro defense fund:** Louis S. Weiss to WNS, 5/21/1934, in
      WNSP, box 1; WNS to Louis S. Weiss, 5/25/1934, in ibid. See WNS Int. by Martin,
      9/8/1970, p. 5.

76 **asked Thacher for permission:** WNS COH, 3/22/1977, pp. 29–30; Fox, *Visit with Whitney North Seymour*, 12.

76 **"complete control":** WNS to Judge Clifton Alexander Woodrum, 1/9/1942, p. 1, in WNSP, box 1. See Gellhorn 1955 COH, pp. 289–90; Gellhorn 1977 COH, pp. 15–16; WNS Int. by Martin, 9/8/1970, p. 4; Gellhorn Int. by Martin, 9/10/1970, p. 3; Gellhorn to Martin, 5/6/1970, p. 2; Martin, *The Angelo Herndon Case*, 141.

76 **Seymour worried:** WNS Int. by Martin, 9/8/1970, p. 4; Ginger, *Carol Weiss King*, 180.

76 **100 communists:** *NYT*, 11/8/1932, 1, 13; *WP*, 11/8/1932, 1, 3; *ADW*, 11/9/1932, 1, 4.

76 **"the best possible defense":** "Statement of Relationship between International Labor Defense Legal Committee and Attorneys," n.d., pp. 3–4, WNSP, box 1 (CWK handwritten on front: "I thought this might interest you especially pages 3–4. C.K.").

76 **"the basic rights of free speech":** Anna Damon to WNS, 8/31/1934, in WNSP, box 1. See ILD Press Release, 8/30/1934, in ILDP, reel 17, p. 673; ILD Press Release, 8/31/1934, in ibid., p. 674; *DW*, 9/1/1934, 3.

77 **On August 9:** Petition for Rehearing to Georgia Supreme Court, 8/17/1934, at 2, Georgia Supreme Court Record, no. 9871, p. 1081.

77 **Russell denied the request:** Petition for Rehearing to Georgia Supreme Court, 8/17/1934, at 4–5.

77 **Georgia Supreme Court's rules:** Petition for Rehearing to Georgia Supreme Court, 8/17/1934, at 1–2, 5; Rule 40, Rules of the Supreme Court of the State of Georgia 9–10 (1934).

77 **On August 20:** Deputy Clerk to Justice R. C. Bell, 8/20/1934, Georgia Supreme Court Record, no. 9871, p. 1179. Justice S. Price Gilbert did not vote on the motion: see ibid.; *DW*, 8/21/1934, 1; *ADW*, 8/21/1934, 1; *AC*, 8/21/1934, 4; WNS to Clerk Z. D. Harrison, 8/29/1934, Georgia Supreme Court Record, no. 9871, p. 1180.

77 **a clear and present danger:** Schenck v. United States, 249 U.S. 47, 52 (1919). See *IJA Bulletin*, 8/1934, 3.

77 **"it must appear clearly":** Petition for Rehearing to Georgia Supreme Court, 8/20/1934, at 1, Georgia Supreme Court Record, no. 9871, p. 1092 (quoting Herndon Trial Record, at 195).

77 **advocated "immediate serious violence":** Herndon v. State, 174 S.E. 597, 608–9 (Ga. 1934).

77 **"necessary to guilt":** Petition for Rehearing to Georgia Supreme Court, 8/20/1934, at 2 (quoting Herndon v. State, 174 S.E. at 610).

77 **contradicted the U.S. Supreme Court's:** Petition for Rehearing to Georgia Supreme Court, 8/20/1934, at 4 (citing Schenk v. United States, 249 U.S. at 52; Fiske v. Kansas, 274 U.S. 380 [1927]; Stromberg v. California, 283 U.S. 359 [1931]).

78 **permitted defendants to raise:** Petition for Rehearing to Georgia Supreme Court, 8/20/1934, at 4 (citing Schenk, 249 U.S. at 52; Fiske v. Kansas, 274 U.S. 380 [1927]; Stromberg v. California, 283 U.S. 359 [1931]); *IJA Bulletin*, 8/1934, 3, 3n12.

78 **"within a reasonable time":** Herndon v. State, 176 S.E. 620, 622 (Ga. 1934).

78 **"a clear and imminent danger" & "does not fail for want":** Herndon v. State, 176 S.E. 623–24 (Ga. 1934) (quoting Whitney v. California, 274 U.S. 357, 373 [1927] [Brandeis, J., concurring]).

78 **Pleasantly surprised:** WNS to William Sutherland, 10/5/1934, in WNSP, box 1.

78 **Seymour obtained an order:** WNS to William Sutherland, 12/21/1934, at 1, Georgia Supreme Court Record, no. 9871, p. 1183.

78   On December 26: Herndon v. Georgia, Petition for Appeal and Assignment of
      Errors, 12/26/1934, October Term 1934 U.S. Supreme Court Record, at 201–4.

78   January 19, 1935: Herndon v. Georgia, no. 665, Statement as to Jurisdiction,
      1/19/1935.

78   free speech and assembly & unconstitutionally vague: Herndon v. Georgia, no.
      665, Statement as to Jurisdiction, 1/19/1935, at 9.

79   reviewed the charges and evidence: Herndon v. Georgia, no. 665, Statement as to
      Jurisdiction, 1/19/1935, at 3–8.

79   The state supreme court's rulings: Herndon v. Georgia, no. 665, Statement as to
      Jurisdiction, 1/19/1935, at 8–17.

79   "a substantial Federal question": Herndon v. Georgia, no. 665, Statement as to
      Jurisdiction, 1/19/1935, at 12.

79   it reserved consideration: Journal of the Supreme Court of the United States, Octo-
      ber Term 1934, 2/11/1935, at 140; Brief for Appellant, Herndon v. Georgia, October
      Term 1934 U.S. Supreme Court, at 2.

80   he would jump bail: PC, 8/25/1934, 10.

80   "never missed" an "opportunity" & "Uncle Tom": DW, 8/28/1934, 5. See DW,
      8/27/1934, 2.

80   embellishing Herndon's life story: YCKWC; ADW, 9/7/1934, 4; BAA, 9/8/1934, 5;
      BAA, 9/15/1934, 5; BAA, 9/22/1934, 5; BAA, 9/29/1934, 5; BAA, 10/6/1934, 5; BAA,
      10/13/1934, 5; BAA, 10/20/1934, 5; BAA, 10/27/1934, 5; BAA, 11/10/1934, 5; BAA,
      11/17/1934, 5.

80   Herndon hit the lecture circuit: DW, 9/4/1934, 5; DW, 11/16/1934, 3; Wesley Ran-
      dall to AH, 12/3/1934, in AHP, box 1, folder 3; Wesley Randall to AH, 12/14/1934,
      pp. 1–2, in ibid. (listing West Coast cities). See W. Burghardt Turner and Joyce
      Moore Turner, eds., Richard B. Moore, Caribbean Militant in Harlem: Collected
      Writings, 1920–1972 (1988), 60–61.

80   "one of the most enthusiastic audiences" & "the fight has just begun": CDef,
      9/29/1934, 13.

80   Mason Opera House: Western Worker, 11/22/1934, 1, 5. See California Eagle,
      11/24/1934, in ILDP, reel 17, p. 108.

81   refused to contribute: Negro Liberator, 2/1/1935, 3.

81   spouting communist propaganda: ADW, 12/11/1934, 1, 5.

81   Tom Mooney: Richard H. Frost, The Mooney Case (Stanford, CA: Stanford Uni-
      versity Press, 1968), 80–102, 173–93.

81   "a treat" & "no illusions" & "still determined to help": Labor Defender, 1/1935,
      8–9. See DW, 1/16/1935, 5.

81   moved by the "militancy" & "vehemently protested": Labor Defender, 3/1935, 16.

82   "hundreds of thousands": DW, 4/6/1935, 4.

82   cases of Clarence Norris and Haywood Patterson: Norris v. Alabama, 294 U.S.
      587, 597–99 (1935); Patterson v. Alabama, 294 U.S. 600, 607 (1935).

82   the justices saw for themselves: Benno C. Schmidt Jr., "Juries, Jurisdiction, and
      Race Discrimination: The Lost Promise of Strauder v. West Virginia," Texas Law
      Review 61, no. 8 (1983): 1476–82; Dan T. Carter, Scottsboro: A Tragedy of the Amer-
      ican South (1979), 319.

82   legal team decided to stay the course: ADW, 4/3/1935, 1, 5; WNS Int. by Martin,
      9/8/1970, pp. 5–6 (recalling desire to put "best foot forward" on free speech and
      assembly and not detract from those claims with jury issue); Gellhorn Int. by Mar-

tin, 9/10/1970, p. 4 (recalling that the Court would not have taken up case about jury issue "alone").

82   eighteen communists: *NM*, 4/23/1935, 3; ILD Press Release, 8/1/1935, p. 2, in ILDP, reel 17, p. 720.

82   police arrested two white women: *DW*, 9/8/1934, 2; *DW*, 9/17/1934, 2; *DW*, 9/20/1934, 4; *ADW*, 9/30/1934, 1; *AC*, 10/3/1934, 5; *AC*, 10/4/1934, 7; *DW*, 10/4/1934, 1, 2; Martin, *The Angelo Herndon Case*, 124.

82   raided communist meetings: *ADW*, 10/16/1934, 1, 4–5; *ADW*, 10/17/1934, 1, 5; *AJ*, 10/17/1934, 17; Martin, *The Angelo Herndon Case*, 121–39.

82   Urban League: *ADW*, 10/16/1934, 1, 4; *ADW*, 10/20/1934, 1; *ADW*, 10/23/1934, 1, 3; *DW*, 10/26/1934, 5; *ADW*, 10/26/1934, 1, 4; *BAA*, 10/27/1934, 8; *CDef*, 11/17/1934, 3.

83   "Not only are the rights": *NM*, 4/23/1935, 3.

83   For several months: WNS to Walter Gellhorn, 3/2/1935, in Gellhorn Papers, box 123 (enclosing brief and asking for feedback from Gellhorn and Wechsler).

83   Filed on March 16, 1935: Herndon Brief for Appellant, October Term 1934 U.S. Supreme Court, at 62.

83   four main arguments: Herndon Brief for Appellant, October Term 1934 U.S. Supreme Court, at 2, 10–13.

83   After reviewing the facts: Herndon Brief for Appellant, October Term 1934 U.S. Supreme Court, at 3–10.

83   drafted by Wechsler: Wechsler COH, pp. 127–28.

83   the clear and present danger test: Herndon Brief for Appellant, October Term 1934 U.S. Supreme Court, at 13–16. See Schenck v. United States 249 U.S. 47, 52 (1919).

83   a constitutional "command." Other Supreme Court decisions: Herndon Brief for Appellant, October Term 1934 U.S. Supreme Court, at 16–21 (quoting Whitney v. California, 274 U.S. 357, 376-77 [1927] [Brandeis, J., concurring]).

83   In contrast to California & revised in 1866: Herndon Brief for Appellant, October Term 1934 U.S. Supreme Court, at 21–38.

84   not intended to be used & "The present record": Herndon Brief for Appellant, October Term 1934 U.S. Supreme Court, at 38–39.

84   section drafted by Gellhorn: WNS to Gellhorn, 3/2/1935; Wechsler COH, pp. 127–28.

84   "sufficiently definite": Herndon Brief for Appellant, October Term 1934 U.S. Supreme Court, at 40.

84   several Supreme Court decisions: Herndon Brief for Appellant, October Term 1934 U.S. Supreme Court, at 42–47.

84   evidence did not support & The literature seized & Black Belt thesis: Herndon Brief for Appellant, October Term 1934 U.S. Supreme Court, at 47–59.

84   "properly raised" & petition for rehearing: Herndon Brief for Appellant, October Term 1934 U.S. Supreme Court, at 59–62.

85   state of Georgia argued & "unanticipated ruling": State of Georgia, Brief for Appellee, October Term 1934 U.S. Supreme Court, at 5–6, 11–26.

86   was consistent with & "dangerous tendency" & Brandeis and Holmes: State of Georgia, Brief for Appellee, October Term 1934 U.S. Supreme Court, at 26–39 (citing Gilbert v. Minnesota, 254 U.S. 325 [1920]).

86   Reconstruction-era roots & Black Belt: State of Georgia, Brief for Appellee, October Term 1934 U.S. Supreme Court, at 39–42.

86   **no more vague:** State of Georgia, Brief for Appellee, October Term 1934 U.S. Supreme Court, at 42–47.

86   **Finally, the evidence:** State of Georgia, Brief for Appellee, October Term 1934 U.S. Supreme Court, at 47–67.

86   **a long line of sightseers:** *DW*, 4/13/1935, 2; *WashTrib*, 4/20/1935, 9.

86   **"Mr. Angelo Herndon" & second row:** *DW*, 4/16/1935, 5. See *Labor Defender*, 10/1936, 13.

87   **"looked like god":** Robert H. Jackson, "Lunch at the White House on Saturday, Dec. 31, 1938," p. 4, Robert H. Jackson Papers, box 81, folder 3.

87   **"Angelo Herndon versus":** *DW*, 4/16/1935, 5.

87   **"at any time in the future":** *DW*, 4/13/1935, 2. See *Newsweek*, 4/20/1935, 25.

88   **"The basic constitutional rights":** *WashTrib*, 4/20/1935, 9.

88   **Seymour's performance was "splendid":** *DW*, 4/16/1935, 5. See *Newsweek*, 4/20/1935, 25.

88   **"a brilliant and eloquent plea":** *The Nation*, 5/8/1935, 540.

88   **"ranting and raving" & "open call":** *The Nation*, 5/8/1935, 540. See *DW*, 4/13/1935, 2; *WashTrib*, 4/20/1935, 9; *BAA*, 4/20/1935, 10 (recording LeCraw's use of racial epithets).

88   **"Maybe what they" & "Can you confiscate" & "Can this be political" & "We thought that was settled":** *DW*, 4/13/1935, 2. Louis Colman's account in *DW* is the most detailed source of quotations in the absence of an oral argument transcript. Supreme Court oral argument was not regularly recorded before 1955.

89   **"Nigras":** *The Nation*, 5/8/1935, 540.

89   **"The membership book" & "The idea of a separate country":** *DW*, 4/13/1935, 2.

89   **"seemed to irritate":** *Newsweek*, 4/20/1935, 25.

89   **a 6–3 opinion:** The justices discussed Herndon's case at their April 27 private conference and then voted: McReynolds Docket Book, *Herndon v. Georgia*, October Term 1934 U.S. Supreme Court; Roberts Docket Book, *Herndon v. Georgia*, ibid.; Stone Docket Book, *Herndon v. Georgia*, ibid. There are no extant conference notes explaining why the justices voted that way.

89   **should have been raised & general constitutional objection & refusal to revisit & March 18, 1933 & "It follows":** Herndon v. Georgia, 295 U.S. 441, 442–46 (1935) (citing Carr v. State, 169 S.E. 201 [Ga. 1933] [Carr II]). On *Carr II*, see above note to chapter 3, "Atlanta Six."

90   **Justice Cardozo:** Andrew L. Kaufman, *Cardozo* (1998); Richard Polenberg, *The World of Benjamin Cardozo* (1997).

90   **emphasized the differences & "the protection" & "challenge the unexpected ruling":** Herndon v. Georgia, 295 U.S. at 446–47 (Cardozo, J., dissenting).

90   **"has color" & Atlanta Six case & "an unequivocal rejection" & "If the rejection" & "the questions":** Herndon v. Georgia, 295 U.S. at 448–55 (Cardozo, J., dissenting).

91   **"sick chicken case":** A.L.A. Schechter Poultry Corp. v. United States, 295 U.S. 495 (1935).

91   **"horse-and-buggy definition":** Franklin Delano Roosevelt, Press Conference, 5/31/1935, p. 28, Franklin Delano Roosevelt Library, Press Conference, ser. 1, no. 209; *NYT*, 6/1/1935, 1, 6.

91   **"The jurisdictional disposition":** FF to LDB, 5/24/[1935], p. 2, in FFLC, box 29.

91   **"harsh":** FF and Henry M. Hart Jr., "The Business of the Supreme Court at October Term, 1934," *Harvard Law Review* 49, no. 1 (1935): 68, 93*n*65. See FF, "Mr. Jus-

tice Cardozo and Public Law," *Harvard Law Review* 52, no. 3 (1939): 440, 463–64 (praising Cardozo's *Herndon v. Georgia* dissent); Kendall Thomas, *"Rouge et Noir* Reread: A Popular Constitutional History of the Angelo Herndon Case," *Southern California Law Review* 65, no. 6 (1992): 2599, 2669–78, 2684–87 (criticizing FF and Hart for failing to distinguish between "rules" and "decisions").

91   newspapers, left-wing magazines: *Cincinnati Post,* 5/21/1935, 6; *Richmond Times-Dispatch,* 5/22/1935, 8; *Pittsburgh Press,* 5/23/1935, 10; *The Nation,* 5/29/1935, 623; *The New Republic,* 5/29/1935, 58; *St. Louis Star-Times,* 6/3/1953, in ILDP, reel 17, p. 462; *BP,* n.d., in ibid., p. 482; *BP,* 5/21/1935, in ibid., p. 485.

91   Black press: *NYAN,* 5/25/1935, 10, in ILDP, reel 17, p. 497; *Denver Star,* 6/8/1935, in ibid., p. 493; *CDef,* 6/1/1935, 16; *Richmond Planet,* 6/1/1935, in ILDP, reel 17, p. 477; *BAA,* 6/1/1935, in ibid., p. 484; *BAA,* 6/8/1935, 4; *PC,* 6/10/1935, 10; *The Crisis,* 7/1935, 209; *Cleveland Call and Post,* n.d., p. 6, in ILDP, reel 17, p. 489; *Louisiana Weekly,* n.d., in ibid., p. 470.

92   "All honor is due": *New York Post,* 5/22/1935, in ILDP, reel 17, p. 481.

92   "Herndon Jailed for Demanding": *DW,* 6/6/1935, 3. See *WES,* 6/2/1935, A16; *WES,* 6/3/1935, 4; *NYHT,* 6/4/1935, 7; *Northwest Enterprise* (Seattle), 6/13/1935, 1, 2.

92   "bring to the attention": *BAA,* 6/8/1935, 2.

92   northeastern colleges: *DW,* 5/11/1935, 4; *DW,* 5/13/1935, 2; *BAA,* 5/18/1935, 23; *NYA,* 5/18/1935, 2.

92   "those ghostly-looking men": *DW,* 5/29/1935, 3.

93   "What the Supreme Court": *Labor Defender,* 6/1935, 5.

Chapter Six: The Civil Rights Lawyer

95   Leroy Braxton appealed: Leroy M. Braxton to Walter White, 2/2/1933, in NAACPP, pt. 12, ser. C, reel 3, p. 47.

95   "exclusive control of the case": Walter White to Leroy Braxton, 2/3/1933, in NAACPP, pt. 12, ser. C, reel 3, p. 45.

96   "sabotaging maneuvers" & "lying attack": ILD Press Release, 2/23/1933, in ILDP, reel 17, p. 622. See AH to William Patterson, 2/13/1933, in AHP, box 1, folder 1 (alerting ILD to letter from NAACP to Leroy Braxton).

96   pursuing a united front: James W. Ford, "The United Front in the Field of Negro Work," *The Communist,* 2/1935, 158–74.

96   Popular Front: In August 1935, the Comintern endorsed a worldwide Popular Front at the Seventh Comintern Congress: Harvey Klehr and John Earl Haynes, *The American Communist Movement: Storming Heaven Itself* (1992), 78–79.

96   "to discuss with you": AH to NAACP, 5/24/1935, in NAACPP, pt. 8, ser. A, reel 8, p. 630.

96   "deeply interested": Walter White to AH, 5/27/1935, in NAACPP, pt. 8, ser. A, reel 8, p. 629.

96   The committee contacted: Memorandum from the Secretary re the Angelo Herndon Case, 6/4/1935, NAACPP, pt. 8, ser. A, reel 8, p. 640. See Walter White to Arthur B. Spingarn, 5/27/1935, in ibid., p. 628; Walter White to CHH, 5/27/1935, in ibid, p. 636; Walter White to Arthur Spingarn, 6/3/1935, in ibid., p. 638.

96   "a poor record" & "they have brought": CHH to Walter White, 5/25/1935, in NAACPP, pt. 1, reel 16, p. 420.

97   **Odd Fellows:** *Washington Bee*, 7/22/1911, 4; CHHP, box 163-3, folders 5–6, 11–16; photograph, 1907–8, National Museum of African American History and Culture, Washington, D.C.

97   **they socialized together:** BJD to CHH, 6/12/1933, in CHHP, box 163-26, folder 9; *CDef*, 5/6/1933, 17 (noting CHH visited BJD in New York City).

97   **Phi Beta Kappa:** 1915 Amherst College *Olio*, p. 244; Amherst College Graduation Program, 6/30/1915, WLHP, box 17, folder 11; *WES*, 3/17/1915, in ibid.; *Amherst (MA) Student*, 3/15/1915, p. 1, in ibid., folder 5; *Crisis*, 7/1915, 140, in ibid., box 23, folder 3. On Houston, see Genna Rae McNeil, *Groundwork: Charles Hamilton Houston and the Struggle for Civil Rights* (1983); Rawn James Jr., *Root and Branch: Charles Hamilton Houston, Thurgood Marshall, and the Struggle to End Segregation* (New York: Bloomsbury, 2010); Kenneth Mack, *Representing the Race: The Creation of the Civil Rights Lawyer* (2012), 42–45; Bruce A. Kimball and Daniel R. Coquillette, *The Intellectual Sword: Harvard Law School, the Second Century* (2020), 184–86; José Felipé Anderson, *Genius for Justice: Charles Hamilton Houston and the Reform of American Law* (2022).

97   **Dunbar's widow:** Alice N. Dunbar to CHH, 6/24/1916, in WLHP, box 1, folder 8.

97   **civil rights lawyer:** During his first year of law school, CHH corresponded with NAACP officials about working that summer for the civil rights organization for free: CHH to Mr. Johnson, 2/15/1920, in NAACPP, pt. I.C., box 113, folder 20; Walter White to CHH, 3/8/1920, in ibid.; CHH to Walter White, 3/15/1920, in ibid.; Walter White to CHH, 3/17/1920, in ibid.; CHH to Walter White, 3/18/1920, in ibid.; CHH to Walter White, 5/23/1920, in ibid; Walter White to CHH, 5/26/1920, in ibid.; Walter White to Mary Ovington, 6/10/1920, in ibid.

97   **second lieutenant:** Snow to Lt. Col. A. H. Carter, 8/26/1918, tel., WLHP, box 20, folder 15.

97   **court-martial:** *PC*, 8/24/1940, 13. See CHH Diary, 5/15/1918, WLHP, box 20, folder 17.

98   **White American soldiers:** CHH to Mary Houston, 10/10/1918, pp. 13–16, in WLHP, box 4, folder 8; CHH to William LePre Houston, 10/12/1918, pp. 8–10, in ibid., box 8, folder 2; CHH Diary, 1/5/1919 and 1/6/1919, ibid., box 20, folder 17.

98   **lynched in retaliation:** *PC*, 9/21/1940, 13; *PC*, 9/28/1940, 13.

98   **he improved his grades:** Roscoe Pound to U.S. Veterans' Bureau, 9/27/1921, in WLHP, box 18, folder 8.

98   **some of the other editors:** CHH to William LePre Houston, 1/8/[1922], p. 9, in WLHP, box 8, folder 10.

98   **Dunbar Law Club:** Dunbar Law Club, moot case, Hercules v. Strong Firearms Co. 1919, WLHP, box 15. The Dunbar Law Club was named for Donald Earl Dunbar, a 1917 law graduate killed in World War I: *Harvard Alumni Bulletin*, 2/5/1920, 443. See McNeil, *Groundwork*, 52; Kimball and Coquillette, *The Intellectual Sword*, 184; David A. Canton, *Raymond Pace Alexander: A New Negro Lawyer Fights for Civil Rights in Philadelphia* (Jackson: University Press of Mississippi, 2010), 16 (attributing formation of club to Houston and Black law student Raymond Pace Alexander).

98   **Houston impressed leading members:** Pound to U.S. Veterans' Bureau, 9/27/1921; Acting Dean Edward Warren to U.S. Veterans' Bureau, 1/19/1922, pp. 1–2, in WLHP, box 18, folder 8; Roscoe Pound to Judge Fenton Booth, 12/31/1923, in CHHP, box 163-12, folder 18; Joseph Beal to CHH, 6/13/1923, in ibid., box 163-5, folder 16; FF to CHH, 1/3/1924, in ibid., box 163-19, folder 11.

98   received his doctorate: CHH to U.S. Veterans' Bureau, 1/19/1921, pp. 1–2, in
        WLHP, box 18, folder 8; CHH, "Notice and Hearing as a Condition Precedent to
        Governmental Action: Preliminary Report" (1923), Harvard Law School Library,
        Red Set.

98   Sheldon Traveling Fellowship: Prof. L. B. R. Briggs to CHH, 3/20/1923, in WLHP,
        box 18, folder 7.

98   transforming Howard's law school: CHH, "Message to Friends," 4/12/1926, pp.
        1–5, WLHP, box 15, folder 8.

98   Black lawyers as "social engineers": McNeil, Groundwork, 67–72 (citing CHH,
        "Survey of the Status and Activities of Negro Lawyers in the United States," and
        CHH, "Personal Observations on the Summary of Studies in Legal Education as
        Applied to the Howard University School of Law"); CHH, "The Need for Negro
        Lawyers," Journal of Negro Education 4, no. 1 (Jan. 1935): 49–52.

98   vice dean: Emmett J. Scott to CHH, 8/10/1929, in WLHP, box 2, folder 6.

98   William Hastie: CHH to William Hastie, 3/10/1930, pp. 1–2, in WLHP, box 3,
        folder 7; CHH to William Hastie, 4/7/1930, in ibid.

99   all-Black defense team: CHH to Walter White, 10/17/1933, p. 1, in NAACPP, pt. 8,
        reel 7, p. 6; "Memorandum from Mr. White re Long Distance Telephone Conversa-
        tion with Mr. Charles H. Houston," 11/1/1933, p. 1, ibid., pt. 1, reel 16, p. 286; Wal-
        ter White, A Man Called White (Athens: University of Georgia Press, 1995), 152–53.

99   George Crawford: McNeil, Groundwork, 89–95; Mack, Representing the Race,
        83–110; Patricia Sullivan, Life Every Voice: The NAACP and the Making of the
        Civil Rights Movement (2009), 164–68; David Bradley, The Historic Murder Trial
        of George Crawford: Charles H. Houston, the NAACP, and the Case That Put All-
        White Southern Juries on Trial (2014).

99   arrested for burglary: Boston Globe, 1/19/1933, 5.

99   James A. Lowell: Boston Globe, 4/25/1933, 12.

99   reversed on appeal: Hale v. Crawford, 65 F.2d 739 (1933).

99   Houston betrayed Crawford: The Nation, 6/27/1934, 730–32; The Nation, 7/4/1934,
        17–19; NM, 1/8/1935, 9–15. See DW, 8/1/1934, 8; DW, 9/28/1934, 3; McNeil, Ground-
        work, 102–5; Mack, Representing the Race, 173–80.

99   Bernard Ades: BAA, 12/16/1933, 12; BAA, 3/24/1934, 2; McNeil, Groundwork, 95–
        99; Mack, Representing the Race, 114–18.

100   Houston declined to represent: CHH to Bernard Ades, 5/1/1934, in CHHP, box
        163-37, folder 2; Bernard Ades to CHH, 5/9/1934, in ibid.; WashTrib, 5/17/1934, 1–2;
        BAA, 5/19/1934, 11.

100   a pragmatic legal strategist: Kenneth Robert Janken, White: The Biography of Wal-
        ter White, Mr. NAACP (2003), 178–79.

100   Willie Peterson's death sentence: Sullivan, Lift Every Voice, 170–72; Melanie S. Mor-
        rison, Murder on Shades Mountain: The Legal Lynching of Willie Peterson and the
        Struggle for Justice in Jim Crow Birmingham (2018), 134–41. Houston abided by the
        wishes of Peterson's white counsel not to attend the pardon board hearing: ibid., 162–
        67. Governor Benjamin M. Miller commuted Peterson's sentence to life in prison:
        ibid., 178–84. Houston was not satisfied and wanted to prove his innocence: ibid., 182.

100   a brief to the U.S. Attorney General: CHH to Attorney General, 10/13/1933, in
        NAACPP, pt. 7, reel 8, p. 141; "Memorandum Report to the International Labor
        Defense, American Civil Liberties Union, and National Association for the
        Advancement of Colored People," 10/13/1933, pp. 1–3, ibid., pp. 143–45; Sullivan,
        Lift Every Voice, 172–73.

100 "must be won": CHH to Walter White, 7/21/1933, in NAACPP, pt. 6, reel 23, p. 1141.

100 "mark a social crisis": CHH to Dr. R. R. Moton, 7/29/1933, p. 1, in NAACPP, pt. 6, reel 23, p. 1150.

100 petty squabbles: William Patterson to Walter White, 7/19/1934, pp. 1–2, in NAACPP, pt. 6, reel 2, pp. 572–73; Walter White to William Patterson, 7/20/1934, in ibid., p. 571.

100 words of encouragement: CHH to Samuel Leibowitz, 11/28/1933, tel., CHHP, box 163-26, folder 11.

100 he advised King: CHH to CWK, 5/31/1934, in CHHP, box 163-26, folder 12; CWK to CHH, 6/1/1934, in ibid.

100 executive committee: CWK to CHH, 6/1/1934; CHH to Thurgood Marshall, 11/25/1935, in NAACPP, pt. 2, reel 3, p. 521; Ann Fagan Ginger, *Carol Weiss King: Human Rights Lawyer, 1895–1952* (1993), 168.

100 fund-raising appeal: CHH to Walter White, 1/16/1935, in NAACPP, pt. 1, reel 16, p. 361; Walter White to CHH, 1/16/1935, in ibid., reel 26, p. 254; "An Appeal for Funds" (memo), 1/12/1935, CHHP, box 163-26, folder 13; CWK to CHH, 1/12/1935, in ibid.

100 In February 1935, he appeared: CHH to CWK, 2/6/1935, in CHHP, box 163-26, folder 13; CHH to Claude Barnett, 2/7/1935, in ibid. (also in Claude Barnett Papers, reel 6, p. 465).

100 similar appearance for Seymour and King: WNS to CHH, 5/28/1935, in WNSP, box 1.

101 brought the organization: NAACP Minutes of Board of Directors Meeting, 6/10/1935, p. 3, NAACPP, pt. 1, reel 2, p. 664.

101 communist cause: Walter White to CHH, 7/26/1935, pp. 1–2, in NAACPP, pt. 1, reel 26, pp. 402–3.

101 could not file a brief: CHH to Walter White, 6/4/1935, tel., NAACPP, pt. 8, ser. A, reel 8, p. 635; "Memorandum from the Secretary re the Angelo Herndon Case," 6/4/1935, ibid., p. 640; "Memorandum from the Secretary re the Angelo Herndon Case," 6/5/1935, ibid., p. 641; "Memorandum re the Angelo Herndon Case," 6/4/1935, ibid., p. 642; Walter White to James Marshall, 6/5/1935, pp. 1–2, in ibid., pp. 643–44.

101 withheld consent: A. T. Walden to Walter White, 6/8/1935, tel., NAACPP, pt. 8, ser. A, reel 8, p. 660. See Walter White to A. T. Walden, 6/5/1935, pp. 1–2, in ibid., pp. 645–46.

101 Two white members: James Marshall to Walter White, 6/10/1935, in NAACPP, pt. 8, ser. A, reel 8, p. 653.

101 "deeply interested": Walter White to Charles Evans Hughes, 6/11/1935, tel., NAACPP, pt. 8, ser. A, reel 8, p. 662.

101 "strictly enforced": Charles Elmore Cropley to Walter White, 6/12/1935, tel., ibid., p. 661.

101 not optimistic: "Memorandum re Angelo Herndon Case," 6/4/1935.

102 preferred the electric chair: Sasha Small, *Hell in Georgia* (New York: International Labor Defense, 1935), 4–5, NAACPP, pt. 8, ser. A, reel 8, p. 689; *DW*, 8/13/1935, 1, 2; *DW*, 8/14/1935, 1–2; *DW*, 8/15/1935, 1–2, *DW*, 8/16/1935, 1–2; *DW*, 10/30/1935, 3.

102 he was a dead man: *New York Post*, 10/15/1935, in NAACPP, pt. 8, ser. A, reel 8, p. 768.

102 Justice Roberts granted: Roberts Order, 6/11/1935, Herndon Georgia Supreme Court Record, no. 9871, p. 1107; AH to Walter White, 6/12/1935, in NAACPP, pt. 8, ser. A, reel 8, p. 655.

102 two-month speaking tour: "Herndon Tour," NAACPP, pt. 8, ser. A, reel 8, p. 669.

102 "the only way": *DW*, 6/28/1935, 1, 2. See William Patterson to Walter White, n.d. [ca. 7/15/1935], p. 1, in NAACPP, pt. 8, ser. A, reel 8, p. 771.

102 the ILD's petition: *Labor Defender*, 10/1935, 9.

103 Donald Gaines Murray: Murray v. Pearson, June 18, 1935, Stenographer's Record, at 3–16.

103 a Maryland trial judge ordered: *WashTrib*, 7/29/1935, 9; Pearson v. Murray, 169 Md. 478, 479–80 (1936).

103 Houston took a sabbatical: *The Crisis*, 7/1935, 208.

103 By the end of the summer: CHH to Walter White, 7/17/1935, in NAACPP, pt. 8, ser. A, reel 8, p. 670; Walter White to CHH, 7/27/1935, in ibid., p. 674; Walter White to James Marshall, 8/2/1935, in ibid., p. 677; Walter White to WNS, 8/2/1935, in ibid., p. 675.

103 Thurgood Marshall: CHH to Thurgood Marshall, 9/16/1935, in NAACPP, pt. 8, ser. A, reel 8, p. 679; George W. Lawrence, president of National Bar Association, to CHH, 9/20/1935, in ibid., p. 721.

103 King selected the other people: CWK to CHH, 9/30/1935, in NAACPP, pt. 8, ser. A, reel 8, p. 748.

103 "I wonder": *NYT*, 10/8/1935, 2.

104 The NAACP's special counsel rose: *NYT*, 10/8/1935, 2; *WashTrib*, 10/19/1935, 8; *CDef*, 10/19/1935, 4.

104 "tacit consent": NAACP Motion for Leave to File Amicus Brief, Herndon v. Georgia, October Term 1934 U.S. Supreme Court, at 2. See CWK to CHH, 9/30/1935.

104 "without authority": M. J. Yeomans to CHH, 9/18/1935, in NAACPP, pt. 8, ser. A, reel 8, p. 685.

104 Houston reprinted: NAACP Motion for Leave to File Amicus Brief, at 2n*.

104 The justices granted: Journal of the Supreme Court of the United States, October Term 1935, 10/7/1935, at 3.

104 "wrong" & "conclusively demonstrated": NAACP Amicus Brief, Herndon v. Georgia, October Term 1934 U.S. Supreme Court, at 7, 14.

104 "not be of very great help": CHH to Mary Fox, League for Industrial Democracy, 9/19/1935, in NAACPP, pt. 8, ser. A, reel 8, p. 682. See NAACP Amicus Brief, Herndon v. Georgia, October Term 1934 U.S. Supreme Court, at 13.

104 eighteen pages & the Atlanta Six cases: Petition of Appellant for Rehearing, Herndon v. Georgia, October Term 1934 U.S. Supreme Court, 6/13/1935, at 12–17.

105 "the widespread interest": CHH to Fox, 9/19/1935.

105 On October 14: 296 U.S. 661 (1935); Journal of the Supreme Court of the United States, October Term 1935, 10/14/1935, at 40.

106 "I haven't lost hope": ILD Press Release, 10/16/1935, in ILDP, reel 17, p. 857.

106 front-page news: *ADW*, 10/16/1935, 1; *BAA*, 10/19/1935, 1; *NYAN*, 10/19/1935, 1; *WashTrib*, 10/19/1935, 1.

106 two million people: *DW*, 10/16/1935, 3, 6; *DW*, 10/19/1935, 5; *NYA*, 10/26/1935, 2, 6.

106 400 Columbia law students: *NYT*, 10/17/1935, 11.

106 college newspaper editors: *NYHT*, 10/27/1935, 14A; *WP*, 10/27/1935, 10.

106 "a shameful blow": *DW*, 10/29/1935, 3.

106 "I am not guilty": *NYT*, 10/22/1935, 15.

106 "Let us achieve": *DW*, 10/25/1935, 2. See *NYHT*, 10/24/1935, 11.

106 boarded a train: *NM*, 11/5/1935, 15–16; Joseph North, *No Men Are Strangers* (1958), 80–83. Though several of the Scottsboro defendants hailed from Georgia, AH

and North most likely stayed at the home of Viola Montgomery, mother of Olen, because she had attended AH's trial.

107 **Herndon prepared to turn himself:** ILD Press Release, 10/28/1935, in ILDP, reel 17, p. 833.

107 **"You know, the nearer":** *NM*, 11/5/1935, 16.

107 **"morally and socially indefensible":** "Memorandum from CHH Re: Herndon Case," 11/4/1935, NAACPP, pt. 8, ser. A, reel 8, p. 750. See CHH to CWK, 10/18/1935, in ibid., p. 726.

107 **the chain gang looming:** ILD Press Release, 10/29/1935, pp. 1–2, in ILDP, reel 17, pp. 834–35; *DW*, 10/30/1935, 3.

Chapter Seven: The Guilty Judge

109 **turned his new client over:** *ADW*, 10/29/1935, 1; *AC*, 10/29/1935, 7; *AJ*, 10/29/1935, 8.

109 **Lawyers Club of Atlanta:** *AJ*, 6/12/1932, 6.

109 **commander of Fulton County's American Legion:** *AC*, 5/25/1933, 19.

110 **Sutherland, Tuttle, and Brennan:** *AJ*, 7/19/1933, 9.

110 **Seymour enlisted Sutherland:** WNS to William Sutherland, 10/5/1934, in WNSP, box 1; WNS to William Sutherland, 9/30/1935, in ibid.; ILD Press Release, 10/29/1935, in ILDP, reel 17, p. 834; WNS Int. by Charles H. Martin, 9/8/1970, p. 2, Charles H. Martin Papers; Elbert Tuttle OH, Georgia State University, 4/10/1992, p. 8. See William Sutherland to Walter Gellhorn, 8/22/1934, p. 1, in Walter Gellhorn Papers, box 123; William Sutherland to Walter Gellhorn, 8/24/1934, in ibid. (suggesting Sutherland and his firm had been minimally involved in the case a year earlier regarding the petition for rehearing with the Georgia Supreme Court).

110 **Ben Davis Jr.:** *Negro Liberator*, 5/1/1935, 5–6; *BAA*, 11/23/1935, 6.

110 **John Geer:** 1940 Census, Kentucky, Jefferson County, Louisville, E.D. 121–196, sheet 62B, line 41. Geer died of complications from diabetes in 1946 at age forty-one: Geer death certificate, Kentucky Death Records, 11/12/1946.

110 **two white women charged:** *DW*, 9/17/1934, 2; *Negro Liberator*, 9/22/1934, 3; *ADW*, 9/30/1934, 1; "Report on the Atlanta Situation," 11/2/1934, pp. 2–3, RGASPI, fond 515, reel 281, delo 3628.

110 **Sutherland possessed the pedigree:** *AJ*, 8/11/1933, 1, 4; Tuttle OH, 4/10/1992, p. 3; Will W. Alexander COH, pp. 207a–208a. See William A. Sutherland, "The Child Labor Cases and the Constitution," *Cornell Law Quarterly* 8, no. 4 (1922): 8.

110 **"a hard-boiled lawyer":** Talladega College president Buell G. Gallagher to Walter White, 12/3/1935, in NAACPP, pt. 8, ser. A, reel 8, p. 765. See Walter White to WNS, 12/9/1935, in ibid., p. 757 (quoting Gallagher's letter).

110 **"stereotyped prejudices":** Tuttle OH, 4/10/1992, pp. 1–4. See Anne Emanuel, *Elbert Parr Tuttle: Chief Jurist of the Civil Rights Revolution* (2011), 14–51; Jack Bass, *Unlikely Heroes* (1981), 32–34.

111 **Tuttle belonged to the Republican Party:** Ashton G. Ellett, "Recasting Conservativism: Georgia Republicans and the Transformation of Southern Politics Since World War II" (PhD diss., University of Georgia, 2017).

111 **1000 white people:** Tuttle OH, 4/10/1992, pp. 5–8.

111 **five minutes of deliberation & Two days before:** *AJ*, 6/14/1931, B2.

111 *Moore v. Dempsey:* 261 U.S. 86, 90–91 (1923).

111 **Fifth Circuit Court of Appeals:** Downer v. Dunaway, 53 F.2d 586, 592 (5th Cir. 1931); *AJ*, 10/5/1931, 3.

111 **The second time:** Downer v. Dunaway, 1 F. Supp. 1001, 1003 (M.D. Ga. 1932).

111 **in March 1934 died:** *AJ*, 3/16/1934, 8.

111 **"serious doubt":** Tuttle OH, 4/10/1992, p. 7. See Elbert P. Tuttle, "Reflections on the Law of Habeas Corpus," *Journal of Public Law* 22, no. 2 (1973): 325, 325–29; Emanuel, *Elbert Parr Tuttle,* 1–7; Bass, *Unlikely Heroes,* 35–37; Anne S. Emanuel, "Lynching and the Law in Georgia Circa 1931: A Chapter in the Career of Judge Elbert Tuttle," *William and Mary Bill of Rights Journal* 5, no. 1 (1996): 215.

112 **Leo Frank:** Steve Oney, *And the Dead Shall Rise: The Murder of Mary Phagan and the Lynching of Leo Frank* (2003). See Steve Oney to CVW, 3/18/1999, in CVWP, box 40, folder 480; Steve Oney to CVW, 4/14/1999, pp. 1–2, in ibid.

112 **an impassioned closing argument:** *Argument of Hugh M. Dorsey at the Trial of Leo M. Frank* (Macon, GA: N. Christophulos, 1914).

112 **7–2 vote:** Frank v. Mangum, 237 U.S. 309 (1915).

112 **"marked by doubt":** https://www.famous-trials.com/leo-frank/35-clemency decision; Oney, *And the Dead Shall Rise,* 499–502. See Stephen J. Goldfarb, "The Slaton Memorandum," *American Jewish History* 88, no. 3 (Sept. 2000): 325–39.

112 **prominent white citizens:** Oney, *And the Dead Shall Rise,* 513–72.

113 **Jasper County plantation:** Pete Daniel, "We Are Going to Do Away with These Boys . . . ," *American Heritage* 23, no. 3 (Apr. 1972).

113 **"In some counties" & "it seems that we stand indicted":** Hugh M. Dorsey, *A Statement from Governor Hugh M. Dorsey as to the Negro in Georgia* (Atlanta, n.p.: 1921), pp. 1–2. See *AJ*, 4/22/1921, 2; *AC*, 4/23/1921, 7; Timothy J. Pitts, "Hugh M. Dorsey and 'The Negro in Georgia,'" *Georgia Historical Quarterly* 89, no. 2 (Summer 2005): 185–212.

113 **Released a few days later:** *AC*, 4/24/1921, 1, 8.

113 **"slander on the state":** *AC*, 5/15/1921, 1.

113 **Even without impeachment:** *AC*, 6/25/1921, 3.

113 **fifty-eight Black men & "the hands of those":** *AC*, 6/26/1921, E6–E7. See Pitts, "Hugh M. Dorsey," 208.

113 **named a city court judge:** *AJ*, 9/12/1926, 1; *AC*, 9/12/1926, 1; *AC*, 9/14/1926, 6.

113 **Fulton County superior court judge:** *AC*, 5/2/1935, 7.

114 **appointed Tuttle solicitor pro tem:** *AC*, 9/21/1935, 17.

114 **a convicted perjurer sentenced:** *AC*, 10/23/1935, 5.

114 **Tuttle declined to present:** *AC*, 10/26/1935, 1, 3; *AJ*, 10/27/1935, 5.

114 **the perfect opportunity:** Tuttle Int. by Steve Oney, 6/24/1987, p. 2, Steve Oney Papers, box 25; Oney, *And the Dead Shall Rise,* 614, 701. See Tuttle OH, 4/10/1992, p. 9; Tuttle, "Reflections on the Law of Habeas Corpus," 330; WNS Int. by Martin, 9/8/1970, pp. 1–2 (believing Judge Dorsey "felt enough compunction" about Leo Frank's case); Charles H. Martin, *The Angelo Herndon Case and Southern Justice* (1976), 161–62n50 (attributing decision to Tuttle based on 2/6/1970 interview with Joseph Brennan). But see David Entin, "Angelo Herndon" (master's thesis, University of North Carolina–Chapel Hill, 1963), 56, 56n4 (Herndon prosecutor John Hudson claimed that the Fulton County solicitor general's office wanted the habeas petition to go to Dorsey because the new judge was up for reelection in 1936— and was unsuccessfully challenged by Hudson; based on interview with Hudson, 1/31/1963); Martin, *The Angelo Herndon Case,* 162n50 (arguing Hudson had been

mistaken because the defense chose which judge to present the habeas motion to and that Hudson may have conflated the 1935 petition with a 1936 hearing).

114 **he and Sutherland filed a petition:** *AC*, 10/29/1935, 7; *AJ*, 10/29/1935, 8; *ADW*, 10/29/1935, 1, 2; ILD Press Release, 10/29/1935, pp. 1–2, in ILDP, reel 17, pp. 834–35.

114 **nearly thirty Black inmates & "breaking into jail" & speak in California:** *NM*, 12/17/1935, 15 (thirty-two prisoners). See AH to Sasha Small, 11/20/1935, p. 1, in AHP, box 1, folder 2 (about thirty); *LML*, 326 (thirty-five).

114 **slept in bunk beds:** *BAA*, 11/16/1935, 1–2.

115 **playing cards & dreamed about it:** AH to Small, 11/20/1935, pp. 1–2. See *DW*, 11/8/1935, 1–2.

115 **denied his books and magazines:** AH to Anna Damon, 11/4/1935, pp. 1–2, in AHP, box 1, folder 2.

115 **Prison conditions:** *LML*, 325–26; *ADW*, 12/8/1935, 6.

115 **he had been "re-incarcerated":** AH to Anna Damon, 10/31/1935, p. 1, in AHP, box 1, folder 2.

115 **asked the sheriff & *The Letters of Sacco and Vanzetti*:** WNS Int. by Martin, 9/8/1970, pp. 2–3; Martin, *The Angelo Herndon Case*, 162, 162n51 (citing WNS Int.).

115 **"a youthful college student":** *ADW*, 11/13/1935, 2.

115 **so many Black spectators:** *DW*, 11/14/1935, 1–2; *DW*, 11/19/1935, 4.

116 **overthrow the government by "force" & only twenty-three:** *PC*, 11/16/1935, 6.

116 **"with the same brilliant forcefulness":** *DW*, 11/14/1935, 1.

116 **Holmes's dissent & "very noticeable effect":** WNS to LDB, 11/15/1935, in WNSP, box 3.

116 **"fine and powerful" argument:** J. Walter LeCraw to Charles H. Martin, 5/7/1970, p. 2, in Martin Papers (on file with author).

116 ***The Communist Position on the Negro Question* & nearly three hours:** *ADW*, 11/14/1935 2. See *AJ*, 11/13/1935, 13; *AC*, 11/14/1935, 11.

116 **"sought to foster" & "overthrow of republican government":** *DW*, 11/14/1935, 2.

116 **"This idea" & "I now have":** *ADW*, 11/14/1935, 2.

117 **"It is unusual that Georgia":** *PC*, 11/16/1935, 6.

117 **a persistent cough:** *Cleveland Call and Post*, 11/21/1935, 3.

117 **"not optimistic":** *PC*, 11/16/1935, 6.

117 **Shortly after noon:** *ADW*, 11/14/1935, 1.

117 **the decision would come:** *ADW*, 11/14/1935, 1; AH to Anna Damon, 11/18/1935, p. 1, in AHP, box 1, folder 2; AH to Small, 11/20/1935, p. 1.

117 **The wait:** AH to Anna Damon, 11/27/1935, p. 1, in AHP, box 1, folder 2; AH to Anna Damon, 11/29/1935, p. 1, in ibid.

117 **a bout of tonsilitis:** AH to Anna Damon, 11/22/1935, p. 1, in AHP, box 1, folder 2.

117 **"I shall be":** BJD to AH, 11/1/1935, p. 2, in AHP, box 1, folder 2.

117 **"too vague and indefinite":** Herndon v. Lowry, Habeas Corpus Judgment, 12/7/1935, October Term 1936 U.S Supreme Court Record, at 90.

118 **Leo Frank case:** *Washington Daily News*, 12/9/1935, in ILDP, reel 18, p. 10; *Cleveland Eagle*, 1/3/1936, in ILDP, reel 17, p. 385.

118 **"states have laws":** *AC*, 12/8/1935, 6.

118 **A little before noon & A turnkey told Herndon:** *DW*, 12/9/1935, 1.

118 **Shortly before 1:00 p.m. & bath towel & take off his hat:** *ADW*, 12/8/1935, 1, 6.

118 **Treasury bonds & "You can go now":** *ADW*, 12/8/1935, 6.

118   Auburn Avenue: *ADW*, 12/8/1935, 6.

118   "Excuse me" & Tarzan movie & Edward R. Kane: *DW*, 12/9/1935, 2.

118   Washington's Union Station: *DW*, 12/9/1935, 1.

119   In Philadelphia & wired the Scottsboro defendants: *DW*, 12/9/1935, 2.

119   In Newark, forty members: *DW*, 12/9/1935, 1.

119   Around 4:10 p.m. & "This must, this will": *DW*, 12/9/1935, 1–2.

119   *Angelo Herndon Jones*: *NYT*, 12/16/1935, 22; Langston Hughes to Noël Sullivan, 1/29/1936, *Selected Letters of Langston Hughes*, ed. Arnold Rampersad and David Roessel (New York: Knopf, 2015), 189.

119   Hughes saw Herndon: Langston Hughes to Matt and Evelyn Crawford, 1/4/1936, *Letters from Langston: From the Harlem Renaissance to the Red Scare and Beyond*, ed. Evelyn Louise Crawford and MaryLouise Patterson (2016), 121–22; *BAA*, 1/11/1936, 8.

119   "the old and rich": Langston Hughes "Kids Who Die," in *The Collected Poems of Langston Hughes*, ed. Arnold Rampersad and David Roessel (New York: Knopf, 1994), 210–11; *DW*, 2/2/1936, 2 (originally titled "They're Our Kids!").

119   "stirring and challenging victory" & "it is going to be": CHH to WNS, 12/17/1935, in NAACPP, pt. 8, ser. A, p. 761.

119   request the "assistance": WNS to CHH, 12/19/1935, in NAACPP, pt. 8, ser. A, p. 763.

120   objected on evidentiary grounds: October Term 1936 U.S. Supreme Court Record, at 91–95, and Georgia Supreme Court Record, nos. 11216 and 11226, pp. 248–51; *AJ*, 12/11/1935, 1; *ADW*, 12/12/1935, 1; *DW*, 12/13/1935, 1.

120   counter objections: October Term 1936 U.S. Supreme Court Record, at 95–99, and Georgia Supreme Court Record, nos. 11216 and 11226, pp. 256–60.

120   Both sides wrote their briefs: *DW*, 1/17/1936, 1. The Georgia Supreme Court briefs from 1936 are not in the record.

120   "the doctrine of violence" & "black belt republic" & "the communist party": *AC*, 1/25/1936, 18.

120   "This case" & "When a man" & "if this case": *AC*, 1/25/1936, 18.

121   "in 1932 the state was secure": *AC*, 1/25/1936, 18. The count of 28 votes was an error: see Herndon v. Lowry, Brief for Appellant, October Term 1936 U.S. Supreme Court, at 43 (correctly noting that the Communist Party presidential candidate William Foster received only 23 votes in Georgia in 1932).

121   they had already ruled: *AC*, 1/25/1936, 18.

121   "especially touched": WNS to RNB, 5/13/1936, in WNSP, box 3.

121   advised Sutherland to contact: WNS to William Sutherland, 5/21/1936, in WNSP, box 3.

121   "The foregoing provisions": Lowry v. Herndon, 186 S.E. 429, 430 (Ga. 1936).

121   "The decision" & "we are calling": *NYHT*, 6/14/1936, 7.

122   observed that eighteen other: *NYHT*, 6/14/1936, 7; *DW*, 6/25/1936, 5; *SW*, 6/1936, 1.

122   "marks a crisis": CHH to NAACP board of directors, 7/20/1936, in NAACPP, pt. 8, ser. A, reel 8, p. 781.

122   That fall, the board of directors: NAACP Board of Directors Meeting Minutes, 9/14/1936, p. 4, NAACPP, pt. 1, reel 2, p. 764. By the end of the year, the NAACP had also reluctantly joined the Scottsboro Defense Committee: Dan T. Carter, *Scottsboro: A Tragedy of the American South* (1979), 330–35; James Goodman, *Stories of Scottsboro* (1994), 244–45.

122   "The decision": *Labor Defender*, 7/1936, 10.

122 **sixty days, until August 17:** Sutherland Tuttle & Brennan to Walter Gellhorn, 6/16/1936, tel., Gellhorn Papers, box 123; Elbert Tuttle to Walter Gellhorn, 6/16/1936, in ibid.; *ADW*, 6/27/1936, 1.

Chapter Eight: The Justice under Fire

126 **dismissed the factual differences & "[f]reedom of contract is the general rule":** Morehead v. Tipaldo, 298 U.S. 587, 605–09, 610–11 (1936).

126 **"No Man's Land":** *NYT*, 6/3/1936, 1.

126 **Roosevelt's comments made front-page news:** *NYT*, 6/3/1936, 1; *Los Angeles Times*, 6/3/1936, 1; *CT*, 6/3/1936, 1; *BaltSun*, 6/3/1936, 1.

126 **"an ingrained conservative":** FF to LDB, 5/24/1935, p. 1, in FFLC, box 29.

126 **son of a wagonmaker:** Burt Solomon, "The Original Justice Roberts," *Journal of Supreme Court History* 34, no. 2 (2009): 196, 197; Josephus Roberts, 1880 Census, Pennsylvania, Philadelphia County, Philadelphia, E.D. 440, p. 29, line 49.

126 **Germantown Academy:** *PI*, 6/14/1890, 6.

126 **class valedictorian:** *PI*, 6/12/1895, 10.

127 **highest honors:** Edwin R. Keedy, "Owen J. Roberts and the Law School," *University of Pennsylvania Law Review* 104, no. 3 (1955): 318; *Philadelphia Times*, 6/8/1898, 8.

127 **returned as an instructor:** *Philadelphia Times*, 9/29/1898, 5.

127 **made him an assistant professor:** *PI*, 10/18/1901, 11.

127 **the city's assistant district attorney:** *PI*, 6/5/1903, 6; *PI*, 7/3/1904, 5; 1 *American Law School Review* 168 (1902).

127 **he commanded the courtroom:** *PI*, 6/1/1904, 4.

127 **As a special federal prosecutor:** *PI*, 5/17/1918, 10; *PI*, 9/28/1918, 1; *PI*, 12/19/1918, 2.

127 **regulate the coal industry:** *PI*, 2/28/1922, 3.

127 **Lincoln University:** George Wharton Pepper, "Owen J. Roberts—The Man," *University of Pennsylvania Law Review* 104, no. 3 (1955): 372, 375; Solomon, "The Original Justice Roberts," 198.

127 **Rittenhouse Square & dairy farm:** Owen J. Roberts, 1930 U.S. Census, Pennsylvania, Philadelphia County, Philadelphia, E.D. 280, sheet 21A, line 12; Solomon, "The Original Justice Roberts," 198.

127 **special prosecutor & George Wharton Pepper:** *PI*, 2/16/1924, 1, 18; *BaltSun*, 2/16/1924, 2; *CT*, 2/16/1924, 3; *NYT*, 2/19/1924, 2; *WP*, 11/9/1928, 2.

127 **Teapot Dome scandal:** Laton McCartney, *The Teapot Dome Scandal: How Big Oil Bought the Harding White House and Tried to Steal the Country* (New York: Random House, 2009).

128 **John J. Parker:** Brad Snyder, *The House of Truth: A Washington Political Salon and the Foundations of American Liberalism* (2017), 519–23; Brad Snyder, *Democratic Justice: Felix Frankfurter, the Supreme Court, and the Making of the Liberal Establishment* (2022), 195–97.

128 **American Federation of Labor objected:** *Confirmation of Hon. John J. Parker to Be an Associate Justice of the Supreme Court of the United States, Hearing Before the Subcommittee on the Senate Judiciary Committee*, 71st Cong., 2nd sess., 4/5/1930, p. 28. See FFLC, box 59; UMW v. Red Jacket Consol. Coal & Coke Co., 18 F.2d

839 (4th Cir. 1927); Peter Graham Fish, *"Red Jacket* Revisited," *Law and History Review* 5, no. 1 (1987): 51.

128 **The NAACP, opposing a:** *Confirmation of Hon. John J. Parker,* pp. 74–75 (quoting *Greensboro Daily News,* 4/19/1920).

128 **41–39:** 72 Cong. Rec. 8487 (1930).

128 **progressives hailed:** FF to LDB, 5/10/1930, p. 1, in FFLC, box 29.

128 **"There is a good deal of talk":** FF to Owen J. Roberts, 5/10/1930, in Owen J. Roberts Papers, vol. 1.

128 **Black commentators:** *BAA,* 5/18/1935, 16. See Grovey v. Townsend, 295 U.S. 45 (1935).

128 **Frankfurter and other progressives abhorred:** FF to LDB, 5/24/1935, p. 1.

128 **pension system:** Railroad Retirement Board v. Alton RR Co., 295 U.S. 330, 362 (1935).

128 **the press declared:** *NYHT,* 5/12/1935, A1, A2.

129 **milk prices:** Nebbia v. New York, 291 U.S. 502, 515, 530 (1934).

129 **Agricultural Adjustment Act's payments:** United States v. Butler, 297 U.S. 1, 77–78 (1935). Roberts's friend and sponsor George Wharton Pepper argued for Butler against the constitutionality of the law; ibid., at 23–44.

129 **"Roberts is dejected":** FF, notes on conversation with LDB, 5/20/1936, p. 2, FFLC, box 28.

129 **"local activities":** Owen J. Roberts, *The Court and the Constitution* (1951), 3, 46–49.

129 **"strict constructionist":** *NYHT,* 6/12/1935, 2. See *NYHT,* 5/26/1935, A2; *NYHT,* 6/11/1935, 7; *NYHT,* 6/13/1935, 21.

129 **a stay of Herndon's sentence:** Roberts Order, 6/11/1935, Herndon Georgia Supreme Court Record, no. 9871, p. 1107; *NYHT,* 6/13/1935, 21.

129 **Four Horsemen:** Mark V. Tushnet, *The Hughes Court: From Progressivism to Pluralism, 1931–1940* (2022), 1147–48, 1148n3 (rejecting conventional labels such as "liberal" and "conservative" for members of the Hughes Court as well as the term "Four Horsemen"); G. Edward White, *The Constitution and the New Deal* (2000), 294–98 (rejecting political labels for the Four Horsemen and explaining the origin of the label in 1955 by Yale law professor Fred Rodell); Barry Cushman, "The Secret Lives of the Four Horsemen," *University of Virginia Law Review* 83, no. 3 (Apr. 1997): 559.

130 **Willis Van Devanter:** Robert C. Post, *The Taft Court,* vol. 1, *Making Law for a Divided Nation, 1921–1930* (2023), 225–58; Tushnet, *The Hughes Court,* 19–21; Robert Post, "Willis Van Devanter: Chancellor of the Taft Court," *Journal of Supreme Court History* 45, no. 3 (2020): 287–307; Mark Tushnet, "Willis Van Devanter: The Person," *Journal of Supreme Court History* 45, no. 3 (2020): 308–27.

130 **instrumental role:** LDB–FF Conversations, 11/30/1922, Louis D. Brandeis Papers, Harvard Law School Library, pt. 2, reel 33, p. 277; LDB–FF Conversations, 7/3/1924, pp. 4–5, ibid., pp. 288–89; LDB–FF Conversations, 7/6/1924, pp. 8–9, ibid., pp. 292–93; LDB–FF Conversations, 7/1/1923, pp. 10–11, ibid., pp. 318–19; LDB to FF, 5/26/1937, in *"Half Brother, Half Son": The Letter of Louis D. Brandeis to Felix Frankfurter,* ed. Melvin I. Urofsky and David W. Levy (1991), 597. Of Van Devanter and Brandeis, Chief Justice Hughes remarked, "they are the court": Burton K. Wheeler to Paul A. Freund, 12/21/1962, p. 1, in Burton K. Wheeler Papers, box 1, folder 1:6; John L. Wheeler to Edward K. Wheeler, 12/6/1962, in ibid.; Paul

A. Freund, "Charles Evans Hughes as Chief Justice," *Harvard Law Review*. 81, no 1 (Nov. 1967): 4, 27.

130 **James McReynolds:** John Knox, *The Forgotten Memoir of John Knox*, ed. Dennis J. Hutchinson and David J. Garrow (Chicago: University of Chicago Press, 2002); James E. Bond, *I Dissent: The Legacy of Chief Justice James Clark McReynolds* (Fairfax, VA: George Mason University Press, 1992); Post, *The Taft Court*, 1:259–94; Tushnet, *The Hughes Court*, 21–22.

130 **referred to a Black person as a "darky":** *PC*, 3/27/1937, 1.

130 **turned his back on Black advocates:** Robert L. Carter, "The Long Road to Equality," *The Nation*, 5/3/2004, p. 28 (alleging McReynolds turned his back on CHH during a 1938 graduate school segregation argument).

130 **refused to speak:** Knox, *Forgotten Memoir of John Knox*, 36–37. But see Franz Jantzen, "From the Urban Legend Department: McReynolds, Brandeis, and the Myth of the 1924 Group Photograph," *Journal of Supreme Court History* 40, no. 3 (2015): 325–33 (debunking myth that McReynolds refused to stand next to Brandeis for the official Supreme Court photograph).

130 **made no secret of his dislike:** *Boston Globe*, 8/27/1934, 4.

130 **"Nero at his worst":** New York *Daily News*, 2/19/1935, 10.

130 **joined Butler's dissent:** Powell v. Alabama, 287 U.S. 45, 77 (1932) (McReynolds, J., concurring with Butler's dissent).

130 **George Sutherland:** Hadley Arkes, *The Return of George Sutherland: Restoring a Jurisprudence of Natural Rights* (Princeton, NJ: Princeton University Press, 1994); Joel Francis Paschal, *Mr. Justice Sutherland, a Man Against the State* (Princeton, NJ: Princeton University Press, 1951); Post, *The Taft Court*, 1:39–45, 50–58; Tushnet, *The Hughes Court*, 24–25; Samuel R. Olken, "Justice Sutherland Reconsidered," *Vanderbilt Law Review* 62, no. 2 (2009): 630; Samuel R. Olken, "The Business of Expression: Economic Liberty, Political Factions and the Forgotten First Amendment Legacy of Justice George Sutherland," *William and Mary Bill of Rights Journal* 10, no. 2 (2002): 249; Samuel R. Olken, "Justice George Sutherland and Economic Liberty: Constitutional Conservatism and the Problem of Factions," *William and Mary Bill of Rights Journal* 6, no. 1 (1997): 1.

130 **the 1936 majority opinion:** Carter v. Carter Coal, 298 U.S. 238 (1936).

130 **Pierce Butler:** David J. Danelski, *A Supreme Court Justice Is Appointed* (New York: Random House, 1964); Post, *The Taft Court*, 1:61–66, 70–83; Tushnet, *The Hughes Court*, 25–26; David R. Stras, "Pierce Butler: A Supreme Technician," *Vanderbilt Law Review* 62, no. 2 (2009): 695–725; David Schroeder, "Joining the Court: Pierce Butler," *Journal of Supreme Court History* 35, no. 3 (2010): 144–65; David Schroeder, "More Than a Fraction: The Life and Work of Justice Pierce Butler" (PhD diss., Marquette University, 2009); John Paul Frank, "The Confirmation of Pierce Butler" (master's thesis, University of Wisconsin–Madison, 1940).

131 ***Buck v. Bell:*** Buck v. Bell, 274 U.S. 200, 208 (1927) (Butler, J., dissenting).

131 ***Olmstead v. United States:*** Olmstead v. United States, 277 U.S. 438, 485 (1928) (Butler, J., dissenting).

131 ***Powell v. Alabama:*** Powell v. Alabama, 287 U.S. 45, 73 (1932) (Butler, J., dissenting); Powell v. Alabama, Butler Docket Book, October Term 1932 U.S. Supreme Court, p. 260.

131 **Charles Evans Hughes & nearly defeated:** Merlo J. Pusey, *Charles Evans Hughes* (1951), 1:335–49.

131 **Hoover's surprising choice for chief justice:** Tushnet, *The Hughes Court*, 13–18; Snyder, *The House of Truth*, 517–19.

131   **wrote a concurring opinion:** Carter v. Carter Coal, 298 U.S. 238, 317 (1936)
      (Hughes, C.J., concurring).

131   **factual distinctions:** Morehead v. New York ex rel. Tipaldo, 298 U.S. 587, 618 (1936)
      (Hughes, C.J., dissenting).

131   **independent thinker:** Bailey v. Alabama, 219 U.S. 219, 227 (1911); Frank v. Mangum,
      237 U.S. 309, 345 (1915) (Holmes, J., dissenting).

132   **"vague and indefinite":** Stromberg v. California, 283 U.S. 359, 367–70 (1931).

132   **Jay Near:** Near v. Minnesota, 283 U.S. 697, 713–16, 717–20 (1931); Tushnet, *The
      Hughes Court*, 689–702; Fred W. Friendly, *Minnesota Rag: The Dramatic Story of
      the Landmark Supreme Court Case That Gave New Meaning to Freedom of the
      Press* (New York: Random House, 1981).

132   **Hughes and his wife visited:** Historians disagree whether Hughes visited Roberts in
      the summer of 1935 or 1936. The most contemporaneous evidence, a letter from New
      Deal lawyer Charles Wyzanski, suggested it was the summer of 1936: see Daniel R.
      Ernst, "The Hughes-Roberts Visit Revisited," *Green Bag 2d* 18, no. 1 (2014): 5, 10
      (highlighting letter from Wyzanski to his parents on May 28, 1937, and suggesting it
      was 1936). But see Barry Cushman, "Interpreting Secretary Perkins," *Green Bag* 2d
      18, no. 1 (2014): 13, 22–25 (discounting letter and placing visit in summer of 1935);
      Barry Cushman, "The Hughes-Roberts Visit," *Green Bag 2d* 15, no. 2 (2012): 125.

132   **walked up and down:** Frances Perkins COH, pt. 7, sess. 1: 71–74. Perkins's OH,
      as Daniel Ernst observes, was from the early 1950s. The Wyzanski letter and other
      evidence suggests the visit took place in 1936: Ernst, "The Hughes-Roberts Visit
      Revisited," 6, 8–10.

132   **nicknamed Isaiah:** Thomas G. Corcoran, "Rendezvous with Democracy," Pack
      C/14–17, Thomas G. Corcoran Papers, box 586.

132   **reminded others of Abraham Lincoln:** Joseph P. Lash, ed., *From the Diaries of
      Felix Frankfurter* (1975), 104 (entry of 10/20/1911).

132   **contentious confirmation process:** Snyder, *The House of Truth*, 123–36; Sny-
      der, *Democratic Justice*, 70–75; A. L. Todd, *Justice on Trial: The Case of Louis D.
      Brandeis* (New York: McGraw-Hill, 1964). On Brandeis, see Post, *The Taft Court*,
      1:295–368; Tushnet, *The Hughes Court*, 22–23; Jeffrey Rosen, *Louis D. Brandeis:
      American Prophet* (New Haven: Yale University Press, 2016); Melvin I. Urofsky,
      Louis D. Brandeis (2009); Philippa Strum, *Louis D. Brandeis: Justice for the Peo-
      ple* (1984); Lewis J. Paper, *Brandeis* (Englewood Cliffs, NJ: Prentice-Hall, 1983);
      Alpheus Thomas Mason, *Brandeis: A Free Man's Life* (1946).

133   **Brandeis began to rethink:** LDB–FF Conversations, 8/8/1923, Brandeis Papers,
      pt. 2, reel 33, p. 338. See Melvin I. Urofsky, "The Brandeis-Frankfurter Conversa-
      tions," *Supreme Court Review* 1985 (1985): 299, 323–24.

133   **"It is the function":** Whitney v. California, 274 U.S. 357, 376 (1927) (Brandeis, J.,
      concurring).

133   **Harlan Fiske Stone:** Post, *The Taft Court*, 1:122–60; Tushnet, *The Hughes Court*,
      26–28; Alpheus Thomas Mason, *Harlan Fiske Stone: Pillar of the Law* (1956).

133   **often joined majority opinions:** Connally v. General Const. Co., 269 U.S. 385
      (1926); Whitney v. California, 274 U.S. 357 (1927); Schwimmer v. United States, 279
      U.S. 644 (1929).

133   **he lost all respect:** FF to Marion Denman Frankfurter, 4/22/1936, p. 4, in FFLC,
      box 15.

134   **Stone met privately:** HFS to FF, n.d., with FF's handwritten notes, in Felix Frank-
      furter Papers, Harvard Law School Library, pt. 1, reel 1, p. 199; Snyder, *Democratic
      Justice*, 322, 812.

134   **Benjamin Cardozo:** Tushnet, *The Hughes Court*, 29–31; Andrew L. Kaufman, *Cardozo* (1998); Richard Polenberg, *The World of Benjamin Cardozo* (1997); George S. Hellman, *Benjamin N. Cardozo, American Judge* (New York: McGraw-Hill, 1940). During the 1936 term, Cardozo's law clerk, Joseph Rauh, wrote a memorandum reviewing the evidence against Herndon and urging the reversal of his conviction. He signed it, "Comrade Rauh": "Memorandum, Nos. 474, 475," Frankfurter Papers, Harvard, pt. 1, reel 1, p. 71.

134   **an influential book:** Benjamin N. Cardozo, *The Nature of the Judicial Process* (New Haven: Yale University Press, 1921).

134   **"we here have really ceased":** FF to Marion Denman Frankfurter, 2/17/1937, p. 3, in FFLC, box 15.

134   **"economic tyranny" & "These economic royalists":** Franklin Delano Roosevelt, Democratic National Convention, 6/27/1936, pp. 6, 7–8, Franklin Delano Roosevelt Library, ser. 2 MSF, box 25, file 879a.

135   **"We have sought":** Democratic Party Platform, 6/23/1936, https://www.presidency .ucsb.edu/documents/1936-democratic-party-platform.

135   **"the forces of reaction":** *DW*, 7/7/1936, 2.

135   **on January 25:** FDR Day by Day, 1/25/1936, Roosevelt Library, http://www .fdrlibrary.marist.edu/daybyday/; *NYHT*, 1/26/1936, 8; *AC*, 1/28/1936, 13; Joseph P. Lash, *Eleanor Roosevelt: A Friend's Memoir* (1964), 2–5; Joseph P. Lash, *Eleanor and Franklin* (1971), 544–46.

136   **"when things like that happen":** "The Young Asks Questions and Mrs. Roosevelt Answers" [newspaper clipping], 2/2/1936, in Charles W. Taussig Papers, Roosevelt Library, box 81; Britt Haas, *Fighting Authoritarianism: American Youth Activism in the 1930s* (2018), 79.

136   **"The Nazi Olympics have given" & "The triumph":** *DW*, 8/12/1936, 1.

136   **Owens's triumphant return home:** *DW*, 9/21/1936, 1, 5.

136   **Alf Landon & considered Roosevelt & his resolution:** *DW*, 9/18/1936, 5.

137   **Harlem All People's Party:** *DW*, 8/6/1936, 4.

137   **"Keep Herndon Off the Chain Gang":** *DW*, 9/5/1936, 8.

137   **"a rousing reception":** *DW*, 10/27/1936, 1.

137   **"spoke calmly" & "was frequently":** *DW*, 11/3/1936, 1.

137   **lost badly:** *DW*, 11/5/1936, 4 (showing Herndon won only 327 votes in the Twenty-First District).

137   **"Sometimes I wonder" & "because today":** *Labor Defender*, 10/1936, 13.

138   **On September 11:** October Term 1936 U.S. Supreme Court Record, at 105–11.

138   **a twenty-three-page document:** Herndon v. Lowry, nos. 474 and 475, October Term 1936 U.S. Supreme Court, Statement as to Jurisdiction, 10/20/1936.

138   **drafted by Herbert Wechsler:** Walter Gellhorn to William Sutherland, 7/14/1936, in Walter Gellhorn Papers, box 123.

138   **"the most important case":** ILD Press Release, 10/6/1936, in ILDP, reel 17, p. 879.

138   **"that there would be no Herndon case":** ILD Press Release, 11/19/1936, in ILDP, reel 17, p. 877.

138   **On November 23:** Herndon v. Lowry, Brief for Appellant, October Term 1936 U.S. Supreme Court, at 2; *NYHT*, 11/24/1936, 17.

138   **Herndon was in Milwaukee:** ILD Press Release, 11/24/1936, in ILDP, reel 17, p. 875.

138   **"The name of Angelo Herndon":** *DW*, 11/25/1936, 6.

138   **"National Herndon Day" & "Herndon Defense Meetings":** ILD Press Release, 11/19/1936, p. 876; *DW*, 11/30/1936, 1, 6.

139   "contemplating suicide": *DW*, 12/21/1936, 6.

139   **nationwide speaking tour:** AH to Robert K. Haas, 12/12/1936, in Random House Records, box 85; AH to Robert Haas, 12/24/1936, p. 2, in ibid.; *DW*, 12/31/1936, 3.

139   **Tom Mooney:** AH to Haas, 12/12/1936; Crusader News Agency Press Release, 12/28/1936, p. 3, in Crusader News Agency Papers, reel 1, box 1.

139   **"fiery-cross"** & **"Communism must be destroyed":** Crusader News Agency Press Release, 12/28/1936, p. 1; *CDef*, 1/2/1937, 1.

139   **Elsie Parrish:** Helen J. Knowles, *Making Minimum Wage: Elsie Parrish Versus the West Coast Hotel Company* (2021), 3–6.

140   **Roberts and Hughes voted:** Brandeis Docket Sheet, *West Coast Hotel v. Parrish*, October Term 1936 U.S. Supreme Court; Butler Docket Sheet, *West Coast Hotel v. Parrish*, ibid.; Roberts Docket Sheet, *West Coast Hotel v. Parrish*, ibid.; FF, "Mr. Justice Roberts," *University of Pennsylvania Law Review* 104, no. 3 (Dec. 1955): 311, 315; Barry Cushman, "Inside the 'Constitutional Revolution' of 1937," *Supreme Court Review* 2016 (2017): 367, 376n40; Knowles, *Making Minimum Wage*, 182–83.

140   **Stone's absence from the Court:** Gertrude Jenkins (HFS's secretary) to Herbert Wechsler, 11/12/1936, in Herbert Wechsler Papers, box 100; HFS to Herbert Wechsler, 1/30/1937, in ibid.

140   **150 to 300 people** & **"crime, physical violence"** & **"public and orderly":** De Jonge v. Oregon, 299 U.S. 353, 357–59 (1937).

140   **"Freedom of speech"** & **"peaceable assembly for lawful discussion":** De Jonge v. Oregon, 299 U.S. 353, 364–65 (1937). On *De Jonge*, see *Labor Defender*, 12/1936, 16–17; Tushnet, *The Hughes Court*, 702–6; Mark Tushnet, "The Hughes Court and Radical Political Dissent: The Case of Dirk De Jonge and Angelo Herndon," *Georgia State University Law Review* 28, no. 2 (Winter 2012): 333, 349–59.

141   **narrowly drafted to attract:** Herbert Wechsler COH, pp. 134–35.

141   **"penalize the advocacy"** & **"make the act":** Herndon v. Lowry, Brief for Appellant, October Term 1936 U.S. Supreme Court, at 14–15.

141   **"had personally advocated":** Herndon v. Lowry, Brief for Appellant, at 18.

141   **hold meetings:** Herndon v. Lowry, Brief for Appellant, at 19.

141   **possessing radical literature** & **"can no more be sustained":** Herndon v. Lowry, Brief for Appellant, at 22–26.

141   **"The greater the importance":** Herndon v. Lowry, Brief for Appellant, at 33 (quoting De Jonge, 299 U.S. at 365).

142   *Whitney v. California:* Herndon v. Lowry, Brief for Appellant, at 35 (Whitney, 274 U.S. at 376–77 [Brandeis, J., concurring]).

142   **Herndon's lawyers distinguished:** Herndon v. Lowry, Brief for Appellant, at 37–43; Appendix B, ibid., at 57–73.

142   **not a threat to the state of Georgia:** Herndon v. Lowry, Brief for Appellant, at 43.

142   **"so vague and indefinite":** Herndon v. Lowry, Brief for Appellant, at 46.

142   **"three different and inconsistent ways"** & **"This Court has recently said":** Herndon v. Lowry, Brief for Appellant, at 53–54 (quoting De Jonge, 299 U.S. at 365).

142   **"I'm kind of struck":** Wechsler COH, p. 134.

143   **the evidence supported Herndon's conviction:** Herndon v. Lowry, Brief for Appellee, October Term 1936 U.S. Supreme Court, at 3–6.

143   **a paid organizer:** Herndon v. Lowry, Brief for Appellee, at 9–13.

143   **He was arrested:** Herndon v. Lowry, Brief for Appellee, at 14–16.

143   **distribute copies:** Herndon v. Lowry, Brief for Appellee, at 18–21.

143   **"could not be accomplished":** Herndon v. Lowry, Brief for Appellee, at 23.

143   "set forth an unquestioned plan": Herndon v. Lowry, Brief for Appellee, at 25. See ibid., at 26–31.

143   De Jonge case & "part of a conspiracy": Herndon v. Lowry, Brief for Appellee, at 32–34.

143   did not violate Herndon's right: Herndon v. Lowry, Brief for Appellee, at 7–8, 34.

143   "dangerous tendency": Herndon v. Lowry, Brief for Appellee, at 7, 38–39.

144   "clear or present danger of success": Herndon v. Lowry, Brief for Appellee, at 39.

144   Whitney was convicted: Herndon v. Lowry, Brief for Appellee, at 42–45.

144   The origin of the Georgia insurrection law: Herndon v. Lowry, Brief for Appellee, at 47–53.

144   "dangerous tendency": Herndon v. Lowry, Brief for Appellee, at 53–55.

144   "sufficiently definite and certain": Herndon v. Lowry, Brief for Appellee, at 56–66.

144   "presumed to be" & "overcome the presumption" & asked the justices to affirm: Herndon v. Lowry, Brief for Appellee, at 66–67.

144   Early on the morning: DW, 2/8/1937, 1.

144   left New York by train: DW, 11/17/1939, 1.

144   sat in the center & ILD officials: BAA, 2/13/1937, 2; DW, 2/9/1937, 4.

144   a tension and uneasiness: WP, 2/9/1937, 1; NYT, 2/9/1937, 1.

144   "court-packing plan": Snyder, Democratic Justice, 264–82; Laura Kalman, FDR's Gambit: The Court Packing Fight and the Rise of Legal Liberalism (New York: Oxford University Press, 2022); Jeff Shesol, Supreme Power: Franklin Roosevelt vs. the Supreme Court (2010); Barry Cushman, Rethinking the New Deal Court: The Structure of a Constitutional Revolution (New York: Oxford University Press, 1998); William E. Leuchtenburg, The Supreme Court Reborn: The Constitutional Revolution in the Age of Roosevelt (New York: Oxford University Press, 1995); Joseph Alsop and Turner Catledge, The 168 Days (Garden City, NY: Doubleday Doran, 1938).

145   The morning of February 5: Clerk of Court Charles Elmore Cropley to WNS, 1/19/1937, Herndon v. Lowry, Clerk's Office Files, October Term 1936 U.S. Supreme Court, NARA, box 805, folder 474 (instructing AH's counsel to be in court on February 5). In 1937, oral argument was not scheduled for an exact time; the clerk of the court instructed counsel to be in the courtroom on a specific day and wait for the case to be called.

145   The justices had received: CT, 2/6/1937, 7. Wechsler mistakenly remembered that the Herndon case was February 5, the day the court-packing was announced, but in fact the Herndon argument was three days later: Wechsler COH, pp. 132–33.

145   atmosphere was still tense: WP, 2/9/1937, 1; NYT, 2/9/1937, 1; NYHT, 2/9/1937, 9.

145   "The Chief Justice" & "Oyez! Oyez!": WP, 2/9/1937, 1.

145   Hughes admitted Wechsler: Herbert Wechsler to Charles Elmore Cropley, 1/22/1937, Herndon v. Lowry Clerk's Office Files, October Term 1936 U.S. Supreme Court, NARA, box 805, folder 474; Asst. to Cropley to Herbert Wechsler, 1/23/1937, ibid.

145   Legal observers packed: WNS to Whitney North Seymour Jr., 2/9/1937, p. 1, in WNSP, box 2.

145   expecting an announcement: NYT, 2/9/1937, 1; WES, 2/8/1937, A-3.

145   At 12:27 p.m.: DW, 2/9/1937, 4.

146   without collecting a fee: WNS COH, 3/22/1977, p. 32.

146   "old friends": WNS to Seymour Jr., 2/9/1937, p. 2.

146   "Our dogs": WNS COH, 3/22/1977, p. 28.

146   **turned down Sutherland's request:** WNS to CWK, 8/27/1936, in Angelo Herndon Collection, reel 22, p. 912; CWK to WNS, 8/28/1936, in ibid., p. 918.

146   **"was engaged in lawful":** *NYT*, 2/9/1937, 5. See *BAA*, 2/13/1937, 2.

147   **"advocated taking the land":** *DW*, 2/9/1937, 4.

147   **"Yessir, Herndon is working":** *DW*, 2/9/1937, 4.

147   **whether the law was "void" & Stone asked:** *DW*, 2/9/1937, 4.

147   **McReynolds, Van Devanter, and Sutherland:** *BAA*, 2/13/1937, 2.

147   **"required a reversal" & "with dignity":** *DW*, 2/9/1937, 1, 4.

147   **remarked how tense & first Supreme Court session:** *NYT*, 2/9/1937, 1.

148   **Henry F. Ashurst:** *NYT*, 2/9/1937, 9.

148   **Virginia Railway Company:** *NYT*, 2/9/1937, 1, 5; *WES*, 2/9/1937, 1; *WP*, 2/9/1937, 1, 2; *CT*, 2/9/1937, 9; *BaltSun*, 2/9/1937, 3.

148   **Butler's shorthand conference notes:** Butler Docket Book, Herndon v. Lowry, October Term 1936 U.S. Supreme Court, at 1–2 (including handwritten conference notes). For a helpful transcription of these notes, see Barry Cushman, "Vote Fluidity on the Hughes Court: The Critical Terms, 1934–1936," *University of Illinois Law Review* 2017, no. 1 (2017): 269, 292–93.

148   **Hughes obsessively prepared:** Charles Evans Hughes Autobiographical Notes, CJ Notes 1930–1931, Charles Evans Hughes Papers, box 182, reel 140, p. 19; Freund, "Charles Evans Hughes as Chief Justice," 40; FF, "Chief Justices I Have Known," *Virginia Law Review* 39, no. 7 (Nov. 1953): 883, 901–4.

149   **"immediate" threat:** All quotations in this paragraph are from Butler Docket Book, Herndon v. Lowry, at 1–2.

149   **"of fact" & "established facts" & "to get members" & "principles":** Butler Docket Book, Herndon v. Lowry, at 2.

149   **a 5–4 majority & assigned *Herndon v. Lowry*:** Butler Docket Book, Herndon v. Lowry, at 1–2; Brandeis Docket Book, Herndon v. Lowry, October Term 1936 U.S Supreme Court; Roberts Docket Book, Herndon v. Lowry, ibid.; Stone Docket Book, Herndon v. Lowry, ibid. Technically, the justices voted in reverse order at the end of the discussion: Hughes Autobiographical Notes, CJ Notes 1930–1931, Hughes Papers, box 182, reel 140, p. 19.

149   **"most delicate task":** Hughes Autobiographical Notes, CJ Notes 1930–1931, Hughes Papers, box 182, reel 140, pp. 19–20. See FF, "Chief Justices I Have Known," 904.

149   **"In the Herndon case":** National Committee for the Defense of Political Prisoners, 2/8/1937, ILDP, reel 17, p. 892.

150   **American Youth Congress:** *WP*, 2/20/1937, 4; *DW*, 2/22/1937, 1, 4; *DW*, 2/23/1937, 1, 4; Lash, *Eleanor and Franklin*, 546–48.

150   **At 4:30 p.m.:** FDR Day by Day, 2/20/1937.

150   **"that all depends" & "I am Angelo Herndon":** *NYT* 2/23/1937, 1. See *WashTrib*, 2/27/1937, 5; *BAA*, 2/27/1937, 9, 18; *CDef*, 2/27/1937, 6.

151   **"Although it has come out":** *NYHT*, 3/14/1937, 14.

151   **"no seasoned ghost" & "the innocence":** *The Atlantic Monthly*, 6/1937.

151   **"He tells his story simply":** *NYT*, 3/28/1937, 98.

152   **insisted that he had written:** AH to *NYHT* book review editor Irita Van Doren, 3/15/1937, pp. 1–2, in Random House Records, box 85. Random House and their editors also contributed $125 to the printing of the Supreme Court Record: Carol King to Robert Hart [*sic*], 12/10/1936, in ibid.; Robert K. Haas to CWK, 12/11/1936, in ibid.

152   **347 pages:** AHP, box 1, folders 7–8.

152   **"tentative outline":** Tentative Outline, n.d., pp. 1–12, Random House Records, box 85.

152   **their editorial changes:** Donald S. Klopfer to AH, 7/30/1936, in AHP, box 1, folder 6; Robert K. Haas to AH, 9/22/1936, in ibid.; Robert Haas to AH, 11/6/1936, in ibid.; Robert Haas to AH, 11/11/1936, in ibid.; Robert Haas to AH, 11/23/1936, pp. 1–4, in ibid.; Robert Haas to AH, 11/30/1937, pp. 1–5, in ibid.; AH to Robert Haas, 12/2/1936, pp. 1–2, in ibid.; Robert Haas to AH 12/8/1936, tel., ibid.; Robert Haas to AH, 12/9/1936, tel., ibid.; Robert Haas to AH, 12/16/1936, in ibid.; Robert Haas to AH, 12/28/1936, in ibid.; AH to Donald Klopfer, 8/8/1936, in Random House Records, Box 85; AH to Robert Haas, 10/13/1936; in ibid.; AH to Robert Haas, 12/12/1936, in ibid.; AH to Robert Haas, 12/24/1936, pp. 1–2, in ibid.; Kendall Thomas, "*Rouge et Noir* Reread: A Popular Constitutional History of the Angelo Herndon Case," *Southern California Law Review* 65, no. 6 (1992): 2621*n*78 (believing AH wrote *Let Me Live* based on his correspondence with Random House editors).

152   **a $1000 advance:** *LML* book contract, 5/29/1936, p. 2, AHP, box 1, folder 6.

152   **a book about sharecroppers:** Sharecropper book contract, 8/19/1937, AHP, box 1, folder 6.

152   **his New York lawyers:** WNS to AH, 3/15/1937, in AHP, box 1, folder 6; Herbert Wechsler to AH, 3/16/1937, in ibid.; Walter Gellhorn to AH, 3/17/1937, in ibid.; AH to Walter Gellhorn, 3/30/1937, in Gellhorn Papers, box 123.

152   **"It is a fine":** WNS to AH, 3/15/1937.

152   **"abreast of its work":** Charles Evans Hughes to Burton K. Wheeler, 3/21/1937, p. 1, in Wheeler Papers, box 8, folder 16; *Hearings on S. 1392 Before the Senate Committee on the Judiciary*, 75th Cong., 1st sess., "A Bill to Reorganize the Judicial Branch of the Government," pt. 3, 3/22–25/1937, p. 488.

153   **"freedom of contract":** West Coast Hotel v. Parrish, 300 U.S. 379, 389–91, 400 (1937).

153   **"switch in time that saved nine":** John Q. Barrett, "Attribution Time: Cal Tinney's Quip, 'A Switch in Time'll Save Nine,'" *Oklahoma Law Review* 73, no. 2 (2021): 229.

153   **Legal cognoscenti:** FF to Thomas Reed Powell, 8/14/1946, p. 4, in Thomas Reed Powell Papers, box B, folder B24 ("I now know from certain contemporaneous records about Roberts' 'two votes' on Minimum Wage. The facts would call for a much more complicated statement than his silence in the two cases naturally indicated"); FF, "Mr. Justice Roberts," 313–15 (quoting memorandum that Roberts gave to FF on November 9, 1945). See Michael Ariens, "A Thrice-Told Tale, or Felix the Cat," *Harvard Law Review* 107, no. 3 (1994): 620 (contending memorandum was a forgery); Richard D. Friedman, "A Reaffirmation: The Authenticity of the Roberts Memorandum, or Felix the Non-Forger," *University of Pennsylvania Law Review* 142, no. 6 (1994): 1985 (rebutting forgery claim); Snyder, *Democratic Justice*, 274–75.

153   **National Labor Relations Act:** NLRB v. Jones & Laughlin Steel Corp., 301 U.S. 1, 40–41, 43 (1937).

154   **"In those ten days":** ILD Press Release, 4/12/1937, in ILDP, reel 17, p. 897.

154   **"especially relies" & "advocating forcible subversion" & "must rest":** Herndon v. Lowry, 301 U.S. 242, 250, 253 (1937).

154   **"The power of a state":** Herndon v. Lowry, 301 U.S. at 258–59.

155   **"had a constitutional right" & "If the evidence" & "unemployment and emergency relief":** Herndon v. Lowry, 301 U.S. at 259, 261.

155 "not furnish" & "forcible resistance": Herndon v. Lowry, 301 U.S. at 261–62.

155 "dangerous tendency" & "The statute, as construed": Herndon v. Lowry, 301 U.S. at 262, 263–64.

156 "a reasonably definite" & "attempting to induce": Herndon v. Lowry, 301 U.S. at 264 (Van Devanter, J., dissenting).

156 "It should not be overlooked" & "a negro and a member": Herndon v. Lowry, 301 U.S. at 275, 268 (Van Devanter, J., dissenting).

156 full annual salaries: Judge Glock, "Unpacking the Supreme Court," *Journal of American History* 106, no. 1 (June 2019): 47–71.

156 the past two years: *Time*, May 31, 1937, 17; Tushnet, "Willis Van Devanter," 322–24.

156 the Court's decision on April 26: *NYT*, 4/27/1937, 1; *NYHT*, 4/27/1937, 1; *WP*, 4/27/1937, 1; *BaltSun*, 4/27/1937, 1; *PI*, 4/27/1937, 1; *ADW*, 4/27/1937, 1; *BAA*, 5/1/1937, 1; *NYAN*, 5/1/1937, 1; *PC*, 5/1/1937, 1; *CDef*, 5/1/1937, 1.

157 "The man who set": *New York Post*, 4/27/1937, in ILDP, reel 17, p. 571.

157 "Mr. Justice Roberts": *New York Post*, 4/27/1937, in ILDP, reel 17, p. 571.

157 "confused and difficult" & "Herndon should": *Labor Defender*, 6/1937, 8–9.

158 "The close division": *Labor Defender*, 6/1937, 8. See *IJA Monthly Bulletin*, 5/1937, 130–31.

158 "I do not want to minimize": FF to Charles E. Wyzanski Jr., 4/27/1937, Charles E. Wyzanski Papers, carton 26.

158 "may have done your client": Wechsler COH, p. 133.

159 civil liberties during the rise of fascism: Tushnet, *The Hughes Court*, 4–5; Glenda Elizabeth Gilmore, *Defying Dixie: The Radical Roots of Civil Rights, 1919–1950* (2008), at 195.

159 "rebuilding the prestige": *Washington Daily News*, 4/27/1937, p. 2, in NAACPP, pt. 8, ser. A, reel 8, p. 816.

Chapter Nine: The Harlem Literary Hero

161 "I was prepared" & "felt" & "decisive victory" & "another blow" & "to preserve democracy": *NYHT*, 4/27/1937, 14.

161 "It is done to keep" & "gives southern labor": *DW*, 4/27/1937, 4. See *BAA*, 5/1/1937, 23.

162 "marked transformation": *NYT*, 4/27/1937, 10.

162 "Harlem is happy again" & "Have you heard": *DW*, 4/28/1937, 1.

162 "Herndon's victory": *NYAN*, 5/8/1937, 12.

162 "I am free": *DW*, 5/4/1937, 2.

162 "Negro work": *DW*, 5/5/1937, 2. See *DW*, 5/6/1937, 2.

163 elected Herndon its vice president: *NYT*, 5/6/1937, 18; *DW*, 5/7/1937, 5.

163 "Of course, it will not do": *WP*, 5/21/1937, 20. See *BAA*, 5/29/1937, 18.

163 "to the end": *BAA*, 6/26/1937, 11, 15. See *DW*, 6/16/1937, 2; *Labor Defender*, 7/1/1937, 8. AH was elected to the ILD's national committee: *DW*, 6/26/1937, 6.

164 arrested during a protest: *NYAN*, 9/8/1934, 1; *BAA*, 9/8/1934, 13; *CDef*, 9/8/1934, 2.

164 "thousands of heroic": *DW*, 6/23/1937, 3.

164 to picket and protest: *DW*, 7/17/1937, 2.

164 $8500 for medical aid: *NYT*, 7/20/1937, 12; *DW*, 7/21/1937, 3.

164 a series of articles: *DW*, 8/20/1937, 3; *DW*, 8/21/1937, 2; *DW*, 8/23/1937, 2.

164   **Born on a plantation:** Richard Wright, *Black Boy* (New York: Harper & Brothers, 1945); Michel Fabre, *The Unfinished Quest of Richard Wright* (1993); Margaret Walker, *Richard Wright, Daemonic Genius* (1988); Hazel Rowley, *Richard Wright: The Life and Times* (New York: Henry Holt, 2001).

165   **Ben Davis Jr.:** Earle V. Bryant, ed., *Byline, Richard Wright: Articles from the* Daily Worker *and* New Masses (2015), 5–7; *DW*, 9/23/1936, 1; *DW*. 9/29/1936, 5.

165   **gave him a copy of *Let Me Live*:** Michel Fabre, *The World of Richard Wright* (1985), 24.

165   **autobiographical sketch:** Richard Wright, "The Ethics of Living Jim Crow," in *American Stuff: An Anthology of Prose & Verse by Members of the Federal Writers' Project* (New York: Viking, 1937), 39–52.

165   **"out of Herndon's shadow":** Frederick T. Griffiths, "Ralph Ellison, Richard Wright, and the Case of Angelo Herndon," *African American Review* 35, no. 4 (Winter 2001): 626.

165   **"The Way of Herndon" & "So far as we are aware":** Loren Miller to Richard Wright, n.d., in Richard Wright Papers, box 102, folder 1497. See Fabre, *Unfinished Quest of Richard Wright*, 124; Griffiths, "Ralph Ellison, Richard Wright, and the Case of Angelo Herndon," 616. On Loren Miller, see Kenneth Mack, *Representing the Race: The Creation of the Civil Rights Lawyer* (2012), 181–206; Amina Hassan, *Loren Miller: Civil Rights Attorney and Journalist* (Norman: University of Oklahoma Press, 2015).

165   **"Daughter" & "read Angelo Herndon's":** *DW*, 9/7/1937, 5.

166   **disenchanted with the Communist Party:** Richard Wright, "I Tried to Be a Communist," *The Atlantic*, 8/1944, 61–70, and 9/1944, 48–56.

166   **Herndon greeted them on the stage:** *NYA*, 8/7/1937, 4.

166   **"Let this victory":** *BAA*, 8/7/1937, 22.

166   **"The Shame of America" & "It can be done":** *Labor Defender*, 10/1/1937, 6. See AH, *The Scottsboro Boys: Four Freed! Five to Go!* (1937).

167   **his brother Milton was dead:** *DW*, 10/20/1937, 1, 4.

167   **a bullet in the heart:** *NYAN*, 11/13/1937, 4. See Chris Brooks, "Milton Herndon," The Abraham Lincoln Brigade Archives, https://alba-valb.org/volunteers/milton-herndon/.

167   **head and mouth:** *BAA*, 1/1/1938, 2.

167   **"Any victory that can be won":** *DW*, 10/21/1937, 2.

167   **Herndon's mother, Hattie:** *NYAN*, 10/23/1937, 1.

167   **"My brother's death":** *DW*, 10/20/1937, 4.

167   **Milton's memorial service:** *DW*, 11/22/1937, 4; *DW*, 11/27/1937, 2. See Bryant, *Byline, Richard Wright*, 153, 162, 169–70.

167   **Langston Hughes covered:** *BAA*, 1/1/1938, 2; Langston Hughes, *I Wonder as I Wander* (1964), 372–78.

168   **"be a decisive victory" & "His death will forever":** *Sunday Worker*, 10/31/1937, 5.

168   **antilynching legislation:** *DW*, 11/18/1937, 5.

168   **William Penn Hotel:** *PT*, 12/2/1937, 1, 20; *PC*, 12/4/1937, 1, 4; *NYAN*, 12/4/1937, 21; *Pittsburgh Press*, 12/12/1937, 13.

169   **"What I actually said":** *DW*, 12/29/1937, 6.

169   **front-page news:** *PT*, 3/3/1938, 1; *CDef*, 3/5/1938, 1.

169   **a butcher and a maternity nurse:** 1920 Census, Alabama, Etowah County, Gadsden, E.D. 93, sheet 15B, lines 52–53.

169   **Her father died:** Robert Chellis, AL Death Index, 1908–1959, Jan. 1924, vol. 2, roll 2, p. 589.

169 **Youngstown:** 1930 Census, Ohio, Mahoning County, Youngstown, E.D. 50–59, sheet 9B, lines 92–95.

169 **In the mid-1920s:** *NYAN*, 8/4/1926, 5.

169 **"most attractive" by her peers:** *NYA*, 12/30/1933, 8.

169 **working as a stenographer:** *BAA*, 2/26/1938, 23. See SAC New York to SAC Chicago Memorandum re: Eugene Angelo Braxton Herndon, 7/22/1957, Interview with Joyce Chellis Davis, 5/27/1957, Herndon FBI File, 100-HQ-18143, vol. 1, p. 90.

169 **February 18:** Angelo Herndon Marriage License, 2/18/1938, NY Marriage Licenses, 1908–1910, 1938–1940.

169 **a Union Square rally:** *NYA*, 4/23/1938, 2.

169 *God's Step Children: NYA*, 5/28/1938, 7; *BAA*, 5/28/1938, 10.

170 **"the voice of every progressive":** *DW*, 6/21/1938, 5. See *BAA*, 7/2/1938, 4.

170 **member of the National Committee & communist school:** Herndon dossier, pp. 2a, 3a, Herndon FBI File, 61-HQ-7259, vol. 1, pp. 44, 46.

170 **"There is no doubt":** *Hearings Before a Special Committee on Un-American Activities, House of Representatives*, 75th Cong., 3rd sess., vol. 1, 8/13/1938, p. 268.

170 **Herndon visited southern cities:** *Chattanooga Times Free Press*, 4/24/1939, 3.

170 **the book with Langston Hughes:** AH to Langston Hughes, 2/20/1939, in Langston Hughes Papers, box 79, folder 1510. AH never completed the sharecroppers book: see AH to Donald Klopfer, 12/10/1938, in Random House Records, box 85 (sending the editor a partial manuscript).

170 **"nationally known figures":** *DW*, 5/2/1939, 3.

170 **vice president:** *Young Communist Review*, 6/1939, 16; Henry Winston, *Life Begins with Freedom* (1937), 36–37.

170 **sixth-grade education & salary of $1200:** Angelo Herndon, 1940 Census, New York, New York City, E.D. 31-913, sheet 12B, line 52.

171 **only two Black staff writers & Ted Poston:** *CDef*, 2/3/1940, 12.

171 **Joe Louis:** *DW*, 6/30/1939, 8.

171 **job campaign:** *DW*, 7/2/1939, 4.

171 **housing and employment problems:** *DW*, 7/10/1939, 3.

171 **after their release:** *DW*, 7/24/1939, 4.

171 **suicides among Harlem's:** *DW*, 8/7/1939, 5.

171 **Walter White's speech:** *DW*, 8/9/1939, 3.

171 **Negro Actors Guild:** *DW*, 8/14/1939, 7.

171 **"do everything in his power" & "the silent treatment":** George Hewitt testimony, 7/19/1948, Washington State Un-American Activities Committee (Canwell Committee), p. 295.

171 **not convicted of perjury:** Vern Countryman, *Un-American Activities in the State of Washington* (Ithaca, NY: Cornell University Press, 1951), 286–91, 301–11; *The New Republic*, 7/5/1954, 22.

171 **Nazi-Soviet Pact:** Harvey Klehr, *The Heyday of American Communism: The Depression Decade* (1984), 386–409.

172 **the Party's Bronx chapter:** *DW*, 8/26/1939, 4.

172 **Soviet Union's show trials:** Kelly J. Evans and Jeanie M. Welch, *Witnessing Stalin's Justice: The United States and the Moscow Show Trials* (London: Bloomsbury Academic, 2023); Harvey Klehr and John Earl Haynes, *The American Communist Movement: Storming Heaven Itself* (1992), 90–92.

172 **Hughes and other leading American writers:** *NM*, 5/3/1938, 19; *DW*, 8/14/1939, 2; Evans and Welch, *Witnessing Stalin's Justice*, 126–27; Arnold Rampersad, *The Life of*

Langston Hughes, vol. 1, *1902–1941, I, Too, Sing America* (1986), 338, 374–75. Hughes had witnessed one of the early show trials: Hughes, *I Wonder as I Wander*, 116–17.

172 "a valiant fighter": *DW*, 11/17/1939, 3.

172 "great sacrifice" & "true intent" & "The American people": *DW*, 12/28/1939, 5.

172 "opening our eyes": *WP*, 12/29/1939, 8.

173 American Writers' Congress: Walker, *Richard Wright*, 126–29; Maryemma Graham, *The House Where My Soul Lives: The Life of Margaret Walker* (2022), 194–95; *DW*, 6/2/1939, 7; *DW*, 6/5/1939, 7; *NYAN*, 6/17/1939, 5.

173 a collection of stories: Richard Wright, *Uncle Tom's Children* (1938).

173 improved upon anecdotes: Griffiths, "Ralph Ellison, Richard Wright, and the Case of Angelo Herndon," 627–28.

173 "exposé of what it means": *Young Communist Review*, 6/1938, 28.

173 *Native Son*: Richard Wright, *Native Son* (1940). Bigger Thomas was based in part on the case of Black serial murderer Robert Nixon: Richard Wright, *How "Bigger" Was Born* (1940), 532.

173 the same radical literature & closing argument: Griffiths, "Ralph Ellison, Richard Wright, and the Case of Angelo Herndon," 628–29.

173 "symbol of the whole": *Sunday Worker*, 4/14/1940, 4. See BJD to Richard Wright, 4/17/1940, pp. 1–2, in Wright Papers, box 96, folder 1289.

174 "horrified by the murder": RE to Richard Wright, 4/14/1940, p. 1, in REP, box 76, folder 5 (also in Wright Papers, box 97, folder 1314, and in John Callahan and Marc Conner, eds., *The Selected Letters of Ralph Ellison* [New York: Random House, 2019], 129). Mary Dalton is the namesake of one of the Atlanta Six arrested under the Georgia insurrection law before AH; she is also mentioned in *Let Me Live*: *LML*, 108.

174 Richard Moore: Mark Naison, *Communists in Harlem During the Depression* (1983), 5, 7; W. Burghardt Turner and Joyce Moore Turner, eds., *Richard B. Moore, Caribbean Militant in Harlem: Collected Writings, 1920–1972* (1988).

174 Their initial major offering: *DW*, 9/3/1940, 7.

174 charged that Herndon had misused: Richard B. Moore, "To Set the Record Straight," p. 3, Richard B. Moore Papers, box 7. See Turner and Turner, *Richard B. Moore, Caribbean Militant in Harlem*, 66; Frederick Douglass, *Life and Times of Frederick Douglass* (1941), vii.

174 Lawrence D. Reddick: David A. Varel, *The Scholar and the Struggle: Lawrence D. Reddick's Crusade for Black History and Black Power* (2020), 88; Int. with Lawrence D. Reddick, 2/11/1954, p. 1, SAC Atlanta to FBI Dir., 2/18/1954, Herndon FBI File, 100-HQ-18143, vol. 1, p. 83.

174 "All who yearn": *NM*, 4/15/1941, 23.

175 "He is the most outstanding": *DW*, 11/28/1941, 3.

175 Moore protested to Party officials: Turner and Turner, *Richard B. Moore, Caribbean Militant in Harlem*, 66–67; Richard B. Moore to George B. Murphy Jr., 6/25/1941, Moore Papers, box 7, folder 3.

175 *The Kidnapped and the Ransomed*: Kate E. R. Pickard, *The Kidnapped and the Ransomed* (1856; repr., New York: Negro Publication Society of America, 1942); AH to Langston Hughes, in 1/16/1942, Hughes Papers, box 79, folder 1510.

175 "Now is the time for us": *PC*, 1/10/1942, 5.

176 "a review of Negro thought" & "the need of reflecting" & "devote space": *Negro Quarterly* 1, no. 1 (Spring 1942), in *Negro Quarterly: A Review of Negro Life and Culture* (1969), 3–4.

176   "disposes of the idyllic" & "Wright replies": *Negro Quarterly* 1, no. 1 (Spring 1942), in *Negro Quarterly*, 86–87.

176   "Mr. Ralph Ellerson": AH to RE, 11/25/1941, in REP, box 60, folder 5.

177   a review of William Attaway's novel: *Negro Quarterly* 1, no. 1 (Spring 1942), in *Negro Quarterly*, 87–92.

177   launch party: AH to RE, 2/18/1942, in REP, box 60, folder 5; invitation to launch party, 3/8/1942, REP, box 60, folder 6; AH to Langston Hughes, 2/18/1942, in Hughes Papers, box 79, folder 1510; Arnold Rampersad, *Ralph Ellison* (2007), 153; Lawrence Jackson, *Ralph Ellison: Emergence of Genius, 1913–1952* (2002), 264.

177   his job with the Federal Writers' Project: Maryemma Graham and Amritjit Singh, eds., *Conversations with Ralph Ellison* (1995), 296; RE to Henry Louis Gates Jr., 2/2/1985, p. 2, in REP, box II-27, folder 16; Rampersad, *Ralph Ellison*, 153–54.

177   *The Waste Land*: Graham and Singh, *Conversations with Ralph Ellison*, 292. On Ellison, see Rampersad, *Ralph Ellison*, 3–142; Jackson, *Ralph Ellison*, 1–236; Lawrence Patrick Jackson, "Ralph Ellison's Early Life and Intellectual Foundation, 1914–1941" (PhD diss., Stanford University, 1997).

177   Alain Locke and Langston Hughes: Graham and Singh, *Conversations with Ralph Ellison*, 292; Ralph Ellison, *Shadow and Act* (New York: New American Library, 1965), 162.

177   Wright encouraged: RE to Richard Wright, 10/27/[1937], pp. 1–2, in Wright Papers, box 97, folder 1314; RE to Richard Wright, 11/8/1937, pp. 1–2, in ibid.; RE to John Callahan, 5/12/1985, pp. 1–2, in REP, box 40, folder 7; Graham and Singh, *Conversations with Ralph Ellison*, 293–94.

177   moved to Dayton, Ohio: RE to Wright, 10/27/[1937], p. 1; Ellison, *Shadow and Act*, 14, 168.

177   "the first philosophical novel": *NM*, 8/5/1941, 22. See RE to Richard Wright, 4/14/1940, pp. 1–2, in Wright Papers, box 97, folder 1314; RE to Richard Wright, 4/22/1940, pp. 1–3, in ibid.

178   "devoted entirely to the review": *DW*, 3/9/1942, 7.

178   "Double Victory" campaign: *PC*, 2/14/1942, 1.

178   "We've got to lick" & "Negroes, you see" & "The Quarterly sprang": *DW*, 3/9/1942, 7.

178   "the Four Freedoms": *Negro Quarterly* 1, no. 2 (Summer 1942), in *Negro Quarterly*, i–v. See Fanny Ellison to Carol Polsgrove, 1/9/1969, p. 2, in REP, box 110, folder 6; Jansen B. Werner, "Black America's Double War: Ralph Ellison and 'Critical Participation' During World War II," *Rhetoric and Public Affairs* 18, no. 3 (Fall 2015): 441–70.

178   Ellison also solicited excerpts: RE to Richard Wright, 3/24/1942, in Wright Papers, box 97, folder 1314.

178   submissions from white writers: RE to Sanora Babb, 4/10/1942, *The Selected Letters of Ralph Ellison*, ed. John F. Callahan and Marc Conner (2019), 150; RE to Stanley Hyman, 6/22/1942, in Stanley Edgar Hyman Papers, box 6, folder 30; RE to Stanley Hyman, 7/15/1942, pp. 1–3, in ibid.; RE to Stanley Hyman, n.d. [ca. 1942–1943], p. 2, in ibid.

179   "What we are doing": *NYAN*, 4/10/1943, 24.

179   musicians including: Program, Third Annual Cavalcade of American Folk Music, 6/26/1942, REP, box 60, folder 5; *DW*, 6/25/1942, 8; *NYT*, 6/27/1942, 9.

179   Orson Welles: Charles Collins and AH to Friend, 10/17/1942, in REP, box 60, folder 5 (also in Hughes Papers, box 79, folder 1510); *DW*, 10/22/1942, 5; Assis-

tant Director P. E. Foxworth to FBI Dir., 11/9/1942, and Assistant Director
Foxworth to FBI Dir., 11/19/1942, Negro Labor Victory Committee FBI File,
100-HQ-115471.

179 **lost money:** RE to Langston Hughes, 12/11/1942, *Selected Letters of Ralph Ellison*,
154.

179 **series of pamphlets:** AH to John Pittman, 3/9/1943, in Pittman Papers, box 1, folder
23; RE to Sanora Babb, 7/4/1943, p. 1, in REP, box 37, folder 9 (also in *Selected Letters of Ralph Ellison*, 162); *PC*, 8/7/1943, 15.

179 **Philadelphia & "getting considerable criticism":** Memo, 4/11/1943, Confidential
Informant in E. E. Conroy, SAC New York, to FBI Dir., 4/15/1943, Herndon FBI
File, 61-HQ-7259, vol. 1, pp. 96–98. In April 1942, Hoover directed the Bureau to
reopen its surveillance on AH—undoubtedly because of the launch of the *Negro
Quarterly*: Hoover to SAC NY, 4/11/1942, ibid., p. 67.

180 **Ellison's weekly paychecks:** RE to Gates, 2/2/1984, p. 2; Graham and Singh, *Conversations with Ralph Ellison*, 296.

180 **the *Quarterly*'s creditors:** Stanley Burnshaw, Dryden Press, to RE, 4/2/1943, in
REP, box 60, folder 5.

180 **checks bounced:** Louis Katz, Harlem Check Cashing Corp., to RE, 4/8/1943, in
REP, box 60, folder 5.

180 **"Herndon's job":** RE to Sanora Babb, 7/4/1943, p. 2. See Rampersad, *Ralph Ellison*,
153; Jackson, *Ralph Ellison*, 264.

180 **May 1943:** Rose Poindexter Ellison to RE, 5/24/1943, p. 1, in REP, box 16, folder 9
("Your very good friend Angelo called and wanted to know where his good friend
was...").

180 **Vermont before joining the merchant marine:** RE to Babb, 7/4/1943, p. 2; RE to
Gates, 2/2/1984, p. 2.

180 **good terms:** AH to RE, n.d. [ca. 5/17/1944], in REP, box 37, folder 2.

180 **"self-serving statement" & "not fighting" & "not a Communist" & "deferment"
& "dyed-in-the-wool":** *NYWT*, 8/5/1943, 3. See *CT*, 8/6/1943, 1; *NYHT*, 8/6/1943,
5. Woltman won the Pulitzer Prize in 1947 for his stories on communist infiltration
of the Methodist Church.

180 *Daily Worker*: *DW*, 8/7/1943, 3.

180 **"my contribution":** *NYHT*, 8/11/1943, 8.

181 **Herndon appealed:** *NYWT*, 8/11/1943, 3, 8; *CT*, 8/11/1943, 17.

181 **not giving up:** *NYT*, 8/20/1943, 7.

181 **Herndon lost:** *NYHT*, 8/31/1943, 15; *CT*, 8/31/1943, 2; *NYT*, 8/31/1943, 19.

181 **five-foot-ten:** AH, World War II Draft Card, p. 2, serial no. 3421, order no. 675,
World War II U.S. Draft Cards for Young Men, 1940–1947, New York City,
Hass–Hersey.

181 **reclassified 4-F:** *NYHT*, 11/2/1943, 25.

181 **"charge[d] him" & "very bitter":** Confidential FBI Informant re: Angelo Herndon,
8/10/1943, Herndon FBI File, 61-HQ-7259, vol. 1, p. 102. See Conroy to FBI Dir.,
8/12/1943, ibid., p. 101.

181 **"no responsibility":** *NYWT*, 9/9/1943, 3. See "C.P. Statement on Herndon Negro
Quarterly," n.d., REP, box 60, folder 6; *NYAN*, 9/18/1943, 1.

181 **The order was drafted:** R. Campbell Carden Report on Herndon, 10/9/1943, p. 7,
Herndon FBI File, 61-HQ-7259, vol. 1, p. 117 (also in 100-HQ-18143, vol. 1, p. 32).

182 **"neglecting the cause":** *NYWT*, 9/9/1943, 3; Carden Report on Herndon, 10/9/1943,
p. 7; *NYAN*, 9/18/1943, 1.

182 "side tracked the struggle": Confidential Informant on Angelo Herndon, 10/9/1943, Herndon FBI File, 61-HQ-7259, vol. 1, p. 121.

182 San Francisco: Carden Report on Herndon, 10/9/1943, p. 7.

182 "critical participation": *Negro Quarterly* 1, no. 4 (Winter–Spring 1943), in *Negro Quarterly*, 298.

182 "We are fighting" & "Our conception" & "What we need": AH, "Frederick Douglass: Negro Leadership and War," *Negro Quarterly* 1, no. 4 (Winter–Spring 1943), in *Negro Quarterly*, 305, 323–24. See AH, *"Frederick Douglass*: Symbol of Freedom," in *There Were Giants in the Land* (1942), 137–41.

183 "The South Moves West" & "This westward shift": *The South Moves West* (February 1944), pp. 1, 3, Schomburg Center for Research in Black Culture. See *People's Observer*, 11/26/1943, 4; Lawrence P. Jackson, *The Indignant Generation: A Narrative History of African American Writers and Critics, 1934–1960* (2010), 523n10 (citing 4/1999 letter from Negro Publication Society board member Ernest Kaiser).

183 "the rumor": *BAA*, 3/15/1947, 4.

183 "tried to translate": RE to Babb, 7/4/1943, pp. 1–2.

183 "Herndon's attempt": RE to Gates, 2/2/1984, p. 2.

184 borrowed money: Report by Leo Anthony Schon, 9/18/1944, p. 2, Herndon FBI File, 100-HQ-18143, vol. 1, p. 42.

184 "a center": Report by Leo Anthony Schon, 2/18/1944, p. 3, Herndon FBI File, 100-HQ-18143, vol. 1, p. 37.

184 "not financed": *People's Advocate*, 1/5/1944, 2, Schomburg Center for Research in Black Culture, reel 1.

184 praising the Black press: *People's Advocate*, 1/24/1944, 2, Schomburg Center for Research in Black Culture, reel 1. This is one of two extant issues.

184 "was dropped" & "developing a nationalist line": *People's World*, 3/21/1944, 1; Report to FBI Dir., 3/22/1944, Herndon FBI File, 61-HQ-7259, vol. 2, p. 4 (quoting memorandum from William Schneiderman, secretary of California Communist Party, 3/16/1944); *DW*, 3/25/1944, 3.

184 William Henry McClendon: *People's Observer*, 11/26/1943, 1, Schomburg Center for Research in Black Culture; Report by Schon, 9/18/1944, p. 3, vol. 1, p. 149.

184 stopped publishing in May: Report by Schon, 9/18/1944, p. 6, vol. 1, p. 152.

184 moved to Portland & efforts to raise money: SAC Portland to FBI Dir., 6/17/1946, Herndon FBI File, 100-HQ-18143, vol. 1, p. 2; SAC NY to FBI Dir., 7/12/1946, Herndon FBI File, 100-HQ-18143, vol. 1, p. 21; *The Oregonian*, 7/24/1944, 5; *The Oregonian*, 9/17/1944, 17; *The Oregonian*, 9/21/1944, 5; *Seattle Post-Intelligencer*, 9/23/1944, 7.

185 Browder had proposed changing: Klehr, *The Heyday of American Communism*, 410–12; Edward P. Johanningsmeier, *Forging American Communism: The Life of William Z. Foster* (1994), 297–308.

185 Anna Damon leapt: *DW*, 5/19/1944, 5; *DW*, 5/20/1944, 9; *PI*, 5/20/1944, 15; *People's Voice*, 5/27/1944, 12.

185 had already broken with: Frank Marshall Davis, *Livin' the Blues* (Madison: University of Wisconsin Press, 1992), 243–44; Barbara Foley, *Wrestling with the Left: The Making of Ralph Ellison's* Invisible Man (2010), 359n29; Barbara Foley, "The Rhetoric of Anticommunism in *Invisible Man*," *College English* 59, no. 5 (Sept. 1997): 538.

185 published the first of two: Wright, "I Tried to Be a Communist."

185 "he's to be pitied" & "You'll hear": AH to Richard Wright, 8/23/1944, in Wright Papers, box 98, folder 1372. See *DW*, 8/6/1944, 6.

185   "Sorry I did not get": AH to RE, n.d. [ca. 5/17/1944].

186   "she had not seen": Ida Guggenheimer to RE, 2/22/1945, p. 1, in REP, box 49, folder 5.

186   remarried: Joyce Chellis Davis, 8/4/1945, New York Marriage Index 1945, cert. no. 36107, p. 189.

186   Claudia Jones: Marika Sherwood, *Claudia Jones: A Life in Exile* (1999), 21; Erik S. McDuffie, *Sojourning for Freedom: Black Women, American Communism, and the Making of Black Left Feminism* (2011), 96–100.

186   Carol Weiss King & subpoenaed Herndon: SAC NY to FBI Dir., 9/30/1948, Herndon FBI File, 100-HQ-18143, vol. 1, p. 51; Claude Lightfoot to Tillie Carr, 9/28/1948, ibid., p. 53.

186   "I have never" & "The accused is a Negro": Angelo Herndon statement, 9/30/1948, pp. 1, 5, Civil Rights Congress Records, box 9, A167.

186   "As the symbol of man's struggle": Angelo Herndon statement, 9/30/1948, p. 6. See American Committee for Protection of Foreign Born Press Release (cosponsored with Civil Rights Congress), 10/1/1948, in Civil Rights Congress Records, box 9, A167; *DW*, 10/1/1948, 3, 11.

187   Sometime in 1945: SAC Portland to FBI Dir., 6/17/1946, Herndon FBI File, 100-HQ-18143, vol. 1, p. 2 (suggesting AH left Portland in the spring of 1945).

187   moved in with his brother Leroy: SAC NY to FBI Dir., 7/12/1946, Herndon FBI File, 100-HQ-18143, vol. 1, p. 21; G. R. McSwain, SAC Chicago, to FBI Dir., 8/16/1946, ibid., p. 23; SAC San Francisco to FBI Dir., 9/10/1946, ibid., p. 24; SAC Chicago to FBI Dir., 1/14/1947, ibid., p. 25.

187   "He looks well": RE to Ellen Wright, 9/23/1946, p. 1, in REP, box 76, folder 6 (also in *The Selected Letters of Ralph Ellison*, pp. 224–25).

187   "But for the cynicism": RE to Gates, 2/2/1984, p. 2.

187   "Why there's Ralph Ellison!": RE to Odette Harper Hines, 4/23/1984, pp. 1–2, in REP, box 51, folder 6.

187   *Invisible Man*: Ralph Ellison, *Invisible Man* (1952). See Griffiths, "Ralph Ellison, Richard Wright, and the Case of Angelo Herndon," 621–22 (identifying subtle influences on *Invisible Man* from *Let Me Live*); RE to Callahan, 5/12/1985, p. 10 (disclaiming AH's influence on his protagonist).

Epilogue: Home Sweet Home

189   Ralph Ellison and the rest: "Swindle Suspect Identified as Ex-Red Angelo Herndon," *Jet*, 4/29/1954, pp. 6–7, in REP, box 189, folder 2.

189   "with any large sums" & Ishmael Flory: SA Raymond E. Horgan to SAC, 6/9/1953, p. 1, Herndon FBI File, 100-HQ-18143, vol. 1, p. 78.

190   charged with embezzlement: People v. Gene Braxton, Witness memorandum to Clerk, Grand Jury No. 127, 54CR-978, Cook County Criminal Archives; Braxton v. Salter & Gutknecht, Complaint, at 5 (E.D. Ill. 10/3/1956), NARA, Chicago, RG 21, USDC Chicago Civil Case 56C1750.

190   birth name, Gene Braxton: "Swindle Suspect Identified," pp. 6–7.

190   trial was postponed: People v. Gene Braxton, Memorandum of Orders, 6/28/1954, 54CR-978 (continued until 9/9/1954).

190 **Gloria E. Wilson:** People v. Gene Braxton, Appearance Form, 4/22/1954, at 2, 54CR-978; *CT,* 7/4/1959, 8; *CT,* 11/10/1987, A6.

190 **advised him to plead guilty & two to seven years & one to ten years & eight to ten years & two to six years:** Braxton v. Salter & Gutknecht, Complaint, at 5–6 (E.D. Ill. 10/22/1956).

190 **ushered & reviewed the witness testimony:** Braxton v. Salter & Gutknecht, Complaint, at 6 (E.D. Ill. 10/22/1956).

191 **agreed to waive & two to six years:** People v. Braxton, Penitentiary Mittimus, at 1–2 (Cook County 9/10/1954), Cook County Criminal Archives, 54CR-978.

191 **#35956 & "his disloyal counsel" & "a trial conducted" & "deprived of his" & $150,000:** Braxton v. Salter & Gutknecht, Complaint, at 7–9 (E.D. Ill. 10/22/1956).

191 **leave to file his complaint:** Clerk of Court Roy H. Johnson to Gene Braxton, Order, (E.D. Ill 10/23/1956,), NARA, Chicago, USDC Chicago Civil Case 56C1750.

191 **motion to dismiss:** Braxton v. Salter & Gutknecht, Motion, at 1–3 (E.D. Ill. 11/20/1956), NARA, Chicago, USDC Chicago Civil Case 56C1750.

191 **Judge Igoe dismissed:** Braxton v. Salter & Gutknecht, Memorandum, 11/20/1956, NARA, Chicago, USDC Chicago Civil Case 56C1750; Braxton v. Salter & Gutknecht, Memorandum of Orders, ibid.

191 **moved to certify the case:** Braxton v. Salter & Gutknecht, Motion to Certify and Transmit Record on Appeal, at 1–2, Memorandum (E.D. Ill. 12/4/1956), NARA, Chicago, USDC Chicago Civil Case 56C1750.

192 **denied Herndon's motion:** Memorandum (E.D. Ill. 12/4/1956), NARA, Chicago, USDC Chicago Civil Case 56C1750; Clerk Roy H. Johnson to Gene Braxton, 12/4/1956, ibid.; Docket, ibid.

192 **the U.S. Supreme Court:** Griffin v. Illinois, 351 U.S. 12 (1956).

192 **Adam Clayton Powell Jr.'s former seat:** *DW,* 11/11/1943, 1; *NYT,* 11/11/1943, 1; *CCFH,* 101–17; Gerald Horne, *Black Liberation/Red Scare: Ben Davis and the Communist Party* (2001), 97–118.

192 **Ben Sr.:** *NYAN,* 11/3/1945, 1, 24; *CCFH,* 145–60.

192 **reelected in November 1945:** *NYT,* 11/15/1945, 1; *DW,* 11/16/1945, 4; *DW,* 11/18/1945, 16; *CCFH,* 140–44; Horne, *Black Liberation/Red Scare,* 154–66.

192 **"I certainly do not expect":** *Investigation of Un-American Propaganda Activities in the United States, Committee on Un-American Activities, House of Representatives,* 79th Cong., 1st sess., 9/26/1945, p. 14; *DW,* 9/27/1945, 1–2.

193 **charged under the Smith Act:** *NYT,* 7/21/1948, 1, 3; *NYT,* 7/22/1948, 1, 2; *DW,* 7/22/1948, 1, 2, 3, 11; *CCFH,* 180–86; Horne, *Black Liberation/Red Scare,* 207–9.

193 **repeatedly interrupted & communist literature:** Dennis v. United States Record, reel 4, pp. 8341–52, Conspiracy Trials in America, 1919–1953, pt. 20, Pickler Memorial Library, Truman State University, Kirksville, MO.

193 **attempted to impeach & "crooked record":** Dennis v. United States Record, reel 4, pp. 8492–8502.

193 **In 1943, Wyatt:** *AC,* 8/6/1943, 2; *NYT,* 2/7/1960, 84.

193 **the Nuremberg tribunal:** https://encyclopedia.ushmm.org/content/en/article/subsequent-nuremberg-proceedings-case-8-the-rusha-case.

193 **Party's literature as weapons:** Dennis v. United States Record, reel 5, pp. 12444–45; *CCFH,* 190; Michal R. Belknap, "Why *Dennis v. United States* Is a Landmark Case," *Journal of Supreme Court History* 34, no. 3 (2009): 289; William M. Wiecek, "The Legal Foundations of Domestic Anticommunism: The Background of *Den-*

nis v. United States," Supreme Court Review 2001 (2001): 375; Michal R. Belknap, "*Dennis v. United States*: Great Case or Cold War Relic?" *Journal of Supreme Court History* 18, no. 1 (1993): 41.

193 **represent himself:** Dennis v. United States Record, reel 5, pp. 11925–35, 12437, and reel 6, pp. 13624–33; *DW*, 10/4/1949, 1, 9; *NYT*, 10/4/1949, 19; *DW*, 10/6/1949, 3.

193 **the jury convicted:** *NYT*, 10/15/1949, 1, 3; Horne, *Black Liberation/Red Scare*, 210–26.

193 **"I will not":** *DW*, 10/24/1949, 4; *DW*, 10/30/1949, 6. See *NYHT*, 10/22/1949, 7; *CCFH*, 181.

193 **His fellow city council members:** *DW*, 11/29/1949, 3; *NYT*, 11/29/1949, 1, 8; Horne, *Black Liberation/Red Scare*, 240–43.

194 **in *Dennis v. United States*:** Dennis v. United States, 341 U.S. 494 (1951).

194 **"Why, I think" & "because you are a Negro":** *NYAN*, 7/7/1951, 28. See *DW*, 7/8/1951, 3; Horne, *Black Liberation/Red Scare*, 251 ("I do not have the 13th, the 14th and the 15th Amendments. They are not kept in this country").

194 **federal prison in Terre Haute:** *NYT*, 7/11/1951, 9; *DW*, 7/15/1951, 3; *CCFH*, 187–94; Horne, *Black Liberation/Red Scare*, 254–66.

194 **a memoir in longhand:** *DW*, 1/4/1956, 8; *DW*, 3/11/1956, 3; *NYT*, 7/24/1960, BR-24; *DW*, 3/22/1969, M-2; Horne, *Black Liberation/Red Scare*, 269–70.

194 **On March 1, 1955:** *DW*, 3/1/1955, 1; *NYT*, 3/2/1955, 1; *DW*, 3/10/1955, 3, 5; Horne, *Black Liberation/Red Scare*, 266–70.

194 **Smith Act trial in Pittsburgh:** *DW*, 8/4/1953, 1, 6; *DW*, 8/5/1953, 1, 6; Horne, *Black Liberation/Red Scare*, 263–65.

194 **Soviet Union's invasion of Hungary:** *DW*, 11/28/1956, 5; Horne, *Black Liberation/Red Scare*, 274.

194 **elected national secretary:** *DW*, 12/20/1959, 1; Horne, *Black Liberation/Red Scare*, 300–301; SAC NY to FBI Dir., 8/13/1964, "Benjamin J. Davis Jr.," pp. 1–2, CPUSA, 100-3-104-34, NY, sect. 10, FBI File (describing national secretary position as "mostly ornamental" and depriving BJD of opportunity to lead the Party).

195 **spoke at Harvard Law School:** *DW*, 4/29/1962, 2, 11; *Ben Davis on the McCarran Act at the Harvard Law Forum* (1962), 4–5.

195 **Dean Erwin Griswold:** Erwin Griswold to BJD, 2/26/1957, Benjamin J. Davis Papers, reel 1; Erwin Griswold to BJD, 2/17/1958, pp. 1–3, ibid.; Erwin Griswold to BJD, 4/30/1958, pp. 1–4, ibid.; Erwin Griswold to BJD, 3/14/1960, ibid.

195 **"I leave Harvard":** *DW*, 4/29/1962, 11.

195 **led to his decision:** *DW*, 4/29/1962, 11; *CCFH*, 81.

195 **"you can't kill a man":** *BAA*, 1/28/1933, 9.

195 **Tom Watson:** CVW, *Thinking Back: The Perils of Writing History* (1986), 29–42; James C. Cobb, *C. Vann Woodward: America's Historian* (2022), 30–82; John Herbert Roper, *C. Vann Woodward, Southerner* (1987), 78–102; CVW, *Tom Watson: Agrarian Rebel* (New York: Macmillan, 1938).

196 **two groundbreaking books:** Cobb, *C. Vann Woodward: America's Historian*, 105–27; CVW, *Thinking Back*, 43–79; CVW, *Reunion and Reaction: The Compromise of 1877 and the End of Reconstruction* (Boston: Little, Brown, 1951); CVW, *Origins of the New South, 1877–1913* (Baton Rouge: Louisiana State University Press, 1951); *NYT*, 5/16/1952, 24.

196 **John Hope Franklin:** CVW to Lester J. Cappon, 1/31/1949, tel., *CVWL*, p. 116; CVW to John Hope Franklin, 2/4/1949, ibid., p. 122; CVW to John Hope Franklin, 2/23/1949, in ibid., p. 123; CVW, "The Fifteenth Annual Meeting of the Southern

Historical Association," *Journal of Southern History* 16, no. 1 (1950): 43; CVW, *Thinking Back*, 89–90; Cobb, *C. Vann Woodward: America's Historian*, 128–46; Roper, *C. Vann Woodward, Southerner*, 165–69.

196 **advising Thurgood Marshall:** CVW to Howard Jay Graham, 6/16/1954, *CVWL*, p. 137; CVW, *Thinking Back*, 88–89; Cobb, *C. Vann Woodward: America's Historian*, 147–54; Roper, *C. Vann Woodward, Southerner*, 163–65.

196 **series of lectures:** CVW to George B. Tindall, 3/8/1955, *CVWL*, pp. 145–47; CVW, *Thinking Back*, 81–84, 90; CVW, *The Strange Career of Jim Crow* (New York: Oxford University Press, 1955); Cobb, *C. Vann Woodward: America's Historian*, 154–83. On the book's critics and CVW's responses, see David M. Potter, "C. Vann Woodward," in *Pastmasters: Some Essays on American Historians*, ed. Marcus Cunliffe and Robin W. Winks (1969), 395–407; Cobb, *C. Vann Woodward: America's Historian*, 184–200.

196 **800,000 copies:** Cobb, *C. Vann Woodward: America's Historian*, 206.

196 **voting rights march:** Walter Johnson, "Historians Join the March on Montgomery," *South Atlantic Quarterly* 79, no. 2 (Spring 1980): 160, 164, in CVWP, box 90, folder 3.

196 **heard Martin Luther King Jr.:** Martin Luther King Jr., "Address at the End of the March from Selma to Montgomery," 3/25/1965, King Institute, https://kinginstitute .stanford.edu/our-god-marching; Cobb, *C. Vann Woodward*, 182–83.

197 **"communist influence" & "a Socialist":** U.S. Naval Intelligence Investigation Report on C. Vann Woodward, Office of the Secretary of Defense, 8/22/1951 interview with John Hudson, pp. 3–4 (on file with author); Cobb, *C. Vann Woodward: America's Historian*, 307. Hudson's recollections are suspect because he claimed that CVW was at the November 1934 trials of Nathan Yagol and Mrs. R. W. Ailing, but by that time CVW was a graduate student at the University of North Carolina.

197 **blocked Marxist historian Herbert Aptheker:** Cobb, *C. Vann Woodward: America's Historian*, 312–41; Roper, *C. Vann Woodward, Southerner*, 268–91.

197 **National Association of Scholars:** Cobb, *C. Vann Woodward: America's Historian*, 388.

197 **prominent report:** Chairman's Letter to the Fellows of the Yale Corporation, 12/23/1974, https://yalecollege.yale.edu/get-know-yale-college/office-dean/reports/ report-committee-freedom-expression-yale.

197 **fielded questions:** CVW to Wilma Dykeman Stokely, 12/1/1959, *CVWL*, p. 200; CVW to David Entin, 2/25/1963, ibid., pp. 234–35; CVW Int. by John Herbert Roper, 7/18/1978, pp. 3–4, John Herbert Roper Papers, folder 10; CVW, *Thinking Back*, 86–87.

197 **National Lawyers Guild:** Craig Thompson, "The Communist's Dearest Friend," *Saturday Evening Post*, 2/17/1951, 93; Ann Fagan Ginger, *Carol Weiss King: Human Rights Lawyer, 1895–1952* (1993), 219–21.

197 **American Committee for Protection of Foreign Born:** Ginger, *Carol Weiss King*, 195–96, 458. See Records of the American Committee for Protection of Foreign Born, box 3, folder 6, box 16, folder 6, and box 19, folder 10.

197 **Harry Bridges:** Bridges v. Wixon, 326 U.S. 135 (1945); Ginger, *Carol Weiss King*, 256–87, 325–62, 405–8, 412–21; Peter Afrasiabi, *Burning Bridges: America's 20-Year Crusade to Deport Labor Leader Harry Bridges* (2016), 67–105, 139–52.

198 **William Schneiderman:** Schneiderman v. United States, 320 U.S. 118 (1943); Carol King, "The Willkie I Knew," *NM*, 10/24/1944, 10–11, 26–27; Ginger, *Carol Weiss*

King, 363–80, 398–401; William Schneiderman, *Dissent on Trial* (Minneapolis: MEP Publications, 1983), 79–104.

198   **the FBI opened an investigation:** Carol Weiss King FOIA Files; Carol Weiss King Collection; Ginger, *Carol Weiss King*, 325–27, 518.

198   **King's former client:** Ginger, *Carol Weiss King*, 479.

198   **John Zydok:** Ginger, *Carol Weiss King*, 530–33, 537–38; Carlson v. Landon, 342 U.S. 524 (1952).

198   **"probably defended more Reds":** Thompson, "The Communists' Dearest Friend," 30. See Ginger, *Carol Weiss King*, 516.

198   **denying that she was a member:** *Hearings Before the House Select Committee on Immigration and Nationalization*, 1/12/1938, 75th Cong., 3rd sess., pp. 11–14 (testimony of Carol Weiss King); RNB COH, 1954, p. 139; Ginger, *Carol Weiss King*, 326, 333–34, 432, 526.

199   **the Supreme Court case of Joseph George Strecker:** *NYT*, 10/18/1938, 1, 10; *NYHT*, 2/11/1939, 10A; *NYT*, 2/11/1939, 9; *DW*, 4/18/1939, 1, 4; Kessler v. Strecker, 307 U.S. 22 (1939).

199   **board of the ACLU & cochaired the Lawyers' Committee:** Eleanor M. Fox, ed., *A Visit with Whitney North Seymour* (1984), 14.

199   **American Bar Association special committee:** "Report of the Special Committee on Individual Rights as Affected by National Security," *Annual Report of the ABA* 79 (1954): 329–32; WNS, "Congressional Investigations," *Texas Bar Journal* 18, no. 3 (1955): 111–46.

199   **public servants:** Fox, *Visit with Whitney North Seymour*, 31–53

199   **Association of the Bar of the City of New York:** *NYHT*, 5/10/1950, 7; *NYT*, 2/25/1959, 25; Fox, *Visit with Whitney North Seymour*, 18, 86–87.

200   **civic and social causes:** Fox, *Visit with Whitney North Seymour*, 25–27, 88.

200   **after-dinner speaker:** Fox, *Visit with Whitney North Seymour*, 64–78.

200   **"I've tried to recognize":** Fox, *Visit with Whitney North Seymour*, 98.

200   **the case of Fred Korematsu:** John L. Burling to Herbert Wechsler, 9/9/1944, pp. 1–2, in NARA, DOJ, RG 60, Violation of Curfew Litigation Case Files, 1942–1982, no. 146-42-7, section 2, box 7; Edward Ennis to Herbert Wechsler, 9/11/1944, in ibid; Transcript Fisher-Wechsler Telephone Conversation at 11:30 a.m., 10/2/1944, NARA, War Department Files, RG 107, Papers of John J. McCloy, Box 9, Folder I–M; Edward Ennis to Herbert Wechsler, 9/30/1944, in NARA, RG 21, United States v. Korematsu, 1981, Exhibit B; Wechsler COH, pp. 3-191–3-202; Korematsu v. United States, 323 U.S. 214 (1944); Brad Snyder, *Democratic Justice: Felix Frankfurter, the Supreme Court, and the Making of the Liberal Establishment* (2022), 446–47; Peter Irons, *Justice at War: The Story of the Japanese Interment Cases* (1993), 284–92.

200   **assisted U.S. Judge Francis Biddle:** Wechsler COH, pp. 4-203–4-273, 5-274–5-276; Telford Taylor, *The Anatomy of the Nuremberg Trials* (New York: Knopf, 1992).

200   *New York Times v. Sullivan:* Wechsler COH, 5-298–5-315; New York Times Co. v. Sullivan, 376 U.S. 254 (1964); Anthony Lewis, *Make No Law: The Sullivan Case and the First Amendment* (New York: Random House, 1991); Samantha Barbas, *Actual Malice: Civil Rights and Freedom of the Press in New York Times v. Sullivan* (Oakland: University of California Press, 2023).

201   **tarred him as a radical:** 88 Cong. Rec. 5442 (June 22, 1942) (Rep. Richard B. Wigglesworth [R-MA]) (attacking Wechsler for work with ILD and International Juridical Association); WNS to Rep. Clifton A. Woodrum (D-VA), 1/9/1942, pp. 1–2, in WNSP, box 1 (defending Wechsler and their work on the Herndon and Strecker cases).

201 **longer career in public life:** Wechsler COH, pp. 3-175–3-176.

201 **"neutral principles":** Wechsler COH, pp. 5-337–5-352; Norman Silber and Geoffrey Miller, "Toward 'Neutral Principles' in the Law: Selections from the Oral History of Herbert Wechsler," *Columbia Law Review* 93, no. 4 (1993): 854; Herbert Wechsler, "Toward Neutral Principles of Constitutional Law," *Harvard Law Review* 73, no. 1 (1959): 1–35.

201 **Charles Hamilton Houston:** Wechsler, "Toward Neutral Principles," 34.

201 **Model Penal Code:** Wechsler COH, pp. 5-316–5-326; R. Ammi Cutter, "Herbert Wechsler and the American Law Institute," *Columbia Law Review* 78, no. 5 (1978): 959; Anders Walker, "American Oresteia: Herbert Wechsler, the Model Penal Code, and the Uses of Revenge," *University of Wisconsin Law Review* 2009 (2009): 1018; Anders Walker, "The New Common Law: Courts, Culture, and the Localization of the Model Penal Code," *Hastings Law Review* 62, no. 6 (2011): 1633; David Wolitz, "Herbert Wechsler, Legal Process, and the Jurisprudential Roots of the Model Penal Code," *Tulsa Law Review* 51, no. 3 (2016): 633.

201 **his casebook with Henry Hart:** Henry M. Hart Jr. and Herbert Wechsler, *The Federal Courts and the Federal System* (Brooklyn: Foundation Press, 1953); Richard H. Fallon Jr., "Reflections on the Hart and Wechsler Paradigm," *Vanderbilt Law Review* 47, no. 4 (1994): 953, 956.

201 **"a crisis in the development":** CHH to NAACP Board of Directors, 7/20/1936, in NAACPP, pt. 8, ser. A, reel 8, p. 781.

202 **Donald Murray's admission:** *BAA*, 3/22/1947, 4; Pearson v. Murray, 182 A. 590 (Md. 1936); José Felipé Anderson, *Genius for Justice: Charles Hamilton Houston and the Reform of American Law* (2022), 64–70; Genna Rae McNeil, *Groundwork: Charles Hamilton Houston and the Struggle for Civil Rights* (1983), 138–43.

202 **Lloyd Gaines's case:** *BAA*, 11/12/1938, 1, 3; Missouri ex rel. Gaines v. Canada, 305 U.S. 337 (1938); Anderson, *Genius for Justice*, 73–75; McNeil, *Groundwork*, 143–51.

202 **railroad union had violated:** *BAA*, 11/18/1944, 1, 2; Steele v. Louisville & N. R. Co., 323 U.S. 192 (1944); *BAA*, 9/27/1947, 4; Anderson, *Genius for Justice*, 120–23; McNeil, *Groundwork*, 156–71.

202 **racially restrictive covenants:** *BAA*, 6/21/1947, 4; *BAA*, 9/27/1947, 4; *BAA*, 10/11/1947, 4; *BAA*, 12/13/1947, 4; *BAA*, 1/24/1948 1, 12; Hurd v. Hodge, 334 U.S. 24 (1948); Anderson, *Genius for Justice*, 127–37; McNeil, *Groundwork*, 176–85.

202 **"Racism must go":** *BAA*, 1/24/1948, 1.

202 **toll on Houston's health:** McNeil, *Groundwork*, 148–49.

202 **Hollywood Ten:** *BAA*, 11/1/1947, 4; José Felipé Anderson, "Freedom of Association, the Communist Party, and the Hollywood Ten: The Forgotten First Amendment Legacy of Charles Hamilton Houston," *McGeorge Law Review* 40, no. 1 (2009): 25; Anderson, *Genius for Justice*, 141–52; McNeil, *Groundwork*, 204–6.

203 **Esther McCready:** *BAA*, 9/27/1947, 4; Anderson, *Genius for Justice*, 175–79; McNeil, *Groundwork*, 199–200.

203 **hospital bed:** *BAA*, 4/22/1950, 6; McCready v. Byrd, 73 A.2d 8 (Md. 1950).

203 **Marshall always gave credit:** Mark V. Tushnet, ed., *Thurgood Marshall: His Speeches, Writings, Arguments, Opinions, and Reminiscences* (2001), 206, 272–76, 415–16, 418, 423; Ken Gormley, "A Mentor's Legacy," *American Bar Association Journal* 78, no. 6 (June 1992): 62–66.

204 **a 1936 reelection challenge:** *AC*, 9/1/1936, 1, 11. In 1950, Walter LeCraw, the other assistant solicitor who had prosecuted Herndon, narrowly lost an election

for a judgeship even though LeCraw's brother was a former Atlanta mayor: *ADW*, 6/27/1950, 1; *ADW*, 6/30/1950, 4.

204 **Whitney North Seymour's recommendation:** WNS to Elbert P. Tuttle, 4/30/1936, pp. 1–2, in WNSP, box 3; Elbert P. Tuttle to WNS, 4/25/1936, in ibid.; WNS to William Sutherland, 4/13/1936, pp. 1–3, in ibid.

204 **Monroe Bridwell and John Johnson:** Elbert Tuttle OH, Georgia State University, 9/21/1992, pp. 15–18; Anne Emanuel, *Elbert Parr Tuttle: Chief Jurist of the Civil Rights Revolution* (2011), 124–27.

204 **"right to be heard":** Johnson v. Zerbst, 304 U.S. 458, 463 (1938) (quoting Powell v. Alabama, 287 U.S. 45, 68, 60 [1932]).

204 **Tuttle volunteered:** *AC*, 7/10/1945, 12; *AC*, 7/15/1945, 1B; *AC*, 3/6/1946, 5.

204 **general counsel of the Treasury Department:** *AC*, 1/14/1953, 1, 8.

204 **nominated Tuttle to serve:** Jack Bass, *Unlikely Heroes* (1981), 30–31; *AC*, 7/7/1954, 1.

205 **he ordered the admission:** Holmes v. Danner, 191 F. Supp. 394 (M.D. Ga. 1961); Bass, *Unlikely Heroes*, 217 23.

205 **"unconstitutional and void" & Stokely Carmichael:** Carmichael v. Allen, 267 F. Supp. 985, 993–94 (N.D. Ga. 1966) (per curiam). Herndon prosecutor Walter LeCraw represented the Fulton County solicitor general and sheriff in the Carmichael case: ibid., at 986.

205 **"switch in time":** John Q. Barrett, "Attribution Time: Cal Tinney's Quip, 'A Switch in Time'll Save Nine,' " *Oklahoma Law Review* 73, no. 2 (2021): 229.

205 **Yet as Roberts revealed eight years later:** FF to Thomas Reed Powell, 8/14/1946, p. 4, in Thomas Reed Powell Papers, box B, folder B24; FF, "Mr. Justice Roberts," *University of Pennsylvania Law Review* 104, no. 3 (Dec. 1955): 311, 313–15 (quoting memorandum that Roberts gave to FF on November 9, 1945).

205 **resigned in disgust:** FF to Learned Hand, 6/15/1961, p. 2, in Learned Hand Papers, box 105D, folder 105-26.

206 **congratulatory letter:** Snyder, *Democratic Justice*, 468–73.

206 **lacked the intellectual equipment:** FF to HFS, 7/22/1945, p. 2, in Harlan Fiske Stone Papers, box 75.

206 **"the indisputable facts":** Korematsu v. United States, 323 U.S. 214, 225–26 (1944) (Roberts, J., dissenting).

206 **Strecker's deportation case:** Kessler v. Strecker, 307 U.S. 22 (1939).

206 **With the notable exception:** Grovey v. Townsend, 295 U.S. 45 (1935); Smith v. Allwright, 321 U.S. 649, 666 (1944) (Roberts, J., dissenting) (insisting on following *Grovey*).

206 **"The power of a state":** Herndon v. Lowry, 301 U.S. 242, 258 (1937).

207 **"I remembered Angelo Herndon":** James Baldwin, "Nobody Knows My Name," (1961), in *The Price of the Ticket: Collected Nonfiction, 1948–1985* (New York: St. Martin's, 1985), 184.

207 **Transferred to the Cook County jail & released no later than:** SA Edwin W. Flint to SAC Chicago, 3/23/1956, Herndon FBI File, 100-HQ-18143, vol. 1, p. 89; Herndon Criminal Record, 9/6/1967, Department of Justice, FBI, ibid., p. 108.

207 **working as a cook:** SA Henry F. Burns Jr., 9/15/1967, p. 9, Herndon FBI File, 100-HQ-18143, vol. 1, 168. On Lightfoot, see Claude M. Lightfoot, *Chicago Slums to World Politics: The Autobiography of Claude M. Lightfoot* (New York: New Outlook, 1985); Claude M. Lightfoot, *Ghetto Rebellion to Black Liberation* (New York: International Publishers, 1968).

207 **he recited a poem:** *CDef*, 2/9/1963, 14.

207 **rejoined the Communist Party:** FBI memorandum, 5/2/1967, p. 5, Herndon FBI File, 100-HQ-18143, vol. 1, p. 100; memorandum, 5/3/1967, p. 1, ibid., p. 104.

207 **Afro-American Book Store:** Ian Rocksborough-Smith, *Black Public History in Chicago: Civil Rights Activism from World War II into the Cold War* (Urbana: University of Illinois Press, 2018), 88.

207 **Henry Winston:** *DW*, 5/14/1967, in Communist Party of the United States of America Records, box 84, folder 18. See also *DW*, 6/18/1967, in ibid. (AH mourning loss of *Daily Worker* writer Mike Gold).

207 **"on a trip":** Memorandum, 9/11/1967, Herndon FBI File, 100-HQ-18143, vol. 1, p. 179.

207 **FBI could not find him:** SA Henry F. Burns Jr., 9/15/1967, Herndon FBI File, 100-HQ-18143, vol. 1, p. 160; SA Henry F. Burns Jr. to SAC Chicago, 10/3/1967, ibid., p. 175; SAC Chicago to FBI Dir., 12/28/1967, ibid., p. 190.

207 **described Herndon as a "drifter":** SAC Chicago to FBI Dir., 10/19/1967, p. 2, Herndon FBI File, 100-HQ-18143, vol. 1, p. 184.

207 **who had a "mental problem":** SAC Chicago to FBI Dir., 9/27/1969, p. 1, Herndon FBI File, 100-HQ-18143, vol. 1, p. 214; SAC Chicago to FBI Dir., 1/29/1969, p. 1, ibid., p. 225.

207 **"the history of the Negro":** SAC Chicago to FBI Dir., 11/22/1968, Herndon FBI File, 100-HQ-18143, vol. 1, p. 220.

207 **Louise Thompson Patterson:** Louise Patterson to Friends of Ben Davis, 5/23/1969, in Communist Party USA Records, box 79, folder 31; memorandum, 5/14/1969, Herndon FBI File, 100-HQ-18143, vol. 1, pp. 248, 252; memorandum, 6/4/1969, ibid., p. 262; Keith Gilyard, *Louise Thompson Patterson: A Life of Struggle for Justice* (2017).

207 **"to relate the present-day struggles":** Louise Patterson to AH, 5/26/1969, in Louise Thompson Patterson Papers, box 16, folder 3; Gilyard, *Louise Thompson Patterson*, 192.

207 **hyped Herndon's appearance:** *DW*, 5/24/1969, 4; *DW*, 5/30/1969, 8; *DW*, 6/3/1969, 4; *DW*, 6/7/1969, 11.

209 **"You've got to fight":** *DW*, 6/10/1969, 11. See SA John P. Di Marchi to SAC NY, 7/3/1969 re: 6/8/1969 Davis tribute, pp. 1–3, Herndon FBI File, 100-HQ-18143, vol. 1, pp. 263–65; *Daily World Magazine*, 7/5/1969, M-10.

209 **small reception:** SA John P. Di Marchi to SAC NY, 7/10/1969 re: 6/8/1969 reception for Herndon, pp. 1–3, Herndon FBI File, 100-HQ-18143, vol. 1, pp. 267–69; SA John P. Di Marchi to SAC NY, 7/7/1969, pp. 1–3, ibid., pp. 271–73.

209 **declined interview requests:** John Hammond Moore, "The Angelo Herndon Case, 1932–1937," *Phylon* 32, no. 1 (1971): 61, 61n4 (citing 5/7/1967 letter from Herndon); Charles H. Martin, *The Angelo Herndon Case and Southern Justice* (1976), xv.

209 **J. Edgar Hoover:** FBI Dir. to John H. Moore, 3/30/1967, Angelo Herndon FBI File, 61-HQ-7259, vol. 2, p. 42 (claiming material was "confidential"); John H. Moore to FBI Dir., 3/26/1967, ibid., p. 43; Moore, "The Angelo Herndon Case, 1932–1937," 61, 61n4.

209 **living in Chicago:** William L. Patterson to Charles H. Martin, 5/25/1970, p. 2, in Charles H. Martin Papers.

209 **living in New York:** Memorandum, 12/30/1971, Herndon FBI File, 100-HQ-18143, vol. 1, p. 303; SAC Chicago to FBI Dir., 1/26/1972, ibid., p. 304.

209 **stopped surveilling him in 1972:** SAC Chicago to Acting FBI Dir., 10/30/1972, Herndon FBI File, 100-HQ-18143, vol. 1, p. 314.

209   **residing in Milwaukee:** AH, 1987 Milwaukee Public Record Voter Registration.

209   **Sweet Home, Arkansas:** AH, Social Security Death Index, 12/9/1997.

210   *Carolene Products***:** United States v. Carolene Prods. Co., 304 U.S. 144, 152–53n4 (1938).

211   **"fear of serious injury":** Whitney v. California, 274 U.S. 357, 376 (1927) (Brandeis, J., concurring).

211   **"a man because of":** *BAA*, 1/28/1933, 9.

SELECTED BIBLIOGRAPHY

MANUSCRIPTS

American Civil Liberties Union Papers, Seeley G. Mudd Manuscript Library, Princeton University, Princeton, NJ

Records of the American Committee for Protection of Foreign Born, New York University, Tamiment Library and Robert F. Wagner Labor Archive, New York, NY

Louis Dembitz Brandeis Papers, Harvard Law School Library, Historical and Special Collections, Cambridge, MA

Louis D. Brandeis Papers, University of Louisville Library, Louisville, KY

Civil Rights Congress Records, Schomburg Center for Research in Black Culture, New York, NY

Commission for Interracial Cooperation Papers, 1919–1944, Library of Congress, Washington, DC

Communist Party of the United States of America Records, New York University, Tamiment Library and Robert F. Wagner Labor Archive, New York, NY

Cook County Criminal Archives, Chicago, IL

Crusader News Agency Papers, Schomburg Center for Research in Black Culture, New York, NY

Daily Worker Collection, New York University, Tamiment Library and Robert F. Wagner Labor Archive, New York, NY

Benjamin J. Davis Jr., Small Materials Collection, Harvard Law School Library, Historical and Special Collections, Cambridge, MA

Benjamin J. Davis Papers, Schomburg Center for Research in Black Culture, New York, NY

Hugh M. Dorsey Sr. Papers, Atlanta History Center, Atlanta, GA

Early Presidents Collection, Georgia Institute of Technology, Archives and Special Collections, Atlanta, GA

Ralph Ellison Papers, Library of Congress, Washington, DC

James W. Ford Papers, New York University, Tamiment Library and Robert F. Wagner Labor Archive, New York, NY

Felix Frankfurter Papers, Harvard Law School Library, Historical and Special Collections, Cambridge, MA

Felix Frankfurter Papers, Library of Congress, Washington, DC

Walter Gellhorn Papers, Columbia University, Rare Book and Manuscript Library, New York, NY

Ida Guggenheimer Papers, Schomburg Center for Research in Black Culture, New York, NY

Learned Hand Papers, Harvard Law School Library, Historical and Special Collections, Cambridge, MA

Angelo Herndon Collection, Schomburg Center for Research in Black Culture, New York, NY

Angelo Herndon Papers, Schomburg Center for Research in Black Culture, New York, NY

Herndon v. Georgia, U.S. Supreme Court Briefs and Records, October Term 1934

Herndon v. Lowry, U.S. Supreme Court Briefs and Records, October Term 1936

J. Edgar Hoover Official and Confidential File, Federal Bureau of Investigation Files, National Archives and Records Administration, College Park, MD

Gerald Horne Papers, Schomburg Center for Research in Black Culture, New York, NY

Charles Evans Hughes Papers, Library of Congress, Washington, DC

Langston Hughes Papers, Beinecke Library, Yale University, New Haven, CT

Charles H. Houston Papers, Howard University, Washington, DC

William LePre Houston Family Papers, Library of Congress, Washington, DC

Stanley Edgar Hyman Papers, Library of Congress, Washington, DC

International Labor Defense Papers, Schomburg Center for Research in Black Culture, New York, NY

Robert Houghwout Jackson Papers, Library of Congress, Washington, DC

Claudia Jones Memorial Collection, Schomburg Center for Research in Black Culture, New York, NY

Carol Weiss King Collection, University of Michigan Library, Special Collections Research Center, Ann Arbor, MI

Carol Weiss King FOIA Files, New York University, Tamiment Library and Robert F. Wagner Labor Archive, New York, NY

Jay and Si-Lan Chen Leda Papers, New York University, Tamiment Library and Robert F. Wagner Labor Archive, New York, NY

Charles H. Martin Collection on Angelo Herndon, Georgia State University, Atlanta, GA

Charles H. Martin Papers for *The Angelo Herndon Case and Southern Justice* (privately held)

Clarina Michaelson Papers, New York University, Tamiment Library and Robert F. Wagner Labor Archive, New York, NY

Richard B. Moore Papers, Schomburg Center for Research in Black Culture, New York, NY

National Association for the Advancement of Colored People Papers, Library of Congress, Washington, DC

National Negro Congress Papers, Schomburg Center for Research in Black Culture, New York, NY

Steve Oney Papers, Georgia Historical Society, Savannah, GA

Louise Thompson Patterson Papers, Emory University, Woodruff Library, Atlanta, GA

People's Advocate, Schomburg Center for Research in Black Culture, New York NY

John Pittman Papers, New York University, Tamiment Library and Robert F. Wagner Labor Archive, New York, NY

Thomas Reed Powell Papers, Harvard Law School Library, Historical and Special Collections, Cambridge, MA

Glenn W. Rainey Papers, Emory University, Woodruff Library, Atlanta, GA

Random House Records, Columbia University, Rare Book and Manuscript Library, New York, NY

Raoul Family Papers, Emory University, Woodruff Library, Atlanta, GA

Owen J. Roberts Papers, Library of Congress, Washington, DC

Franklin D. Roosevelt Papers, Franklin D. Roosevelt Presidential Library, Hyde Park, NY

John Herbert Roper Papers, University of North Carolina, Wilson Special Collections Library, Chapel Hill, NC

Richard B. Russell Sr. Papers, University of Georgia, Richard B. Russell Library for Political Research and Studies, Athens, GA

Russian State Archive of Social and Political History, Files of the Communist Party of the USA in the Comintern Archives, Library of Congress. Washington, DC

Whitney North Seymour Papers, New York Public Library, New York, NY

The South Moves West, February 1944, Schomburg Center for Research in Black Culture, New York, NY

Harlan Fiske Stone Papers, Library of Congress, Washington, DC

Supreme Court Docket Books, Curator's Office, Supreme Court of the United States, Washington, DC

Supreme Court of the United States, Clerk's Office Files, National Archives and Record Administration, Washington, DC

Charles W. Taussig Papers, Franklin D. Roosevelt Presidential Library, Hyde Park, NY

Elbert P. Tuttle Papers, Emory University, Woodruff Library, Atlanta, GA

U.S. Census Records, 1870–1950

U.S. District Records, Northern District, Illinois, National Archives, Chicago, IL

Willis Van Devanter Papers, Library of Congress, Washington, DC

Austen T. Walden Papers, Atlanta History Center, Atlanta, GA

Herbert Wechsler Papers, Columbia University, Rare Book and Manuscript Library, New York, NY

Burton K. Wheeler Papers, Montana State University, Bozeman, MT

C. Vann Woodward Papers, Yale University Library, Manuscripts and Archives, New Haven, CT

Richard Wright Papers, Beinecke Library, Yale University, New Haven, CT

Charles E. Wyzanski Jr. Papers, Massachusetts Historical Society, Boston, MA

ORAL HISTORIES

Author Interviews

Angelo Braxton, nephew of Angelo Herndon, by telephone, June 22, 2023

Charles H. Martin, by telephone, June 8, 2023

Atlanta History Center

Nanny L. Washburn

Columbia Oral Histories

Will W. Alexander

Roger Nash Baldwin

Walter Gellhorn, 1955 and 1977

Thurgood Marshall

Frances Perkins

Whitney North Seymour Sr., March 22, 1977

Herbert Wechsler

C. Vann Woodward

Georgia State University

Elbert Tuttle, April 10, 1992 and September 21, 1992

Howard University, Moorland-Spingarn Research Center, Ralph J. Bunche Oral History Collection

William L. Patterson, February 28, 1970

University of North Carolina, Southern Oral History Program Collection

Don West, January 22, 1975

GOVERNMENT RECORDS

FBI Files

Angelo Herndon, 61-HQ-7159, vol. 1–2; 100-HQ-18143, vol. 1; 100-WFO-47734
Carol Weiss King, 100-NY-25773
CPUSA (Communist Party USA), 100-3-104-34, NY, sect. 10
Negro Labor Victory Committee, 100-HQ-115471

Navy Criminal Investigatory Service File

C. Vann Woodward—June 25,1951, 100-HQ-409893-2

BOOKS

Afrasiabi, Peter. *Burning Bridges: America's 20-Year Crusade to Deport Labor Leader Harry Bridges*. Brooklyn: Thirlmere Books, 2016.

Anderson, José Felipé. *Genius for Justice: Charles Hamilton Houston and the Reform of American Law*. Durham, NC: Carolina Academic Press, 2022.

Bass, Jack. *Unlikely Heroes*. New York: Simon & Schuster, 1981.

Ben Davis on the McCarran Act at the Harvard Law Forum. New York: Gus Hall–Benjamin J. Davis Defense Committee, 1962.

Bradley, David. *The Historic Murder Trial of George Crawford: Charles H. Houston, the NAACP, and the Case That Put All-White Southern Juries on Trial*. Jefferson, NC: McFarland, 2014.

Brown-Nagin, Tomiko. *Courage to Dissent: Atlanta and the Long History of the Civil Rights Movement*. New York: Oxford University Press, 2011.

Bryant, Earle V., ed. *Byline, Richard Wright: Articles from the* Daily Worker *and* New Masses. Columbia: University of Missouri Press, 2015.

Burden-Stelly, Charisse. *Black Scare/Red Scare: Theorizing Capitalist Racism in the United States*. Chicago: University of Chicago Press, 2023.

Callahan, John F., and Marc Conner, eds. *The Selected Letters of Ralph Ellison*. New York: Random House, 2019.

Carle, Susan D. *Defining the Struggle: National Organizing for Racial Justice, 1880–1915*. New York: Oxford University Press, 2013.

Carter, Dan T. *Scottsboro: A Tragedy of the American South*. Rev. ed. Baton Rouge: Louisiana State University Press, 1979.

Cobb, James C. *C. Vann Woodward: America's Historian*. Chapel Hill: University of North Carolina Press, 2022.

Damon, Anna. *Victory: Decision of the United States Supreme in the Case of Angelo Herndon, April 1937*. New York: International Labor Defense, 1937.

Davis, Benjamin J. *Communist Councilman from Harlem: Autobiographical Notes Written in a Federal Penitentiary*. New York: International Publishers, 1969.

Douglass, Frederick. *Life and Times of Frederick Douglass*. New York: Pathway Press, 1941.

Emanuel, Anne. *Elbert Parr Tuttle: Chief Jurist of the Civil Rights Revolution*. Athens: University of Georgia Press, 2011.

Fabre, Michel. *The Unfinished Quest of Richard Wright*. Trans. Isabel Barzun. 2nd ed. Urbana: University of Illinois Press, 1993.

——— . *The World of Richard Wright*. Jackson: University Press of Mississippi, 1985.

Ferguson, Karen. *Black Politics in New Deal Atlanta*. Chapel Hill: University of North Carolina Press, 2002.

Foley, Barbara. *Wrestling with the Left: The Making of Ralph Ellison's* Invisible Man. Durham, NC: Duke University Press, 2010.

Fox, Eleanor M., ed. *A Visit with Whitney North Seymour*. New York: William Nelson Cromwell Foundation, 1984.

Gilmore, Glenda Elizabeth. *Defying Dixie: The Radical Roots of Civil Rights, 1919–1950*. New York: W. W. Norton, 2008.

Gilyard, Keith. *Louise Thompson Patterson: A Life of Struggle for Justice*. Durham, NC: Duke University Press, 2017.

Ginger, Ann Fagan. *Carol Weiss King: Human Rights Lawyer, 1895–1952*. Niwot: University Press of Colorado, 1993.

Goluboff, Risa L. *The Lost Promise of Civil Rights*. Cambridge, MA: Harvard University Press, 2007.

Goodman, James. *Stories of Scottsboro*. New York: Pantheon, 1994.

Graham, Maryemma. *The House Where My Soul Lives: The Life of Margaret Walker*. New York: Oxford University Press, 2022.

Graham, Maryemma, and Amritjit Singh, eds. *Conversations with Ralph Ellison*. Jackson: University Press of Mississippi, 1995.

Griswold, Erwin N. *Ould Fields, New Corne*. St. Paul, MN: West Publishing, 1992.

Haas, Britt. *Fighting Authoritarianism: American Youth Activism in the 1930s*. New York: Fordham University Press, 2018.

Haywood, Harry. *Black Bolshevik: Autobiography of an Afro-American Communist*. Chicago: Liberator Press, 1978.

Herndon, Angelo. *Let Me Live*. New York: Random House, 1937.

——— . *The Scottsboro Boys: Four Freed! Five to Go!* New York: Workers Library Publishers, 1937.

——— . *You Cannot Kill the Working Class*. New York: International Labor Defense and League for Struggle of Negro Rights, 1934.

Horne, Gerald. *Black Liberation/Red Scare: Ben Davis and the Communist Party*. Rev. ed. New York: International Publishers, 2021.

——— . *Black Revolutionary: William Patterson and the Globalization of the African American Freedom Struggle*. Urbana: University of Illinois Press, 2013.

———. *The Final Victim of the Blacklist: John Howard Lawson, Dean of the Hollywood Ten*. Berkeley: University of California Press, 2006.

Hughes, Charles Evans. *The Autobiographical Notes of Charles Evans Hughes*. Edited by David J. Danelski and Joseph S. Tulchin. Cambridge, MA: Harvard University Press, 1973.

Hughes, Langston. *I Wonder as I Wander: An Autobiographical Journey*. New York: Hill & Wang, 1964.

———. *Letters from Langston: From the Harlem Renaissance to the Red Scare and Beyond*. Edited by Evelyn Louise Crawford and MaryLouise Patterson. Oakland: University of California Press, 2016.

Investigation of Communist Propaganda: Hearings Before a Special Committee to Investigate Communist Activities in the United States of the House of Representatives, 71st Cong., 2nd sess., pt. 6, vol. 1. Washington, DC: GPO, 1930.

Irons, Peter H. *Justice at War: The Story of the Japanese American Internment Cases*. Berkeley: University of California Press, 1993.

Isserman, Maurice. *Reds: The Tragedy of American Communism*. New York: Basic Books, 2024.

Jackson, Lawrence. *The Indignant Generation: A Narrative History of African-American Writers and Critics*. Princeton, NJ: Princeton University Press, 2010.

———. *Ralph Ellison: Emergence of Genius*. New York: John Wiley & Sons, 2007.

Janken, Kenneth Robert. *White: The Biography of Walter White, Mr. NAACP*. New York: New Press, 2003.

Johanningsmeier, Edward P. *Forging American Communism: The Life of William Z. Foster*. Princeton, NJ: Princeton University Press, 1994.

Jones, Claudia. *Ben Davis: Fighter for Freedom*. Brooklyn: National Committee to Defend Negro Leadership, 1954.

Kaufman, Andrew L. *Cardozo*. Cambridge, MA: Harvard University Press, 1998.

Kelley, Robin D. G. *Hammer and Hoe: Alabama Communists During the Great Depression*. Chapel Hill: University of North Carolina Press, 1990.

Kelly, Brian. *Race, Class, and Power in the Alabama Coalfields, 1908–1921*. Urbana: University of Illinois Press, 2001.

Kennedy, David M. *Freedom from Fear: The American People in Depression and War, 1929–1945*. New York: Oxford University Press, 1999.

Kimball, Bruce A., and Daniel R. Coquillette. *The Intellectual Sword: Harvard Law School, the Second Century*. Cambridge, MA: Belknap Press of Harvard University Press, 2020.

Klarman, Michael. *From Jim Crow to Civil Rights: The Supreme Court and the Struggle for Racial Equality*. New York: Oxford University Press, 2004.

Klehr, Harvey. *Communist Cadre: The Social Background of the American Communist Party Elite*. Palo Alto, CA: Hoover Institution Press, 1978.

———. *The Heyday of American Communism: The Depression Decade*. New York: Basic Books, 1984.

Klehr, Harvey, and John Earl Haynes. *The American Communist Movement: Storming Heaven Itself.* New York: Twayne, 1992.

Klehr, Harvey, John Earl Haynes, and Fridrikh Igorevich Firsov. *The Secret World of American Communism.* New Haven: Yale University Press, 1995.

Knowles, Helen J. *Making Minimum Wage: Elsie Parrish Versus the West Coast Hotel* Company. Norman: University of Oklahoma Press, 2021.

Lash, Joseph P. *Eleanor and Franklin.* New York: W. W. Norton, 1971.

———. *Eleanor Roosevelt: A Friend's Memoir.* Garden City, NY: Doubleday, 1964.

Lash, Joseph P., ed. *From the Diaries of Felix Frankfurter.* New York: W. W. Norton, 1975.

Lawson, Elizabeth. *20 Years on the Chain Gang?: Angelo Herndon Must Go Free.* New York: International Labor Defense, 1935.

Lorence, James J. *A Hard Journey: The Life of Don West.* Urbana: University of Illinois Press, 2007.

———. *The Unemployed People's Movement: Leftists, Liberals and Labor in Georgia, 1929–1941.* Athens: University of Georgia Press, 2009.

Mack, Kenneth. *Representing the Race: The Creation of the Civil Rights Lawyer.* Cambridge, MA: Harvard University Press, 2012.

Martin, Charles H. *The Angelo Herndon Case and Southern Justice.* Baton Rouge: Louisiana State University Press, 1976.

Mason, Alpheus Thomas. *Brandeis: A Free Man's Life.* New York: Viking, 1946.

———. *Harlan Fiske Stone: Pillar of the Law.* New York: Viking, 1956.

McDuffie, Erik S. *Sojourning for Freedom: Black Women, American Communism, and the Making of Black Left Feminism.* Durham, NC: Duke University Press, 2011.

McNeil, Genna Rae. *Groundwork: Charles Hamilton Houston and the Struggle for Civil Rights.* Philadelphia: University of Pennsylvania Press, 1983.

Morrison, Melanie S. *Murder on Shades Mountain: The Legal Lynching of Willie Peterson and the Struggle for Justice in Jim Crow Birmingham.* Durham, NC: Duke University Press, 2018.

Naison, Mark. *Communists in Harlem During the Depression.* Urbana: University of Illinois Press, 2004.

Negro Quarterly: A Review of Negro Life and Culture, Numbers 1–4, 1942–1943. New York: Negro University Press, 1969.

North, Joseph. *No Men Are Strangers.* New York: International Publishers, 1958.

O'Brien, Michael, ed. *The Letters of C. Vann Woodward.* New Haven: Yale University Press, 2013.

Oney, Steve. *And the Dead Shall Rise: The Murder of Mary Phagan and the Lynching of Leo Frank.* New York: Pantheon, 2003.

Painter, Nell Irvin. *The Narrative of Hosea Hudson: His Life as a Negro Communist in the South.* Cambridge, MA: Harvard University Press, 1979.

Patterson, William L. *Ben Davis: Crusader for Freedom and Socialism.* New York: New Outlook Publishers, 1967.

Phillips, Harlan B., ed. *Felix Frankfurter Reminisces.* New York: Reynal, 1960.

Polenberg, Richard. *The World of Benjamin Cardozo.* Cambridge, MA: Harvard University Press, 1997.

Post, Robert C. *The Taft Court.* Vol. 1, *Making Law for a Divided Nation, 1921– 1930.* Cambridge: Cambridge University Press, 2023.

Pusey, Merlo J. *Charles Evans Hughes.* 2 vols. New York: Macmillan, 1951.

Rampersad, Arnold. *The Life of Langston Hughes.* Vol. 1, *1902–1941, I, Too, Sing America.* New York: Oxford University Press, 1986.

———. *Ralph Ellison.* New York: Alfred A. Knopf, 2007.

Roberts, Owen J. *The Court and the Constitution.* Cambridge, MA: Harvard University Press, 1951.

Roper, John Herbert. *C. Vann Woodward, Southerner.* Athens: University of Georgia Press, 1987.

Schlesinger, Arthur, Jr. *The Vital Center: The Politics of Freedom.* Boston: Houghton Mifflin, 1949.

Sherwood, Marika. *Claudia Jones: A Life in Exile.* London: Lawrence & Wishart, 1999.

Shesol, Jeff. *Supreme Power: Franklin Roosevelt vs. the Supreme Court.* New York: W. W. Norton, 2010.

Simon, James F. *FDR and Chief Justice Hughes: The President, the Supreme Court, and the Epic Battle over the New Deal.* New York: Simon & Schuster, 2012.

Smith, J. Clay, Jr. *Emancipation: The Making of the Black Lawyer, 1844–1944.* Philadelphia: University of Pennsylvania Press, 1993.

Snyder, Brad. *Democratic Justice: Felix Frankfurter, the Supreme Court, and the Making of the Liberal Establishment.* New York: W. W. Norton, 2022.

———. *The House of Truth: A Washington Political Salon and the Foundations of American Liberalism.* New York: Oxford University Press, 2017.

Solomon, Mark. *The Cry Was Unity: Communists and African Americans, 1917– 36.* Jackson: University Press of Mississippi, 1998.

Spivak, John L. *On the Chain Gang.* New York: International Publishers, 1932.

Street, James H. *Look Away!: A Dixie Notebook.* New York: Viking, 1936.

Strum, Philippa. *Louis D. Brandeis: Justice for the People.* Cambridge, MA: Harvard University Press, 1984.

Sullivan, Patricia. *Days of Hope: Race and Democracy in the New Deal Era.* Chapel Hill: University of North Carolina Press, 1996.

———. *Lift Every Voice: The NAACP and the Making of the Civil Rights Movement.* New York: New Press, 2009.

Sutherland, Arthur E. *The Law at Harvard: A History of Ideas and Men, 1817– 1967.* Cambridge, MA: Belknap Press, 1967.

Turner, W. Burghardt, and Joyce Moore Turner, eds. *Richard B. Moore, Carib-*

bean Militant in Harlem: Collected Writings, 1920–1972. Bloomington: Indiana University Press, 1988.

Tushnet, Mark V. *The Hughes Court: From Progressivism to Pluralism, 1931–1940.* Cambridge: Cambridge University Press, 2022.

——— . *Making Civil Rights Law: Thurgood Marshall and the Supreme Court, 1936–1961.* New York: Oxford University Press, 1996.

Tushnet, Mark V., ed. *Thurgood Marshall: His Speeches, Writings, Arguments, Opinions, and Reminiscences.* Chicago: Lawrence Hill Books, 2001.

Urofsky, Melvin I. *Louis D. Brandeis: A Life.* New York: Pantheon, 2009.

Urofsky, Melvin I., and David W. Levy, eds. *"Half Brother, Half Son": The Letters of Louis D. Brandeis to Felix Frankfurter.* Norman: University of Oklahoma Press, 1991.

——— , eds. *Letters of Louis D. Brandeis.* 5 vols. Albany: State University of New York Press, 1971–1978.

Varel, David A. *The Scholar and the Struggle: Lawrence D. Reddick's Crusade for Black History and Black Power.* Chapel Hill: University of North Carolina Press, 2020.

Walker, Margaret. *Richard Wright, Daemonic Genius: A Portrait of the Man, a Critical Look at his Work.* New York: Warner Books, 1988.

Ware, Gilbert. *William Hastie: Grace Under Pressure.* New York: Oxford University Press, 1984.

Washburn, Nanny. *75 Years of Struggle!: The Life of Nanny Washburn.* Chicago: Liberator Press, 1975.

Wechsler, James A. *The Age of Suspicion.* New York: Random House, 1953.

White, G. Edward. *The Constitution and the New Deal.* Cambridge, MA: Harvard University Press, 2000.

Winston, Henry. *Life Begins with Freedom.* New York: New Age Publishers, 1937.

Woodrum, Robert H. *"Everybody Was Black Down There": Race and Industrial Change in the Alabama Coalfields.* Athens: University of Georgia Press, 2007.

Woodward, C. Vann. *Thinking Back: The Perils of Writing History.* Baton Rouge: Louisiana University Press, 1986.

ARTICLES

Childs, Dennis. " 'An Insinuating Voice': Angelo Herndon and the Invisible Genesis of the Radical Prison Slave's Neo-Slave Narrative." *Callaloo* 40, no. 4 (Fall 2017): 30–56.

Cushman, Barry. "Inside the 'Constitutional Revolution' of 1937." *The Supreme Court Review* 2016 (2017): 367–409.

——— . "The Secret Lives of the Four Horsemen." *University of Virginia Law Review* 83, no. 3 (Apr. 1997): 559–645.

———. "Vote Fluidity on the Hughes Court: The Critical Terms, 1934–1936." *University of Illinois Law Review* 2017, no. 1 (2017): 269–306.

Emanuel, Anne S. "Lynching and the Law in Georgia Circa 1931: A Chapter in the Career of Judge Elbert Tuttle." *William and Mary Bill of Rights Journal* 5, no. 1 (1996): 215–48.

Frankfurter, Felix. "Chief Justices I Have Known." *Virginia Law Review* 39, no. 7 (Nov. 1953): 883–906.

———. "Mr. Justice Roberts." *University of Pennsylvania Law Review* 104, no. 3 (Dec. 1955): 311–17.

Frankfurter, Felix, and Henry M. Hart Jr. "The Business of the Supreme Court at October Term, 1934." *Harvard Law Review* 49, no.1 (1935): 68–107.

Freund, Paul A. "Charles Evans Hughes as Chief Justice." *Harvard Law Review* 81, no. 1 (Nov. 1967): 4–43.

Friedman, Richard D. "Chief Justice Hughes' Letter on Court-Packing." *Journal of Supreme Court History* 1 (1997): 76–86.

———. "A Reaffirmation: The Authenticity of the Roberts Memorandum, or Felix the Non-Forger." *University of Pennsylvania Law Review* 142, no. 6 (June 1994): 1985–96.

Gell, Aaron. "The Red and the Black: What the Forgotten Story of Angelo Herndon Tells Us about Cop City." *The Baffler*, no. 72 (Jan. 2024).

Green, James R. "Past and Present in Southern History." *Radical History Review* 36 (1986): 80–100.

———. "Rewriting Southern History: An Interview with C. Vann Woodward." *Southern Exposure* 12 (1984): 87–93.

Griffiths, Frederick T. "Ralph Ellison, Richard Wright, and the Case of Angelo Herndon." *African American Review* 35, no. 4 (Winter 2001): 615–36.

Herndon, Angelo. "Frederick Douglass: Symbol of Freedom." In *There Were Giants in the Land: Twenty-Eight Historic Americans as Seen by Twenty-Eight Contemporary Americans*, 137–41. New York: Farrar & Rinehart, 1942.

Kaufman, Andrew L. "Cardozo's Appointment to the Supreme Court." *Cardozo Law Review* 1, no. 1 (Spring 1979): 23–54.

Keedy, Edwin R. "Owen J. Roberts and the Law School." *University of Pennsylvania Law Review* 104, no. 3 (Dec. 1955): 318–21.

Kelley, Robin D. G. "The Great Depression." In *Four Hundred Souls*, ed. Ibram X. Kendi and Keisha N. Blain, 292–96. New York: One World, 2021.

———. "1929–1934: The Great Depression." In *Did It Happen Here? Perspectives on Fascism and America*, ed. Daniel Steinmetz-Jenkins, 149–53. New York: W. W. Norton, 2024.

Lorence, James J. "Mobilizing the Reserve Army: The Communist Party and the Unemployed in Atlanta, 1929–1934." In *Radicalism in the South Since Reconstruction*, ed. Chris Green, Rachel Rubin, and James Smethurst, 57–80. New York: Palgrave Macmillan, 2006.

Martin, Charles H. "Angelo Herndon and Southern Justice." In *American Political Trials*, ed. Michal R. Belknap, 159–77. Rev. ed. Westport, CT: Greenwood Press, 1994.

———. "Communists and Blacks: The ILD and the Angelo Herndon Case." *Journal of Negro History* 64, no 2 (Spring 1979): 131–41.

McCloy, John J. "Owen J. Roberts' Extra Curiam Activities." *University of Pennsylvania Law Review* 104, no. 3 (Dec. 1955): 350–53.

Moore, John Hammond. "The Angelo Herndon Case, 1932–1937." *Phylon* 32, no. 1 (1971): 60–71.

———. "Communists and Fascists in a Southern City: Atlanta." *South Atlantic Quarterly* 67, no. 3 (Summer 1968): 437–54.

Pepper, George Wharton. "Owen J. Roberts—The Man." *University of Pennsylvania Law Review* 104, no. 3 (Dec. 1955): 372–79.

Pitts, Timothy J. "Hugh M. Dorsey and 'The Negro in Georgia.'" *Georgia Historical Quarterly* 89, no. 2 (Summer 2005): 185–212.

Potter, David M. "C. Vann Woodward." In *Pastmasters: Some Essays on American Historians*, ed. Marcus Cunliffe and Robin W. Winks, 375–407. New York: Harper & Row, 1969.

Pusey, Merlo J. "The Nomination of Charles Evans Hughes as Chief Justice." *1982 Yearbook, Supreme Court Historical Society*: 95–100.

Pye, David Kenneth. "Complex Relations: An African American Attorney Navigates Jim Crow Atlanta." *Georgia Historical Quarterly* 91, no. 4 (Winter 2007): 453–77.

Roper, John Herbert. "C. Vann Woodward's Early Career: The Historian as Dissident Youth." *Georgia Historical Quarterly* 64, no. 1 (Spring 1980): 7–21.

Silber, Norman, and Geoffrey Miller. "Toward Neutral Principles in the Law: Selections from the Oral History of Herbert Wechsler." *Columbia Law Review* 93, no. 4 (1993): 854–931.

Solomon, Burt. "The Original Justice Roberts." *Journal of Supreme Court History* 34, no 2 (2009): 196–203.

Thomas, Kendall. "*Rouge et Noir* Reread: A Popular Constitutional History of the Angelo Herndon Case." *Southern California Law Review* 65, no. 6 (1992): 2599–2704.

Thompson, Craig. "The Communist's Dearest Friend." *Saturday Evening Post*, Feb. 17, 1951, 30, 91–93.

Tushnet, Mark. "The Hughes Court and Radical Political Dissent: The Case of Dirk De Jonge and Angelo Herndon." *George State University Law Review* 28, no. 2 (Winter 2012): 333–78.

Tuttle, Elbert P. "Reflections on the Law of Habeas Corpus." *Journal of Public Law* 22, no. 2 (1973): 325–33.

Urofsky, Melvin I. "The Brandeis-Frankfurter Conversations." *The Supreme Court Review* 1985 (1985): 299–340.

Walker, Anders. "'Neutral' Principles: Rethinking the Legal History of Civil Rights, 1934–1964." *Loyola University Chicago Law Journal* 40, no. 3 (Spring 2009): 385–436.

THESES AND DISSERTATIONS

Ellett, Ashton G. "Recasting Conservativism: Georgia Republicans and the Transformation of Southern Politics Since World War II." PhD diss., University of Georgia, 2017.

Entin, David. "Angelo Herndon." Master's thesis, University of North Carolina–Chapel Hill, 1963.

Ferguson, Karen J. "The Politics of Inclusion: Black Activism in Atlanta During the Roosevelt Era." PhD diss., Duke University, 1996.

Mack, Kenneth Walker. "Race Uplift, Professional Identity and the Transformation of Civil Rights Lawyering and Politics, 1920–1940." PhD diss., Princeton University, 2005.

Martin, Charles Henry. "The Angelo Herndon Case and Georgia Justice, 1930–1937." PhD diss., Tulane University, 1972.

Naison, Mark D. "The Communist Party in Harlem: 1928–1936." PhD diss., Columbia University, 1976.

Pye, David Kenneth. "Legal Subversives: African American Lawyers in the Jim Crow South." PhD diss., University of California–San Diego, 2010.

Soliman, Maryan. "Inciting Free Speech and Racial Equality: The Communist Party and Georgia's Insurrection Statute in the 1930s." PhD diss., University of Pennsylvania, 2014.

Uhlmann, Jennifer Ruthanne. "The Communist Civil Rights Movement: Legal Activism in the United States, 1919–1946." PhD diss., University of California–Los Angeles, 2007.

ILLUSTRATION CREDITS

PHOTO INSERT

1   1932 leaflet: Tamiment Library.

1   Ben Davis Jr. and Herndon: Estate of Robert Disraeli.

2   Fulton Tower: Atlanta Journal-Constitution Photographic Archive/Georgia State University.

2   Provisional Committee meeting flyer: Stuart A. Rose Manuscript, Archives, and Rare Book Library, Emory University.

2   Protesters on Pennsylvania Avenue, May 8, 1933: Bettmann/Contributor/Getty Images.

3   Milton Herndon with Ruby Bates and several Communist Party leaders (right): Bettmann/Contributor via Getty Images.

3   Herndon carried up the stairs of Penn Station: Daily Worker Collection/Tamiment Library.

4   A cheering throng at Penn Station: Bettmann/Getty Images.

4   Walter Gellhorn and Herbert Wechsler: Columbia Law Library Archives.

5   Herndon at International Labor Defense rally, New York City, October 1935: Baltimore Afro-American.

5   Judge Hugh Dorsey: Kenan Research Center, Atlanta History Center.

6   Herndon at the November 12, 1935, habeas corpus hearing: AP Images.

6   The International Labor Defense 1935 pamphlet: Tamiment Library.

7   Herndon, Anna Damon, and Joseph Gelders: AP Images.

7   Front pages: Baltimore Afro-American; Daily Worker Collection.

8   Ralph Ellison: Uncredited/Library of Congress Prints and Photographs Division.

8   *The Negro Quarterly,* edited by Herndon and Ellison: Uncredited/Author's collection.

THROUGHOUT THE TEXT

INDEX

Page numbers in *italics* refer to illustrations.